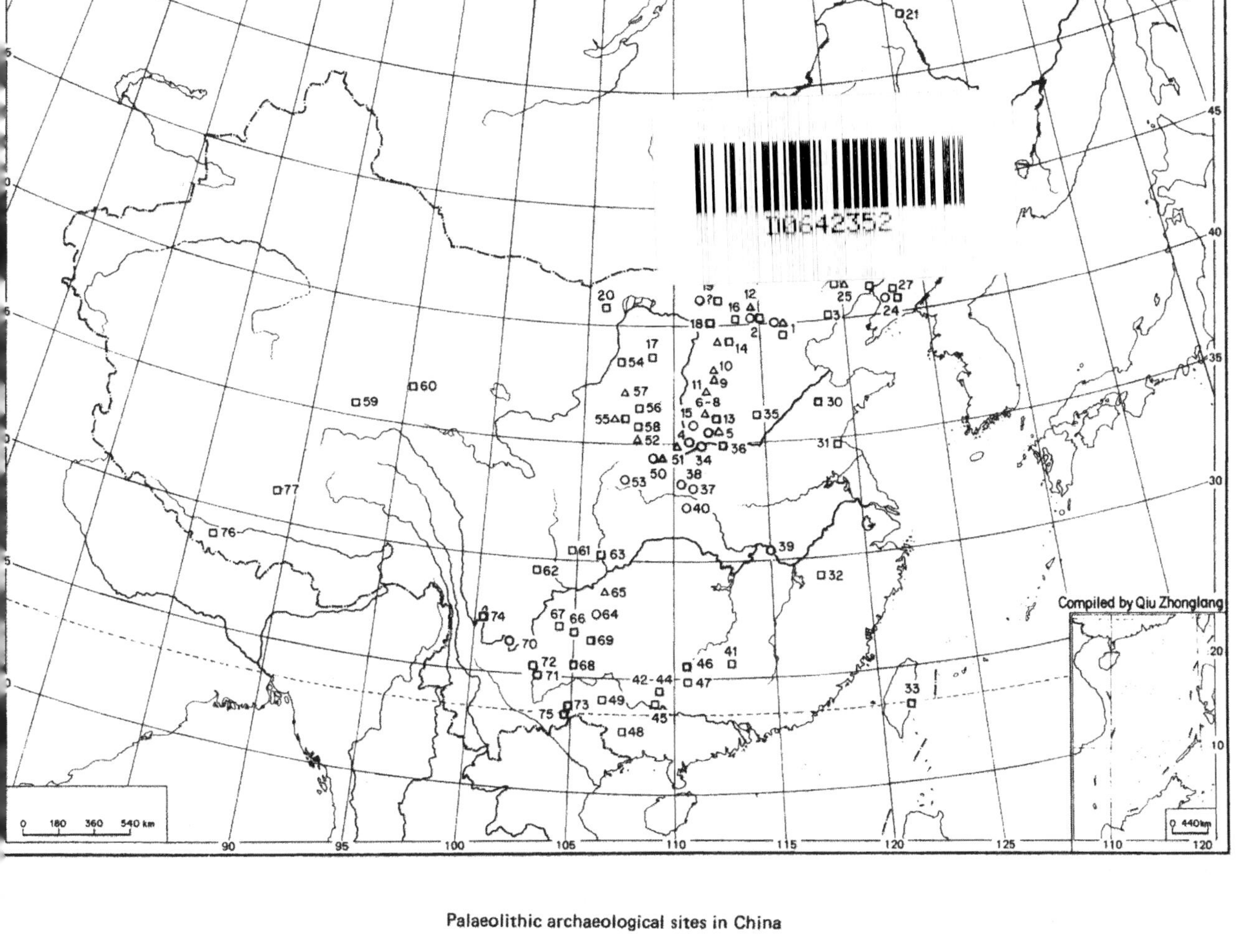

Palaeolithic archaeological sites in China

1. Zhoukoudian, Beijing
2. Yangyuan, Hebei
3. Qian'an, Hebei
4. Kehe and Xihoudu, Shanxi
5. Yuanqu, Shanxi
6. Dingcun, Shanxi
7. Houma, Shanxi
8. Quwo, Shanxi
9. Jiaocheng, Shanxi
10. Taiyuan, Shanxi
11. Huoxian, Shanxi
12. Xujiayao, Shanxi
13. Xiachuan, Shanxi
14. Shiyu, Shanxi
15. Wanrong, Shanxi
16. Datong, Shanxi
17. Salawusu (Sjara-osso-gol), Inner Mongolia
18. Qingshuihe, Inner Mongolia
19. Dayao, Inner Mongolia
20. Alashan, Inner Mongolia
21. Shibazhan, Heilongjiang
22. Ha'erbin, Heilongjiang
23. Yushu, Jilin
24. Jinniushan, Liaoning
25. Gezidong, Liaoning
26. Lingyuan, Liaoning
27. Haicheng, Liaoning
28. Jinxian, Liaoning
29. Benxi, Liaoning
30. Yiyuan, Shandong
31. Donghai, Jiangsu
32. Leping, Jiangxi
33. Changbin, Taiwan
34. Sanmenxia, Henan
35. Xiaonanhai, Henan
36. Luoyang, Henan
37. Yunxian, Hubei
38. Yunxi, Hubei
39. Shilongtou, Hubei
40. Fangxian, Hubei
41. Guiyang, Hunan
42–44. Sites in the Liuzhou-Liujiang area, Guangxi
45. Laibin, Guangxi
46. Guilin, Guangxi
47. Lipu, Guangxi
48. Changzuo, Guangxi
49. Baise, Guangxi
50. Lantian, Shaanxi
51. Dali, Shaanxi
52. Changwu, Shaanxi
53. Hanzhong, Shaanxi
54. Shuidonggou, Ningxia
55. Zhenyuan, Gansu
56. Qingyang, Gansu
57. Huanxian, Gansu
58. Jinchuan, Gansu
59. Kekexili, Quighai
60. Ge'ermu (Golmud), Qinghai
61. Ziyang, Sichuan
62. Fulin, Sichuan
63. Tongliang, Sichuan
64. Guanyindong, Guizhou
65. Tongzi, Guizhou
66. Shuicheng, Guizhou
67. Weining, Guizhou
68. Xingyi, Guizhou
69. Pu'ding, Guizhou
70. Yuanmou, Yunnan
71. Lunan, Yunnan
72. Chenggong, Yunnan
73. Xichou, Yunnan
74. Lijiang, Yunnan
75. Maguan, Yunnan
76. Dingri, Xizang (Tibet)
77. Shenzha, Xizang (Tibet)

○ Early Palaeolithic
△ Middle Palaeolithic
□ Late Palaeolithic

Paleoanthropology and Paleolithic Archaeology in the People's Republic of China

Paleoanthropology and Paleolithic Archaeology in the People's Republic of China

中国古人类学与旧石器时代考古学

Edited by

WU RUKANG
JOHN W. OLSEN

LONDON AND NEW YORK

Publisher's Note
The publisher has gone to great lengths to ensure the quality of this book but points out that some imperfections from the original may be apparent.

First published 2009 by Left Coast Press, Inc.

Published 2016 by Routledge
2 Park Square, Milton Park, Abingdon, Oxon OX14 4RN
711 Third Avenue, New York, NY 10017, USA

Routledge is an imprint of the Taylor & Francis Group, an informa business

Replaces edition of this book produced by Emerald Group Publishing under ISBN 978-0-12-601720-5 in 2007. Originally published by Academic Press in 1985.

Library of Congress Cataloguing-in-Publication Data available from the publisher.

ISBN 13: 978-1-59874-458-3 paperback

This book is respectfully dedicated to the memory of
the pioneers of Chinese vertebrate palaeontology and palaeoanthropology,

YANG ZHONGJIAN
(1897–1979)
and
PEI WENZHONG
(1904–1982)

Contents

7 *Homo sapiens* Remains from Late Palaeolithic and Neolithic China

WU XINZHI AND ZHANG ZHENBIAO

8 China's Earliest Palaeolithic Assemblages

JIA LANPO

9 The Early Palaeolithic of China

ZHANG SENSHUI

10 The Middle Palaeolithic of China

QIU ZHONGLANG

11 The Late Palaeolithic of China

JIA LANPO AND HUANG WEIWEN

Contributors

Contributors to the book at the Institute of Vertebrate Palaeontology and Palaeoanthropology, Beijing, July 1983. Sitting (left to right): Jia Lanpo, John W. Olsen, Wu Rukang. Standing (left to right): Xu Chunhua, Qiu Zhonglang, Lin Shenglong, Han Defen, Gai Pei, Qi Guoqin, Wu Maolin, Dai Jiasheng, Zhang Yinyun, Chen Yan, Wang Linghong, Xu Qinghua, Liu Zeng, Dong Xingren. Authors not present: Wu Xinzhi, Wang Yuping, Zhang Zhenbiao, Huang Weiwen. (Photograph by Yi Min.)

Numbers in parentheses indicate the pages on which the authors' contributions begin.

DONG XINGREN (董 兴 仁) (79), Institute of Vertebrate Palaeontology and Palaeoanthropology, Chinese Academy of Sciences, Beijing, People's Republic of China

GAI PEI (盖 培) (225), Institute of Vertebrate Palaeontology and Palaeoanthropology, Chinese Academy of Sciences, Beijing, People's Republic of China

HAN DEFEN (韩德芬) (267), Institute of Vertebrate Palaeontology and Palaeoanthropology, Chinese Academy of Sciences, Beijing, People's Republic of China

HUANG WEIWEN (黄慰文) (211, 259), Institute of Vertebrate Palaeontology and Palaeoanthropology, Chinese Academy of Sciences, Beijing, People's Republic of China

JIA LANPO (贾兰坡) (135, 211, 259), Institute of Vertebrate Palaeontology and Palaeoanthropology, Chinese Academy of Sciences, Beijing, People's Republic of China

LIN SHENGLONG (林圣龙) (1), Institute of Vertebrate Palaeontology and Palaeoanthropology, Chinese Academy of Sciences, Beijing, People's Republic of China

OLSEN, JOHN W. (243), Department of Anthropology, University of Arizona, Tucson, Arizona 85721

QIU ZHONGLANG (邱中郎) (187), Institute of Vertebrate Palaeontology and Palaeoanthropology, Chinese Academy of Sciences, Beijing, People's Republic of China

WANG LINGHONG (王令红) (29), Institute of Vertebrate Palaeontology and Palaeoanthropology, Chinese Academy of Sciences, Beijing, People's Republic of China

WANG YUPING (汪宇平) (243), The Inner Mongolia Museum, Hohhot, Inner Mongolia Autonomous Region, People's Republic of China

WU MAOLIN (吴茂霖) (91), Institute of Vertebrate Palaeontology and Palaeoanthropology, Chinese Academy of Sciences, Beijing, People's Republic of China

WU RUKANG (吴汝康) (1, 53, 79), Institute of Vertebrate Palaeontology and Palaeoanthropology, Chinese Academy of Sciences, Beijing, People's Republic of China

WU XINZHI (吴新智) (29, 91, 107), Institute of Vertebrate Palaeontology and Palaeoanthropology, Chinese Academy of Sciences, Beijing, People's Republic of China

XU CHUNHUA (许春华) (267), Institute of Vertebrate Palaeontology and Palaeoanthropology, Chinese Academy of Sciences, Beijing, People's Republic of China

XU QINGHUA (徐庆华) (53), Institute of Vertebrate Palaeontology and Palaeoanthropology, Chinese Academy of Sciences, Beijing, People's Republic of China

ZHANG SENSHUI (张森水) (147), Institute of Vertebrate Palaeontology and Palaeoanthropology, Chinese Academy of Sciences, Beijing, People's Republic of China

ZHANG YINYUN (张银运) (69), Institute of Vertebrate Palaeontology and Palaeoanthropology, Chinese Academy of Sciences, Beijing, People's Republic of China

ZHANG ZHENBIAO (张振标) (107), Institute of Vertebrate Palaeontology and Palaeoanthropology, Chinese Academy of Sciences, Beijing, People's Republic of China

List of Figures

List of Tables

Foreword

For too long, the formidable barrier of language has limited access to Chinese studies relevant to human evolution and Pleistocene archaeology to all but a handful of interested non-Chinese scientists. This volume provides redress in 15 well-chosen surveys of the current state of knowledge of these fields. As a consequence, it affords both valuable historical perspective and a welcome introduction to the wealth and diversity of new research results that will be of fundamental importance to all students of the human past. Sixteen of the 18 authors (with the exception of the junior co-editor and Wang Yuping of the Inner Mongolia Museum) are members of the Institute of Vertebrate Palaeontology and Palaeoanthropology of the Chinese Academy of Sciences in Beijing, a remarkable organization that has provided impetus for the splendid progress in Cenozoic studies made over the past 35 years.

The 15 chapters are devoted to a historical overview of past and recent palaeoanthropological studies, the development of chronological frameworks, the composition and biostratigraphy of Pleistocene vertebrate faunas, the pongid and hominid palaeontological records (5 chapters), and Pleistocene prehistoric archaeology (7 chapters). Useful maps of fossil localities and archaeological sites are provided in endpapers, and individual chapters provide illustrations of important fossil materials or appropriate archaeological specimens, as the case may be.

Continental Asia, and China in particular, has contributed in important and fundamental ways to the documentation of the diversity of late Cenozoic phenomena relevant to an appreciation of palaeoenvironmental circumstances; faunal diversification, deployment, and extinctions; the evolution of hominoid, including hominid, primates; and Pleistocene human culture history. The roots of such developments extend back some six decades to the first fruitful collaborations between Chinese and Western scientists. Following an interruption of more than a decade, prior to and subsequent to World War II, such researches were successfully renewed, as evidenced by the various contributions in this volume.

The Miocene of China has been poorly known until recent years. There are now some six major faunal horizons (zones) attributed to the Neogene on the basis of various localities in northern and southern China. From the middle Miocene onward there appear to be increasingly close faunal relationships with western Asia and Europe, as well as with sub-Himalayan Asia. In Yunnan the faunal localities of Kaiyuan, and particularly Shihuiba (Lufeng), have afforded remains of hominoid primates in contexts that appear to be correlative with the Chinji and Nagri "zones" of the Siwaliks sequence (between about 11 and 8 mya, respectively). The abundance of cranial–gnathic–dental remains from the latter locality afford a unique body of evidence relevant to the study of hominoid structure and diversity, and at the same time (considering the new hominoids from the Potwar Plateau of Pakistan) have posed new problems in the interpretation of the phylogenetics and systematics of the higher primates.

The first evidence of the enigmatic gigantic pongid, *Gigantopithecus,* also derived from China. Through intensive searches in the 1950s, further dental remains of this creature were recovered from several localities in Guangxi and also Hubei (in the latter instance, at the Jianshi locality), with direct evidence of co-association with *Homo erectus.* The Lengzhai (Liucheng) locality produced the first mandibular parts, along with a great abundance of isolated teeth, which substantially added to our knowledge of this still-imperfectly known primate of the South Asian Lower and Middle Pleistocene.

The earliest human occupation of eastern Asia remains very inadequately documented. There is increasing evidence for human presence in the late Lower Pleistocene (upper Matuyama [R] chron) in Shanxi (Xihoudu locality), as well as in the upper Nihewan Formation (Hebei), in situations in which extinct species comprise a predominance of the faunal associations. Several of these occurrences afford evidence of fire and bone breakage, possibly including butchery, and comprise lithic assemblages distinct from those of subsequent, Middle Pleistocene (Brunhes [N] chron) age. However, except for the Donggutuo (Hebei) lithic assemblage, which closely resembles that from Zhoukoudian Locality 1, there are still no really substantial and diverse archaeological occurrences in well-documented Lower Pleistocene contexts.

Human occupation sites of Middle Pleistocene age are now substantially better represented in various parts of China, particularly in the North. The huge Zhoukoudian Locality 1 still represents the single most important occurrence because of repeated human visitations through 11 major depositional units that span a period of some 300,000 years, its abundance of archaeological and faunal residues, and, of course, its unique sample of *Homo erectus* remains. A monograph on this most important locality is expected to appear soon in China and will reflect the diversity of studies elucidating its formation, infilling, varied occupations by carnivores and early humans, and the advances in deciphering its relative and radiometric age. Still earlier occurrences of *Homo erectus* derive from localities in the Lantian area (Shaanxi), where nearly 30 archaeological sites are documented, and from Yuanmou (Yunnan). Teeth attributed to *Homo erectus* are now known from other cave sites in Hubei, Henan, Shandong, and Anhui. In Anhui the newly found Longtandong site (Hexian) has afforded one of the best-preserved *Homo erectus* calvaria yet known from China. Caves with later Middle Pleistocene occupations are now also known from Hubei, Guizhou, and Liaoning provinces. The most important stratified archaeological occurrences of such age are still those in the valley of the Fen River (Shanxi), as well as in some comparable situations in Shaanxi and Henan. Intensified studies of the massive loessic succession of northern China, including palaeomagnetic, thermoluminescent, and oxygen isotopic studies, have recently advanced substantially our understanding of the sequence of Pleistocene events in this part of eastern Asia and will ultimately make possible a firm correlation with the deep-sea sequence derived from Pacific cores.

In recent years a central problem in palaeoanthropology has been understanding the emergence of *Homo sapiens*. A number of sites in northern China and the Maba site in southern China have provided human remains, though usually both sparse and fragmentary, of presumed late Middle to earlier Upper Pleistocene age. Three localities—Dali (Shaanxi), Xujiayao (Shanxi), and Maba (Guangdong)—have yielded significant human cranial and dental remains that document an overall morphological structure distinctive from the well-known *Homo erectus* pattern. Most Chinese palaeoanthropologists concerned with this problem believe that certain shared primitive characters indicate an immediate ancestor–descendent relationship between these succedent taxa. Two of the aforementioned sites have provided important lithic assemblages considered to be of a "Middle" Palaeolithic aspect: from a total of 21 such recently recorded occurrences there is emerging a substantial archaeological documentation that was unavailable heretofore. Comparative study of the lithic technology and composition of these assemblages is now required in order to elucidate points of similarity and differences vis-à-vis assemblages from broadly comparable time ranges in India and Pakistan on the one hand, and Soviet Asia on the other. Unfortunately, there is still almost no close temporal control for the sites of this interval.

For many years the archaeology of late Pleistocene China was an almost unknown quantity. The only evidence derived from Shuidonggou (Ningxia Hui Autonomous Region) in the Ordos Desert, and from some meager data from the Shaanxi and Shanxi loesslands. This is no longer the case. There are now a number of such sites known throughout China, with significant artifactual assemblages, substantial faunal associations, and well-defined stratigraphic radiometric contexts. These assemblages show considerable diversity regionally and temporally, and the sites themselves often afford significant evidence of the past environments to which the last Pleistocene populations adjusted. As rightly stated here, these occurrences merit treatment in their own right, rather than in the terms that have been generated to accommodate European and West Asian manifestations, terms that tend to obscure the distinctiveness of some of the Chinese materials. Nonetheless, detailed comparisons with penecontemporaneous occurrences elsewhere in northern and central Asia are very much to be desired in the future.

Finally, it is a pleasure and privilege to congratulate the editors and contributors to this volume for making available to a worldwide audience such a broad-ranging overview of the accomplishments and status of researches into the human past in China. I thank the editors for their kindness in offering me the opportunity to contribute this brief foreword to the volume.

F. Clark Howell

Preface

Normalization of diplomatic relations between the People's Republic of China and many countries in the West has resulted in increased communication between the scientific communities of China and the English-speaking world. In palaeoanthropology and archaeology, for example, it is now well known that the pace of research in China in these fields has been intense during the past two decades. Unfortunately, a formidable language barrier has prevented most scholars in the West from gaining access to critical published materials, and as a consequence Chinese data are rarely included in detailed discussions of hominoid and hominid phylogeny and Pleistocene prehistory in the English language. Notable exceptions of course exist (e.g., Aigner 1981; Chang 1977; Howells and Tsuchitani 1977; Jia 1980; Zhang *et al.* 1980), but for the most part hominoid and hominid palaeontology and Palaeolithic archaeology in China remain poorly understood in the West.

This volume was conceived and implemented as a cooperative Sino-American project and its function is twofold. First, a systematic attempt has been made to present a series of original articles, specifically prepared for this volume and based on recently acquired data, that outline aspects of hominoid and hominid evolution and Pleistocene prehistory in China. Each of these articles has been written by the scholars principally involved in the collection and analysis of the relevant data, and as such they represent a unique treatment of these subjects in the English language.

Second, this book is intended to function as a forum from which the leading figures of contemporary Chinese palaeoanthropology and Palaeolithic archaeology can speak directly to the international scholarly community about their views on topics of mutual interest. This volume reflects the interpretation of archaeological and palaeoanthropological data *in China.* Because a vital influence on the growth of any scientific discipline is the cultural milieu in which it develops, we believe that, by allowing Chinese scientists the opportunity to express their own conclusions within their own interpretive framework, researchers in the West will gain a better perspective on current theoretical approaches to these fields in China.

Extant journals specializing in the translation of Chinese archaeological reports seldom include Pleistocene cultural remains in their contents. English-speaking physical anthropologists interested in recent developments in the interpretation of the Chinese fossil hominoid and hominid records have had even fewer sources to consult. The partial rectification of this regrettable situation is one of the principal goals of this volume. Although the book is primarily directed toward physical anthropologists and Pleistocene prehistorians, we anticipate that a broad spectrum of individuals interested in the current development and application of scientific method and theory in China will also find the text of value.

The presentation of conflicting interpretations of palaeoanthropological and archaeological data contradicts the popular notion that contemporary Chinese science is essentially a monolithic entity from which only standardized policy statements may be expected. We believe the dynamic character of modern Chinese research in these fields is reflected in the articles we have chosen to include.

This book is not intended to be encyclopedic. Rather, we present a range of articles that reflect the priorities and interests of China's contemporary anthropologists. This volume is an interim report, not the final word on any of the topics addressed.

The text is conceptually subdivided into two major sections, one dealing with recent palaeoanthropological discoveries and their interpretation, and the other with the illumination of China's rich Pleistocene archaeological record. Both sections proceed chronologically in an attempt to render the volume useful as both a textbook and a reference work. New interpretations of previously analyzed material are also included. Zhang Yinyun's reanalysis of the Jianshi "australopithecine" molars (Chapter 4) and the reinterpretation of China's *Ramapithecus* and *Sivapithecus* fossils by Wu Rukang and Xu Qinghua (Chapter 3) are cases in point.

With the exception of the reference sections, which retain reference titles in their original form, the *Hanyu Pinyin* system of romanization has been employed throughout the book. Also known as the Chinese Phonetic Alphabet, this system is now officially sanctioned by the Chinese government and is being adopted by the world's major libraries, having largely supplanted both the Wade–Giles and Yale orthographies.

Because of the complexity of Chinese bibliographic references, a few words of explanation are in order. The titles of bibliographic entries derived from English abstracts published in Chinese journals have been reproduced in their original form to facilitate their location by those not familiar with the Chinese language.

For journals that do not possess a formal English or Latin title, and in instances where these translated renditions may be easily confused with many other serials bearing the same title, the *Hanyu Pinyin* title alone is presented. Hence, the journal *Kaogu* appears in the reference sections in this romanized form rather than as its English equivalent, *Archaeology*.

A list of the romanized titles of Chinese journals and their English or Latin versions may be found at the end of this preface. The principal journals referred to in this book have also been listed in the reference sections under their *Hanyu Pinyin* romanized titles in cases where the history of publication of these serials might cause confusion. For example, the journal *Gu Jizhuidongwu Xuebao (Vertebrata PalAsiatica)* was first published in 1957 and contains articles primarily in non-Chinese languages. In 1961 it was combined with the Chinese language publication *Gu Jizhuidongwu yu Gu Renlei*, and took the latter's Chinese name but retained the Latin designation *Vertebrata PalAsiatica*. Since 1961 the journal has been published mainly in Chinese with foreign language abstracts, mostly English and Russian.

Gu Jizhuidongwu yu Gu Renlei was first published in 1959 and was, until 1961, concurrently released as a journal distinct from *Gu Jizhuidongwu Xuebao* under the Latin title *Palaeovertebrata et Palaeoanthropologia*. Two volumes totaling six issues of this journal were published from 1959 to 1961. The volume and issue numbers established in 1957 with the initial publication of *Gu Jizhuidongwu Xuebao* have been continued in the post-1961 issues of *Gu Jizhuidongwu yu Gu Renlei (Vertebrata PalAsiatica)*. It should be noted that *Vertebrata PalAsiatica* was not published from 1967 to 1972, hence Volume 10 was issued during 1966 and publication resumed with Volume 11 in 1973.

Readers wishing to consult these journals, especially those published between 1959 and 1961, should be aware that their complex history of publication has resulted, in many Western libraries, in simply cataloging them all under the single designation *Vertebrata PalAsiatica*. Those interested in bibliographic matters will find two internal publications of the Institute of Vertebrate Palaeontology and Palaeoanthropology (IVPP) to be of great assistance. These are the *Contributions from the Institute of Vertebrate Palaeontology and Palaeoanthropology, Academia Sinica (Zhongguo Kexueyuan Gu Jizhuidongwu yu Gu Renlei Yanjiusuo Zhuzuo Mulu Huibian)*, published in 1963 and 1979, which provides a compilation of most of this institute's scientific works through the 1970s. In addition, a new serial, *Renleixue Xuebao (Acta Anthropologica Sinica)*, was initiated in 1982 to provide a specialized outlet for anthropological data.

We have produced this book in the hope that it will make a contribution toward a better understanding within the international scholarly community of the style and content of current Chinese research on palaeoanthropology and Palaeolithic archaeology. The rapprochement between the People's Republic of China and many Western nations has fostered mutual interest in the expansion of scholarly contacts. We compiled the present volume in the spirit of such strengthened academic ties in 1984 to commemorate the fifty-fifth anniversary of the first discovery of *Homo erectus* fossils at Zhoukoudian. We hope that continued cooperative ventures will soon necessitate the publication of a revised, expanded edition!

References

Aigner, Jean S.
1981 *Archaeological remains in Pleistocene China.* Forschungen zur Allgemeinen und Vergleichrenden Archäologie, Band 1. Munich: Verlag C. H. Beck.
Chang, Kwang-chih
1977 *The archaeology of ancient China.* Third edition. New Haven: Yale University Press.
Howells, William W., and Patricia J. Tsuchitani
1977 *Paleoanthropology in the People's Republic of China.* Report No. 4, Committee on Scholarly Communication with the People's Republic of China. Washington, D.C.: National Academy of Sciences.
Jia Lanpo (Chia Lan-po)
1980 *Early man in China.* Beijing: Foreign Languages Press.
Zhang Senshui, Gu Yumin, Bao Yixin, Shen Wenlong, Wang Zhefu, Wang Chunde, and Du Zhi
1980 *Atlas of primitive man in China.* Beijing: Science Press. New York: Van Nostrand Reinhold.

Hanyu Pinyin titles of Chinese journals and their English or Latin equivalents

Dicengxue Zazhi—Acta Stratigraphica Sinica
Dizhi Kexue—Scientia Geologica Sinica
Dizhi Xuebao—Acta Geologica Sinica
Kaogu—Archaeology
Kaogu Xuebao—Acta Archaeologica Sinica
Renleixue Xuebao—Acta Anthropologica Sinica
Wenwu—Cultural Relics
Xinhua Wenzhai—New China Digest
Zhiwu Xuebao—Acta Botanica Sinica
Zhongguo Disiji Yanjiu—Quaternaria Sinica

Acknowledgments

I

The publication of this book reflects the combined efforts of scholars in both China and the United States. I am grateful to the L. S. B. Leakey Foundation for sponsoring my initial visit to China in 1981, during which the basic outline for this text was formulated. My extended stay in China during 1983, entailing both fieldwork and editorial activities, was sponsored by the National Academy of Science's Committee on Scholarly Communication with the People's Republic of China. I wish to thank in particular Albert Feuerwerker, Mary Brown Bullock, and Robert Geyer for their generous support and encouragement.

My work in China was conducted under the auspices of the National Cultural Relics Bureau, the Inner Mongolia Museum, and the Institute of Vertebrate Palaeontology and Palaeoanthropology (IVPP), a branch of the Chinese Academy of Sciences. Fieldwork in the Hobq Desert was made possible through the able assistance of the staff of the Inner Mongolia Museum in Hohhot, particularly Wen Hao, Wang Xiaohua, Wang Yuping, Ge Jingwei, Li Rong, and Bai Yuren.

Local authorization for fieldwork was kindly granted in Hohhot by A'rigun of the Inner Mongolia Bureau of Culture and in Baotou by Zha'rigelatu of the Municipal Bureau of Culture. Zheng Long and Liu Huanzhen of the Baotou City Cultural Relics Management Bureau were principally responsible for providing logistical support in the field. Their selfless devotion to the project is deeply appreciated.

In Beijing, my colleagues at the IVPP deserve special thanks for their unflagging hospitality and attention to my comfort and well-being (both academic and physical). Among those to whom I owe the greatest debt of thanks are Wu Rukang (my co-editor), Zhou Mingzhen, Jia Lanpo, Qiu Zhonglang, Qi Guoqin, Gai Pei, Gu Yumin, and Huang Wanbo. I deeply appreciate having had the opportunity to work closely with so many fine scholars.

I am indebted to Professor John D. Evans, Professor F. R. Hodson, and the staff of the Institute of Archaeology, University of London, for providing me with the stimulating academic environment in which the final translation and editing of this book were conducted.

I have benefitted greatly from discussions with my colleagues M. B. Schiffer, A. J. Jelinek, I. C. Glover, D. R. Brothwell, S. K. M. Allan, S. J. Olsen, S. L. Olsen, J. S. Aigner, D. E. Savage, R. L. Ciochon, A. S. Walker, and F. C. Howell.

Tan Aiqing skillfully helped me through the vagaries of handwritten Chinese and technical terminology. Her contribution to the finished English text is gratefully acknowledged, although I accept personal responsibility for any errors in translation that may have crept into the final draft.

John W. Olsen

II

The preparation of this volume was conducted at the Institute of Vertebrate Palaeontology and Palaeoanthropology under the auspices of the Chinese Academy of Sciences (Academia Sinica). We wish particularly to thank Liu Zeng, Chen Yan, and Dai Jiasheng for contributing most of the illustrations for this text. IVPP photographers Wang Zhefu, Du Zhi, and Zhang Jie provided the photographs.

Each of the contributing authors receives our thanks for promoting the spirit of scholarly cooperation in which this volume was conceived and executed.

Wu Rukang

John W. Olsen

1

Chinese Palaeoanthropology: Retrospect and Prospect

WU RUKANG AND LIN SHENGLONG

Introduction

Palaeoanthropological research in China, including the allied pursuits of Palaeolithic archaeology and the study of fossil apes and hominids, has taken its place in the mainstream of world palaeoanthropology. A combination of China's unique geographic location and abundant fossil and archaeological materials has allowed great strides to be taken in palaeoanthropological research over the course of the past few decades. This article presents a historical review of Chinese palaeoanthropological studies, as well as a delineation of some of the principal directions in which we foresee the field moving.

Because China was inexorably locked in a semifeudal and semicolonial social order for a considerable portion of its modern history, palaeoanthropological research is a relatively recent development there. Prior to the 1920s, only an enigmatic fossil tooth purchased by the German palaeontologist Max Schlosser in a Chinese apothecary shop (Schlosser 1903) provided any real evidence of the possible antiquity of the human occupation of China. In 1920 Emile Licent collected four chipped-stone artifacts in northern Qingyang Prefecture, Gansu Province, in the Upper Pleistocene loess and gravels that characterize the region (Teilhard and Licent 1924). In 1924 Pierre Teilhard de Chardin and Licent also recorded the discovery of quartzite artifacts in association with the fossil cranium of *Coelodonta antiquitatis,* which the missionary F. Schotte had located several years previously about 5 km east of Shuidonggou in the Ningxia Hui

ISBN 0-12-601720-4

Autonomous Region. These artifacts were the first Palaeolithic cultural remains discovered in China.

In 1922 and 1923 Teilhard's and Licent's geological investigations led to the discovery of three Palaeolithic localities at Shuidonggou, Ningxia; Youfangtou, in Yulin Prefecture, Shaanxi; and Dagouwan, Inner Mongolia. Subsequent excavations at Shuidonggou and Dagouwan yielded large quantities of stone artifacts and fossil animal remains. Among the fossils discovered at Dagouwan was a human incisor, which came to be known as Ordos Man. This specimen, and two other earlier hominid teeth discovered at approximately the same time at Zhoukoudian, near Beijing, were the first human fossils of Pleistocene age to be recovered anywhere on the East Asian mainland (Boule *et al.* 1928; Licent *et al.* 1926; Teilhard and Licent 1924).

Teilhard was soon joined in the field by Yang Zhongjian (C. C. Young). Collections of stone artifacts were made at many scattered localities in western Shanxi and northern Shaanxi in 1929, and in Inner Mongolia, Gansu, and Xinjiang in 1930–1931 (Teilhard and Yang 1930, 1932).

As important as these sporadic discoveries were to the demonstration of the antiquity of human activity in China, it was the recovery in 1921 of Middle Pleistocene hominid remains at Zhoukoudian Locality 1 that captured the world's attention (Wu and Lin 1983). In 1921 and 1923 the Austrian palaeontologist Otto Zdansky conducted short-term excavations in Locality 1. He recovered two teeth that he subsequently assigned to the genus *Homo* (Zdansky 1927), arousing the interest of scholars in China and abroad. As a result of this burgeoning interest, large-scale excavations were initiated at Zhoukoudian in 1927 under the leadership of the Geological Survey of China. In the first year of excavation an extremely well-preserved hominid lower molar was discovered, which the Canadian anatomist Davidson Black (1927) named *Sinanthropus pekinensis*, or "Beijing Man" (commonly known as Peking Man and now classified as *Homo erectus pekinensis*). In December 1929 the Chinese scientist Pei Wenzhong discovered the first complete calvarium of Beijing Man, thus firmly establishing *Sinanthropus* in the corpus of world palaeoanthropological data (Pei 1929).

Excavations continued at Zhoukoudian until the outbreak of the Sino–Japanese War in 1937. Intensive investigation during those years revealed large numbers of hominid fossils, which were thought to represent at least 40 individuals. Most of the anatomical studies of the original Zhoukodian finds were published by Franz Weidenreich (1936a,b, 1937, 1939b, 1941, 1943).

In 1930 Pei Wenzhong identified for the first time stone artifacts in Locality 1 (Pei 1931; Teilhard and Pei 1932). Simultaneously, colleagues also discovered ash lenses and burned bones and stones that were taken as evidence of fire utilization (Black 1931). This series of discoveries in the Locality 1 deposits confirmed that Beijing Man had the ability to utilize fire and fabricate stone tools. Over the years, more than 100,000 stone artifacts have been discovered in Locality 1, greatly enhancing our understanding of *Homo erectus pekinensis* and his culture.

In 1890–1892 fossils of *Homo erectus* were discovered by Dubois in Java, but for many years afterward controversy raged in palaeoanthropological circles over whether "Java Man" was an ape or human. The discovery near Beijing of *Sinanthropus* fossils in association with lithic artifacts, irrefutable evidence of fire utilization, and massive quantities of vertebrate fossils, all of which could be relatively accurately dated on geological and biostratigraphic grounds, finally established the position of *Homo erectus* in the scheme of evolution leading to modern humans.

The Zhoukoudian discoveries also unequivocally demonstrated the presence of tool- and fire-using hominids in North China in Middle Pleistocene times, a realization that had a major effect on the palaeoanthropological theories of the day.

In addition to Locality 1, important Palaeolithic cultural relics and mammalian fossils have been unearthed at Zhoukoudian Locality 3 (Pei 1936), Locality 4 (Pei 1939a), Locality 13 (Pei 1934), Locality 15 (Pei 1938), and the Upper Cave (Pei 1939b, 1940).

In the Upper Cave, or Shandingdong, the remains of at least eight individual *Homo sapiens sapiens* were discovered, including three well-preserved crania (one male and two females). Weidenreich's analysis (1939a) of the Upper Cave crania concluded that they typified three different racial elements, best described as primitive Mongoloid, Melanesoid, and Eskimoid types. Although Weidenreich's interpretations of the data are open to criticism, his pioneering analysis of the Upper Cave human remains demonstrated the possibility of substantial racial diversity in Upper Pleistocene North China.

Before Chinese Liberation in 1949, virtually no identifiable human fossils or Palaeolithic remains were known from the Northeast, then referred to as Manchuria. In South China, however, Nels C. Nelson collected stone artifacts in the area of the Yangzi River (Nelson 1926), most of which ultimately proved to be of Neolithic and Mesolithic or Terminal Palaeolithic origin.

As early as 1913, J. H. Edgar began his collection of stone-age artifacts in Sichuan Province in China's Southwest (Edgar 1933–1934). Under Edgar's guidance, G. T. Bowles and D. C. Graham continued his research, concluding that some of the artifactual assemblages they encountered were indeed Palaeolithic (Bowles 1933; Graham 1935). In later years, Pei Wenzhong reanalyzed the material, leading him to conclude that some of the Sichuan material was probably not the product of human activity and that other specimens were of Neolithic origin (Pei 1955).

The early 1930s also witnessed the discovery of chipped-stone tools and flakes in Sichuan, Guangxi, and Yunnan, although at the time no means existed for determining the absolute antiquity of these finds (Bian and Jia 1938; Pei 1935; Teilhard and Yang 1935; Teilhard *et al.* 1935).

Regarding the study of Chinese fossil primates, the Dutch palaeontologist G. H. R. von Koenigswald made a major contribution to the field through his discovery in 1935 of large primate teeth in the collections of "dragon bones" of

Chinese apothecary shops in Hong Kong. These important fossils, given the binomial designation *Gigantopithecus blacki* by Koenigswald (1935), have been the subject of intensive research since their initial discovery (see Chapter 4, this volume).

Before the Liberation, a number of comprehensive essays dealing with Chinese fossil hominids and Palaeolithic cultures were published by both Chinese and foreign scholars (e.g., Black *et al.* 1933; Boule *et al.* 1928; Movius 1949; Pei 1937, 1939c; Teilhard 1941; Terra 1941).

Owing to the limitations of the social conditions that characterized China during the first half of the twentieth century, palaeoanthropology progressed at a very slow pace prior to Liberation. Although numerous Palaeolithic sites were discovered and scattered artifacts were collected during this pre-Liberation period, systematic excavations were conducted only at Shuidonggou, Dagouwan, and Zhoukoudian in North China. The vast territories of South China, the West, and the Northeast were virtually unknown in terms of their Pleistocene prehistory, and many chronological lacunae existed in the record of human activity in China.

In spite of these shortcomings the work accomplished during this period, especially the investigations conducted at Zhoukoudian, laid a sound foundation for subsequent developments in the field. The present state of affairs in Chinese palaeoanthropology is a result of the combined research efforts of both Chinese and foreign scholars. The revolutionary changes in the Chinese social system that accompanied Liberation in 1949 created conditions favorable for the development of the sciences in China. The past three decades have witnessed the rapid growth of palaeoanthropology in China (Wu Rukang 1980, 1982).

The Discovery and Analysis of Fossil Apes in China

Because humans are known to have descended from fossil apes, the extinct forms that are thought to provide evidence of this transition have captured the attention of palaeoanthropologists the world over. In 1956 and 1957, a total of 10 teeth were recovered from Upper Miocene lignite deposits near Xiaolongtan Village in Kaiyuan County, Yunnan. The teeth bore strong similarities to the dentition of *Dryopithecus punjabicus* recovered in the Siwalik deposits of the Indian subcontinent. Although morphologically similar in many ways to *D. punjabicus*, the Kaiyuan teeth nonetheless exhibit a number of distinctive features; hence they were given the specific designation *D. keiyuanensis* (Wu Rukang 1957, 1958a).

Although the Kaiyuan teeth represent the first remains of *Dryopithecus* to be reported from China, recent additional finds of this animal have been made at Sihong in Jiangsu Province (Gu and Lin 1983), providing more evidence of the distribution of this form.

Since the early 1960s when Simons and Pilbeam incorporated the genus *Ramapithecus* within the family Hominidae, this fossil primate has been the subject of great interest to palaeoanthropologists. In 1975 remains of large and small hominoids, classified as *Sivapithecus yunnanensis* and *Ramapithecus lufengensis*, respectively, were discovered in Upper Miocene lignite beds near Shihuiba Village in Lufeng County, Yunnan (Xu *et al.* 1978; Xu and Lu 1979). Since then, eight excavations have been conducted, yielding large quantities of fossil ape remains, including complete crania of both the large and small hominoids.

Morphologically, these hominoids appear similar to the modern orangutan and quite different from either the gorilla or chimpanzee. It is therefore possible that the Lufeng hominoids represent forms ancestral to *Pongo* (Wu *et al.* 1983), although *Ramapithecus* also exhibits many features similar to early hominids. This body of data from Lufeng is currently being subjected to intensive study (see Chapter 3, this volume). As these analyses continue in conjunction with the recovery of additional fossils at Shihuiba, we hope the phylogenetic position of these primates may be clarified.

For many years after Koenigswald's original discovery of teeth of *Gigantopithecus* in 1935, the provenance, stratigraphic relationships, geological age, and systematic position of these fossils remained a mystery. In 1956 three teeth of *Gigantopithecus* were discovered in Niushuishan Hei Cave in Daxin County, Guangxi. In the same year a cave in Lengzhai Mountain, Liucheng County, Guangxi, yielded a mandible of this animal. Subsequent excavations in the Liucheng locality produced a total of three mandibles and over 1000 isolated teeth of *Gigantopithecus*, as well as large quantities of mammalian fossils. Biostratigraphic and lithostratigraphic data suggested a Lower Pleistocene age for the Liucheng assemblage (Pei and Wu 1956; Wu 1962).

Since 1965 *Gigantopithecus* remains, consisting entirely of dental and mandibular elements, have also been found at Wuming, Guangxi (1965); Jianshi, Hubei (1968, 1970); and Bama, Guangxi (1973). The geological age of the fossiliferous deposits in these three localities is probably Middle Pleistocene (Xu *et al.* 1974; Zhang Yinyun *et al.* 1973, 1975).

As the result of many years of fieldwork and laboratory analysis, we have pinpointed many of the localities in South China's karst region, from which the *Gigantopithecus* teeth sold as "dragon bones" were originally derived. We also have a much clearer idea of their geological age, spatial distribution, and span of existence.

The systematic position of *Gigantopithecus* continues to be a problematic issue. Some scholars persist in their contention that *Gigantopithecus* represents an extinct branch of the hominid evolutionary line. Others maintain it was a specialized pongid. What is certain is that the remains of *Gigantopithecus* reflect an evolutionary dead-end and should not therefore be considered the direct ancestor of either the hominids or pongids. An extreme view was proposed by Weidenreich (1945, 1946), who believed *Gigantopithecus* to be a form of giant human. Obviously, all extant hominid fossils refute such a conclusion, but the idea of *Gigantopithecus*–*Homo* links persists.

As far as we know, *Gigantopithecus* existed from the Pliocene through the

Middle Pleistocene. Its area of distribution apparently extended in a belt from the Indian subcontinent to Guangxi and Hubei in China. Unfortunately, at present we have no postcranial *Gigantopithecus* fossils for examination, but variation in the rather large collection of dentition available suggests this species was characterized by significant morphological change through time, perhaps including a gradual increase in overall body size.

Mention should be made of several Lower Pleistocene primate molars discovered near Jianshi, Hubei. These teeth, originally described as having affinities with the gracile australopithecines (Gao 1975), have recently been reanalyzed and are thought to fall within the range of morphological variation of *Homo erectus* (see Chapter 4, this volume).

The discovery of such abundant fossil-primate remains demonstrates that South China may yet yield important evidence relating to the radiation of hominids in a pantropical belt. The continued exploration of these areas and the analysis of the derived fossil materials will inevitably deepen our understanding of hominid origins and development.

The Discovery and Analysis of Fossil Hominids in China

When excavation was resumed at Zhoukoudian after Liberation, new fossils of *Homo erectus pekinensis* were added to the suite of previously known specimens. In 1949 and 1951 five teeth and two fragments of limb bones were recovered in Locality 1 (Wu and Jia 1954). In 1958 a complete female mandible was discovered (Wu and Zhao 1959), and in 1966 occipital and frontal fragments were found that, when combined with fossils found in 1934, formed a nearly complete calvarium. An isolated tooth was unearthed at the same time (Qiu *et al.* 1973).

On the basis of previously accumulated data and recent reanalyses, basic questions relating to the cranial capacity and stature of *H. erectus pekinensis*, as well as to the role of *H. erectus* in the process of human evolution, are systematically being answered (e.g., Wu and Dong n.d.; Wu and Lin 1983).

From 1978 to 1980, under the leadership of the Institute of Vertebrate Palaeontology and Palaeoanthropology (IVPP), Chinese Academy of Sciences, a new campaign of multidisciplinary studies, including both excavations and laboratory analyses, was carried out at the Zhoukoudian site. More than 120 people from 17 institutions—including research organizations and universities specializing in palaeoanthropology, archaeology, palaeobiology, glaciology, karst geology, pedology, stratigraphy, palynology, and chronology—were involved in the project. Preliminary results of this research program have already been forthcoming and are included in this volume.

In 1963 a *H. erectus* mandible was recovered in reddish Pleistocene clays near Chenjiawo Village on Xiehong Commune in Lantian County, Shaanxi. In 1964 a calvarium and facial bones were unearthed in a similar deposit near Gongwangling, some 15 km east of Lantian. Subsequent investigations indicate *H. erectus lantienensis*, or "Lantian Man," was more primitive than his descendants who inhabited Zhoukoudian Locality 1 and than the early *Homo* from the Trinil beds of Java. Lantian Man most closely resembles the remains of *Pithecanthropus robustus* from the Javanese Djetis beds, and its geological age, while still Middle Pleistocene, considerably antedates the Zhoukoudian Locality 1 deposits (Wu 1964, 1966).

The left and right upper medial incisors of an adult *H. erectus* bearing striking similarities to the Zhoukoudian population were discovered in the brown clay beds of the Yuanmou Formation at Shangnabang Village in Yuanmou County, Yunnan (Hu 1973; Zhou and Hu 1979). On biostratigraphic and lithostratigraphic grounds, the stratum yielding the Yuanmou teeth is thought to be of late Lower Pleistocene antiquity. A palaeomagnetic date of 1.7 million years BP (Li *et al.* 1976) has recently been called into question by scholars who believe the Yuanmou hominid-bearing deposit is younger than the Matuyama–Brunhes boundary and may be only 500,000–600,000 years old or less (Liu and Ding 1983).

Recently another important *H. erectus* fossil, a nearly complete calvarium, was found in Longtan Cave, Hexian County, Anhui. This specimen, which appears morphologically advanced, may be correlated with the hominid population that inhabited the upper levels of Zhoukoudian Locality 1 (Huang *et al.* 1981, 1982; Wu and Dong 1982).

Numerous isolated teeth of *H. erectus* have also come to light in recent years at a number of localities. Among these finds are those from Yunxian, Hubei (Wu and Dong 1980; Xu 1978); Yunxi, Hubei (Qunli 1983; Xiangjiang 1977); Xichuan, Henan (Wu and Wu 1982); Nanzhao, Henan (Qiu *et al.* 1982); Yiyuan, Shandong (Meng 1982); and Chaoxian, Anhui (Anonymous 1982). On the basis of these finds we may conclude that *H. erectus* was distributed throughout the greater portion of China, principally during the Middle Pleistocene, but perhaps in the late Lower Pleistocene as well.

All China's fossils of early *H. sapiens* have been found since 1949 and include discoveries made at five major localities: Dingcun, Shanxi; Changyang, Hubei; Maba, Guangdong; Xujiayao, Shanxi; and Dali, Shaanxi.

The fossils of the Dingcun hominid were found in 1954 in the sandy gravel beds at Locality 54.100 near Dingcun Village, Xiangfen County, Shanxi. The finds included an upper medial incisor, an upper lateral incisor, and a lower second molar of a 12- or 13-year-old boy (Pei *et al.* 1958). In 1976 a partial right parietal of an approximately 2-year-old child was recovered at the same locality (Wu Xinzhi 1976).

Many morphological similarities link *H. erectus pekinensis*, the Dingcun *H. sapiens*, and modern Mongoloids. For example, the shovel-shaped incisors present on these fossil specimens are characteristic of Mongoloid populations. In addition, sawtooth traces on the parietals indicate Wormian bones were probably originally present and these lines of evidence suggest that the Dingcun hominid may be the link between Beijing Man and modern Mongoloids.

The remains of Changyang Man were discovered in a rock-shelter near Xiazhongjiawan Village in Changyang County, Hubei. The fossil assemblage consists of a left maxilla fragment and two teeth (Jia 1957a).

The calvarium of the Maba *H. sapiens* was discovered in 1958 in Shizishan Cave, Qujiang County, Guangdong. This specimen, owing to its excellent state of preservation, has not only provided an expanded view of the distribution of early Upper Pleistocene hominids, but is also an important link in the development of Chinese hominids (Wu and Peng 1959).

The Xujiayao hominid remains were found in 1976 and 1977 near Xujiayao Village, Yanggao County, Shanxi, on the border of Yangyuan County, Hebei. The human fossils include three fragmentary parietals, two occipitals, and a left maxilla with partial dentition. In addition, a number of parietal fragments and isolated teeth were recovered, representing a total of at least 10 individuals (Jia *et al.* 1979; Wu Maolin 1980).

In 1978 a nearly complete hominid cranium was discovered in the gravel beds of the third terrace of the Luo River in Dali County, Shaanxi. This specimen, thought to represent a very archaic form of *H. sapiens,* is an important link between China's *H. erectus* and *H. sapiens sapiens* populations (Wang Yongyan *et al.* 1979; Wu Xinzhi 1981).

In addition to the finds of early *H. sapiens* made at these five principal localities, a number of other isolated specimens have also been recovered. These include two human teeth of probable early Upper Pleistocene antiquity discovered at Tongzi, Guizhou (Wu Maolin *et al.* 1975).

In 1973 a single tooth was discovered in the New Cave (Locality 4) at Zhoukoudian (Gu 1978). Other early *H. sapiens* finds include those from Guojiuyan, Changyang County, Hubei (Li 1981); the Gezidong, Kazuo County; and Miaohoushan, Benxi County—both of the latter in Liaoning Province (Zhang Zhenhong 1981).

The principal discoveries of Pleistocene *H. sapiens sapiens* made after the Liberation include the Ziyang, Sichuan Province, and Liujiang, Guangxi Province, hominids. The older locality of Ordos Man in Inner Mongolia has also produced new fossils, and recent research has been conducted on the casts of the Zhoukoudian Upper Cave human remains.

The well-preserved cranium, minus the basicranium, of an old female was found in 1951 during construction of a railway bridge in Ziyang County, Sichuan (Pei and Wu 1957). The absolute dating of this specimen is somewhat in doubt; a recent radiocarbon date placed an associated wood sample well within the Holocene.

In 1958 human remains were discovered in a small cavern on Tongtianyan Mountain in Liujiang County, Guangxi (Wu 1959a). The finds included a complete cranium, a right innominate, a sacrum, and vertebrae thought to be those of a middle-age male. In addition, two female femoral fragments were discovered. The Liujiang cranium exhibits many Mongoloid features and has proven especially important in tracing lines of racial diversification within China.

In 1922 a lateral incisor of a child was found at Dagouwan in Wushen Banner, Inner Mongolia, within the larger area known as the Ordos or Hetao Region. In 1956 the distal half of a left femur and a fragmentary right parietal were found near Dishaogouwan Village, also in Wushenqi, which added substantially to our knowledge of the history of human activity in this area of China (Wu 1958b).

The Upper Cave at Zhoukoudian, near Beijing, yielded in 1933 a series of *H. sapiens sapiens* burials. Although the original fossil specimens were lost during World War II, diligent research has been conducted on the series of excellent casts that survive. Chinese palaeoanthropologists declared in 1960 that the Upper Cave humans represented a primitive Mongoloid type and closely resemble modern Chinese, Inuit, and American Indian populations (Wu Xinzhi 1960, 1961).

Cranial fragments thought to be between 10,000 and 30,000 years old have recently been reported from Cailiaoxi, Zuozhen in Tainan County, Taiwan Province (Lian 1981). These fossils are the first Pleistocene human fossils to be discovered in Taiwan.

A large number of Chinese localities have yielded smaller samples of Pleistocene *H. sapiens sapiens* fossils. The most important of these sites include: Jinniushan, Liaoning (Zhang 1981); Jianping, Liaoning (Wu Rukang 1961); Suoxian, Shanxi (Jia *et al.* 1972); Xintai, Shandong (Wu and Zong 1973); Dantu, Jiangsu (Li *et al.* 1982); Jiande, Zhejiang (Han and Zhang 1978); Laibin, Guangxi (Jia and Wu 1959); Guilin, Guangxi (Wang *et al.* 1982); Lipu, Guangxi (Wu *et al.* 1962); Du'an, Guangxi (Guangxi Zhuang Autonomous Region Museum 1973; Zhao *et al.* 1981); Chenggong, Yunnan (Zhang *et al.* 1978); Xichou, Yunnan (Chen and Qi 1978); Shuicheng, Guizhou (Cao 1978); Maomaodong, Guizhou (Cao 1982a,b); Lingshan, Guangdong (Gu 1962); Fengkai, Guangdong (Song *et al.* 1981); Yushu, Jilin (Division of Higher Vertebrates, IVPP 1959); Sihong, Jiangsu (Wu and Jia 1955a); and Lijiang, Yunnan (Li Youheng 1961; Yunnan Provincial Museum 1977).

At present the difficulty of determining the exact geological age of many of these finds hinders their integration into a comprehensive synthesis, and it is possible that some of these hominids may ultimately prove to be of early Holocene age.

The discovery of these remains of later *H. sapiens* has provided important information concerning the origin of modern human races, especially the Mongoloids. Research continues in conjunction with archaeological approaches directed toward understanding the chronology and dynamics of ethnogenesis in China.

These representative data reflect the abundance of fossil apes, hominoids, and hominids that characterizes China. As a result of nearly half a century of work both in the field and in the laboratory, much information has been gathered on the origin and development of the hominid line in East Asia. Further, it has been demonstrated that tool-using hominids, present in China since at least early Middle Pleistocene times and perhaps much earlier, constitute the basal stock from which the various Chinese national minorities ultimately emerged.

Since 1949 a number of essays have been published dealing with the analysis of specific finds and the interpretation of China's fossil primate record (e.g., Wu Rukang 1959b, 1980, 1982; Wu Rukang and Jia 1955b; Wu Xinzhi and Zhang 1978). The results of this research indicate substantial continuity in the development of the Mongoloid physical type as well as in the phylogenetic relationships among the various stages of hominid development. This is shown with particular clarity in the development of the shovel-shaped incisor, the structure of the zygomatic arches, the broad nose, and the mandibular torus. In addition to these morphological similarities, sufficient characters are retained to allow easy distinction of the various stages of hominid evolution. It is most important to note that although the modern Mongoloid race seems to be a product of only the past few tens of thousands of years of evolution, its origins may be traced into the earlier Pleistocene to fossils such as those from Yuanmou, Yunnan (Wu and Zhang 1978).

The Discovery and Analysis of Palaeolithic Cultural Remains in China

Since the founding of the People's Republic of China in 1949, rapid progress has been made in the study of China's Pleistocene prehistory and numerous new materials have been discovered.

Early Palaeolithic

For over three decades Chinese archaeologists have been diligently searching for evidence of human cultural remains in Lower Pleistocene contexts. In 1960 important finds were made at Xihoudu, Ruicheng County, Shanxi (Jia and Wang 1978; see Chapter 8, this volume) and in 1978 at Xiaochangliang in the Nihewan Basin of Yangyuan County, Hebei (You *et al.* 1980). Additionally, during the winter of 1973 three quartz scrapers were discovered at the site in Yunnan Province where the remains of Yuanmou Man were found (Wen 1978). All three of these sites have yielded artifacts in reportedly Lower Pleistocene strata, although this chronological placement is by no means universally accepted.

China's Middle Pleistocene archaeological record is, however, abundant and well documented. Many seasons of excavation have been conducted since the Liberation at China's most important Early Palaeolithic site, Zhoukoudian near Beijing (Jia 1959b; Qiu *et al.* 1973; Wu and Lin 1983; Zhao and Dai 1961; Zhao and Li 1960). The Palaeolithic remains from Locality 1 at Zhoukoudian have been the subject of intensive study and a large series of publications have resulted (e.g., Jia 1956, 1957b, 1959a,b, 1960, 1961, 1962, 1964; Pei 1955, 1959, 1960, 1961, 1962; Qiu *et al.* 1973; Qiu and Li 1978; Zhang 1962). In recent years Pei Wenzhong and Zhang Senshui have concentrated their efforts on the systematic study of all the stone artifacts recovered from Zhoukoudian to date. The results of their research are now awaiting publication.

In addition to Zhoukoudian a number of new Early Palaeolithic localities have been discovered in China, including Kehe, Shanxi (Jia *et al.* 1962); Gongwangling, Shaanxi (Dai 1966; Dai and Xu 1973; Jia *et al.* 1966); and the lower beds at Jinniushan, Liaoning (Jinniushan Combined Excavation Team 1976, 1978).

Based on a somewhat limited sample, it appears that the Gongwangling, Lantian, material is closely related to the Early Palaeolithic Kehe and Middle Palaeolithic Dingcun cultures. However, the stone artifacts from Jinniushan's Early Palaeolithic levels strongly resemble those from Zhoukoudian Locality 1 in terms of flaking techniques and retouch employed. The illumination of patterns of cultural interrelationships in the Pleistocene is an important research topic in Chinese prehistory today. These sites have provided many of the basic data essential to this sort of analysis.

South China has also begun to yield important Early Palaeolithic assemblages. In 1964, the Guanyindong site in Qianxi County, Guizhou, was found to preserve a record of Middle Pleistocene human activity (Li Yanxian and Wen 1978; Pei *et al.* 1965). In 1971 and 1972 the Shilongtou site in Daye County, Hubei, produced the first Early Palaeolithic remains ever discovered on the middle and lower reaches of the Yangzi River (Li Yanxian *et al.* 1974).

Scattered prehistoric remains attributed to the Early Palaeolithic have also been found in Shanxi, Henan, and Shaanxi (Huang 1964; Jia *et al.* 1961; Qiu 1958b; Tang *et al.* 1982; Wang and Hu 1961; Wang *et al.* 1959b; Zong 1980).

Middle Palaeolithic

For many years the Middle Palaeolithic constituted the weak link in China's Pleistocene prehistory. Very few sites were known; consequently, little data existed linking earlier and later Palaeolithic assemblages. Today a number of important Middle Palaeolithic localities are known, including those of the famous Dingcun Culture, the type site of which is located in Xiangfen County, Shanxi (Pei *et al.* 1958). In 1972 nearly 200 Middle Palaeolithic artifacts were discovered at the site of Yaotougou in Changwu County, Shaanxi. Subsequent analyses of the derived cultural materials suggest a developmental relationship with the later Pleistocene archaeological assemblage from Shuidonggou to the west. Owing to its peculiar features, the excavators of the Yaotougou materials have assigned them a distinctive cultural designation—the Jing-Wei Culture (Gai and Huang 1982).

In 1973 and 1975 more than 280 stone artifacts were discovered in association with traces of fire utilization in the Gezidong, Kazuo County, Liaoning. These cultural remains are thought to bear direct affinities with the earlier *Sinanthropus* Industry of Zhoukoudian Locality 1 (Gezidong Excavation Team 1975).

One of China's most important Middle Palaeolithic localities, the Xujiayao site in Shanxi, produced more than 10,000 stone artifacts and human fossils between 1974 and 1976 (Jia and Wei 1976; Jia *et al.* 1979). The techniques of fabrication and the style of many of the artifacts share features in common with those produced by *H. erectus* at Zhoukoudian.

In 1978, 181 stone artifacts were recovered in association with the early *H. sapiens* Dali cranium in Shaanxi (Wu and You 1979).

Middle Palaeolithic collections have also been reported from the following localities: Jiangjiawan and Sigoukou, Zhenyuan County, Qingyang Prefecture, Gansu (Xie and Zhang 1977); New Cave (Locality 4), Zhoukoudian, Beijing (Gu 1978); Locality 22, Zhoukoudian, Beijing (Zhang 1963); various sites in Shanxi (Jia and Wang 1957; Jia *et al.* 1961; Tang 1981; Wang Zeyi 1965; Wang *et al.* 1959a; Wang and Wang 1960); and Shaanxi (Dai and Ji 1964; Jia *et al.* 1966).

Thus far few Middle Palaeolithic remains have been discovered in South China. One of the most likely candidates is the Huiyan Cave site in Tongzi County, Guizhou, although excavations in 1971 and 1972 only produced a dozen stone artifacts and traces of fire utilization (Wu Maolin *et al.* 1975).

Late Palaeolithic

Upper Pleistocene, Late Palaeolithic archaeological localities are relatively abundant in China. Prior to Liberation, artifacts excavated at Shuidonggou, Ningxia, and at Dagouwan, Inner Mongolia, were collectively referred to as *Ordos Culture,* and were thought to be of Middle Palaeolithic affinity. However, as early as 1955 Pei Wenzhong pointed out the many dissimilarities in the stone assemblages from these two localities and called into question the applicability of a covering term such as *Ordos Culture.* Current research indicates that the Shuidonggou assemblage is clearly Late Palaeolithic and many scholars, including its excavator, Wang Yuping (1962), believe the Dagouwan collection may be even younger (Jia *et al.* 1964; Qiu and Li 1978).

North China has produced a wealth of Late Palaeolithic cultural remains. In 1960 as many as 7000 stone artifacts, ornaments, and traces of fire were unearthed in the Xiaonanhai rockshelter near Anyang, Henan. The small tools that characterize the Xiaonanhai assemblage may constitute the Pleistocene forerunners of Chinese microlithic cultures of the Holocene (An 1965; Zhou 1965).

In 1965 more than 15,000 cultural relics were found at the Shiyu site in Suoxian, Shanxi. Microliths and small flakes comprise the bulk of the assemblage, and some researchers believe the significance of the Shiyu materials lies in the possibility of its being a link between the small-flake tool industry of Zhoukoudian Locality 1 and the truly microlithic industries of the later prehistoric period (Jia *et al.* 1972).

The Xiachuan site in Qinshui County, Shanxi, yielded large quantities of stone artifacts during excavations conducted there between 1972 and 1975 (Wang *et al.* 1978). A total of 1800 artifacts, mostly microliths, have been analyzed from Xiachuan. The artifacts lead scholars to classify the assemblage as typical Late Palaeolithic microlithic of the sort characterized by the occurrence of the wedge-shaped cores that enjoyed a wide sphere of distribution in Northeast Asia and North America in the late Upper Pleistocene.

The site of Hutouliang in Yangyuan County, Hebei has yielded large quantities of Late Palaeolithic stone tools and ornaments. Many parallels may be drawn between the Hutouliang assemblage and that from Shiyu, Shanxi, suggesting both are members of a more-generalized North Chinese small-tool tradition (Gai and Wei 1977).

In South China an important Late Palaeolithic site has been identified at Fulin in Hanyuan County, Sichuan. During excavations in 1972 more than 5000 stone artifacts were recovered, including small cores, flakes, and tools (Yang 1961; Zhang 1977). In 1973, 53 stone artifacts and evidence of fire were unearthed in Xiaohui Cave, Shuicheng County, Guizhou. This assemblage is characterized by artifacts exhibiting edge crushing, an unusual occurrence in South China. The geological age of the site is clearly Upper Pleistocene and it is tentatively thought that both Middle and Late Palaeolithic assemblages are present (Cao 1978).

At the Maomaodong site in Xingyi County, Guizhou, more than 4000 stone artifacts, 14 antler and bone implements, and abundant traces of fire utilization were excavated in 1974 (Cao 1982a,b; Zhang and Cao 1980). Edge crushing is in evidence and most pieces exhibit retouch on their ventral surfaces. The Maomaodong assemblage fills an important geographic gap in our understanding of Late Palaeolithic China and seems in many ways related to its contemporary at Xiaohui Cave.

The Tongliang site in Sichuan, which bears many similarities to Guanyindong, produced over 300 stone artifacts during excavations in 1976 (Li Xuanmin and Zhang 1981; Zhang *et al.* 1982).

In addition to the important sites discussed above, cultural relics of Late Palaeolithic or probable Late Palaeolithic affiliation have been discovered in the following regions and localities: Shanxi Province (Jia *et al.* 1961; Wang Jian 1960; Wang Xiangqian *et al.* 1983); Shangchaozui, Hebei (Gai and Wei 1974; Wei 1978); Dayao, Inner Mongolia (Inner Mongolia Museum and Inner Mongolia Cultural Relics Work Team 1977; Wang 1980); Lantian area, Shaanxi (Jia *et al.* 1966); Liujiacha, Gansu (Gansu Provincial Museum 1982); Jujiayuan and Luofangzi, Gansu (Xie and Zhang 1977); Xinyuan, Shandong (Dai and Bai 1966); Xincai, Henan (Pei 1956); Shibazhan, Heilongjiang (Anonymous 1978; Wei and Yu 1981); Jinniushan, Liaoning (Upper Bed) (Jinniushan Combined Excavation Team 1978); Xibajianfang, Liaoning (Liaoning Provincial Museum 1973); Daxianzhuang, Jiangsu (Li *et al.* 1980); Guiyang, Hunan (Zhang 1965); Sijiacun, Yunnan (Wen 1978); Yiliang, Yunnan (Li and Huang 1962; Pei and Zhou 1961); Mujiaqiao, Yunnan (Lin and Zhang 1978); Longtanshan, Yunnan (Hu 1977);

Leping, Jiangxi (Huang and Ji 1963); Suixian, Hubei (Wang 1961); Shangsongcun, Guangxi (Li and You 1975); Liujiang, Liuzhou, Changzuo, Laibin, and Guilin, Guangxi (Jia and Qiu 1960; Jia and Wu 1959; Wang *et al.* 1982); and Baxian Cave, Taiwan (Song 1969).

China's frontier regions have also yielded quantities of Late Palaeolithic remains, including Dingri, Tibet (Zhang 1976); Kekexili, Qinghai (Qiu 1958a); Qingshuihe, Inner Mongolia (Zhang 1959, 1960); and Alashan, Inner Mongolia (Dai *et al.* 1964).

It is obvious from even this incomplete listing that our knowledge of China's Upper Pleistocene prehistory has increased enormously since Liberation and on the basis of these acquired data scholars have begun to formulate explanatory models for the Chinese Palaeolithic (Jia 1978; Pei 1955, 1959). Foreign researchers have also begun to participate actively in the study of Chinese Pleistocene prehistory (Aigner 1981; Chang 1977; Olsen 1982; Olsen *et al.* 1982). In recent years scholars have turned their attention to the exploration of problems concerning the origins of China's Palaeolithic cultural traditions and China may now be said to be in its second decade of advanced theoretical discussion of these points (Jia *et al.* 1972; Zhang 1977).

The Future of Chinese Palaeoanthropology and Palaeolithic Archaeology

Having provided a summary of important events in the historical development of these fields in China, we turn now to a discussion of the directions in which research on the Pleistocene primates and cultural assemblages of China may proceed.

Although palaeoanthropology and Palaeolithic archaeology have advanced greatly in China over the course of the past 50 years, we now face new problems and questions whose resolution calls for our combined efforts.

The problem of human origins is a central question in palaeoanthropology the world over. Thanks to a cooperative approach fostered by the world palaeoanthropological community we have already gained a great deal of understanding of the problem of human origins. Discoveries made in recent years point out the complicated nature of the process of hominid evolution, and no comprehensive solutions have been formulated regarding the chronology, geography, or specific ecology of human evolution.

Yunnan Province, known for its rich Tertiary coal deposits, has yielded the remains of *Dryopithecus* and two other hominoids tentatively classified as *Ramapithecus* and *Sivapithecus*. The Lufeng locality in particular promises to continue to yield well-preserved hominoid fossils, and it is hoped that the continued analysis of these specimens will provide some of the data necessary for illuminating the divergence of ape and hominid phylogeny.

Large numbers of fossils of *Gigantopithecus* have also been found in China. Questions concerning its systematic position and living habits, including mode of locomotion and dietary preferences, have not yet been solved. On the basis of existing clues, fieldwork will continue in Guangxi, Hubei, Hunan, and Guizhou to provide additional specimens for study. Existing fossils must continue to be diligently analyzed by utilizing new multivariate statistical approaches and other metrical studies.

Fossils of the australopithecinae have been discovered in large numbers on the African continent. In Guangxi and Hubei, morphologically peculiar primate teeth have been found, which some scholars ascribe to the australopithecinae. Although this opinion is by no means universal, further study of these enigmatic finds is clearly warranted.

Koenigswald (1952) put forth the idea that a variety of *Homo erectus*, "*Sinanthropus officinalis*," was present in South China during the Middle Pleistocene. In 1957 he erected a new genus and species, "*Hemanthropus peii*," to describe a tooth slightly smaller than those of *Gigantopithecus* that he had purchased in a traditional Chinese medicine shop in Hong Kong. Because of the very small sample sizes involved and the lack of precise provenance information for these specimens, a final conclusion concerning the validity of Koenigswald's hypotheses cannot yet be drawn. We hope that continued explorations of the Tertiary and Quaternary strata of South China will yield the sort of data necessary to answer these and related questions.

Palaeoanthropological research conducted in Africa indicates the history of the genus *Homo* is a very long one, extending back over 1.5 million years to the time of *H. habilis*. Whether *Homo* was also present in East Asia at such an early age is as yet unknown and this subject will be pursued by Chinese palaeoanthropologists in the future.

The fossils of *H. erectus* that are found in many regions of the Old World retain many secrets. We cannot be certain of the relationships among all these Middle Pleistocene hominids, nor can we adequately explain the transitional process from *H. erectus* to early *H. sapiens*. Did this transition take place concomitant with racial diversification in many areas, or did *H. sapiens* evolve from his predecessor in only one or two specific locales? How did modern *H. sapiens sapiens* evolve in various regions, and what were the dynamics of the diversification of human races? These questions, and many others, have no positive answers yet. Because fossils of *H. erectus* and both early and late *H. sapiens* are found in substantial numbers in China, we hope to make valuable contributions in the future to the resolution of these and related problems.

The evolution of human culture is closely related to tbe evolution of the human biological organism. Although many Palaeolithic localities and cultures have already been identified in China, many regions are still virtually unknown in terms of their Pleistocene prehistory. Palaeolithic archaeology in South China is still a weak link and the vast territories of Tibet, Qinghai, Xinjiang, and western Inner Mongolia have barely been touched by prehistorians. In response to this deficiency, Chinese archaeologists plan to concentrate their efforts on gathering data to fill in these temporal and geographic lacunae.

Chronological questions are still of major interest to Chinese prehistorians. Although the application of chronometric dating techniques has become commonplace in China in the past decade, many important Palaeolithic localities are still inadequately dated. The data we have accumulated need to be tested and corrected when necessary to provide a reliable chronological framework into which new Palaeolithic discoveries may be integrated.

The exploration of Pleistocene technological and cultural traditions in China is little more than a decade old, but already the complexity of this process has become apparent. Recent discoveries of important Palaeolithic cultures bearing distinctive regional features (e.g., Gai and Huang 1982; Li Xuanmin and Zhang 1981) suggest that the relationships among geographically separated cultural assemblages may prove to be a useful field of study in the future. In addition to a regional approach to Palaeolithic archaeology within China, comparative studies relating the Chinese Palaeolithic sequence to those in neighboring areas should receive more emphasis in the future.

The infusion of scientific methodology and technology into Chinese palaeoanthropology has revolutionized our data gathering and analytic capabilities. Current research on human evolution and Palaeolithic archaeology is no longer limited to mere descriptive studies. For example, behavioral questions are more and more becoming an integral part of palaeoanthropological research in China. As we now know, human ancestors differed from the anthropoid apes not only in terms of their physical traits and the simple ability to fabricate tools, but had also formed a unique suite of behavioral responses to their living circumstances, such as bipedal locomotion, increased use of the fore limbs, active food sharing, the division of labor, and the establishment of a home base. In addition, subsistence strategies such as cooperative hunting, the gathering of edible vegetal resources, and the preparation of food prior to consumption (i.e., cooking, cutting, grinding, etc.) increased the need for and facilitated the development of tools, weapons, and language. Though one or several of these behavioral traits may occasionally be observed in nonhuman animals, these characteristics as a suite culminated in the hominids. A behavioral approach to the study of Pleistocene hominids provides a more comprehensive and, some would say, profound picture of the human evolutionary process. The analysis of behavior patterns, as reflections of the production activities and social structures that spawned them, will constitute a major research goal for Chinese palaeoanthropologists in the future.

Human evolution consists of the integration of a number of complex features, including anatomy, psychology, biology, technology, economy, and culture. With the development of specialized fields such as taphonomy, palaeoecology, hunter–gatherer ethnology, and modern primate ethology as clues to fossil hominid behavior, palaeoanthropology has become more capable of extracting useful data from the Plio–Pleistocene record.

The multidisciplinary approach to palaeoanthropological studies exemplified by the Olduvai Gorge and Koobi Fora research projects in East Africa has yielded large amounts of important information (Isaac 1978a,b, 1983; Leakey 1971). We have recognized the effectiveness of this multidisciplinary approach and plan to integrate it more thoroughly into Chinese palaeoanthropology in the future.

References

Aigner, Jean S.

1981 *Archaeological remains in Pleistocene China.* Forschungen zur Allgemeinen und Vergleichrenden Archäologie, Band 1. Munich: Verlag C. H. Beck.

An Zhimin

1965 Trial excavations of the Palaeolithic cave of Hsiao-nan-hai, Anyang, Honan. *Acta Archaeologica Sinica* 1:1–28.

Anonymous

1978 The Palaeolithic site discovered at You'an, Heilongjiang. *Renmin Ribao* January 24:4. Beijing.

1982 The excavation of 400,000 year old *Homo erectus* fossils at Chaoxian, Anhui. *Xinhua Wenzhai (New China Digest)* 8:87.

Bian, M. N. (M. N. Bien) and Jia Lanpo (Chia Lan-po)

1938 Cave and rock-shelter deposits in Yunnan. *Bulletin of the Geological Society of China* 18(3–4):325–348.

Black, Davidson

1927 On a lower molar hominid tooth from the Chou Kou Tien deposit. *Palaeontologia Sinica* Series D 7(1):1–28.

1931 Evidences of the use of fire by *Sinanthropus. Bulletin of the Geological Society of China* 11(2):107–108.

Black, Davidson, P. Teilhard de Chardin, Yang Zhongjian (C. C. Young), and Pei Wenzhong (Pei Wen-chung)

1933 Fossil Man in China. *Memoirs of the Geological Survey of China*, Series A 11:1–166.

Boule, M., H. Breuil, E. Licent, and P. Teilhard de Chardin

1928 *Le Paléolithique de la Chine.* Archives de l'Institute de Paléontologie Humaine, Memoire 4:1–138. Paris: Masson et Cie.

Bowles, G. T.

1933 A preliminary report of archaeological investigations on the Sino–Tibetan border of Szechwan. *Bulletin of the Geological Society of China* 13:119–148.

Cao Zetian

1978 Palaeolithic site at Xiaohuidong in Suicheng, Guizhou. *Vertebrata PalAsiatica* 16(1):67–72.

1982a On the Palaeolithic artifacts from Maomaodong (the rock-shelter site), Guizhou province. *Vertebrata PalAsiatica* 20(2):36–41.

1982b The preliminary study of bone tools and antler spades from the rock-shelter site of Maomaodong. *Acta Anthropologica Sinica* 1(1):18–29.

Chang, Kwang-chih

1977 *The archaeology of ancient China.* 3rd edition. New Haven: Yale University Press.

Chen Dezhen and Qi Guoqin

1978 Fossil human and associated mammalian fauna from Xizhou, Yunnan. *Vertebrata PalAsiatica* 16(1):33–46.

Dai Erjian

1966 The palaeoliths found at Lantian Man locality of Gongwangling and its vicinity. *Vertebrata PalAsiatica* 10(1):30–34.

Dai Erjian and Bai Yunzhe

1966 A palaeoliths found in one cave in Shantung. *Vertebrata PalAsiatica* 10(1):82–84.

Dai Erjian, Gai Pei, and Huang Weiwen

1964 The chipped stone tools of the Alashan Desert. *Vertebrata PalAsiatica* 8(4):414–416.

Dai Erjian and Ji Hongxiang

1964 Discovery of palaeoliths at Lantian, Shensi. *Vertebrata PalAsiatica* 8(2):151–161.

Dai Erjian and Xu Chunhua

1973 New finds of palaeoliths from Lantien. *Acta Archaeologica Sinica* 2:1–11.

Division of Higher Vertebrates, Institute of Vertebrate Palaeontology and Palaeoanthropology (IVPP)

1959 Pleistocene mammalian fossils from the northeastern provinces. *Memoirs of the Institute of Vertebrate Palaeontology and Palaeoanthropology* Series A 3:1–82.

Edgar, J. H.

1933–1934 Prehistoric remains in Hsikang or Eastern Tibet. *Journal of the West China Border Research Society* 6:56–61.

Gai Pei and Huang Wanbo

1982 Middle Palaeolithic remains found in Zhangwu county, Shaanxi. *Acta Anthropologica Sinica* 1(1):30–34.

Gai Pei and Wei Qi

1974 Discovery of a stone artifact from Lower Pleistocene Nihowan. *Vertebrata PalAsiatica* 12(1):69–74.

1977 Discovery of the Late Palaeolithic site at Hutouliang, Hebei. *Vertebrata PalAsiatica*15(4):287–300.

Gansu Provincial Museum

1982 The Palaeolithic site at Liujiacha, Huanxian county, Gansu province. *Acta Archaeologica Sinica* 1:35–48.

Gao Jian

1975 Australopithecine teeth associated with *Gigantopithecus*. *Vertebrata PalAsiatica* 13(2):81–87.

Gezidong Excavation Team

1975 Discovery of Palaeolithic artifacts in Gezidong Cave in Liaoning province. *Vertebrata PalAsiatica* 13(2):122–136.

Graham, David C.

1935 Implements of prehistoric man in the West China Union University Museum of Archaeology. *Journal of the West China Border Research Society* 7:47–56.

Gu Yumin

1962 Report on the fossil bearing cave deposits of Lingshan, Kwangtung. *Vertebrata PalAsiatica* 6(2):193–201.

1978 The New Cave Man of Zhoukoudian and his living environments. In *Gurenlei Lunwenji (Collected Papers of Palaeoanthropology)*, edited by the Institute of Vertebrate Palaeontology and Palaeoanthropology, Chinese Academy of Sciences. Beijing: Science Press. Pp. 158–174.

Gu Yumin and Lin Yipu

1983 First discovery of *Dryopithecus* in East China. *Acta Anthropologica Sinica* 2(4):305–314.

Guangxi Zhuang Autonomous Region Museum

1973 The discovery of human teeth and mammalian fossils at Du'an, Guangxi. *Vertebrata PalAsiatica* 11(2):221–223.

Han Defen and Zhang Senshui

1978 A hominid canine and mammalian material from the Pleistocene of Zhejiang. *Vertebrata PalAsiatica* 16(4):255–263.

Hu Chengzhi
1973 Ape-man teeth from Yuanmou, Yunnan. *Acta Geologica Sinica* 1:65–71.
Hu Shaojing
1977 Palaeoliths discovered in Chenggong county, Yunnan province. *Vertebrata PalAsiatica* 15(3):225.
Huang Wanbo, Fang Dusheng, and Ye Yongxiang
1981 Observations on the *Homo erectus* calvarium discovered at Longtandong, Hexian, Anhui. *Kexue Tongbao* 26(24):1508–1510.
1982 Preliminary study on the fossil hominid skull and fauna from Hexian, Anhui. *Vertebrata PalAsiatica* 20(3):248–256.
Huang Wanbo and Ji Hongxiang
1963 Discovery of "*Ailuropoda–Stegodon*" Fauna from Loping district, northeast Kiangsi. *Vertebrata PalAsiatica* 7(2):182–189.
Huang Weiwen
1964 On a collection of palaeoliths from Sanmen area in western Honan. *Vertebrata PalAsiatica* 8(2):162–181.
Inner Mongolia Museum and Inner Mongolia Cultural Relics Work Team
1977 Report on the excavation of a stone workshop in the eastern suburbs of Hohhot. *Wenwu* 5:7–15.
Isaac, Glynn Ll.
1978a The archaeological evidence for the activities of early African hominids. In *Early Hominids of Africa*, edited by Clifford J. Jolly. New York: St. Martin's Press. Pp. 219–254.
1978b Food sharing and human evolution: archaeological evidence from the Plio–Pleistocene of East Africa. *Journal of Anthropological Research* 34(3):311–325.
1983 Aspects of the evolution of human behavior: an archaeological perspective. *Canadian Journal of Anthropology* 3(2):233–243.
Jia Lanpo (Chia Lan-po)
1956 New views on the stone tools of Peking Man. *Kaogu Tongxun* 6:1–8.
1957a Notes on the human and some other mammalian remains from Changyang, Hupei. *Gu Jizhuidongwu Xuebao (Vertebrata PalAsiatica)* 1(3):247–258.
1957b The examination of interrelations among China's Early Palaeolithic cultures. *Kaogu Tongxun* 1:1–6.
1959a Report on the excavation of *Sinanthropus* site in 1958. *Gu Jizhuidongwu yu Gu Renlei (Palaeovertebrata et Palaeoanthropologia)* 1(1):21–26.
1959b Notes on the bone implements of *Sinanthropus*. *Acta Archaeologia Sinica* 3:1–5.
1960 The stone artifacts of *Sinanthropus* and its relationship with the contemporary cultures in North China. *Gu Jizhuidongwu yu Gu Renlei (Palaeovertebrata et Palaeoanthropologia)* 2(1):45–50.
1961 On the characteristics of the stone artifacts of *Sinanthropus* and the problem of pseudo-tools—a response to Mr. Pei Wenzhong. *Xinjianshe* 9:18–24.
1962 *Sinahtropus* is not the most primitive man—another response to Mr. Pei Wenzhong. *Xinjianshe* 7:54–67.
1964 *Sinanthropus* and culture. *Zhishi Congshu*. Beijing: China Bookstore.
1978 *The original inhabitants of the Chinese mainland.* Tianjin: People's Press.
Jia Lanpo (Chia Lan-po), Gai Pei, and Huang Weiwen
1966 The Palaeoliths of the Lantian, Shaanxi region. In *Shaanxi Lantian Xinshengjie Huiyi Lunwenji (Symposium on the Lantian Cenozoic of Shaanxi Province)* Compiled by the Institute of Vertebrate Palaeontology and Palaeoanthropology. Beijing: Science Press. Pp. 151–156.
Jia Lanpo (Chia Lan-po), Gai Pei, and Li Yanxian
1964 New materials from the Shuidonggou Palaeolithic site. *Vertebrata PalAsiatica* 8(1):75–83.
Jia Lanpo (Chia Lan-po), Gai Pei, and You Yuzhu
1972 Report of excavation in Shi Yu, Shanxi—a Palaeolithic site. *Acta Archaeologica Sinica* 1:39–60.

Jia Lanpo (Chia Lan-po) and Qiu Zhonglang

1960 On the age of the chipped stone artifacts in Kwangsi caves. *Gu Jizhuidongwu yu Gu Renlei (Palaeovertebrata et Palaeoanthropologia)* 2(1):64–68.

Jia Lanpo (Chia Lan-po) and Wang Jian (Wang Chien)

1978 *Hsihoutu—A culture site of early Pleistocene in Shansi province.* Beijing: Cultural Relics Press.

Jia Lanpo (Chia Lan-po) and Wang Zeyi

1957 The discovery of the Jiaocheng, Shanxi Palaeolithic culture. *Kaogu Tongxun* 5:12–18.

Jia Lanpo (Chia Lan-po), Wang Zeyi, and Qiu Zhonglang

1961 Palaeoliths of Shansi. *Memoirs of the Institute of Vertebrate Palaeontology and Palaeoanthropology* Series A 4:1–48.

Jia Lanpo (Chia Lan-po), Wang Zeyi, and Wang Jian (Wang Chien)

1962 K'oho—An Early Palaeolithic site in south-western Shansi. *Memoirs of the Institute of Vertebrute Palaeontology and Palaeoanthropology* Series A 5:1–40.

Jia Lanpo (Chia Lan-po) and Wei Qi

1976 A Palaeolithic site at Hsu-chia-yao in Yangkao county, Shansi province. *Acta Archaeologica Sinica* 2:97–114.

Jia Lanpo (Chia Lan-po), Wei Qi, and Li Chaorong

1979 Report on the excavation of Hsuchiayao Man site in 1976. *Vertebrata PalAsiatica* 17(4):277–293.

Jia Lanpo (Chia Lan-po) and Wu Rukang (Woo Ju-kang)

1959 Fossil human skull base of Late Palaeolithic stage from Ch'ilinshan, Leipin district, Kwangsi, China. *Gu Jizhuidongwu yu Gu Renlei (Palaeovertebrata et Palaeoanthropologia)* 1(1):16–18.

Jinniushan Combined Excavation Team

1976 New material of Pleistocene mammalian fossils in Jinniushan from Yingkou, Liaoning province and their significance. *Vertebrata PalAsiatica* 14(2):120–127.

1978 A preliminary study of Palaeolithic artifacts of Jinniushan, Yingkou, Liaoning. *Vertebrata PalAsiatica* 16(2):129–136.

Koenigswald, G. H. R. von

1935 Eine fossile Saugetier-fauna mit Simia aus Südchina. *Proceedings Koninklijke Akademie van Wetenschappen Amsterdam* 38:872–879.

1952 *Gigantopithecus blacki* von Koenigswald, a giant fossil hominoid from the Pleistocene of southern China. *Anthropological Papers of the American Museum of Natural History* 43:295–325.

1957 Remarks on *Gigantopithecus* and other hominoid remains from southern China. *Proceedings Koninklijke Akademie van Wetenschappen Amsterdam* B 60:153–159.

Leakey, Mary D.

1971 *Olduvai Gorge, Volume 3, Excavation in Beds I and II, 1960–1963.* Cambridge: Cambridge University Press.

Li Pu, Qian Fang, Ma Xinghua, Pu Qingyu, Xing Lisheng, and Ju Shiqiang

1976 A preliminary study of the age of Yuanmou Man by palaeomagnetic techniques. *Scientia Sinica* 6:579–591.

Li Tianyuan

1981 The discovery of human fossils at Guojiuyan, Changyang county, Hubei. *Vertebrata PalAsiatica* 19(2):194.

Li Wenming, Zhang Zufang, Gu Yumin, Lin Yipu, and Yan Fei

1982 A fauna from Lianhua Cave, Dantu, Jiangsu. *Acta Anthropologica Sinica* 1(2):169–179.

Li Xuanmin and Zhang Senshui

1981 On Palaeolithic culture of Tongliang county. *Vertebrata PalAsiatica* 19(4):359–371.

Li Yanxian and Huang Weiwen

1962 Preliminary report on the investigation of the Palaeolithic artifacts from Yiliang district, Yunnan province. *Vertebrata PalAsiatica* 6(2):182–192.

Li Yanxian, Lin Yipu, Ge Zhigong, and Zhang Zufang
1980 On a collection of chipped stone artifacts from Donghai, Jiangsu. *Vertebrata PalAsiatica* 18(3):239–246.

Li Yanxian and Wen Benheng
1978 The discovery and significance of the Guanyindong Palaeolithic culture, Qianxi, Guizhou. In *Gurenlei Lunwenji (Collected Papers of Palaeoanthropology)*, edited by the Institute of Vertebrate Palaeontology and Palaeonanthropology, Chinese Academy of Sciences. Beijing: Science Press. Pp. 77–93.

Li Yanxian and You Yuzhu
1975 On the discovery of palaeoliths in Baise, Guangxi. *Vertebrata PalAsiatica* 13(4):225–228.

Li Yanxian, Yuan Zhenxin, Dong Xingren, and Li Tianyuan
1974 Report on the excavation of a Palaeolithic station known as Shilongtou at Daye, Hubei. *Vertebrata PalAsiatica* 12(2):139–157.

Li Youheng
1961 A Pleistocene mammalian locality in the Likiang Basin, Yunnan. *Vertebrata PalAsiatica* 2:143–149.

Lian Zhaomei
1981 On the occurrence of fossil *Homo sapiens* in Taiwan. *Bulletin of the Department of Archaeology and Anthropology, Taiwan University* 42:53–74.

Liaoning Provincial Museum
1973 The Xibajianfang Palaeolithic site in Lingyuan county. *Vertebrata PalAsiatica* 11(2):223–226.

Licent, E., P. Teilhard de Chardin, and D. Black
1926 On a presumably Pleistocene human tooth from the Sjara-osso-gol deposits. *Bulletin of the Geological Society of China* 5(3–4):285–290.

Lin Yipu and Zhang Xingyong
1978 Mammalian fossils and palaeoliths from Lijiang basin, Yunnan. *Diceng Gushengwu Lunwenji (Professional Papers of Stratigraphy and Palaeontology)* 7:80–85.

Liu Dongsheng and Ding Menglin
1983 Discussion on the age of "Yuanmou Man." *Acta Anthropologica Sinica* 2(1):40–48.

Meng Zhenya
1982 The *Homo erectus* fossils discovered in Yiyuan county, Shandong. *Huashi* 3:32.

Movius, Hallam L., Jr.
1949 The Lower Palaeolithic cultures of southern and eastern Asia. *Transactions of the American Philosophical Society*, New Series 38, part 4 (1948):329–420.

Nelson, Nels C.
1926 Prehistoric man of central China. *Natural History* 26(6):570–579.

Olsen, John W.
1982 Archaeological research in Inner Mongolia. *L. S. B. Leakey Foundation News* 22:7–8.

Olsen, Stanley J., John W. Olsen, and Qi Guoqin
1982 The position of *Canis lupus variabilis* from Zhoukoudian in the ancestral lineage of the domestic dog, *Canis familiaris*. *Vertebrata PalAsiatica* 20(3):264–267.

Pei Wenzhong (Pei Wen-chung)
1929 An account of the discovery of an adult *Sinanthropus* skull in the Chou Kou Tien deposit. *Bulletin of the Geological Society of China* 8(3):203–205.
1931 Notice of the discovery of quartz and other stone artifacts in the Lower Pleistocene hominid-bearing sediments of the Choukoutien cave deposit. *Bulletin of the Geological Society of China* 11(2):109–146.
1934 Reports on the excavation of the Locality 13 in Choukoutien. *Bulletin of the Geological Society of China* 13(3):359–367.
1935 On a Mesolithic (?) industry of the cave of Kwangsi. *Bulletin of the Geological Society of China* 14(3):393–412.

1936 On the mammalian remains from Locality 3 at Choukoutien. *Palaeontologia Sinica* Series C, 7(5):1–120.

1937 Palaeolithic industries in China. In *Early Man*, edited by George Grant MacCurdy. New York: Lippincott. Pp. 221–232.

1938 A preliminary study of a new Palaeolithic station known as Locality 15 within the Choukoutien region. *Bulletin of the Geological Society of China* 19(2):147–187.

1939a New fossil materials and artifacts collected from the Choukoutien region during the years 1937–1939. *Bulletin of the Geological Society of China* 19(3):207–234.

1939b The Upper Cave Industry of Choukoutien. *Palaeontologia Sinica*, New Series D 9:1–41.

1939c An attempted correlation of Quaternary geology, palaeontology, and prehistory in Europe and China. *Occasional Paper No. 2*, Institute of Archaeology, University of London.

1940 The Upper Cave fauna of Choukoutien. *Palaeontologia Sinica*, New Series C 10 (Whole Series No. 125):1–100.

1955 The Palaeolithic cultures of China. In *Zhongguo Renlei Huashi de Faxian yu Yanjiu*, edited by the Institute of Vertebrate Palaeontology and Palaeoanthropology, Chinese Academy of Sciences. Beijing: Science Press. Pp. 53–89.

1956 Quaternary mammalian fossils from Hsintsai, south-eastern part of Honan. *Gushengwu Xuebao (Acta Palaeontologica Sinica)* 4(1):77–100.

1959 Palaeolithic studies. In *Shinianlai de Zhongguo Kexue—Gushengwuxue (1949–1959)*. Beijing: Science Press. Pp. 115–125.

1960 On the problem of the "bone implements" from the Choukoutien *Sinanthropus* site. *Acta Archaeologica Sinica* 2:1–9.

1961 Reflections on the "pseudo-tool" question—discussions on a few problems in *Sinanthropus* culture. *Xinjianshe* 7:12–23.

1962 Is *Sinanthropus* the most primitive "man" after all? *Xinjianshe* 4:28–41.

Pei Wenzhong (Pei Wen-chung) and Wu Rukang (Woo Ju-kang)

1956 New materials of *Gigantopithecus* teeth from South China. *Gushengwu Xuebao (Acta Palaeontologica Sinica)* 4(4):477–490.

1957 Tzeyang Man. *Memoirs of the Institute of Vertebrate Palaeontology and Palaeoanthropology*, Series A 1:1–71.

Pei Wenzhong (Pei Wen-chung), Wu Rukang (Woo Ju-kang), Jia Lanpo (Chia Lan-po), Zhou Mingzhen (Chow Min-chen), Liu Xianting, and Wang Zeyi

1958 Report on the excavation of Palaeolithic sites at Ting-tsun, Hsiangfenhsien, Shansi province, China. *Memoirs of the Institute of Vertebrate Palaeontology and Palaeoanthropology* Series A 2:1–111.

Pei Wenzhong (Pei Wen-chung), Yuan Zhenxin, Lin Yipu, and Zhang Yinyun

1965 Discovery of Palaeolithic chert artifacts in Kuan-yin-tung Cave in Chien-Hsihsien of Kweichow province. *Vertebrata PalAsiatica* 9(3):270–279.

Pei Wenzhong (Pei Wen-chung) and Zhou Mingzhen (Chow Min-chen)

1961 Discovery of palaeoliths in Yunnan. *Vertebrata PalAsiatica* 2:139–142.

Qiu Zhonglang

1958a Discovery of palaeoliths on the Tsinghai-Tibet Plateau. *Gu Jizhuidongwu Xuebao (Vertebrata PalAsiatica)* 2(2–3):157–163.

1958b Discovery of palaeoliths in Yuan-chu county of Shansi province. *Gu Jizhuidongwu Xuebao (Vertebrata PalAsiatica)* 2(4):281–291.

Qiu Zhonglang, Gu Yumin, Zhang Yinyun, and Zhang Senshui

1973 Newly discovered *Sinanthropus* remains and stone artifacts at Choukoutien. *Vertebrata PalAsiatica* 11(2):109–131.

Qiu Zhonglang and Li Yanxian

1978 Chinese Palaeolithic archaeology in the past 26 years. In *Gurenlei Lunwenji (Collected Papers of Palaeoanthropology)*, edited by the Institute of Vertebrate Palaeontology and Palaeoanthropology, Chinese Academy of Sciences. Beijing: Science Press. Pp. 43–66.

Qiu Zhonglang, Xu Chunhua, Zhang Weihua, Wang Rulin, Wang Jianzhong, and Zhao Chengfu
1982 A human fossil tooth and fossil mammals from Nanzhao, Henan. *Acta Anthropologica Sinica* 1(2):109–117.
Qunli
1983 Discovery of additional *Homo erectus* teeth in Bailongdong, Yunxi county, Hubei. *Acta Anthropologica Sinica* 2(2):203.
Schlosser, Max
1903 Die fossilen Saugetiere Chinas nebst einer Odontographie der recenten Antilopen. *Abhandlungen der Bayerischen Akademie der Wissenschaften München*, Band 22 (1):3–220.
Song Fangyi, Qiu Licheng, and Wang Linghong
1981 Preliminary investigation of the Huangyandong site, Fengkai, Guangdong. *Vertebrata PalAsiatica* 19(1):98.
Song Wenxun
1969 The Changbin Culture (note). *Zhongguo Minzuxue Tongxun* 9.
Tang Yingjun, Zong Guanfu, and Xu Qingi
1982 Discovery of Palaeolithic artifacts in Wanrong, Shanxi. *Acta Anthropologica Sinica* 1(2):156–159.
Tang Zong
1981 The Dongyaowen site, Yongji county, Shanxi. *Vertebrata PalAsiatica* 19(2):195.
Teilhard de Chardin, Pierre
1941 Early Man in China. *Institut de Géo-Biologie Publication 7*, Pp. 1–99.
Teilhard de Chardin, Pierre and Emile Licent
1924 On the discovery of a Palaeolithic industry in northern China. *Bulletin of the Geological Society of China* 3(1):45–50.
Teilhard de Chardin, Pierre and Pei Wenzhong (Pei Wen-chung)
1932 The lithic industry of the *Sinanthropus* deposits in Choukoutien. *Bulletin of the Geological Society of China* 11(4):315–364.
Teilhard de Chardin, Pierre and Yang Zhongjian (C. C. Young)
1930 Preliminary observations on Pre-Loessic and Post-Pontian formations in western Shansi and northern Shensi. *Memoirs of the Geological Survey of China*, Series A 8:1–54.
1932 On some Neolithic (and possibly Palaeolithic) finds in Mongolia, Sinkiang and West China. *Bulletin of the Geological Society of China* 12(1):83–104.
1935 The Cenozoic sequence in the Yangtze Valley. *Bulletin of the Geological Society of China* 14(2):161–178.
Teilhard de Chardin, P., Yang Zhongjian (C. C. Young), and Pei Wenzhong (Pei Wen-chung)
1935 On the Cenozoic formations of Kwangsi and Kwangtung. *Bulletin of the Geological Society of China* 14(2):179–210.
Terra, Helmut de
1941 Pleistocene formations and Stone Age man in China. *Institut de Géo-Biologie Publication 6*, Pp. 1–54.
Wang Jian (Wang Chien)
1960 On the discovery of the palaeoliths at Kulung, Yangcheng, Shansi. *Gu Jizhuidongwu yu Gu Renlei (Palaeovertebrata et Palaeoanthropologia)* 2(1):56–58.
Wang Jian (Wang Chien), Wang Xiangqian, and Chen Zheying
1978 Archaeological reconnaissances at Hsia Chuan in Chin Shui county, Shansi province. *Acta Archaeologica Sinica* 3:259–288.
Wang Linghong, Peng Shulin, and Chen Yuanzhang
1982 On the human fossils and stone artifacts found in Baojiyan Cave, Guilin. *Acta Anthropologica Sinica* 1(1):30–35.
Wang Shancai
1961 Palaeolithic artifacts discovered at Suixian, Hubei. *Kaogu* 7:363.
Wang Xiangqian, Ding Jianping, and Tao Fuhai
1983 Microliths from Xueguan, Puxian county, Shanxi. *Acta Anthropologica Sinica* 2(2):162–171.

Wang Yongyan, Xue Xiangxu, Yue Leping, Zhao Jufa, and Liu Shuntang
1979 Discovery of Dali fossil man and its preliminary study. *Kexue Tongbao* 24(7):303–306.
Wang Yuping
1962 The Palaeolithic site at Shuidonggou Village. *Kaogu* 11:588–589.
1980 The Dayao Culture stone workshop in the east suburbs of Hohhot. In *Zhongguo Kaoguxuehui Diyici Nianhui Lunwenji,* edited by the Archaeological Society of China. Beijing: Cultural Relics Press. Pp. 1–13.
Wang Zeyi
1965 Palaeoliths from Huoxian, Shansi. *Vertebrata PalAsiatica* 9(4):399–402.
Wang Zeyi and Hu Jiarui
1961 Palaeolithic implements from P'ing Lu, Shansi. *Kaogu* 12:643, 668.
Wang Zeyi, Hu Jiarui, and Li Yujie
1959a Some palaeoliths found in Nan-liang, Hou-ma, Shansi province. *Gu Jizhuidongwu yu Gu Renlei (Palaeovertebrata et Palaeoanthropologia)* 1(4):187–188.
Wang Zeyi, Qiu Zhonglang, and Bi Chuzhen
1959b Report on the excavation of a Palaeolithic site from Nan-hai-yu, Yuan-ch'u, Shansi. *Gu Jizhuidongwu yu Gu Renlei (Palaeovertebrata et Palaeoanthropologia)* 1(2):88–91.
Wang Zeyi and Wang Jian (Wang Chien)
1960 On the discovery of the palaeoliths at Gujiao, Shansi. *Gu Jizhuidongwu yu Gu Renlei (Palaeovertebrata et Palaeoanthropologia)* 2(1):59–60.
Wei Qi
1978 New discoveries in the Nihewan sequence and their stratigraphic significance. In *Gurenlei Lunwenji (Collected Papers of Palaeoanthropology),* edited by the Institute of Vertebrate Palaeontology and Palaeoanthropology, Chinese Academy of Sciences. Beijing: Science Press. Pp. 136–150.
Wei Zhengyi and Yu Zhigeng
1981 New Palaeolithic artifacts discovered at Shibazhan, Huma. *Qiushi Xuekan* 1.
Weidenreich, Franz
1936a The mandibles of *Sinanthropus pekinensis:* a comparative study. *Palaeontologia Sinica,* Series D 7(3):1–162.
1936b Observations on the form and proportions of the endocranial casts of *Sinanthropus pekinensis,* other hominids, and the great apes: a comparative study of brain size. *Palaeontologia Sinica,* Series D 7(4):1–50.
1937 The dentition of *Sinanthropus pekinensis:* a comparative odontography of the hominids. *Palaeontologia Sinica,* New Series D 1:1–180.
1939a On the earliest representatives of modern mankind recovered on the soil of East Asia. *Bulletin of the Natural History Society of Peking* 13:161–174.
1939b Six lectures on *Sinanthropus pekinensis* and related problems. *Bulletin of the Geological Society of China* 19(1):1–110.
1941 The extremity bones of *Sinanthropus pekinensis. Palaeontologia Sinica,* New Series D 5:1–150.
1943 The skull of *Sinanthropus pekinensis:* a comparative study on a primitive hominid skull. *Palaeontologia Sinica,* New Series D 10:1–484.
1945 Giant early man from Java and South China. *Anthropological Papers of the American Museum of Natural History* 40:1–134.
1946 *Apes, giants, and early man.* Chicago: University of Chicago Press.
Wen Benheng
1978 Palaeolithic artifacts found in the Yuanmou Basin, Yunnan. In *Gurenlei Lunwenji (Collected Papers of Palaeoanthropology),* edited by the Institute of Vertebrate Palaeontology and Palaeoanthropology, Chinese Academy of Sciences. Beijing: Science Press. Pp. 126–133.
Wu Maolin
1980 Human fossils discovered at Xujiayao site in 1977. *Vertebrata PalAsiatica* 18(3):229–238.

Wu Maolin, Wang Linghong, Zhang Yinyun, and Zhang Senshui
1975 Fossil human teeth and associated fauna from northern Guizhou. *Vertebrata PalAsiatica* 13(1):14–23.

Wu Rukang (Woo Ju-kang)
1957 *Dryopithecus* teeth from Keiyuan, Yunnan province. *Gu Jizhuidongwu Xuebao (Vertebrata PalAsiatica)* 1(1):25–32.
1958a New materials of *Dryopithecus* from Keiyuan, Yunnan. *Gu Jizhuidongwu Xuebao (Vertebrata PalAsiatica)* 2(1):38–42.
1958b Fossil human parietal bone and femur from Ordos, Inner Mongolia. *Gu Jizhuidongwu Xuebao (Vertebrata PalAsiatica)* 2(4):208–212.
1959a Human fossils found in Liukiang, Kwangsi, China. *Gu Jizhuidongwu yu Gu Renlei (Palaeovertebrata et Palaeoanthropologia)* 1(3):97–104.
1959b Palaeoanthropology. In *Shinianlai de Zhongguo Kexue—Gushengwuxue (1949–1959).* Beijing: Science Press. Pp. 103–113.
1961 Fossil human humerus from Chienping, Liaoning province. *Vertebrata PalAsiatica* 4:287–290.
1962 The mandibles and dentition of *Gigantopithecus. Palaeontologia Sinica,* New Series D 11:1–94.
1964 Mandible of the *Sinanthropus*-type discovered at Lantian, Shensi—*Sinanthropus lantianensis. Vertebrata PalAsiatica* 8(1):1–17.
1966 The hominid skull of Lantian, Shensi. *Vertebrata PalAsiatica* 10(1):1–22.
1980 Thirty years of palaeoanthropology in China (1949–1979). *Vertebrata PalAsiatica* 18(1):1–8.
1982 Paleoanthropology in China, 1949–79. *Current Anthropology* 23(5):473–477.

Wu Rukang (Woo Ju-kang) and Dong Xingren
1980 The teeth from Yunxian, Hubei. *Vertebrata PalAsiatica* 18(2):142–149.
1982 Preliminary study of *Homo erectus* remains from Hexian, Anhui. *Acta Anthropologica Sinica* 1(1):2–13.
n.d. Reflections on and prospects for the study of *Homo erectus pekinesis.* In *Multidisciplinary studies at the Peking Man site,* edited by Wu Rukang et al. In press.

Wu Rukang (Woo Ju-kang) and Jia Lanpo (Chia Lan-po)
1954 New discoveries about *Sinanthropus pekinensis* in Choukoutien. *Gushengwu Xuebao (Acta Palaeontologica Sinica)* 2(3):267–288.
1955a Fossil human femur fragment of Hsiatsaohwan. *Gushengwu Xuebao (Acta Palaeontologica Sinica)* 3(1):67–68.
1955b The discovery of various human fossils in China and their significance in human evolution. In *Zhongguo Renlei Huashi de Faxian yu Yanjiu.* Beijing: Science Press. Pp. 39–52.

Wu Rukang (Woo Ju-kang) and Lin Shenglong
1983 Peking Man. *Scientific American* 248(6):78–86.

Wu Rukang (Woo Ju-kang) and Peng Ruce
1959 Fossil human skull of early Paleoanthropic stage found at Mapa, Shaokuan, Kwangtung province. *Gu Jizhuidongwu yu Gu Renlei (Palaeovertebrata et Palaeoanthropologia)* 1(4):159–164.

Wu Rukang (Woo Ju-kang) and Wu Xinzhi
1982 Human fossil teeth from Xichuan, Henan. *Vertebrata PalAsiatica* 20(1):1–9.

Wu Rukang (Woo Ju-kang), Xu Qinghua, and Lu Qingwu
1983 Morphological features of *Ramapithecus* and *Sivapithecus* and their phylogenetic relationships—morphology and comparison of the crania. *Acta Anthropologica Sinica* 1(4):155–158.

Wu Rukang (Woo Ju-kang) and Zhao Zikuei
1959 New discovery of *Sinanthropus* mandible from Choukoutien. *Gu Jizhuidongwu Xuebao (Vertebrata PalAsiatica)* 3(4):169–172.

Wu Xinzhi
1960 On the racial type of Upper Cave Man of Choukoutien. *Gu Jizhuidongwu yu Gurenlei (Palaeovertebrata et Palaeoanthropologia)* 2(2):141–149.
1961 Study on the Upper Cave Man of Choukoutien. *Vertebrata PalAsiatica* 3:181–211.
1976 Turning grief into strength: excavating Neoanthropus fossils at Dingcun. *Vertebrata PalAsiatica* 14(4):270.
1981 The well preserved cranium of an early *Homo sapiens* from Dali, Shaanxi. *Scientia Sinica* 2:200–206.

Wu Xinzhi and You Yuzhu
1979 A preliminary observation of Dali Man site. *Vertebrata PalAsiatica* 17(4):294–303.

Wu Xinzhi and Zhang Yinyun
1978 Chinese palaeoanthropological multidisciplinary studies. In *Gurenlei Lunwenji (Collected Papers of Palaeoanthropology)*, edited by the Institute of Vertebrate Palaeontology and Palaeoanthropology, Chinese Academy of Sciences. Beijing: Science Press. Pp. 28–42.

Wu Xinzhi, Zhao Zikuei, Yuan Zhenxin, and Shen Jiayu
1962 Report on palaeoanthropological expedition of the north-eastern part of Kwangsi. *Vertebrata PalAsiatica* 6(4):408–418.

Wu Xinzhi and Zong Guanfu
1973 A human tooth and mammalian fossils of late Pleistocene in Wuzhutai, Xintai, Shantung. *Vertebrata PalAsiatica* 11(1):105–107.

Xiangjiang
1977 The discovery of *Homo erectus* teeth at Yunxi, Hubei. *Vertebrata PalAsiatica* 15(2): rear endpaper.

Xie Junyi and Zhang Luzhang
1977 Palaeolithic artifacts in Qingyang district, Gansu. *Vertebrata PalAsiatica* 15(3):211–222.

Xu Chunhua
1978 The excavation of the Yunxian *Homo erectus* locality in Hubei. In *Gurenlei Lunwenji (Collected Papers of Palaeoanthropology)*, edited by the Institute of Vertebrate Palaeontology and Palaeoanthropology, Chinese Academy of Sciences. Beijing: Science Press. Pp. 175–179.

Xu Chunhua, Han Kangxin, and Wang Linghong
1974 Discovery of *Gigantopithecus* teeth and associated fauna in western Hupei. *Vertebrata PalAsiatica* 12(4):293–309.

Xu Qinghua and Lu Qingwu
1979 The mandibles of *Ramapithecus* and *Sivapithecus* from Lufeng, Yunnan. *Vertebrata PalAsiatica* 17(1):1–13.

Xu Qinghua, Lu Qingwu, Pan Yuerong, Qi Guoqin, Zhang Xingyong, and Zheng Liang
1978 On the fossil mandible of *Ramapithecus lufengensis*. *Kexue Tongbao* 23(9):554–556.

Yang Ling
1961 Discovery of the palaeoliths from Fulinchen, Hanyuan, Szechuan. *Vertebrata PalAsiatica* 6(2):139–142.

You Yuzhu, Tang Yingjun, and Li Yi
1980 New discovery of palaeoliths in the Nihewan Formation. *Quaternaria Sinica* 5(1):1–13.

Yunnan Provincial Museum
1977 Note on Lijiang Man's skull from Yunnan. *Vertebrata PalAsiatica* 15(2):157–161.

Zdansky, Otto
1927 Preliminary notice on two teeth of a hominid from a cave in Chihli (China). *Bulletin of the Geological Society of China* 5(3–4):281–284.

Zhang Senshui
1959 Discovery of Late Palaeolithic artifacts in Inner Mongolia and north-west Shansi. *Gu Jizhuidongwu yu Gu Renlei (Palaeovertebrata et Palaeoanthropologia)* 1(1):31–40.
1960 New materials of palaeoliths from Inner Mongolia. *Gu Jizhuidongwu yu Gu Renlei (Palaeovertebrata et Palaeoanthropologia)* 2(2):129–140.

1962 Some problems concerning the *Sinanthropus* Industry of Choukoutien. *Vertebrata PalAsiatica* 6(3):270–279.

1963 Some palaeoliths from Loc. 22 of Choukoutien. *Vertebrata PalAsiatica* 7(1):84–86.

1965 The discovery of an incised bone awl at Guiyang, Hunan. *Vertebrata PalAsiatica* 9(3):309.

1976 Newly discovered Palaeolithic artifacts from Dingri, Tibet. In *Report on a scientific survey in the Mount Qomolangma area (1966–1968), Quaternary geology*. Beijing: Science Press. Pp. 105–109.

1977 On Fulin Culture. *Vertebrata PalAsiatica* 15(1):14–27.

Zhang Senshui and Cao Zetian

1980 A general discussion of Guizhou Palaeolithic culture. *Guiyang Shiyuan Xuebao* 2:1–11.

Zhang Senshui, Wu Yushu, Yu Qianli, Li Xuanmin, and Yang Xinglong

1982 Discussion of natural environment of Palaeolithic site of Tong-liang. *Vertebrata PalAsiatica* 20(2):165–179.

Zhang Xingyong, Hu Shaojing, and Zheng Liang

1978 The late Pleistocene human teeth from Kunming, Yunnan. *Vertebrata PalAsiatica* 16(4):288–289.

Zhang Yinyun, Wang Linghong, Dong Xingren, and Chen Wenjun

1975 Discovery of a *Gigantopithecus* tooth from Bama district in Kwangsi. *Vertebrata PalAsiatica* 13(3):148–153.

Zhang Yinyun, Wu Maolin, and Liu Jinrong

1973 New discovery of *Gigantopithecus* teeth from Wuming, Kwangsi. *Kexue Tongbao* 18(3):130–133.

Zhang Zhenhong

1981 The human and the culture of the Palaeolithic period from Liaoning district. *Vertebrata PalAsiatica* 19(2):184–192.

Zhao Zhongru, Liu Xingshi, and Wang Linghong

1981 Human fossils and associated fauna of Jiulengshan, Guangxi. *Vertebrata PalAsiatica* 19(1):45–54.

Zhao Zikuei and Dai Erjian

1961 Report on the excavation of the Choukoutien *Sinanthropus* site in 1960. *Vertebrata PalAsiatica* 4:374–379.

Zhao Zikuei and Li Yanxian

1960 Report on the excavation of the Choukoutien *Sinanthropus* site in 1959. *Gu Jizhuidongwu yu Gu Renlei (Palaeovertebrata et Palaeoanthropologia)* 2(1):97–99.

Zhou Benxiong (Chow Ben-shun)

1965 A study of the vertebrate fossils from the Palaeolithic rockshelter of Xiaonanhai, Anyang, Henan. *Acta Archaeologica Sinica* 1:29–50.

Zhou Guoxing and Hu Chengzhi

1979 Supplementary notes on the teeth of Yuanmou Man with a discussion on morphological evolution of mesial upper incisors in hominids. *Vertebrata PalAsiatica* 17(2):149–162.

Zong Guanfu

1980 The discovery of archaic sites in Wanrong county, Shanxi. *Vertebrata PalAsiatica* 18(1):81.

2

Chronology in Chinese Palaeoanthropology

WU XINZHI AND WANG LINGHONG

Introduction

From the discovery of hominid fossils and cultural remains at Zhoukoudian near Beijing in the 1920s until a series of additional finds were made there in the 1960s, the dating of Pleistocene fossil and cultural assemblages in China was based almost exclusively on biostratigraphic methods. However, in the past two decades a variety of new dating techniques has begun to be applied in China including radiometric, palaeomagnetic, fission track, uranium series, and amino-acid racemization dating (Table 2.1).

Beginning in 1965 radiocarbon determinations provided Chinese archaeologists with a series of chronometric dates. These dates, initially generated only by the laboratory of the Institute of Archaeology, Chinese Academy of Social Sciences, coincided well with previously acquired determinations based on more traditional methods such as biostratigraphy and geological correlation. Since then a number of radiocarbon laboratories have been established in China, yielding ^{14}C dates as early as 40,000 BP.

In 1977 chronometric dates based on palaeomagnetic determinations began to be published in China. The multidisciplinary study of the Zhoukoudian fossiliferous localites, begun in 1978, marked a turning point in the application of absolute dating techniques in China. Many laboratories participated in the

ISBN 0-12-601720-4

Table 2.1

CHRONOMETRIC DATES IN CHINESE PALAEOANTHROPOLOGY AND PALAEOLITHIC ARCHAEOLOGY, TO JANUARY 1984

Sample number or reference[a]	Site	Associated culture	Dating technique[b]	^{14}C Half-life[c]	Date BP	Type of sample
Li *et al*. 1977	Yuanmou, Yunnan	Early Palaeolithic	1		1.7 ± 0.1 million	
Cheng *et al*. 1977	Yuanmou, Yunnan	Early Palaeolithic	1		1.63–1.64 million	
Cheng *et al*. 1978	Gongwangling, Shaanxi	Early Palaeolithic	1		1.0 million	
Ma *et al*. 1978	Gongwangling, Shaanxi	Early Palaeolithic	1		0.75–0.80 million	
Li and Lin 1979	Gongwangling, Shaanxi	Early Palaeolithic	2		>0.51 million	Animal bone
Cheng *et al*. 1978	Chenjiawo, Shaanxi	Early Palaeolithic	1		0.53 million	
Ma *et al*. 1978	Chenjiawo, Shaanxi	Early Palaeolithic	1		0.65 million	
Guo *et al*. 1980	Zhoukoudian, Locality 1, Layer 10	Early Palaeolithic	6		0.462 ± 0.045 million	Aspidelite
Zhao *et al*. 1980	Zhoukoudian, Locality 1, Layers 8–9	Early Palaeolithic	4		0.42 ± $^{>0.18}_{0.10}$ million	Mammal dentine
Zhao *et al*. 1980	Zhoukoudian, Locality 1, Layers 1–3	Early Palaeolithic	4		$0.23^{+0.030}_{-0.023}$ million	Mammal dentine
Zhao *et al*. 1980	Zhoukoudian, Locality 1, Layers 1–3	Early Palaeolithic	4		$0.256^{+0.062}_{-0.040}$ million	Deer antler
Xia 1982	Zhoukoudian, Locality 1, Layers 1–3	Early Palaeolithic	4		0.23 million	Bone
Xia 1982	Zhoukoudian, Locality 1, Layers 6–7	Early Palaeolithic	4		0.35 million	Bone
Xia 1982	Zhoukoudian, Locality 1, Layers 8–9	Early Palaeolithic	4		>0.40 million	Bone
Xia 1982	Zhoukoudian, Locality 1, Layer 12	Early Palaeolithic	4		>0.50 million	Bone
Li and Lin 1979	Zhoukoudian, Locality 1, Layer 3	Early Palaeolithic	2		0.37 million	Bone
Li and Lin 1979	Zhoukoudian, Locality 1, Layers 8–9	Early Palaeolithic	2		0.39 million	Bone
Li and Lin 1979	Zhoukoudian, Locality 1, Layer 11, Levels 29–30	Early Palaeolithic	2		0.46 million	Bone

Pei and Sun 1979	Zhoukoudian, Locality 1, Layer 4	Early Palaeolithic	3		0.30 million	Quartz
Pei and Sun 1979	Zhoukoudian, Locality 1, Layer 10	Early Palaeolithic	3		0.61 million	Quartz
Pei 1980	Zhoukoudian, Locality 1, Layer 10	Early Palaeolithic	3		0.52 million	Calcareous soil
Wang *et al.* 1979	Dali, Shaanxi	Middle Palaeolithic	1		<0.73 million	
Wang *et al.* 1979	Dali, Shaanxi, Layer 8	Middle Palaeolithic	3		41,000–71,000	
BKY 80001	Xujiayao, Shanxi	Middle Palaeolithic	4		99,000 ± 6000	Equid dentine
BKY 80002	Xujiayao, Shanxi	Middle Palaeolithic	4		88,000 ± 5000	Equid dentine
BKY 80003	Xujiayao, Shanxi	Middle Palaeolithic	4		102,000 ± 6000	Equid dentine
BKY 80012	Xujiayao, Shanxi	Middle Palaeolithic	4		114,000 ± 17,000	Equid dentine
BKY 81012	Xujiayao, Shanxi	Middle Palaeolithic	4		94,000 ± 7000	Equid enamel
BKY 81014	Xujiayao, Shanxi	Middle Palaeolithic	4		91,000 ± 9000	Rhinoceros enamel
ZK-670-0(1)	Xujiayao, Shanxi	Middle Palaeolithic	5	5730 ± 40	16,920 ± 2000	Rhinoceros bone
ZK-670-0(2)	Xujiayao, Shanxi	Middle Palaeolithic	5	5568 ± 30	16,450 ± 2000	Rhinoceros bone
Chen *et al.* 1982	Xujiayao, Shanxi	Middle Palaeolithic	5		>40,000	
BKY 80027-2	Salawusu, Inner Mongolia	Late Palaeolithic	4		52,800 ± 3800	Bone
BKY 80028-2	Salawusu, Inner Mongolia	Late Palaeolithic	4		44,000 ± 7000	Tooth
BKY 81021	Salawusu, Inner Mongolia	Late Palaeolithic	4		49,500 ± 2200	Rhinoceros enamel
ZK-109-0(1)	Shiyu, Shanxi	Late Palaeolithic	5	5730 ± 40	28,945 ± 1370	*Bubalus* bone
ZK-109-0(2)	Shiyu, Shanxi	Late Palaeolithic	5	5570 ± 30	28,135 ± 1330	*Bubalus* bone
ZK-170-0(1)	Xiaonanhai, Henan	Late Palaeolithic	5	5730 ± 40	13,075 ± 220	Bone
ZK-170-0(2)	Xiaonanhai, Henan	Late Palaeolithic	5	5568 ± 30	12,710 ± 215	Bone
ZK-654-0(1)	Xiaonanhai, Henan, Layer 6	Late Palaeolithic	5	5730 ± 40	24,100 ± 500	Charcoal
ZK-654-0(2)	Xiaonanhai, Henan, Layer 6	Late Palaeolithic	5	5568 ± 30	23,420 ± 500	Charcoal
ZK-655-0(1)	Xiaonanhai, Henan, Layers 2–3	Late Palaeolithic	5	5730 ± 40	11,000 ± 500	Charcoal and animal bone

(*continued*)

Table 2.1 (*Continued*)

Sample number or reference[a]	Site	Associated culture	Dating technique[b]	^{14}C Half-life[c]	Date BP	Type of sample
ZK-655-0(2)	Xiaonanhai, Henan, Layers 2–3	Late Palaeolithic	5	5568 ± 30	10,690 ± 500	Charcoal and animal bone
ZK-136-0(1)	Zhoukoudian, Upper Cave	Late Palaeolithic	5	5730 ± 40	18,865 ± 420	Deer bone
ZK-136-0(2)	Zhoukoudian, Upper Cave	Late Palaeolithic	5	5568 ± 30	18,340 ± 410	Deer bone
ZK-136-0(3)	Zhoukoudian, Upper Cave	Late Palaeolithic	5	5730 ± 40	10,470 ± 360	Bone
ZK-136-0(4)	Zhoukoudian, Upper Cave	Late Palaeolithic	5	5568 ± 30	10,175 ± 360	Bone
ZK-19(1)	Ziyang, Sichuan	Late Palaeolithic (?)	5	5730 ± 40	7500 ± 130	Wood
ZK-19(2)	Ziyang, Sichuan	Late Palaeolithic (?)	5	5730 ± 40	7485 ± 130	Wood
ZK-256(1)	Ziyang, Sichuan	Late Palaeolithic (?)	5	5730 ± 40	6740 ± 120	Wood
ZK-256(2)	Ziyang, Sichuan	Late Palaeolithic (?)	5	5568 ± 30	6550 ± 120	Wood
PV-14(1)	Ziyang, Sichuan	Late Palaeolithic (?)	5 (Gas)	5730 ± 40	7640 ± 140	Wood
PV-14(2)	Ziyang, Sichuan	Late Palaeolithic (?)	5 (Liquid)	5730 ± 40	7310 ± 150	Wood
PV-160	Ziyang, Sichuan	Late Palaeolithic (?)	5	5730 ± 40	39,300 ± 2500	Wood
PV-221	Ziyang, Sichuan	Late Palaeolithic (?)	5	5730 ± 40	37,430 ± 3000	Wood
BKY 76050	Tongliang, Sichuan	Late Palaeolithic	5	?	21,550 ± 310	Wood(?)
PV-128	Tongliang, Sichuan	Late Palaeolithic	5	5730 ± 40	25,450 ± 850	Walnut shell
ZK-384(1)	Xiachuan, Shanxi	Late Palaeolithic	5	5730 ± 40	21,700 ± 1000	Organic mud and charcoal

ZK-384(2)	Xiachuan, Shanxi	Late Palaeolithic	5	5568 ± 30	21,090 ± 1000	Organic mud and charcoal
ZK-385(1)	Xiachuan, Shanxi	Late Palaeolithic	5	5730 ± 40	16,400 ± 900	Charcoal
ZK-385(2)	Xiachuan, Shanxi	Late Palaeolithic	5	5568 ± 30	15,940 ± 900	Charcoal
ZK-494(1)	Xiachuan, Shanxi	Late Palaeolithic	5	5730 ± 40	18,375 ± 480	Organic mud
ZK-494(2)	Xiachuan, Shanxi	Late Palaeolithic	5	5568 ± 30	17,860 ± 480	Organic mud
ZK-497(1)	Xiachuan, Shanxi	Late Palaeolithic	5	5730 ± 40	18,560 ± 480	Peat
ZK-497(2)	Xiachuan, Shanxi	Late Palaeolithic	5	5568 ± 30	18,040 ± 480	Peat
ZK-628(1)	Xiachuan, Shanxi	Late Palaeolithic	5	5730 ± 40	2830 ± 100	Charcoal
ZK-628(2)	Xiachuan, Shanxi	Late Palaeolithic	5	5568 ± 30	2750 ± 100	Charcoal
ZK-634(1)	Xiachuan, Shanxi	Late Palaeolithic	5	5730 ± 40	19,600 ± 600	Charcoal
ZK-634(2)	Xiachuan, Shanxi	Late Palaeolithic	5	5568 ± 30	19,055 ± 600	Charcoal
ZK-638(1)	Xiachuan, Shanxi	Late Palaeolithic	5	5730 ± 40	$36,200^{+3500}_{-2500}$	Charcoal
ZK-638(2)	Xiachuan, Shanxi	Late Palaeolithic	5	5568 ± 30	$35,190^{+3500}_{-2500}$	Charcoal
Wang *et al.* 1983	Xueguan, Shanxi	Late Palaeolithic	5	5730 ± 40	13,550 ± 150	Bone
PV-15(1)	Zhalainur, Inner Mongolia	Late Palaeolithic (?)	5 (Gas)	5730 ± 40	11,770 ± 230	Wood
PV-15(2)	Zhalainur, Inner Mongolia	Late Palaeolithic (?)	5 (Liquid)	5730 ± 40	11,280 ± 200	Wood
PV-15(3)	Zhalainur, Inner Mongolia	Late Palaeolithic (?)	5	5568 ± 30	11,460 ± 230	Bone
PV-4	Hutouliang, Hebei	Late Palaeolithic	5	5730 ± 40	11,000 ± 213	Bone

[a]Key to laboratory abbreviations: BKY, Dating Laboratory, Archaeology Section, Department of History, Beijing University; ZK, Laboratory, Institute of Archaeology, Chinese Academy of Social Sciences; PV, Laboratory, Institute of Vertebrate Palaeontology and Palaeoanthropology, Chinese Academy of Sciences.
[b]Key to dating techniques: 1, palaeomagnetism; 2, amino acid racemization; 3, thermoluminescence; 4, uranium series; 5, ^{14}C; 6, fission track.
[c]With the exception of ZK-19 (2), radiocarbon dates are uncalibrated.

chronological analysis of the Zhoukoudian deposits, utilizing a wide range of investigative techniques. Among these, fission track dating and amino acid racemization were used for the first time in China to establish an archaeological chronology. Based on our accumulated experience, it is evident that the application of numerous dating techniques at individual localities maximizes our ability to compare and confirm chronometric determinations, which is, of course, important in the establishment of a reliable chronological framework for China's Pleistocene prehistory.

With these general considerations in mind, we turn now to a detailed discussion of the application of chronometric dating techniques to China's most important Palaeolithic and fossil ape localities.

Fossil Ape Localities

Dryopithecus, Ramapithecus, and *Sivapithecus*

The Tertiary coal deposits of the Xiaolongtan Colliery in Kaiyuan County, Yunnan, that yielded teeth of *Dryopithecus* in 1956 and 1957 were originally considered to be of Lower Pliocene age (Wu 1957, 1958). A reanalysis of the associated fauna however, suggests the Kaiyuan fossils derive from a stratigraphic context equivalent to the Siwalik Upper Chinji Formation and are therefore more likely of Upper Miocene antiquity (Zhang 1974).

The faunal assemblage associated with the abundant fossils of *Ramapithecus* and *Sivapithecus* at Shihuiba in Lufeng County, Yunnan, has been reported on in detail by Qi Guoqin (1979). Of the 32 species presently identified in the Shihuiba collections, the most significant chronological indicators include *Hipparion* cf. *nagriensis, Ictitherium gaudryi, Chilotherium* sp. nov., *Sivaonyx bathygnathus, Hyotherium* cf. *palaeochoerus,* and *Epimachairodus fires.* These species are associated with the Upper Miocene Nagri Fauna in the Siwaliks as well as in contemporaneous North Chinese and European faunas. Additionally, Miocene Euro–Asiatic species identified at Shihuiba include *Macrotherium salinum, Aceratherium* sp. indet., and *Potamochoerus* cf. *salinus.* This evidence has led to the conclusion that the Lufeng Fauna may be correlated with the Siwalik Nagri Fauna or the European Upper Vallesian or Lower Turolian. Since the Miocene–Pliocene boundary has been revised by international convention to 5 million years BP, the age of the Lufeng Fauna is now considered to be Upper Miocene (Wu *et al.* 1983). As a result of their analysis of rhizomyid rodents from Lufeng and the Siwaliks, Flynn and Qi (1982) reported that, based on the co-occurrence of *Brachyrhizomys nagrii, B. tetracharax,* and *B.* cf. *pilgrimi,* hominoids probably inhabited southern China and Pakistan at about the same time some 8 million years ago.

Archaeological Localities

Early Palaeolithic (*Homo erectus*)

Yuanmou, Yunnan

The study of the geological age of the Yuanmou deposits (formerly known as Makai Valley) in northern Yunnan Province was initiated as early as the 1920s when the discovery of abundant *Equus yunnanensis* fossils led to the Yuanmou Formation's being considered a type section representing Lower Pleistocene alluvial and lacustrine deposits in southwest China (Teilhard 1938).

The hominid remains—two *Homo erectus* incisors—discovered at this site in 1965 were originally thought to be "probably later Lower Pleistocene" (Hu 1973:65). Subsequent excavations have provided more accurate information on the fauna contained within the Yuanmou Formation. Thus far 28 mammalian genera, subdivided into 40 distinct species, have been identified in the Yuanmou deposits. The presence of 9 species considered Tertiary relict forms seems to support the original interpretation of the Yuanmou hominid's Lower Pleistocene antiquity (Lin *et al.* 1978).

Recently Liu and Ding (1983) pointed out an anomalous situation in that the upper strata of the Yuanmou Formation (*sensu lato*) contain more extinct species than do the lower levels. Based on the recognition of a faulted disconformity in the Yuanmou section, the authors explained that the stratum from which the hominid incisors derive is likely to contain faunal elements from earlier stratigraphic levels. Thus the age of the Yuanmou *H. erectus* is not likely to be as early as originally thought (see Chapter 5, this volume).

Recent attempts to clarify the problematic age of the Yuanmou deposits through palaeomagnetic dating have also generated intense controversy. Li Pu and his coauthors (1976) suggest the upper portion of the Yuanmou stratigraphic column may be correlated with the Matuyama Reversed Epoch and the lower with the Gauss Normal Epoch. They conclude that the entire Yuanmou Formation was accumulated between 1.5 ± 0.1 and 3.1 ± 0.1 million years ago. The stratigraphic horizon containing the Yuanmou hominid incisors is thought to fall within the Gilsa Event (1.61–1.79 million years BP) at roughly 1.7 ± 0.1 million years BP.

A subsequent reanalysis of the Yuanmou palaeomagnetic sequence produced nearly identical results; that is, that the Yuanmou Formation was deposited between 1.53 and 3.12 million years BP and that the *H. erectus* fossils derive from a stratum roughly 1.63–1.64 million years old (Cheng *et al.* 1977).

Recently a major reevaluation of the Yuanmou deposits by Liu Dongsheng and Ding Menglin (1983) suggests that the earlier magnetostratigraphic sequence at this site may be explained in a different way. Liu and Ding prefer to correlate the normal polarity member at Yuanmou with the Brunhes Epoch rather than with an event of normal polarity within the Matuyama. Furthermore, they have concluded that the layer yielding the fossils of *H. erectus* is situated at the base of the Brunhes Normal Epoch strata and therefore might not be older than 0.73 million years BP, and possibly only 0.5–0.6 million years old (Figure 2.1).

Li and Lin (1979) determined the alloisoleucine/isoleucine ratio in animal fossils from the hominid-bearing locality at Yuanmou to be 0.80 million years old, suggesting an age much younger than the 1.70 million BP originally proposed. Fluctuations in average temperature of the enclosing sediments during burial may have had a significant influence on these determinations, and, as such fluctuations are not at present quantifiable, the resulting chronometric dates

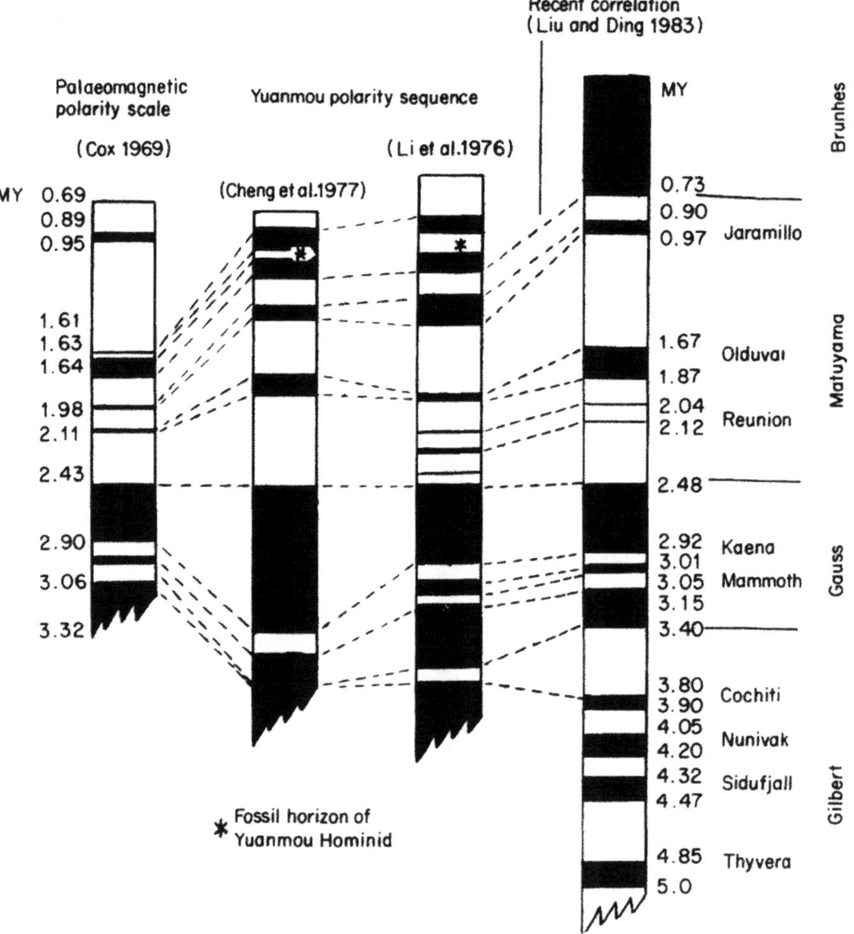

Figure 2.1 Differing interpretations of the correlation between the Yuanmou, Yunnan, palaeomagnetic sequence and the standard polarity scale. (After Liu and Ding 1983.)

must be viewed with caution. However, if we accept the 0.80 alloisoleucine/isoleucine determination as accurate, the inescapable conclusion is that the Yuanmou dentition is not of Early Pleistocene antiquity.

Lantian, Shaanxi

The absolute chronology of the two localities near Lantian in east-central Shaanxi that have produced remains of *H. erectus* is complicated, and various opinions have been expressed on this matter. One of the principal reasons for this long-standing controversy concerns the fact that one of the Lantian localities, Chenjiawo, has produced such a small faunal assemblage that it is not readily comparable with the larger faunal collection from the Gongwangling locality (see Chapter 15, this volume).

Some original descriptions attributed the stratum containing the Chenjiawo mandible to the upper Middle Pleistocene while the Gongwangling hominid-bearing stratum was thought to be of lower Middle Pleistocene age (Jia *et al.* 1966). Subsequent reanalysis and fieldwork have led to a modification of this view, which now suggests that, based on stratigraphic and geomorphological data, the Chenjiawo and Gongwangling fossiliferous strata are broadly contemporaneous in that both may be correlated with lower Middle Pleistocene deposits elsewhere (Wu *et al.* 1966; Zhang *et al.* 1978; Zhou and Li 1965).

Aigner and Laughlin (1973) assigned the Gongwangling *H. erectus* cranium to the middle Mosbachian (or "Cromerian") of roughly 700,000 BP, and attributed the Chenjiawo assemblage to the early part of the Holstein equivalent in China (ca. 300,000 BP). Part of their argument for the temporal distinction between these two sites rests on their understanding of the original paper by Zhou and Li (1965), which describes the fauna collected during excavations at Chenjiawo. They argued that fossils of an extinct pika (*Ochotonoides complicidens*) derive only from stratigraphic units below the remaining Chenjiawo fauna, which may be correlated with the level at Gongwangling that produced the hominid cranium. However, Zhou and Li (1965:382) reported that, "With the exception of one of the upper jaws of *Ochotonoides* which was from a slightly lower level, all the fossils were from the same stratigraphic horizon. However, all of these fossils may be considered to belong to the same mammalian assemblage." In the same paper they reported the discovery of an additional maxilla and mandible of the same animal from the same layer in which the *H. erectus* mandible was found. In fact, no discontinuity is discernable and suggests the various levels in question do not represent different interglacial events as Aigner and Laughlin (1973) suggested.

Unfortunately, magnetostratigraphic evidence has not resolved the problem of the Lantian localities' absolute chronology. One early analysis suggested a correlation between the hominid-bearing stratum at Gongwangling and a period within the Matuyama Reversed Epoch sometime before the Jaramillo Event (Cheng *et al.* 1978). These authors considered the stratum that produced the

Chenjiawo mandible to be attributable to an early phase of the Brunhes Normal Epoch. Based on these determinations—as well as on ancillary lines of evidence, including the relative stratigraphic position of the Lantian hominid fossils and the reconstruction of the average rates of loess deposition in the region—Cheng and his colleagues calculated an absolute age of roughly 1.0 million BP for the Gongwangling cranium, and 0.5 million BP for the Chenjiawo mandible. Based on stratigraphic evidence alone, the former date seems much too early.

Additional archaeomagnetic determinations reported by Ma Xinghua and his colleagues in 1978 yielded a range of 0.75 to 0.80 million BP for the Gongwangling site, and roughly 0.65 million BP for the Chenjiawo *H. erectus* locality.

Mammalian fossils from the layer containing the Gongwangling cranium have also been subjected to amino acid racemization (Li and Lin 1979). These determinations have resulted only in the conclusion that the cranium is older than 0.51 million years BP, but a more precise temporal indication has not been achieved thus far.

In spite of the varying absolute chronologies proposed for the Lantian materials on the basis of a number of analytic techniques, one fact seems apparent: the accumulated data all suggest the Gongwangling cranium antedates the Chenjiawo mandible. At present the duration of the temporal hiatus separating the hominid-bearing deposits at these two localities remains unclear.

Zhoukoudian, Locality 1

Investigations in the fossiliferous limestone fissures at Zhoukoudian in the municipality of Beijing, about 48 km southwest of the city's center, were initiated in the early 1920s. From the beginning, biostratigraphic evidence suggested a Middle Pleistocene age for the bulk of the Locality 1 deposits and an absolute date of roughly 500,000 BP was put forth and widely accepted. Continuing excavations indicated the fissure contained over 40 m of fossiliferous deposits within which significant changes in faunal composition, artifactual inventory, and the character of the hominid fossils themselves were detectable. Clearly, a single absolute date for such a long stratigraphic sequence is a serious oversimplification since the duration of occupation of the cavern by *H. erectus* must also be taken into consideration.

Many scholars approached this problem from a palaeoclimatic perspective by trying to correlate the Zhoukoudian sediments with the European Pleistocene glacial sequence. For example, the Basal Gravels in Locality 1 were considered to be glacial deposits by some authors (Wang and Jia 1952; Xu 1965). Kahlke and Zhou (1961) believed that the major period of *H. erectus* occupation in Locality 1 could be approximately correlated with the closing phases of the European Mindel glaciation (Elster), or the end of the Mindel–Riss interglacial (Holsteinian).

A palynological analysis conducted in 1959 by Kurten on a sample of pollen from matrix adhering to fossil specimens (*Sinomegaceros pachyosteus*) in the Uppsala collection obtained before the Second World War, was employed in conjunction with a more general faunal comparison to arrive at the conclusion that the strata at Zhoukoudian Locality 1 could be correlated with the European Elster II (Mindel II) of approximately 360,000 BP.

A palynological study conducted by Xu Ren (1965) inferred that the climate reflected in the deposits above Layer 11 did not differ significantly from that of the local Zhoukoudian area today. This sedimentary sequence is thought to reflect the events of a single interglacial period. Jia Lanpo (1978) correlates the Basal Gravels at Zhoukoudian with the Dagu (Mindel) glacial period, while all of the strata above the Basal Gravels were, in Jia's view, deposited during the Dagu–Lushan (Mindel–Riss) interglacial. According to Jia, the uppermost strata in Locality 1 (Layers 1–3) contain a faunal assemblage indicating a relatively warm climate.

Zhou Benxiong (1979) studied the fossil rhinocerotids from Locality 1, and based on the stratigraphic distribution of these remains he concluded that Layers 13 and 12 represented a glacial period, Layers 11–9 a transition period into an interglacial, Layers 8–5 the interglacial maximum and Layers 4–1 a transition sequence into a relatively cold climate again. Zhou concluded that the Locality 1 sequence preserves sediments deposited during the closing phases of the second (Dagu) glaciation and the early Dagu–Lushan interglacial, suggesting a chronological range of 680,000 to 370,000 BP.

The absolute dates proposed for the Zhoukoudian Locality 1 deposits include the analyses of Guo Shilun and his colleagues (1980), who derived a ^{238}U fission track date of 0.462 ± 0.045 million years BP on aspidelite (granularity 0.05–0.3 mm) separated from ash collected in Layer 10.

A uranium series date on mammalian dentine from Layers 8–9 yielded a date of $0.42 \pm {}^{>0.18}_{0.10}$ million BP (Zhao *et al.* 1980), while the analysis of a similar sample from Layers 1–3 resulted in a date of $0.23 \pm {}^{0.030}_{0.023}$ million BP. A third uranium series determination derived from deer antlers collected in Layers 1–3 produced a date of $0.256 \pm {}^{0.062}_{0.040}$ million BP.

Subsequently Xia Ming (1982) reexamined the samples from various layers in Locality 1 using the ^{230}Th/^{234}U method. The chronology thus derived is not in accordance with the site's stratigraphy, a contradiction Xia explains as a result of changes in the environment during the deposition of the Locality 1 sediments. Consequently, Xia developed a model for the analysis of the Zhoukoudian sediments utilizing uranium series determinations expressed as ratios of ^{230}Th/^{234}U and ^{234}U/^{238}U. Xia's results suggest the following chronological sequence: Layers 1–3: 0.23 million BP; Layers 6–7: 0.35 million BP; Layers 8–9: more than 0.40 million BP; and Layer 12: more than 0.50 million BP.

Three horizons within the Zhoukoudian Locality 1 stratigraphic profile have also been dated by amino acid racemization (Li and Lin 1979). Fossils from Layer 3 produced a result of 0.37 million BP; those from Layers 8–9, 0.39 million BP; and bones from the twenty-ninth and thirtieth levels of Layer 11 yielded a date of 0.46 million BP.

Two palaeomagnetic studies have been conducted at Zhoukoudian Locality 1. The original analysis of 28 samples from Layers 4–10 all exhibit normal polarity and consequently the authors consider the main deposits at Locality 1 to fall entirely within the Brunhes Normal Epoch (Liu *et al.* 1977). A later palaeomagnetic analysis of the Locality 1 stratigraphic profile indicates that Layers 1–6 and 8–13 are all characterized by normal polarity (Qian *et al.* 1980). Layer 7 however is reversed and the authors suggest this stratum may be correlated with the Japanese Biwa E Event (ca. 400,000 BP) within the Brunhes Normal Epoch (see Derbyshire 1983:181). All Locality 1 deposits below Layer 13 exhibit reversed polarity and are therefore considered to have been deposited during the Matuyama Reversed Epoch.

The ages of five quartz samples extracted from the inclusions of ash deposits at Zhoukoudian have been determined using the thermoluminescence (TL) technique (Pei and Sun 1979). This method suggests the average age of the upper cultural deposits in Layer 4 is 0.30 million BP, while the average age of the samples collected from the lower deposits in Layer 10 is 0.61 million BP. An additional sample derived from the calcareous cap of Layer 10 yielded a TL date of 0.52 million BP (Pei 1980; Pei and Sun 1979).

The combined results of these various approaches to the determination of the absolute chronology of Zhoukoudian Locality 1 can be roughly correlated with one another to derive a synthetic picture. The dates derived from the lower deposits support the conventional estimate of 500,000 BP for these strata, while the upper deposits are certainly older than 200,000 BP. We may say that based on current evidence the duration of the occupation of Locality 1 by *H. erectus* corresponds to the Dagu–Lushan (Mindel–Riss) interglacial, although climatic fluctuations within this long period of time are evident.

In spite of the diverse range of chronometric dates available for the Zhoukoudian Locality 1 deposits, several persistent problems warrant careful consideration. First, racemization dates are influenced by the average temperature that samples are subjected to during burial, since fluctuations in temperature affect the amino acid composition of fossil bone. Since the means for precise determination of a particular stratigraphic sequence's thermal history is not yet available to us, an as-yet-undetermined range of deviation is an inherent feature of these dates.

Second, the absolute reliability of TL dating is also questionable. For example, the age of Locality 4 at Zhoukoudian was determined to be roughly 0.32 million years BP, older than the upper cultural deposits in Locality 1 (Pei and Sun 1979; Pei 1980). This result contradicts biostratigraphic data that seem to indicate Locality 4 postdates the upper deposits in Locality 1 (Gu 1978).

Third, as far as the uranium series determinations are concerned, some of the original investigators themselves have little faith in the dates derived by this method alone. This is, of course, a situation that is not unique to China and suggests that this technique is of great value principally as a means of checking other chronometric determinations and the establishment of rough stratigraphic correlations.

Hexian, Anhui

The Hexian site has yielded a fairly complete *H. erectus* calvarium and a large number of mammalian fossils. Judging from the composition of the fauna, the site is thought to be slightly later than the Middle Pleistocene deposits at Zhoukoudian Locality 1.

Middle Palaeolithic (Early *Homo sapiens*)

With the exception of the late Middle Pleistocene locality at Dali, Shaanxi the various representatives of early *Homo sapiens* and their cultural remains discovered thus far in China are all thought to be of Upper Pleistocene antiquity.

Dali, Shaanxi

The Dali *H. sapiens* cranium, one of the best-preserved late Middle Pleistocene hominid fossils in the world, was discovered in 1978 in the third layer of the Dali stratigraphic section (Wu Xinzhi 1981). Preliminary attempts to clarify the chronology of the Dali sediments by both palaeomagnetic and TL dating have yielded the following results (Wang *et al.* 1979). At the bottom of the Dali section, Layers 1–4, including the stratum that produced the hominid cranium, all exhibit indications of normal polarity that are correlated with the Brunhes Normal Epoch. A single TL date from Layer 8, above the cranium's find-spot, yielded a temporal range of 41,000 to 71,000 BP. Although neither of these determinations provides us with an accurate assessment of the absolute antiquity of the Dali hominid, the TL date at least establishes an upper chronological limit for the specimen.

Xujiayao, Shanxi

After initial excavations at the Xujiayao locality in northern Shanxi in the early 1970s, the deposits, which include both human fossils and an abundant artifactual assemblage, were thought to date between 30,000 and 60,000 BP (Jia and Wei 1976). Subsequent biostratigraphic analyses yielded two mammalian species typical of the Locality 1 deposits at Zhoukoudian (see Chapter 15, this volume). These forms, including the fossil antelope *Spiroceros peii* and vole *Microtus brantioides,* led to the conclusion that the Xujiayao deposits were earlier than had originally been suspected. The Xujiayao faunal assemblage was also found to include such species as *Equus przewalskyi, Coelodonta antiquitatis, Megaloceros ordosianus, Cervus elaphus,* and *Bos primigenius,* which, as forms adapted principally to cold climatic conditions, suggest sedimentary deposition during a glacial

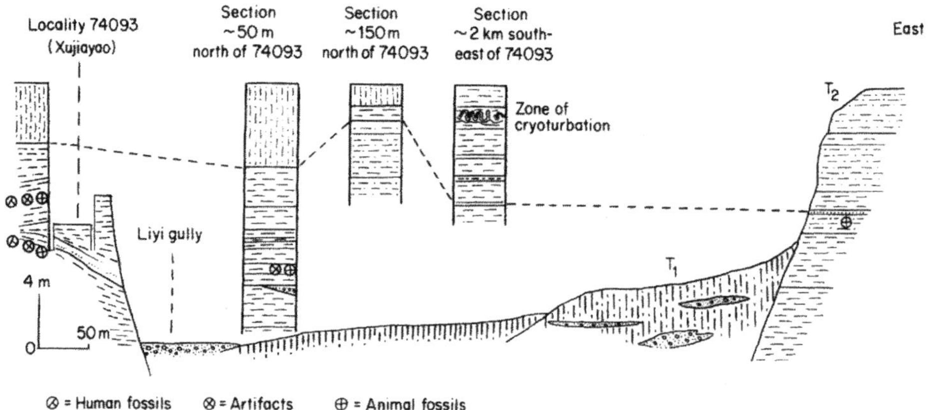

Figure 2.2 Stratigraphic sections in the vicinity of the Xujiayao site, Shanxi. (After Jia *et al.* 1979.)

cycle. In addition, at Locality 74093 a marked zone of cryoturbation occurs above the fossiliferous layer that is believed to have formed during an as-yet-unspecified phase of the Dali (Wurm) glaciation (Figure 2.2). Consequently, the glacial sequence reflected in the fossiliferous deposit below this cryoturbation horizon is correlated with the Lushan (Riss) glacial period. Based on these lines of evidence, Jia Lanpo has concluded that the absolute age of the Xujiayao hominid remains "can be conservatively estimated as 100,000 BP" (Jia *et al.* 1979:293).

Six samples of fossil animal dentition from the Xujiayao site have been subjected to uranium series analysis, yielding an interval concordant ^{230}Th/^{234}U age of roughly 100,000 BP as the youngest possible date for the deposit (Chen *et al.* 1982).

The establishment of an absolute chronology for the Xujiayao site has not been devoid of controversy. For example, a radiocarbon determination generated by the Institute of Archaeology on animal bone from Xujiayao yielded a date of only 16,920 ± 2000 BP (ZK-670-0), a variance that has yet to be adequately explained (Laboratory of the Institute of Archaeology, Chinese Academy of Social Sciences 1981).

These uranium series and radiocarbon dates for Xujiayao represent two interpretive extremes, but other data and opinions also exist. For example, You and Xu (1981) agree that the Xujiayao fossiliferous deposits reflect a relatively cold climate, but they choose to correlate the deposit with the first cold stage of the Dali (Wurm) glaciation rather than with the earlier Lushan (Riss) period, suggesting that the animals typical of Zhoukoudian Locality 1 are not necessarily indicators of great antiquity. In addition, four radiocarbon dates produced in 1978 by Beijing University and the laboratory of the Institute of Vertebrate Palaeontology and Palaeoanthropology suggest a date of more than 40,000 BP for the relevant strata (see Chen *et al.* 1982; You and Xu 1981).

Xindong, Zhoukoudian, Beijing

According to Gu Yumin (1978), the deposits within this fossiliferous cave date to the beginning of the Upper Pleistocene, based on the site's faunal assemblage.

Dingcun, Shanxi

Two contrasting interpretations of the age of Locality 54.100 at Dingcun have been offered. Wang Weijie (1976) and other authors consider the site to be later Middle Pleistocene due to the presence of a thick palaeosol above the fossil-bearing gravels in the stratigraphic section. Pei and his colleagues (1958) hold the opinion that the site dates to the earlier Upper Pleistocene. The Dingcun fauna contains many Upper Pleistocene North Chinese mammalian species such as *Equus hemionus, E. przewalskyi, Bos primigenius,* and *Sinomegaceros* cf. *ordosianus.* In addition, the morphology of the hominid fossils supports an Upper Pleistocene antiquity.

Chronometric interpretations of the important sites of Maba, Guangdong; Changyang, Hubei; and Tongzi, Guizhou, may be found in Chapters 6 and 15 in this volume.

Late Palaeolithic (Late *Homo sapiens*)

Salawusu (Sjara-osso-gol), Inner Mongolia

The later Pleistocene deposits in the Ordos (Hetao) region of southern Inner Mongolia and northern Shaanxi have produced an important sequence of Late Palaeolithic archaeological materials and fossil assemblages. In particular, localities in the Salawusu Valley of Inner Mongolia have yielded abundant archaeological and faunal remains (Qi 1975). The percentage of extinct mammalian species in the Salawusu Fauna (29.6%) is intermediate between that of Dingcun (58.3%) and the Upper Cave at Zhoukoudian (12.1%), suggesting a late Upper Pleistocene age for these assemblages.

Fossilized mammalian dentition and antlers from various stratigraphic horizons have been subjected to uranium series dating that suggests the geological deposits of the Salawusu Formation itself range between 30,000 and 50,000 BP. Based on the stratigraphic position of the *H. sapiens* remains and stone artifacts within this section, an approximate age of 37,000 to 50,000 BP has been suggested for the Salawusu archaeological assemblage (Yuan *et al.* 1983).

Shiyu, Shanxi

Locality 63661, near Shiyu in northern Shanxi Province, has produced a large assemblage of Upper Pleistocene fossils and artifacts since investigations were initiated in 1963. Of the 12 mammalian forms thus far identified in the site's faunal collection, 4 are extinct species (*Crocuta* sp. indet., *Megaloceros ordosianus*, *Bubalus* cf. *wansjocki*, and *Coelodonta antiquitatis*). Based on the composition of this faunal assemblage, it has been suggested that the Shiyu collection antedates that of the Upper Cave at Zhoukoudian (Jia *et al.* 1972).

The only chronometric date yet established for the Shiyu assemblage is a ^{14}C determination on *Bubalus* bone of 28,135 ± 1330 BP (ZK-109), based on a 5570 ± 30 half-life (Laboratory of the Institute of Archaeology, Chinese Academy of Social Sciences 1977).

Xiaonanhai, Henan

The Xiaonanhai cave, some 30 km southwest of Anyang in northern Henan, is characterized by a faunal assemblage that includes 18 vertebrate species, of which 3 are now extinct (*Struthio anderssoni*, *Ursus* cf. *spelaeus*, and *Crocuta crocuta ultima*). According to the analysis of Zhou Benxiong (1965), the Xiaonanhai fauna is clearly of Upper Pleistocene antiquity and may be roughly correlated with that described from Salawusu, Inner Mongolia (Qi 1975) or slightly later, indicating an age somewhat older than the Zhoukoudian Upper Cave fauna.

An early radiocarbon determination on bone derived from a variety of stratigraphic horizons at Xiaonanhai yielded a date of 13,075 ± 220 BP (ZK-170-0) (Laboratory of the Institute of Archaeology, Chinese Academy of Social Sciences 1977). Subsequently, samples of fossil bone taken from provenanced strata were subjected to ^{14}C testing, yielding the following results: Layer 6: 24,100 ± 500 BP (ZK-654); Layers 2–3: 11,000 ± 500 BP (ZK-655) (Laboratory of the Institute of Archaeology, Chinese Academy of Social Sciences 1980). Based on the congruence among the 1977 and 1980 determinations, it is reasonable to conclude that the Xiaonanhai assemblage reflects very late Pleistocene activities in the area.

Zhoukoudian, Upper Cave

Two sets of radiocarbon dates have been published for the Upper Pleistocene deposits in the Upper Cave (Shandingdong) at Zhoukoudian. One specimen, a deer limb-bone excavated from the cave's lower recess in 1934, yielded dates of 18,865 ± 420 BP (ZK-136-0-1), based on the 5730 ± 40 half-life, and 18,340 ± 410 BP (ZK-136-0-2), calculated on a 5568 ± 30 half-life (Laboratory of the Institute of Archaeology, Chinese Academy of Social Sciences 1977). A second sample, fossil specimen No. 109 excavated in 1933 from the cave's upper deposits, has yielded a single date of 10,470 ± 360 BP (ZK-136-0-3), again based on the 5730 ± 40 half-life (Laboratory of the Institute of Archaeology, Chinese Academy of Social Sciences 1980). There are a number of problems involved in the interpretation of the Upper Cave chronology. Most important is the fact that the earlier of the extant radiocarbon dates (ZK-136-0-1 and ZK-136-0-2) were calculated from specimens whose original provenance is thought to have considerably underlain the cave's archaeological deposit. Thus, these ^{14}C dates of 18,000 to 19,000 BP may not provide an accurate chronology for human activity in the Upper Cave. Similarly, the ZK-136-0-3 date is derived from a sample of bone whose exact provenance is unknown. At this point, it seems best to conclude that the archaeological assemblage in the Upper Cave is bracketed by this series of dates but neither extreme is likely to provide an accurate chronological assessment of the cultural remains themselves.

Liujiang, Guangxi

See Chapter 7, this volume.

Ziyang, Sichuan

The Ziyang cranium, discovered in 1951 at Huangshanxi in Ziyang County, Sichuan, was originally thought to be of late Pleistocene antiquity due to the recovery of extinct forms, such as *Rhinoceros* cf. *sinensis* and *Stegodon orientalis*, in apparent association with the hominid fossil. A series of four radiocarbon dates suggests the Ziyang cranium may be considerably younger than was originally suspected: 7485 ± 130 BP (ZK-19) (Laboratory of the Institute of Archaeology, Chinese Academy of Social Sciences 1972); 6740 ± 120 BP (ZK-256) (Laboratory of the Institute of Archaeology, Chinese Academy of Social Sciences 1974); 7640 ± 140 BP and 7310 ± 150 BP (PV-14) (Li *et al.* 1979). All these dates were produced from wood samples thought to have been derived from the same stratigraphic context as the Ziyang cranium, although this is by no means universally accepted. Based on these dates, some scholars now believe that the Ziyang hominid should be correlated with Holocene deposits in the area and that the extinct species from the Ziyang locality are probably early Holocene surviving forms or are not in direct association with the *H. sapiens* cranium (Quaternary Section, Chengdu Institute of Geology 1974). An additional problem concerns the relationship between the wood samples that have been subjected to radiocarbon dating and the stratum in which the hominid remains are thought to have been found. Recently, two radiocarbon dates have been determined on fossil wood collected about 100 m from the Ziyang hominid find-spot in a stratum thought to correspond to that of the cranium. The dates—37,430 ± 3000 BP (PV-221) and 39,300 ± 2500 BP (PV-160)—are obviously well within the Upper Pleistocene (Li and Zhang n.d.). It is possible that the ^{14}C determinations cited previously do not correspond closely to the true antiquity of the Ziyang cranium.

Tongliang, Sichuan

The Palaeolithic site of Tongliang, more than 300 km southeast of Chengdu, is considered to be of middle Upper Pleistocene antiquity due to the recovery of such forms as *Megatapirus augustus*, *Rhinoceros sinensis*, and *Stegodon orientalis* (Zhang *et al.* 1982). Each of the two currently known cultural levels has an associated radiocarbon date that supports the original chronological interpretations based on biostratigraphic data. The upper cultural component at Tongliang is dated to 21,550 ± 310 BP (BKY-76050) (Li and Zhang 1981), while the lower deposit has produced a date of 25,450 ± 850 BP (PV-128) (Li *et al.* 1980).

Xiachuan, Shanxi

The microlithic locality at Xiachuan in Qinshui County, Shanxi, is considered on typological and geomorphological grounds to be a late Upper Pleistocene, Late Palaeolithic site (Wang Jian *et al.* 1978).

The absolute chronology of the Xiachuan site is difficult to interpret at this point. The radiocarbon dates currently available for Xiachuan have yielded a temporal range from 36,200 $\pm\,^{3500}_{2500}$ BP (ZK-638) to 16,400 ± 900 BP (ZK-385) (Laboratory of the Institute of Archaeology, Chinese Academy of Social Sciences 1978, 1979, 1980). In the absence of a larger series of ^{14}C determinations, it is not possible to decide which of these dates is the most accurate or even if they reflect the deposition of archaeological materials over a significant period of time.

Zhalainur (Djalai-Nor), Inner Mongolia

Biostratigraphic evidence, in the form of associated remains of *H. sapiens* and *Mammuthus primigenius,* originally led to the conclusion that the Zhalainur site was a late Pleistocene locality. A radiocarbon date of 11,460 ± 230 (PV-15) on wood from a sand–gravel horizon underlying the stratum containing the human remains suggests it probably dates to the Pleistocene–Holocene boundary (Laboratory, Institute of Vertebrate Palaeontology and Palaeoanthropology 1978). In addition, the presence of *Mammuthus* in the site bears important implications for the question of late Pleistocene–early Holocene megafaunal survival in North China.

Other Localities

In addition to the sites mentioned above, a range of Late Palaeolithic localities in China has been identified as such on the basis of combined geomorphological, physical anthropological, biostratigraphic, and typological data. These sites include Laibin and Lipu, Guangxi (Jia and Qiu 1960; Jia and Wu 1959); Jiande, Zhejiang (Han and Zhang 1978); Wuzhutai, Shandong (Wu and Zong 1973); Maomaodong, Guizhou (Cao 1982); Lijiang, Yunnan (Li 1961; Lin and Zhang 1978); Jianping, Liaoning (Wu 1961); and Zuozhen, Taiwan (Lian 1981).

Conclusions

In this chapter we have endeavored to provide both a history of chronometric dating in China as well as a summary of the more important absolute determinations as they pertain to the Pleistocene prehistory and palaeoanthropology of this region.

Although a great deal of room remains for improvement in the development and application of chronometric dating techniques in China, the data already derived have changed the face of anthropological research in this country in many important respects.

Biostratigraphic analyses and typological studies originally provided us with a relative chronological sequence for China's fossil hominids and Palaeolithic archaeological sites. Absolute dates have proven the original rough estimates are basically correct. In the future, biostratigraphy and typology will continue to be important factors in Chinese palaeoanthropological research, particularly in depositional contexts where chronometric techniques are not applicable or yield ambiguous results. When the strata of a single locality have been accumulated as a result of widely varying depositional processes and the associated faunal assemblages are equally divergent, chronological comparison becomes an especially difficult task. In contrast, chronometric dating provides a common measure applicable to a broad spectrum of depositional environments and, as a result, we believe these techniques will allow us to expand and refine previous accomplishments to meet the needs of anthropological research at a higher level in China.

References

Aigner, J. S. and W. S. Laughlin
1973 The dating of Lantian Man and his significance for analyzing trends in human evolution. *American Journal of Physical Anthropology* 39(1):97–110.

Cao Zetian
1982 On the Palaeolithic artifacts from Maomaodong (the rock-shelter), Guizhou province. *Vertebrata PalAsiatica* 20(2):36–41.

Chen Tiemei, Yuan Sixun, Gao Shijun, Wang Liangxun, and Zhao Guiying
1982 Uranium series dating of Xujiayao (Hsu-chia-yao) site. *Acta Anthropologica Sinica* 1(1):91–95.

Cheng Guoliang, Li Suling, and Lin Jinlu
1977 Discussion of the age of *Homo erectus yuanmouensis* and the event of early Matuyama. *Scientia Geologica Sinica* 1:34–43.

Cheng Guoliang, Lin Jinlu, and Li Suling
1978 A research on the ages of the strata of "Lantien Man". In *Gurenlei Lunwenji (Collected Papers of Palaeoanthropology)*, edited by the Institute of Vertebrate Palaeontology and Palaeoanthropology, Chinese Academy of Sciences. Beijing: Science Press. Pp. 151–157.

Derbyshire, E.
1983 On the morphology, sediments, and origin of the Loess Plateau of central China. In *Megageomorphology*, edited by R. Gardner and H. Scoging. Oxford: Clarendon. Pp. 172–194.

Flynn, L. and Qi Guoqin
1982 Age of the Lufeng, China hominoid locality. *Nature* 298:746–747.

Gu Yumin
1978 New Cave Man of Zhoukoudian and his living environments. In *Gurenlei Lunwenji (Collected Papers of Palaeoanthropology)*, edited by the Institute of Vertebrate Palaeontology and Palaeoanthropology, Chinese Academy of Sciences. Beijing: Science Press. Pp. 158–174.

Guo Shilun, Zhou Shuhua, Meng Wu, Zhang Rongfa, Shun Shengfen, Hao Xiuhong, Liu Sunsheng, Zhang Fang, Hu Ruiying, and Liu Jingfa
1980 The dating of Peking Man by the fission track technique. *Kexue Tongbao* 25(8):384.

Han Defen and Zhang Senshui
1978 A hominid canine and mammalian material from the Pleistocene of Zhejiang. *Vertebrata PalAsiatica* 16(4):255–263.
Hu Chengzhi
1973 Ape-man teeth from Yuanmou, Yunnan. *Acta Geologica Sinica* 1:65–71.
Jia Lanpo (Chia Lan-po)
1978 A note on the weather conditions in Choukoutien area of Peking Man's time. *Acta Stratigraphica Sinica* 2(1):53–56.
Jia Lanpo (Chia Lan-po), Gai Pei, and You Yuzhu
1972 Report of excavation in Shi Yu, Shanxi—a Palaeolithic site. *Acta Archaeologica Sinica* 1:39–60.
Jia Lanpo (Chia Lan-po) and Qiu Zhonglang
1960 On the age of the chipped stone artifacts in Kwangsi caves. *Gu Jizhuidongwu yu Gu Renlei (Palaeovertebrata et Palaeoanthropologia)* 2(1):64–68.
Jia Lanpo (Chia Lan-po) and Wei Qi
1976 A palaeolithic site at Hsu-chia-yao, Yangkao county, Shansi province. *Acta Archaeologica Sinica* 2:97–114.
Jia Lanpo (Chia Lan-po), Wei Qi, and Li Chaorong
1979 Report on the excavation of Hsuchiayao Man site in 1976. *Vertebrata PalAsiatica* 17(4):277–293.
Jia Lanpo (Chia Lan-po) and Wu Rukang (Woo Ju-kang)
1959 Fossil human skull base of Late Palaeolithic stage from Ch'ilinshan, Leipin district, Kwangsi, China. *Gu Jizhuidongwu yu Gurenlei (Palaeovertebrata et Palaeoanthropologia)* 1(1):16–18.
Jia Lanpo (Chia Lan-po), Zhang Yuping, Huang Wanbo, Tang Yingjun, Ji Hongxiang, You Yuzhu, Ding Suyin, and Huang Xueshi
1966 Cenozoic stratigraphy of Lantian, Shaanxi. In *Shaanxi Lantian Xinshengjie Huiyi Lunwenji (Symposium on the Lantian Cenozoic of Shaanxi Province)*. Beijing: Science Press. Pp. 1–31.
Kahlke, Hans-Dietrich and Zhou Benxiong (Chow Ben-shun)
1961 A summary of stratigraphy and palaeontological observations in the lower layers of Choukoutien Locality 1 and on the chronological position of the site. *Vertebrata PalAsiatica* 3:212–240.
Kurten, Bjorn
1959 New evidence on the age of Peking Man. *Gu Jizhuidongwu Xuebao (Vertebrata PalAsiatica)* 3(4):173–175.
Laboratory of the Institute of Archaeology, Chinese Academy of Social Sciences
1972 Report on Carbon-14 dates (1). *Kaogu* 1:52–56.
1974 Report on Carbon-14 dates (3). *Kaogu* 5:333–338.
1977 Report on Carbon-14 dates (4). *Kaogu* 3:200–204.
1978 Report on Carbon-14 dates (5). *Kaogu* 4:280–287.
1979 Report on Carbon-14 dates (6). *Kaogu* 1:89–94.
1980 Report on Carbon-14 dates (7). *Kaogu* 4:372–377.
1981 Report on Carbon-14 dates (8). *Kaogu* 4:363–369.
Laboratory, Institute of Vertebrate Palaeontology and Palaeoanthropology (IVPP)
1978 Carbon-14 date from woody specimens near Zhalainur and its stratigraphical significance. *Vertebrata PalAsiatica* 16(2):144–145.
Li Pu, Qian Fang, Ma Xinghua, Pu Qingyu, Xing Lisheng, and Ju Shiqiang
1976 A preliminary study of the age of Yuanmou Man by palaeomagnetic tecniques. *Scientia Sinica* 6:579–591.
Li Renwei and Lin Daxing
1979 Geochemistry of amino acid of fossil bones from deposits of "Peking Man", "Lantian Man", and "Yuanmou Man" in China. *Scientia Geologica Sinica* 1:56–61.

Li Xingguo, Liu Guanglian, Xu Guoying, Wang Fulin, and Liu Kunshan
1979 Radiocarbon dating of some geological and archaeological samples. *Vertebrata PalAsiatica* 17(2):163–171.
Li Xingguo, Xu Guoying, Wang Fulin, Li Fengchao, Liu Guanglian, Zhang Wending, Liu Kunshan, and Wu Guangzhong
1980 Radiocarbon dating of some geological and archaeological samples (II). *Vertebrata PalAsiatica* 18(4):344–347.
Li Xuanmin and Zhang Senshui
1981 On Palaeolithic culture of Tongliang county. *Vertebrata PalAsiatica* 19(4):359–371.
n.d. Palaeoliths discovered in Ziyang Man Locality B. *Acta Anthropologica Sinica*. In press.
Li Youheng
1961 A Pleistocene mammalian locality in the Lijiang Basin, Yunnan. *Vertebrata PalAsiatica* 2:143–149.
Lian Zhaomei (Lien Chao-mei)
1981 On the occurrence of fossil *Homo sapiens* in Taiwan. *Bulletin of the Department of Archaeology and Anthropology, Taiwan University* 42:53–74.
Lin Yipu, Pan Yuerong, and Lu Qingwu
1978 The Lower Pleistocene mammalian fauna of Yuanmou, Yunnan. In *Gurenlei Lunwenji (Collected Papers of Palaeoanthropology)*, edited by the Institute of Vertebrate Palaeontology and Palaeoanthropology, Chinese Academy of Sciences. Beijing: Science Press. Pp. 101–120.
Lin Yipu and Zhang Xingyong
1978 Mammalian fossils and palaeoliths from Lijiang basin, Yunnan. *Diceng Gushengwu Lunwenji (Professional Papers of Stratigraphy and Palaeontology)* 7:80–85.
Liu Chun, Zhu Xiangyuan, and Ye Sujuan
1977 A palaeomagnetic study on the cave deposites of Zhoukoudian (Choukoutien), the locality of *Sinanthropus*. *Scientia Geologica Sinica* 1:26–33.
Liu Dongsheng and Ding Menglin
1983 Discussion on the age of "Yuanmou Man". *Acta Anthropologica Sinica* 2(1):40–48.
Ma Xinghua, Qian Fang, Li Pu, and Ju Shiqiang
1978 Palaeomagnetic dating of Lantian Man. *Vertebrata PalAsiatica* 16(4):238–243.
Pei Jingxian
1980 An application of thermoluminescence dating to the cultural layers of "Peking Man" site. *Quaternaria Sinica* 5(1):87–95.
Pei Jingxian and Sun Jianzhong
1979 Thermoluminescence ages of quartz in ash materials from *Homo erectus pekinensis* site and its geological implications. *Kexue Tongbao* 24(18):849.
Pei Wenzhong (Pei Wen-chung), Wu Rukang (Woo Ju-kang), Jia Lanpo (Chia Lan-po), Zhou Mingzhen (Chow Min-chen), Liu Xianting, and Wang Zeyi
1958 Report on the excavation of Palaeolithic sites at Ting-tsun, Hsiangfenhsien, Shansi province, China. *Memoirs of the Institute of Vertebrate Palaeontology and Palaeoanthropology* Series A 2:1–111.
Pu Qingyu and Qian Fang
1977 Study of the Yuanmou Man fossil human strata—the Yuanmou Formation. *Acta Geologica Sinica* 1:89–100.
Qi Guoqin
1975 Quaternary mammalian fossils from Salawusu River district, Nei Mongol. *Vertebrata PalAsiatica* 13(4):239–249.
1979 Pliocene mammalian fauna of Lufeng, Yunnan. *Vertebrata PalAsiatica* 17(1):14–22.
Qian Fang, Zhang Jingxin, and Yin Weide
1980 A magnetostratigraphical study of the deposits in "Peking Man Cave". *Kexue Tongbao* 25(4):192.

Quaternary Section, Chengdu Institute of Geology
1974 The geological date of the fossil skull of the Ziyang (Tzeyang) Man. *Acta Archaeologica Sinica* 2:111–123.
Teilhard de Chardin, Pierre
1938 Le Villafranchian d'Asie et la question des Villafranchien. *Compte-rendu Sommaire du Seances de la Societe Geologique de la France* 17:325–328.
Wang Jian (Wang Chien), Wang Xiangqian, and Chen Zheying
1978 Archaeological reconnaissances at Hsia Chuan in Chin Shui county, Shansi province. *Acta Archaeologica Sinica* 3:259–288.
Wang Weijie
1976 On the Quaternary strata of the Dingcun area. In *Papers from the symposium on determining the Tertiary-Quaternary boundary in North China,* edited by the Hebei Provincial Geological Survey, Shijiazhuang. Pp. 27–46.
Wang Xianqian, Ding Jianping, and Tao Fuhai
1983 Microliths from Xueguan, Puxian county, Shanxi. *Acta Anthropologica Sinica* 2(2):162–171.
Wang Yongyan, Xue Xiangxu, Yue Leping, Zhao Jufa, and Liu Shuntang
1979 Discovery of Dali fossil man and its preliminary study. *Kexue Tongbao* 24(7):303–306.
Wang Yuelun and Jia Lanpo (Chia Lan-po)
1952 A survey of Quaternary glacial phenomena at Zhoukoudian. *Acta Geologica Sinica* 32(1):16–25.
Wu Rukang (Woo Ju-kang)
1957 *Dryopithecus* teeth from Keiyuan, Yunnan. *Gu Jizhuidongwu Xuebao (Vertebrata PalAsiatica)* 1(1):25–32.
1958 New materials of *Dryopithecus* from Keiyuan, Yunnan. *Gu Jizhuidongwu Xuebao (Vertebrata PalAsiatica)* 2(1):38–43.
1961 Fossil human humerus from Chienping, Liaoning province. *Vertebrata PalAsiatica* 4:287–290.
Wu Rukang (Woo Jukang), Xu Qinghua, and Lu Qingwu
1983 Morphological features of *Ramapithecus* and *Sivapithecus* and their phylogenetic relationships—morphology and comparison of the crania. *Acta Anthropologica Sinica* 2(1):1–10.
Wu Xinzhi
1981 A well-preserved cranium of an archaic type of early *Homo sapiens* from Dali, China. *Scientia Sinica* 24:530–541.
Wu Xinzhi, Yuan Zhenxin, Han Defen, Qi Tao, and Lu Qingwu
1966 Report on the excavation at Lantian Man locality of Gongwangling in 1965. *Vertebrata PalAsiatica* 10(2):23–29.
Wu Xinzhi and Zong Guanfu
1973 A human tooth and mammalian fossils of late Pleistocene in Wuzhutai, Xintai, Shantung. *Vertebrata PalAsiatica* 11(1):105–106.
Xia Ming
1982 Uranium series dating of fossil bones from Peking Man cave—mixing model. *Acta Anthropologica Sinica* 1(2):191–196.
Xu Ren
1965 The climatic conditions in the Beijing area during the time of Peking Man. *Quaternaria Sinica* 4(1):77–83.
You Yuzhu and Qi Guoqin
1973 New Pleistocene mammalian fossils from Yuanmou, Yunnan. *Vertebrata PalAsiatica* 11(1):66–85.
You Yuzhu and Xu Qingqi
1981 The late Pleistocene mammalian fossils of northern China and correlation with deep-sea sediments. *Vertebrata PalAsiatica* 19(1):77–86.

Yuan Sixun, Chen Tiemei, and Gao Shijun

1983 Uranium series dating of "Ordos Man" and "Sjara-osso-gol Culture". *Acta Anthropologica Sinica* 2(1):90–94.

Zhang Senshui, Wu Yushu, Yu Qianli, Li Xuanmin, and Yang Xinglong

1982 Discussion of natural environment of Palaeolithic site of Tong-liang. *Vertebrata PalAsiatica* 20(2):165–179.

Zhang Yuping

1974 Miocene suids from Kaiyuan, Yunnan and Linchu, Shantung. *Vertebrata PalAsiatica* 12(2):117–123.

Zhang Yuping, Huang Wanbo, Tang Yingjun, Ji Hongxiang, You Yuzhu, Tong Yongsheng, Ding Suyin, Huang Xueshi, and Zheng Jiajian

1978 Cenozoic stratigraphy of the Lantian region, Shaanxi. *Memoirs of the Institute of Vertebrate Palaeontology and Palaeoanthropology*, Series A 14. Beijing: Science Press.

Zhao Shusen, Xia Ming, Zhang Zhenghui, Liu Minglin, Wang Shouxin, Wu Qianfan, and Ma Zhibang

1980 A study of the age of Peking Man by the uranium series method. *Kexue Tongbao* 25(4):182.

Zhou Benxiong (Chow Ben-shun)

1965 The fossil remains of vertebrates unearthed from the Palaeolithic cave deposits at Hsiao-nan-hai in Anyang, Honan province. *Acta Archaeologia Sinica* 1:29–50.

1979 The fossil rhinocerotids of Locality 1, Choukoutien. *Vertebrata PalAsiatica* 17(3):236–258.

Zhou Mingzhen (Chow Min-chen)

1961 An occurrence of *Enhydriodon* at Yuanmou, Yunnan. *Vertebrata PalAsiatica* 2:164–167.

Zhou Mingzhen (Chow Min-chen) and Li Chuankuei

1965 Mammalian fossils in association with the mandible of Lantian Man at Chen-chia-ou in Lantian, Shensi. *Vertebrata PalAsiatica* 9(4):377–393.

3

Ramapithecus and *Sivapithecus* from Lufeng, China

WU RUKANG AND XU QINGHUA

Introduction

It should be made clear that the terms "*Ramapithecus*" and "*Sivapithecus*" are retained in this essay not in their original taxonomic sense, but rather as convenient labels that refer to two categories of hominoid fossils, one small (*Ramapithecus*) and the other larger (*Sivapithecus*).

Since 1975 field teams of the Institute of Vertebrate Palaeontology and Palaeoanthropology (IVPP), Academia Sinica, and the Yunnan Provincial Museum have collected large quantities of *Ramapithecus, Sivapithecus,* and other mammalian fossils at Shihuiba (102°4′E, 25°3′N) in Lufeng County, Yunnan. The fossil locality (IVPP 75033) is situated on the south slope of Miaoshanpo Hill, which is 9 km north of Lufeng City and about 90 km northwest of the provincial capital, Kunming (Figure 3.1).

The geological section of the site (Figure 3.2), which slopes toward the southeast, has been divided into eight layers from the top downward (Wu *et al.* 1982):

Layer 1: Yellow sandy clay with gravel and sand lenses. The clay contains ferromagnesium minerals and quantities of quartz gravels that derive as slopewash from the hill nearby. A thin sandy lense marks the bottom of Layer 1 and a distinct erosional surface separates it from Layer 2. The thickness of Layer 1 varies from 0.6 to 1.3 m and more than 10 fossil mammalian species, including *Hipparion*, are noted in this horizon.

ISBN 0-12-601720-4

Layer 2: Blackish-gray carbonaceous clay and gray-white sand interbedded with thin lignite lenses. The interbedded clays and sands provide a clear, readily interpretable stratigraphic succession. Layer 2 ranges from 1.5 to 2.4 m thick and has produced abundant primate fossils, especially "hylobatids" and lorisids. More than 20 additional fossil mammal taxa as well as mollusk, fish, reptile, and

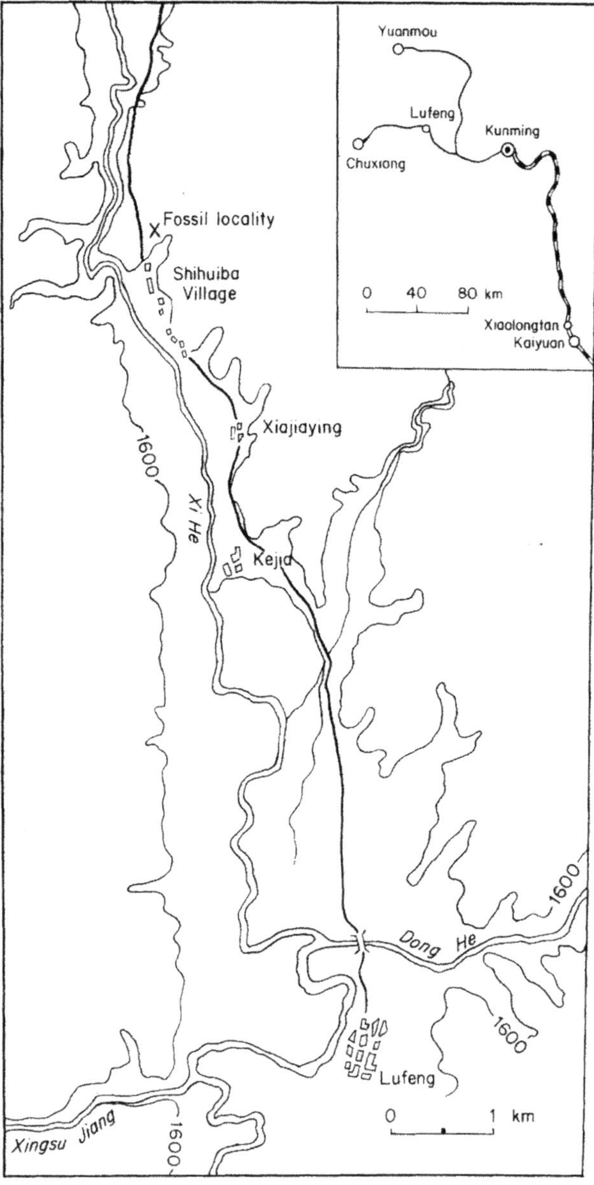

Figure 3.1 The Lufeng, Yunnan, vicinity, indicating the location of the Shihuiba fossil locality. (After Qi 1979.)

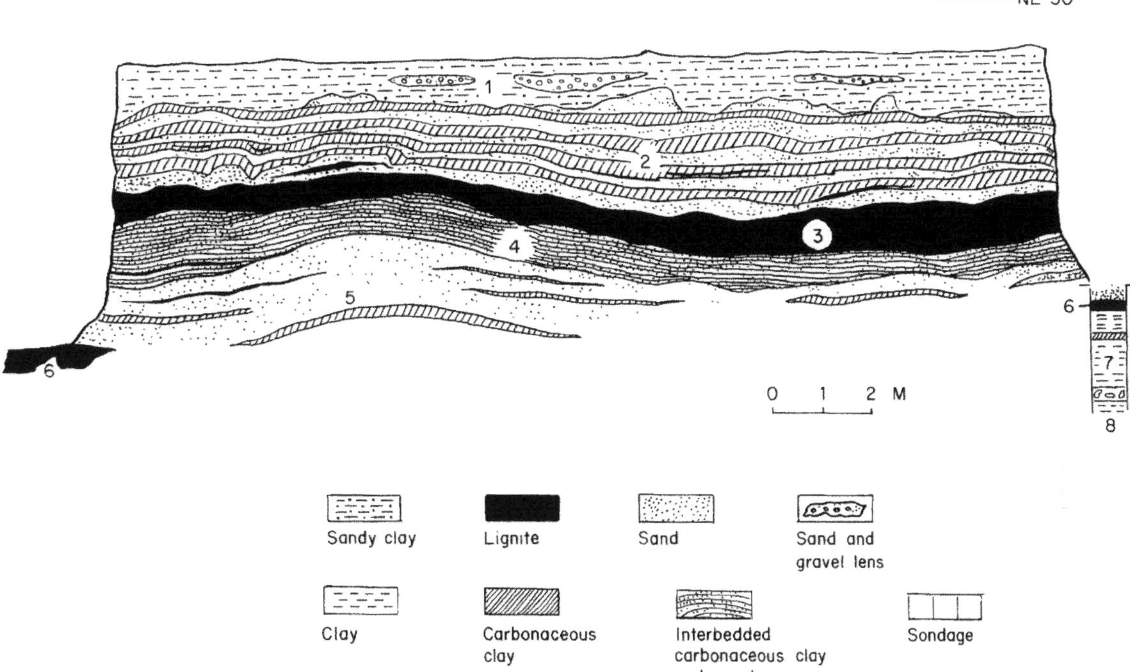

Figure 3.2 1981 geological section at the Shihuiba fossil locality, Lufeng, Yunnan. Numbers refer to layers discussed in the text.

bird remains have been recovered from Layer 2. Segments of fossil tree trunk have also been discovered.

Layer 3: Massive lignite deposit. There are thin carbonaceous clay intercalations in both the upper and lower parts of the stratum. Features that may be fossil rodent burrows (krotoviṇa) or root casts occur in the lignite seam. The thickness of the entire layer is 0.5–1.2 m. Mollusk, fish, reptile, bird, and mammal (including hominoid) fossils are abundant.

Layer 4: Laminated carbonaceous clay and gray-white silt interbedded with lignite lenses. The total thickness of the layer is 0.3–1.0 m. In addition to the remains of hominoids and over 30 other mammalian taxa, a fragment of a tree leaf and tree trunk fossils have also been found.

Layer 5: Gray-white sand with laminated lignite and carbonaceous clay without definite microstratification or cross-bedding. Layer 5 is 1.3–2.3 m thick and has yielded remains of *Ramapithecus, Sivapithecus,* and more than 20 other fossil mammalian species.

Layer 6: Lignite with quartz gravel inclusions, sandy clay, and laminated carbonaceous clay. Thickness is about 0.5 m. Mollusk, fish, reptile, bird, and mammalian fossils (including hominoid) have been recovered.

Layer 7: Gray-white clay enclosing pyritic nodules. The lower part of this

Table 3.1
LUFENG MAMMALS

Primates	Proboscidea
Ramapithecus lufengensis (Xu *et al.* 1978)	*Zygolophodon lufengensis*
Sivapithecus yunnanensis (Xu and Lu 1979)	*Gomphotherium* sp. indet.
"Hylobatinae" gen. et sp. indet.	*Serridentinus* sp. indet.
Lorisiformes family indet.	Perissodactyla
Rodentia	*Hipparion* cf. *nagriensis*
Sciuridae gen. et sp. indet.	*Chilotherium* sp. indet.
Hystrix sp. indet.	*Aceratherium* sp. indet.
Brachyrhizomys nagrii	*Macrotherium salinum*
Brachyrhizomys tetracharax	*Tapirus* sp. indet.
Brachyrhizomys cf. *pilgrimi*	Artiodactyla
Lagomorpha	*Potamochoerus* cf. *salinus*
Leporidae gen. et sp. indet.	*Lophochoerus lufengensis*
Chiroptera	*Hyotherium* cf. *palaeochoerus*
Scaptochirus sp. indet.	Suidae gen. et sp. indet. (1, 2)
Carnivora	*Dorcatherium minus*
Ictitherium gaudryi	*Dorcabune* sp. indet.
Viverridae gen. et sp. indet. (1, 2, 3)	*Palaeomeryx* sp. indet.
Proputorius lufengensis	Cervidae gen. et sp. indet.
Sivaonyx bathygnathus	*Muntiacus* sp. indet.
Lutra sp. indet.	*Metacervulus* cf. *simplex*
Epimachairodus fires	*Antilospira* sp. indet.
Ursavus depereti	*Moschus* cf. *primaevus*
Indarctos sinensis	
Ursinae gen. et sp. indet.	
Pseudaeilurus sp. indet.	

stratum includes relatively large quartz gravels and its total thickness is about 1.6 m. Only a small number of mammalian fossils have been discovered in the upper portion of this layer. No fossil hominoid remains have been recovered here yet.

Layer 8: Yellow-brown and red clay forming the weathered crust of the Precambrian Kunyang Group. Exposed thickness at present is about 0.8 m.

This stratigraphic sequence seems to reflect three distinct depositional environments. Layer 1 is thought to be correlated with a shallow lacustrine niche; the second through the sixth layers with a lacustrine–swamp environment; and Layer 7 with a deep-lake facies. Layer 8 is a product of long-term weathering of Precambrian sediments and bears no palaeoenvironmental data of direct concern here.

The analysis of the Lufeng fauna is currently being undertaken; however, a preliminary list of mammalian forms present has been compiled (Flynn and Qi 1982; Han 1983; Qi 1979, 1983, 1984; Wu *et al.* 1981; Zhang 1982) (Table 3.1).

Many of the Lufeng mammalian species are comparable to those of the Nagri–Dhok Pathan Fauna from the Siwalik Hills of India and Pakistan. The analytic work of Flynn and Qi (1982) on rodent jaws from both areas suggests an age of roughly 8 million years BP (i.e., late Miocene) for the Lufeng Fauna.

Stratigraphic, faunal, and palynological studies all indicate that during the period of late Miocene hominoid occupation, the Lufeng area was characterized by a mixed forest–grassland in close proximity to swamp and lacustrine niches. The climate is thought to have been generally warm and humid.

The Lufeng Small Hominoid (*Ramapithecus*)

Specimens of *Ramapithecus* collected at Lufeng thus far include 3 crania, 4 cranial fragments, 4 mandibles, 16 mandibular and maxillary fragments, 20 dental rows, and 278 isolated teeth.

Crania

The *Ramapithecus* cranium PA-677 (Figures 3.3 and 3.4) was found in the lignite deposits of Layer 3 in December, 1980 (Wu *et al.* 1981, 1983). Although nearly complete, the cranium was compressed to a thickness of only a few centimeters during the process of fossilization. Both of the zygomatic arches and the posterior margin of the cranium are the only major portions of the specimen that are not preserved. All cheek teeth are present *in situ* but the anterior teeth are missing, with the exception of the right lateral incisor.

The PA-677 cranium is rather small and gracile, and from an analysis of this specimen and others from Lufeng, we may formulate the following list of characters considered to be typical of the Lufeng *Ramapithecus*:

1. The temporal crests on both sides are separate, slight, and rounded. They begin at the lateral margin of the supraorbital ridges, run parallel to them, and then turn posteriorly near the midpoint of the ridges. They are robust in the anterior region and gradually become more slender in the posterior direction. They converge slightly in the midposterior portion of the vault and then diverge once again almost immediately.
2. The sagittal crest is weak or absent. In the case of YV-652 it begins near the external occipital protuberance, extends anteriorly, and disappears midway along the vault.
3. The supraorbital ridges are not continuous and are only slightly prominent, with no supraorbital sulcus in evidence.
4. The interobital region is wide and concave while the orbital contours take the form of squares with rounded corners.
5. The lower face is shallow and the infraorbital rims are located slightly below the superior margin of the nasal aperture. The nasoalveolar clivus is very short. The hard palate is shallow and constricted posteriorly, therefore it is less prognathic than in modern apes.
6. The nasal aperture is elongated and pear-shaped.

Figure 3.3 *Ramapithecus* cranium PA-677 from Lufeng, Yunnan. Superior view, ×1.

7. The slight canine juga and shallow canine fossae are consistent with the small size of the canines themselves. The angle of divergence between the canines is less than that observed in *Sivapithecus*.
8. The face of *Ramapithecus* is relatively narrow in comparison to that of *Sivapithecus*, and the zygomatic arches are not expanded as far laterally.

Figure 3.4 *Ramapithecus* cranium PA-677 from Lufeng, Yunnan. Basal view, ×1.

9. The maxillary dental arcade is sub-V shaped, its anterior portion being rounded and then gradually diverging posteriorly.
10. The external occipital protuberance is only slightly developed. The nuchal crests are not marked and the nuchal plane is smooth with a very gracile external occipital crest.

11. The foramen magnum is situated more anteriorly than in extant great apes.

Mandibles

The mandible PA-580 (Figure 3.5) is considered typical of *Ramapithecus* from Lufeng (Xu *et al.* 1978; Xu and Lu 1979). The specimen, discovered in November 1976, is somewhat crushed and twisted. The anterior surface of the mandibular symphysis and the external surface of the body have been damaged, but their internal surfaces are intact. Part of the right ascending ramus remains and all teeth, with the exception of the two medial incisors, are preserved.

The *Ramapithecus* mandible PA-848, discovered in November 1981, is also in a good state of preservation. Unfortunately, like PA-580, this specimen is distorted as a result of lithostatic pressure. In morphology and size it also resembles the PA-580 mandible, but PA-848 preserves both the symphysis and body.

The Lufeng *Ramapithecus* mandibles in general exhibit the following distinguishing characters:

1. The mandibles are relatively gracile with shallow, thin symphyses and bodies.

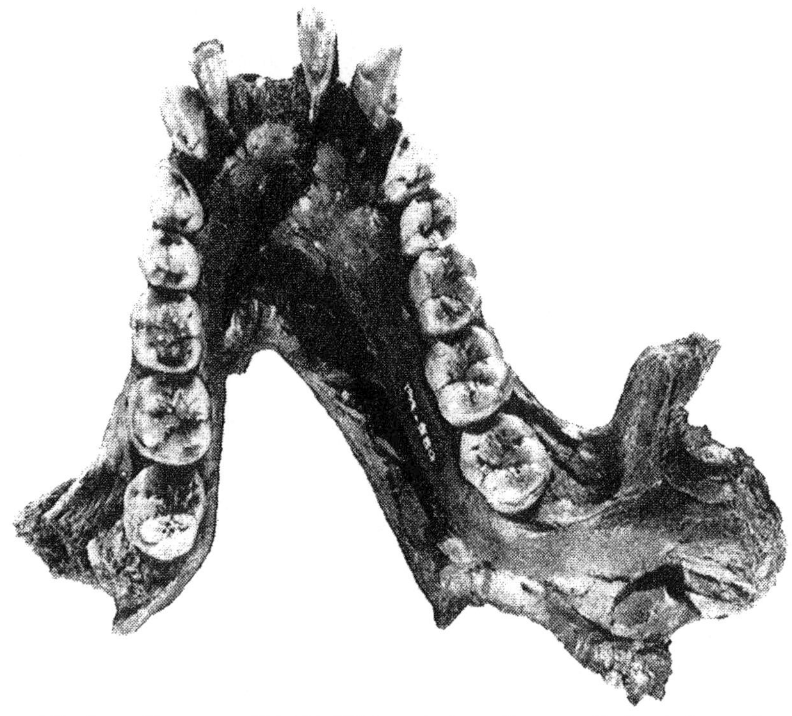

Figure 3.5 *Ramapithecus* mandible PA-580 from Lufeng, Yunnan. Occlusal view, ×1.

2. The anterior margin of the symphysis is rounded and a slight digastric spine is present at the base of the symphysis.
3. The alveolar plane is moderately sloped and the superior transverse torus is poorly developed. The inferior transverse torus is extremely thick and projects posteriorly very far. The genioglossal fossa is wide and shallow. The buccinator grooves are relatively broad.
4. The mandibular dental arcade is sub-V shaped; the anterior tooth row being rounded while both rows of cheek teeth quickly diverge posteriorly.
5. The canines are small and project only slightly beyond the level of the remaining dentition.

Dentition

The teeth of *Ramapithecus* are smaller than those of *Sivapithecus* and the range of variation in size is rather small.

The upper central incisor of *Ramapithecus* is characterized by the great labiolingual breadth of the crown. There is a pronounced tubercle on the basal portion of the lingual surface.

The crown of the upper lateral incisor is particularly small, being only roughly half the size of the central incisor. The upper lateral incisor does not exhibit a developed lingual tubercle.

The upper canine is small and its crown is low with a rather blunt cusp.

The upper third premolar possesses a relatively large paracone and small protocone. The mesiobuccal angle of the crown is markedly developed.

Both cusps of the upper fourth premolar are equal in size. The upper molars each have four relatively low cusps with correspondingly wide fovea. Among the three molars, the second is the largest and the first is the smallest. The distal margin of the crown of the upper third molar is markedly serrate. All molars lack a buccal cingulum and the molar wear gradient is clearly distinguishable. The crenulations on the occlusal surface of the molars are quite complex and the enamel on these teeth is relatively thick.

The lower central and lateral incisors are all nearly equal in size and similar in morphology. The lingual margin of the crown possesses a V-shaped ridge. The lower canine is markedly reduced in both height and robustness.

The lower third premolars are distinctly bicuspid, but the metaconid is much smaller than the protoconid. The mesiodistal dimension of the crown is reduced, therefore the contour of the crown is triangular rather than sectorial.

The crown of the lower fourth premolar is rhomboidal, with the protoconid and metaconid equal in size with large posterior fovea.

The lower molars have five cusps arranged in the typical *Dryopithecus*, or "Y-5," pattern. The molar cusps are low and widely separated with broad fovea.

The lower third molar is a specialized tooth with both a metastylid and a sixth cusp. In addition, the posterior part of the crown is unusually narrow. The occlusal surface of the lower molars are characterized by relatively complex crenulations, thick enamel, and a distinctive wear gradient.

The Lufeng Large Hominoid (*Sivapithecus*)

Fossils described as *Sivapithecus* discovered to date at Lufeng include 2 crania, 2 cranial fragments, 5 mandibles, 20 fragments of upper and lower jaws, 7 dental rows, and 290 isolated teeth. Our analysis of these combined materials permits the following generalizations.

Crania

The well-preserved *Sivapithecus* cranium PA-644 (Figures 3.6 and 3.7) was removed from the lignite deposits of Layer 3 in December 1978 (Lu *et al.* 1981; Wu *et al* 1983; Xu and Lu 1980). The face is nearly complete, although broken. The zygomatic arches are damaged and most of the cranial vault is missing. The foramen magnum is preserved, although perhaps not in its original position due to distortion during fossilization. All the teeth are present in this specimen, although the crown of the left canine is broken.

The other Lufeng *Sivapithecus* cranium, PA-845, is very badly crushed and damaged. Although reconstructable, this specimen does not yet permit the sort of detailed morphometric analysis possible with PA-644.

Although based on a very limited sample, the following characteristics are thought to typify the Lufeng *Sivapithecus* specimens.

1. The crania are large and robust, with well-developed converging temporal crests. These crests originate at the lateral margins of both supraorbital ridges, parallel them, then turn sharply back to converge and join with a median sagittal crest at the middle of the vault.
2. Like *Ramapithecus,* the supraorbital ridges of *Sivapithecus* are not continuous and are only slightly developed, with no apparent supraorbital sulcus. The interorbital region is wide and concave. The orbital margins are very similar to those of *Ramapithecus.*
3. The nasal aperture is exceptionally narrow, but is nonetheless in the shape of an elongated pear, as in *Ramapithecus.* Its lateral borders are bounded inferiorly by prominent canine juga. The concave and rounded nasoalveolar clivus is narrow and short, and a slight anterior nasospinale is visible. The superior margin of the nasal aperture is situated slightly above the plane of the infraorbital rims.
4. Viewed frontally, the canines diverge laterally downward, similar to the pattern seen in the extant orangutan (*Pongo*). The canine fossae are very deep.
5. The roots of the central incisors are curved, producing marked juga, and a deep sulcus is associated with each tooth.

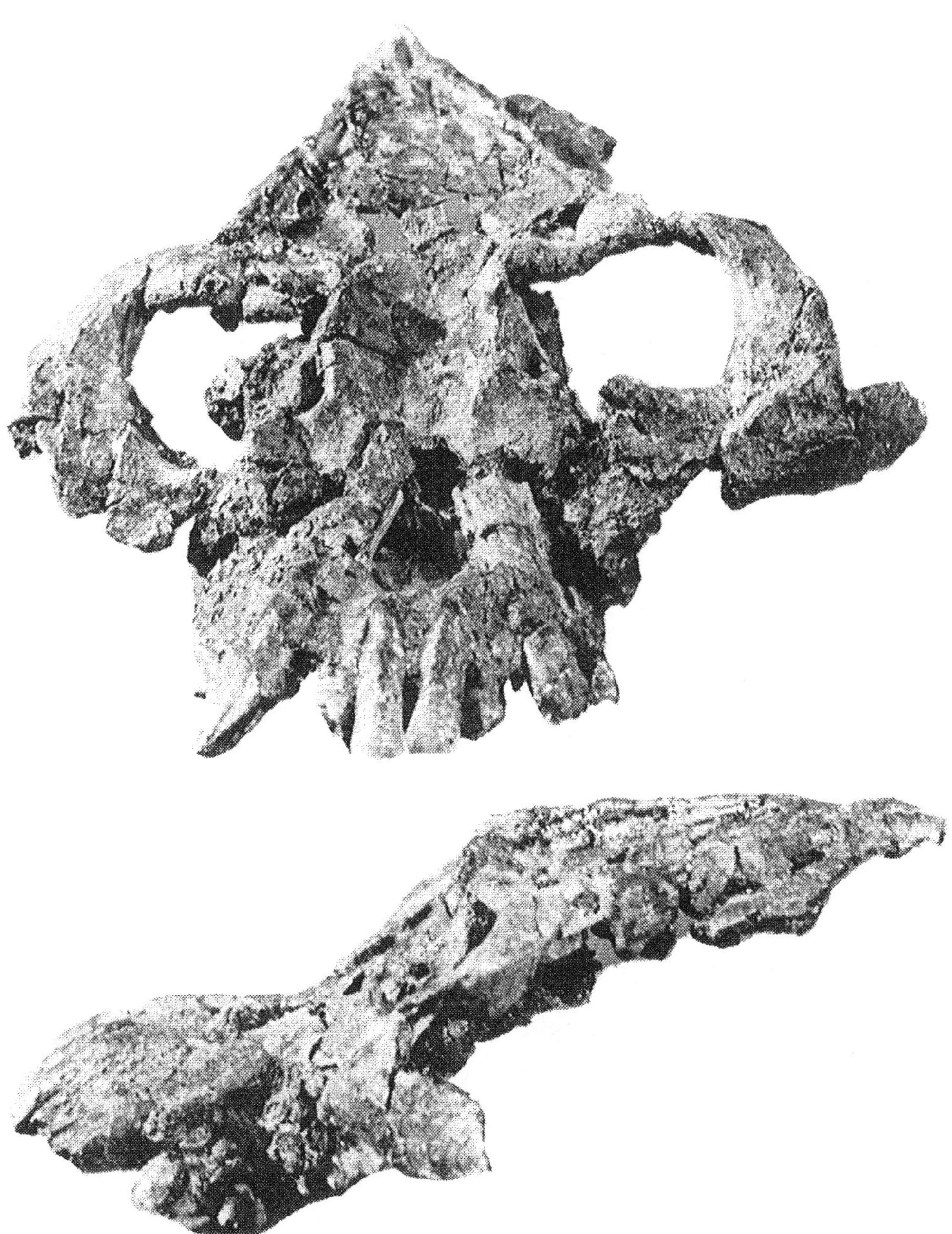

Figure 3.6 (Top) *Sivapithecus* cranium PA-644 from Lufeng, Yunnan. Frontal view, ×1.
Figure 3.7 (Bottom) *Sivapithecus* cranium PA-644 from Lufeng, Yunnan. Left lateral view, ×5/6.

6. The face of the Lufeng *Sivapithecus* is short and wide with both zygomatic arches projecting quite far laterally. Viewed laterally, the facial contour is concave from the supraorbital ridges to the nasoalveolar clivus, and the premaxilla projects upward as in *Pongo*.
7. The dental arcade of the maxilla is somewhat U-shaped and diverges only slightly posteriorly. The canines project markedly beyond the level of the remaining dentition and there is a substantial diastema present between the canine and the lateral incisor.

Mandibles

The large hominoid mandible PA-548 (Figure 3.8) is a typical well-preserved specimen presently classified as *Sivapithecus yunnanensis* (Xu and Lu 1979). Recovered in December 1975, it was the first such mandible to be unearthed at Lufeng. The complete symphysis is preserved as is the mandibular body between the left second molar and the right fourth premolar. The dental battery is complete with the exception of both third molars.

Several other Lufeng large hominoid mandibles (including PA-820, YV-711, and LC-102) are not as well preserved as PA-548; however, an analysis of all these specimens permits the following generalizations to be made about the Lufeng *Sivapithecus* mandibular remains.

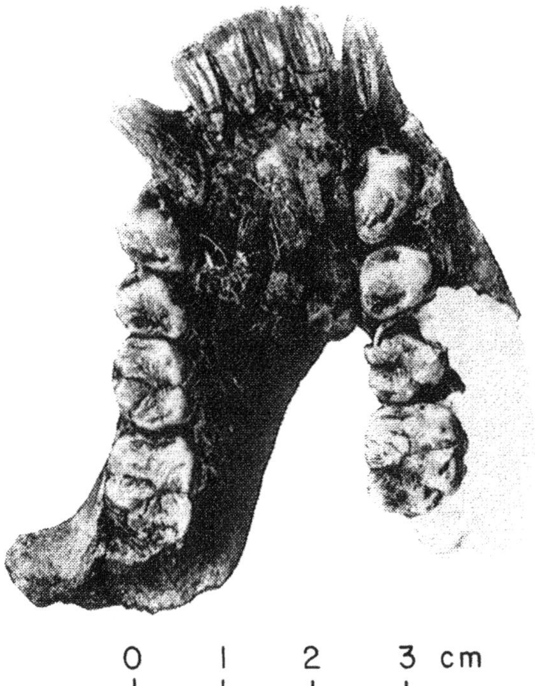

Figure 3.8 *Sivapithecus* mandible PA-548 from Lufeng, Yunnan. Occlusal view, ×1.

The *Sivapithecus* mandibles are much more robust than those of *Ramapithecus*, the symphysis in particular being very deep and thick. The anterior surface of the symphysis is flattened, but its inferior portion is strongly inclined posteriorly. At the base of the symphysis there is a prominent digastric spine, and broad, flat digastric fossae occur on both sides of the spine.

On the posterior, or internal, surface there is a moderately inclined alveolar plane beneath which is situated a poorly developed superior transverse torus and a deep genioglossal fossa. The inferior transverse torus is extremely thick and projects posteriorly.

The mandibular body is thick and deep, gradually becoming shallower toward its posterior limit. The buccinator grooves are broad with poorly developed lateral prominences.

The dental arcade of the mandible is somewhat U-shaped and diverges slightly posteriorly. The canines project significantly beyond the general plane of the tooth row.

Dentition

In general, both the absolute size and the range of variation of the Lufeng *Sivapithecus* dentition are large.

A salient characteristic of the upper central incisors is the very large labiolingual dimension of the crown. The length–breadth indices of some of the teeth exceed 100. Like *Ramapithecus*, the upper central incisors of *Sivapithecus* also exhibit a prominent lingual tubercle on the basal part of the tooth. The upper lateral incisor is much smaller than the central one and it does not possess a lingual tubercle, again similar to *Ramapithecus*.

The upper canine is very large with a high crown and sharp cusp. This tooth is also characterized by a deep vertical groove on the anterior surface and a sharp posterior ridge.

The upper third premolar has a large, high paracone and a small, low protocone. The mesiobuccal angle of the crown projects forward. The occlusal contour of the upper fourth premolar is elliptical. The paracone and protocone are equal in size but the latter is low and blunt.

The morphological features of the upper molars of *Sivapithecus* are similar to those of *Ramapithecus* with the exception that the *Sivapithecus* molar crowns are somewhat higher and larger and the lingual surfaces are rather rounded.

The crowns of the lower incisors of *Sivapithecus* are much higher than those of *Ramapithecus*, but morphologically the two are very similar. In general, the lower central incisor is somewhat smaller than the lateral incisor, particularly in the breadth of the crown. These two incisors are morphologically quite distinct, the cutting edge of the central incisor being horizontal, while the lateral margin of the cutting edge of the lateral incisor slopes downward. The lower canine is large with a high, sharp cusp.

The crown of the lower third premolar is sectorial. In most cases this tooth bears only a single cusp with a small bulge at the medial margin. Some specimens also exhibit a small metaconid, but not as well developed as in *Ramapithecus*.

The lower fourth premolar has two cusps, the distolingual angle of the crown being very pronounced. The morphological characters of the lower molars are similar to those of *Ramapithecus* but the size of the tooth crowns in *Sivapithecus* is much larger. In addition, in *Sivapithecus* the buccal surface of the crown is moderately sloped. The lower third molar usually lacks a metastylid and sixth cusp.

Discussion and Conclusion

In recent years the relationship between *Ramapithecus* and *Sivapithecus* and their phylogenetic positions have been the subject of intense debate (Wu *et al.* 1983). Some authors persist in the view that *Ramapithecus* is a direct ancestor of humans while *Sivapithecus* constitutes the ancestor of living great apes. However, some scholars (Andrews and Cronin 1982) suggest that *Ramapithecus* (=*Sivapithecus*) is related more closely to *Pongo* than to *Homo, Pan,* or *Gorilla* and should not be considered an ancestral hominid.

Lipson and Pilbeam (1982) and Pilbeam (1981, 1982) agree in principal with this latter view but cautiously suggest that if none of the currently recognized ramamorphs (i.e., *Ramapithecus, Sivapithecus*) was the direct ancestor of *Pongo,* another late Miocene Asian ramamorph probably was.

On the other hand, Kay (1982) has suggested that the ramapithecines (including both *Ramapithecus* and *Sivapithecus*) are cladistically hominids. Wu and Oxnard (1983a,b) have demonstrated, based on multivariate statistical analyses performed on a large sample of the Lufeng teeth, that the Lufeng hominoids, *Ramapithecus* and *Sivapithecus,* are of two different types. The full significance of this diversification has yet to be adequately explained and several mechanisms could account for this pattern.

Both the large and small Lufeng hominoids share the following features:

1. poorly developed, discontinuous supraorbital ridges;
2. wide interorbital region, and orbital contours that are square with rounded corners;
3. the upper canines diverge; and
4. the occlusal surfaces of the molars exhibit relatively complex crenulations and rather thick enamel.

These common morphological characters seem to indicate *Ramapithecus* and *Sivapithecus* descended from the same ancestor and should probably be considered variants of the same hominoid (Wu *et al.* 1983). Many features of *Sivapithecus* seem to be closely related to *Pongo* while *Ramapithecus* exhibits morphological characters similar to early forms of *Australopithecus* (e.g., small canines, the anterior position of the foramen magnum, and a weak or absent sagittal crest).

Thus the phylogenetic relationships of *Ramapithecus* may be explained in one of two ways: (1) The Lufeng hominoids designated *Ramapithecus* may be the female form of the larger Lufeng hominoid (*Sivapithecus*). Substantial sexual dimorphism may be an important characteristic of the late Miocene hominoids. (2) The specimens currently classified as *Ramapithecus* may represent a relatively small species more closely related to the common ancestor of humans and the African great apes than is the larger species of *Sivapithecus*.

In 1956 and 1957, 10 isolated teeth of two groups ascribed to the late Miocene hominoid *Dryopithecus keiyuanensis* were discovered at the Xiaolongtan Colliery in Kaiyuan County, Yunnan (Wu 1957, 1958). Bearing similarities to both the small and large hominoids from Lufeng, the Yunnan *Dryopithecus* is generally a bit smaller than the Lufeng specimens. It should also be mentioned that a new species of *Dryopithecus* from Gansu Province is currently being described by both Xue Xiangxu of Xibei (Northwest) University in Xi'an and Eric Delson of the American Museum of Natural History. *Dryopithecus* remains have also been discovered recently at Sihong, Jiangsu (Gu and Lin 1983). At present the exact relationship among these fossil forms is not clear; however, our evidence seems to indicate that during the late Miocene China was inhabited by more than one species of hominoid.

The analysis of the abundant Lufeng fossil materials, apparently deposited over a relatively brief period of time, will, it is hoped, provide the information necessary to answer these pertinent questions.

References

Andrews, P. and J. E. Cronin
1982 The relationships of *Sivapithecus* and *Ramapithecus* and the evolution of the orang-utan. *Nature* 297:541–546.

Flynn, L. and Qi Guoqin
1982 Age of the Lufeng, China hominoid locality. *Nature* 298:746–747.

Gu Yumin and Lin Yipu
1983 First discovery of *Dryopithecus* in East China. *Acta Anthropologica Sinica* 2(4):305–314.

Han Defen
1983 A new species of *Lophochoerus* from Lufeng. *Acta Anthropologica Sinica* 2(1):22–26.

Kay, R. F.
1982 *Sivapithecus simonsi*, a new species of Miocene hominoid, with comments on the phylogenetic status of the Ramapithecinae. *International Journal of Primatology* 3(2):113–173.

Lipson, S. and D. Pilbeam
1982 *Ramapithecus* and hominoid evolution. *Journal of Human Evolution* 11(6):545–548.

Lu Qingwu, Xu Qinghua, and Zheng Liang
1981 Preliminary research on the cranium of *Sivapithecus yunnanensis*. *Vertebrata PalAsiatica* 19(2):101–106.

Pilbeam, D.
1981 New skull remains of *Sivapithecus* from Pakistan. *Memoir of the Geological Survey of Pakistan* 11:1–13.
?2 New hominoid skull material from the Miocene of Pakistan. *Nature* 295:232–234.

Qi Guoqin
1979 Pliocene mammalian fauna of Lufeng, Yunnan. *Vertebrata PalAsiatica* 17(1):14–22.
1983 Description of the carnivora fossils from Lufeng. *Acta Anthropologica Sinica* 2(1):11–21.
1984 First discovery of *Ursavus* in China and note on the Ursidae specimens from the *Ramapithecus* fossil site of Lufeng. *Acta Anthropologica Sinica* 3(1):53–61.

Wu Rukang (Woo Ju-kang)
1957 *Dryopithecus* teeth from Keiyuan, Yunnan. *Gu Jizhuidongwu Xuebao (Vertebrata PalAsiatica)* 1(1):25–32.
1958 New materials of *Dryopithecus* from Keiyuan, Yunnan. *Gu Jizhuidongwu Xuebao (Vertebrata PalAsiatica)* 2(1):38–43.

Wu Rukang (Woo Ju-kang), Han Defen, Xu Qinghua, Lu Qingwu, Pan Yuerong, Zhang Xingyong, Zheng Liang, and Xiao Minghua
1981 *Ramapithecus* skull found first time in the world. *Kexue Tongbao* 26(11):1018–1021.

Wu Rukang (Woo Ju-kang), Han Defen, Xu Qinghua, Qi Guoqin, Lu Qingwu, Pan Yuerong, Chen Wanyong, Zhang Xingyong, and Xiao Minghua
1982 More *Ramapithecus* skulls found from Lufeng, Yunnan—report on the excavation of the site in 1981. *Acta Anthropologica Sinica* 1(2):101–108.

Wu Rukang (Woo Ju-kang) and Charles E. Oxnard
1983a Ramapithecines from China: evidence from tooth dimensions. *Nature* 306(5940):258–260.
1983b *Ramapithecus* and *Sivapithecus* from China: some implications for higher primate evolution. *American Journal of Primatology* 5:303–344.

Wu Rukang (Woo Ju-kang), Xu Qinghua, and Lu Qingwu
1983 Morphological features of *Ramapithecus* and *Sivapithecus* and their phylogenetic relationships—morphology and comparison of the crania. *Acta Anthropologica Sinica* 2(1):1–10.

Xu Qinghua and Lu Qingwu
1979 The mandibles of *Ramapithecus* and *Sivapithecus* from Lufeng, Yunnan. *Vertebrata PalAsiatica* 17(1):1–13.
1980 The Lufeng ape skull and its significance. *China Reconstructs* 29(1):56–57.

Xu Qinghua, Lu Qingwu, Pan Yuerong, Qi Guoqin, Zhang Xingyong, and Zheng Liang
1978 The fossil mandible of *Ramapithecus lufengensis*. *Kexue Tongbao* 23(9):554–556.

Zhang Xingyong
1982 Fossils of Pliocene Elephantoidea from the basin of Lufeng, Yunnan. *Vertebrata PalAsiatica* 20(4):359–365.

4

Gigantopithecus and "*Australopithecus*" in China

ZHANG YINYUN

Gigantopithecus

The generic and specific names *Gigantopithecus blacki* were proposed by G. H. R. von Koenigswald (1935) based on a single lower third molar purchased in a Hong Kong drugstore. Subsequently, Koenigswald collected additional specimens of *Gigantopithecus* dentition but all these fossils lacked provenance and their geological age was uncertain (Koenigswald 1952, 1957).

In 1956 a field team sent by the Laboratory of Vertebrate Palaeontology of the Chinese Academy of Sciences found 3 *Gigantopithecus* teeth *in situ* in Black Cave (Heidong), Daxin County, Guangxi. The team collected an additional 43 isolated *Gigantopithecus* teeth from apothecary shops in Guangdong and Guangxi. At the time these remains were all thought to be of Middle Pleistocene age (Pei and Wu 1956).

At the end of 1956 the famous *Gigantopithecus* Cave (Juyuandong), near Liucheng, Guangxi, was discovered, initiating several years of excavation. The geological deposits within the cavern yielded three *Gigantopithecus* mandibles (Figure 4.1) in addition to about 1000 isolated teeth and an extensive array of associated fossil mammals, facilitating chronological placement of these finds (Gu 1980; Pei 1957; Pei and Li 1958; Wu 1962a). According to the results of an analysis of the Liucheng faunal assemblage, the remains of *Gigantopithecus* were determined to be of early Lower Pleistocene age (Pei 1965; Zhou 1957); however,

ISBN 0-12-601720-4

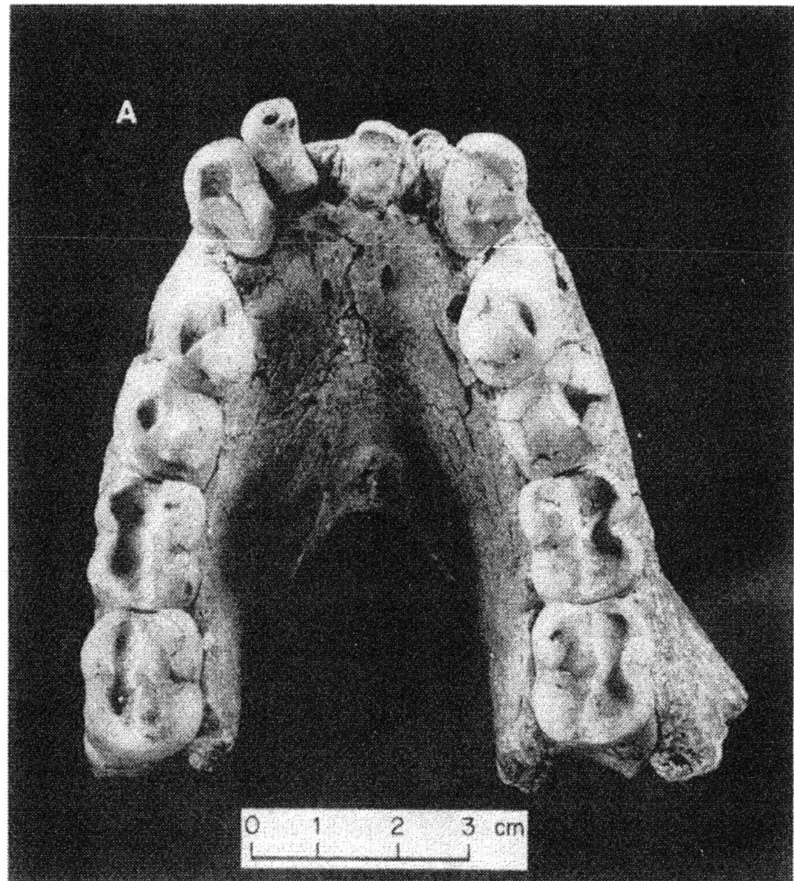

Figure 4.1A *Gigantopithecus* Mandible I from Liucheng, Guangxi; occlusal view.

the equally important *Gigantopithecus* fossils from Heidong, Guangxi, could not yet be reliably dated (Pei 1965).

In 1965 new information on the range of dental morphological variation and chronology was obtained through the discovery of 12 isolated *Gigantopithecus* teeth in a cave deposit in Wuming County, Guangxi. The teeth are larger than their homologues from Liucheng and the associated fauna suggests a later, Middle Pleistocene age for the fossils (Zhang *et al.* 1973).

In 1970 *Gigantopithecus* teeth were also discovered in Jianshi County, southwest Hubei. In all, 5 teeth were recovered from the deposits of Longgudong (Dragon Bone Cave) and more than 200 isolated specimens were collected from local drugstores. The geological age of these specimens is thought to be later than those from Liucheng; possibly as late as the late Lower Pleistocene (Xu *et al.* 1974).

Three years later a lower third molar was unearthed from a cave in Bama

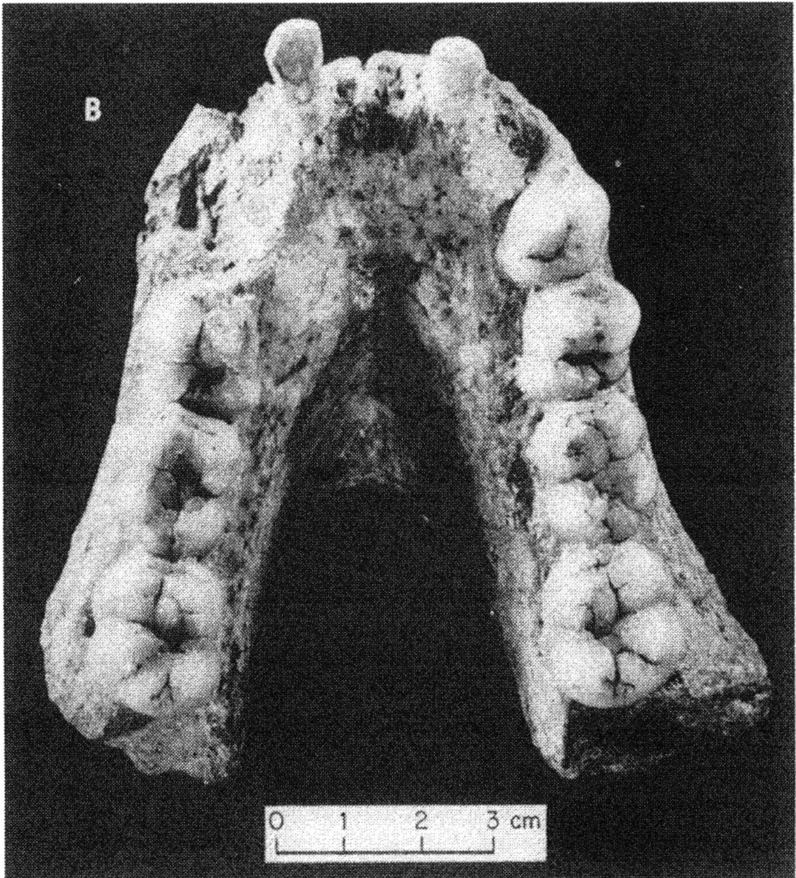

Figure 4.1B *Gigantopithecus* Mandible II from Liucheng, Guangxi; occlusal view.

County, western Guangxi. The associated fauna suggests a Middle Pleistocene date (Zhang *et al.* 1975). Thus, in examining the range of *Gigantopithecus* dentition from Liucheng, Jianshi, Wuming, and Bama, it is clear that a temporal continuum spanning the period from the early Lower Pleistocene to the Middle Pleistocene is represented (Han 1982; Huang 1979; Ji 1977; Li 1981).

The Liucheng, Guangxi, assemblage of *Gigantopithecus* fossils has provided detailed information on the morphological characters of the mandibles and dentition of this extinct form (Wu 1962a). The mandibles are all large and robust, however variations in both dental and mandibular dimensions have been interpreted as evidence of sexual dimorphism. Consequently, Liucheng Mandible I (Figure 4.1A) is thought to be that of a female, while Mandibles II (Figure 4.1B) and III, being larger and more robust, are considered male. The lateral eminence of all three mandibles divides into two weak branches: an upper and a lower. Each side of the mandible is characterized by a single mental foramen, the opening of which faces anteriorly. No definite linea mylohyoidea or torus mandibularis are visible. Likewise, the mentum osseum is absent but the central portion of the anterior surface of the mandible bulges forward. No typical "simian shelf" is present. The lower margin of the mandibular body increases in thickness from posterior to anterior and no definite fossa digastrica is visible. The incisura submentalis is quite distinct. The symphyseal area inclines in the anterosuperior and posteroinferior direction with an average angle of inclination of 55.2°. The index of the position of the foramen supraspinosum averages 28.4. Both the thickness and height of the mandibles are greatest at the symphyses, and their index of robustness averages 46.7 at the mental foramen.

The length–breadth index of the alveolar arch is 154.6 on the average, while the index of the anterior alveolar arch averages 91.4. The mandibles turn back sharply at the canines, but not as sharply as in modern anthropoids. The tooth rows are arranged in a gentle curve that diverges slightly at their posterior limit. The angle of the molar batteries averages 15° and the basal arches are rather wide.

With the exception of the incisors the teeth of *Gigantopithecus* are in general larger and more robust than in any pongids or hominids. In addition, extant *Gigantopithecus* dentition is classifiable into two discrete size categories thought to reflect sexual dimorphism.

The incisor dentition is of particular interest since the tubercle on the lingual surface is so well developed that the labiolingual diameter of the incisors is quite large. The upper canines are also large and robust with conical crowns that are relatively low and broad and the base is surrounded by a comparatively wide cingulum. The crown of the lower canine exhibits a wedgelike aspect in mesial or distal views and, although a cingulum is clearly present, it is not as well developed as in the upper canines. The cingulum on the lower canines forms a triangular prominence on the mesial and distal sides. In all specimens, the diastema is small or inconspicuous.

The occlusal surface of the upper first premolar is pentagonal, with the buccal cusp considerably higher than the lingual. The root is divided into three branches: two buccal and one lingual. The occlusal surface of the upper second premolar is elliptical, the length of the buccal side being nearly equal to that of the lingual side. The buccal cusp is slightly higher and larger than the lingual cusp. As in the case of the first premolar, the root of the second premolar is divided into three branches.

The lower first premolar is semisectorial with well-developed buccal and lingual cusps. The crown of the lower second premolar is nearly cuboid and its root is divided into two branches, one anterior and one posterior.

The crowns of the upper first and second molars are rhomboidal, being slightly wider than they are long. These molars are rather high with all four cusps well developed but blunt and compact. In comparison with the upper first and second molars, the upper third molar is small and its metacone is greatly reduced.

The grinding surfaces of the lower first and second molars are oblong with five main cusps that are all bunodont. Between the metaconid and entoconid a distinct internal accessory tubercle can usually be seen. The ridges on the slope of the cusps are more blunt and fewer in number than those in modern anthropoids.

In the lower third molar, the length far exceeds the width and the breadth of the trigonid is greater than that of the talonid.

The teeth of *Gigantopithecus* from Jianshi, Wuming, Daxin, and Bama are morphologically identical to those from Liucheng, except that the cheek teeth from all these localities are larger than those from Liucheng (Figure 4.2). Given our knowledge of the relative ages of these fossil localities, this sequence provides important insight into evolutionary trends within *Gigantopithecus* dentition (Zhang 1982).

Mammalian fossils associated with *Gigantopithecus* indicate a mixed forest and grassland environment prevailed at each of these localities (Ji 1982; Chapter 15, this volume), thus the evolution of *Gigantopithecus blacki* may have taken place under relatively stable environmental and dietary conditions. Percentages of dental caries and chipping within the genus suggest there may have been little change in diet throughout the known span of *Gigantopithecus* phylogeny (see Wu 1962b; Xu *et al.* 1974: Zhang 1983). Given this apparent homogeneity in diet, the observed increase in *Gigantopithecus* cheek-tooth size through time can hardy be attributed to changes in subsistence (Zhang 1983).

Based on our current understanding of the geological occurrence and evolutionary development of *Gigantopithecus blacki*, it is impossible to concur with Weidenreich (1945, 1946) in his assessment of *Gigantopithecus* as an ancestor of *Homo erectus*. Wu holds the opinion that *Gigantopithecus* belongs to the hominidae as an extinct side branch (Wu 1962a,b), while others believe the genus to be a pongid (e.g., Dong 1962; Pilbeam 1970; Simons and Ettel 1970).

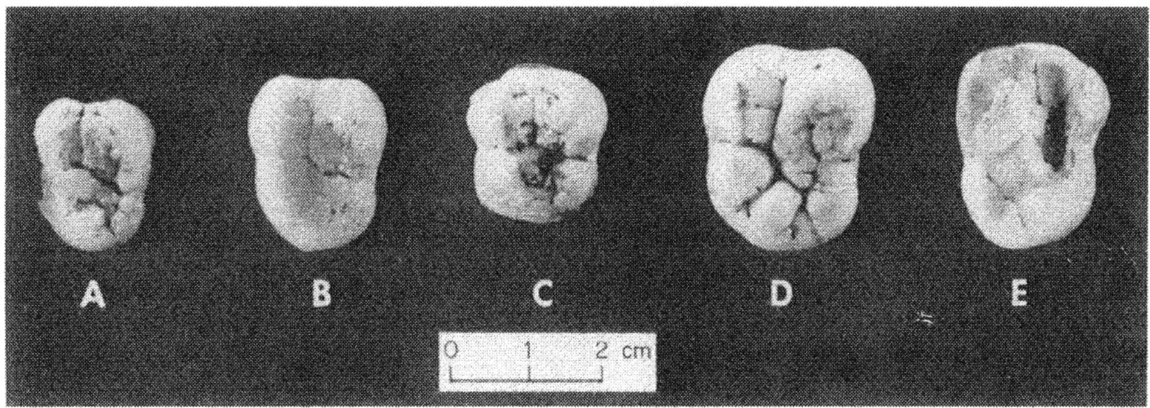

Figure 4.2 Occlusal views of lower third molars of *Gigantopithecus blacki:* A, Jianshi, Hubei; B, Daxin, Guangxi; C, D, Wuming, Guangxi; E, Bama, Guangxi.

Considering the limitations of the extant fossil record, most particularly a lack of postcranial elements, it is still difficult to confirm the taxonomic position of *Gigantopithecus* among the primates. It is true however, that a series of early hominid characters can be found in *Gigantopthecus* mandibles and dentition (Frayer 1973; Gelvin 1980). For example, the mandibular and dental morphology of both *Gigantopithecus* and the australopithecines suggests the development of powerful chewing mechanisms. In addition, *Gigantopithecus* and *Australopithecus* share the following morphological features:

1. The mandibles lack a developed diastema, and no prominent simian shelf is present.
2. The lower third premolar is bicuspid.
3. The molar dentition is bunodont (Wang 1983).
4. The canines are reduced in relation to the molars.

Obviously, based on the scant fossil evidence presently available, the interpretation of such shared characteristics must remain speculative, but it should come as no great surprise if continued research indicates affinities between these fossil genera.

"Australopithecus"

In 1970 three molars (PA-502, PA-503, and PA-504) were found in association with *Gigantopithecus* remains in Jianshi County, southwest Hubei (Gao 1975). An additional molar (PA-507) was collected from a drugstore in Badong, Hubei, in 1968. Originally, these molars were thought to be those of an australopithecine (Gao 1975), but Wolpoff (1979) considered them to be *Homo erectus*. Two of the teeth (PA-502 and PA-503, both lower second molars) appear to be morphologically anomalous and are consequently very difficult to compare with australopithecine dentition. The other two molars—PA-507 (a lower first molar) and PA-504 (a lower second molar)—exhibit two notable characters: the crowns are quite large and the lengths of their occlusal surfaces far exceed their widths. The length/breadth index for PA-507 (118.03) is beyond the range for australopithecines but falls within the range established for African early *Homo* sp. The PA-507 molar is so large and elongated that it might be classifable as *Homo erectus* rather than as *Australopithecus* sp. indet. Judging from their morphology, it is also interesting to note that two of the four Jianshi molars (PA-504 and PA-507) also closely resemble known dentition of the Indonesian form *Meganthropus*, while PA-502 and PA-503 compare favorably with *Pithecanthropus dubius* from Sangiran (Zhang n.d.).

The recent discovery of additional *H. erectus* fossils in China has added greatly to our knowledge of variation within the dentition of this species. For example, the mandible fragments from Hexian, Anhui (Wu and Dong 1982), the teeth from Yunxian, Hubei (Wu and Dong 1980), and the lower fourth premolar from

Nanzhao, Henan (Qiu *et al.* 1982), indicate that early *H. erectus* dentition is relatively large but that the range of variation in mandibular and dental size is rather extreme.

Based on an analysis of these new materials from China, it seems reasonable to conclude that the Jianshi, Hubei, molars, together with some of the early Pleistocene hominid fossils from Indonesia, may be classifiable as *H. erectus* (Zhang n.d.).

Our data from South China indicate that *Gigantopithecus blacki* and *H. erectus* simultaneously shared the same environment and it is very likely these two fossil forms came into contact with one another on occasion. Accepting for the moment our current interpretation of the Jianshi molars as those of *H. erectus,* we are then confronted with at least one locality where remains of *Gigantopithecus* and *Homo* occur together in stratified deposits. It should also be mentioned that as-yet-unpublished data from the *Gigantopithecus* Cave at Liucheng, Guangxi, indicate that *H. erectus* may be present at that site as well. In addition, the cave of Tham Khuyen, Lang Son Province in the Socialist Republic of Vietnam, has also yielded associated fossils of *Gigantopithecus* and *H. erectus* (Hoang *et al.* 1979).

In 1960 Han Defen published a report describing the age composition of the faunal assemblage from the Juyuandong at Liucheng. Noting that the majority of fossil mammals in the cave were represented by the elements of young individuals, some researchers interpreted this phenomenon as a result of *Gigantopithecus* predation. We do not believe this to be the case, especially since our data increasingly indicate the coexistence of *Gigantopithecus* and *H. erectus* in these southern localities. This fact bears significantly on the question of the eventual extinction of *Gigantopithecus* in the Middle Pleistocene. It is possible, although unproven, that intense competition between these two forms resulted in the demise of *Gigantopithecus* stemming from the superior abilities of *H. erectus* to exploit their shared environment through the manufacture and use of tools.

Our analysis of the abundant *Gigantopithecus* remains from South China's karst caverns suggests the genus is characterized by substantial synchronic and diachronic variation. At present, a more complete understanding of the taxonomy and behavior of *Gigantopithecus* is hampered by a lack of postcranial fossil elements. Because *Gigantopithecus* in China is represented only by mandibles and teeth, a wide range of morphological and behavioral questions cannot be addressed.

It is likely that a complex suite of taphonomic factors have influenced the composition of South China's cave faunas. However, our research suggests several processes played an especially important role in the selective preservation of fossil elements, including those of *Gigantopithecus.* Many of the karst caves of South China bear fossil assemblages that seem to have accumulated as a result of fluviatile redeposition. The distribution of some of the *Gigantopithecus* remains in these deposits suggests such a mode of transport and we believe this factor to have been very important in the formation of these fossil assemblages.

In addition, we have no evidence suggesting *Gigantopithecus* inhabited the caverns in which its remains occur. Most likely, carnivores such as the hyaena (*Hyaena licenti*) and rodents such as the porcupine (*Hystrix* spp.) are partly responsible for the deposition and destruction of these fossils. The accidental inclusion of large mammals in these caves is also a possibility, since the original morphology of the caverns may have been such that their entrances were not readily apparent and may have trapped animals as these solution cavities broke through to the surface.

A final taphonomic factor to be considered is the process of breccia formation in the caverns themselves. These deposits are now so highly consolidated that explosives must be employed on occasion to remove overburden. The brecciated fossils are usually highly fragmented as a result of this lithostatic pressure and only very durable elements such as dentition survive prolonged interment. Other processes have undoubtedly contributed to the differential preservation of fossils in these contexts and we hope that further research will help us explain these unusual patterns of element representation.

In conclusion, our research conducted over the past few years has brought to light two significant facts in regard to the larger Pleistocene primates of China. First, *Gigantopithecus blacki* is characterized by substantial variation within synchronic populations, perhaps as a result of sexual dimorphism, and as a function of evolutionary development. Second, current evidence provides no support for the contention that *Australopithecus* fossils are present in China, although we cannot rule out the possibility of their discovery in the future.

References

Dong Tizhen

1962 The systematic position of *Gigantopithecus* among the primates. *Vertebrata PalAsiatica* 6(4):375–383.

Frayer, D. W.

1973 *Gigantopithecus* and its relationship to *Australopithecus*. *American Journal of Physical Anthropology* 39:413–426.

Gao Jian

1975 Australopithecine teeth associated with *Gigantopithecus*. *Vertebrata PalAsiatica* 13(2):81–88.

Gelvin, B. R.

1980 Morphometric affinities of *Gigantopithecus*. *American Journal of Physical Anthropology* 53:541–568.

Gu Yumin

1980 Notes on the burial and distribution of the *Gigantopithecus* fossils in the *Gigantopithecus* Cave of Liucheng, Guangxi. *Vertebrata PalAsiatica* 18(2):150–153.

Han Defen

1960 Age observation on the mammals of *Gigantopithecus* Cave of Liu-Cheng. *Gu Jizhuidongwu yu Gu Renlei (Palaeovertebrata et Palaeoanthropologia)* 2(1):74–76.

Hoang Xuan Chinh, Nguyen Lan Cuong, and Vu The Long

1979 First discoveries of Pleistocenian man, culture and fossilized fauna in Vietnam. In *Recent discoveries and new views on some archaeological problems in Vietnam*, edited by the Committee for Social Sciences of Vietnam. Hanoi: Institute of Archaeology. Pp. 14–20.

Huang Wanbo
1979 On the age of the cave faunas of South China. *Vertebrata PalAsiatica* 17(4):327–342.
Ji Hongxiang
1977 Problems in the division of Quaternary mammalian faunas in South China. *Vertebrata PalAsiatica* 15(4):271–277.
1982 The living environment of the Quaternary mammalian faunas of South China. *Vertebrata PalAsiatica* 20(2):148–154.
Koenigswald, G. H. R. von
1935 Eine fossile Säugetier-fauna mit Simia aus Südchina. *Proceedings Koninklijke Akademie van Wetenschappen Amsterdam* 38:872–879.
1952 *Gigantopithecus blacki* von Koenigswald, a giant fossil hominoid from the Pleistocene of southern China. *Anthropological Papers of the American Museum of Natural History* 43:295–325.
1957 Remarks on *Gigantopithecus* and other hominoid remains from southern China. *Proceedings Koninklijke Akademie van Wetenschappen Amsterdam* B 60:153–159.
Li Yanxian
1981 On the subdivisions and evolution of Quaternary mammalian faunas in South China. *Vertebrata PalAsiatica* 19(1):67–76.
Pei Wenzhong (Pei Wen-chung)
1957 Discovery of *Gigantopithecus* mandibles and other material in Liu-Cheng district of central Kwangsi in South China. *Gu Jizhuidongwu Xuebao (Vertebrata PalAsiatica)* 1(2):65–71.
1965 Excavation of Liucheng *Gigantopithecus* Cave and exploration of other caves in Kwangsi. *Memoirs of the Institute of Vertebrate Palaeontology and Palaeoanthropology*, 7:1–54.
Pei Wenzhong (Pei Wen-chung) and Li Youheng
1958 Discovery of a third mandible of *Gigantopithecus* in Liucheng, Kwangsi, South China. *Gu Jizhuidongwu Xuebao (Vertebrata PalAsiatica)* 2(4):193–200.
Pei Wenzhong (Pei Wen-chung) and Wu Rukang (Woo Ju-kang)
1956 New materials of *Gigantopithecus* teeth from South China. *Gushengwu Xuebao (Acta Palaeontologica Sinica)* 4(4):477–490.
Pilbeam, D. R.
1970 *Gigantopithecus* and the origins of Hominidae. *Nature* 225:516–519.
Qiu Zhonglang, Xu Chunhua, Zhang Weihua, Wang Rulin, Wang Jianzhong, and Zhao Chengfu
1982 A human fossil tooth and fossil mammals from Nanzhao, Henan. *Acta Anthropologica Sinica* 1(2):109–117.
Simons, E. L. and P. C. Ettel
1970 *Gigantopithecus. Scientific American* 221(1):76–84.
Wang Linghong
1983 Distinguishing first from second molars of *Gigantopithecus* by multivariate analysis. *Acta Anthropologica Sinica* 2(1):39–47.
Weidenreich, Franz
1945 Giant early man from Java and South China. *Anthropological Papers of the American Museum of Natural History* 40:1–134.
1946 *Apes, giants, and man.* Chicago: University of Chicago Press.
Wolpoff, M. H.
1979 The Krapina dental remains. *American Journal of Physical Anthropology* 50(1):67–114.
Wu Rukang (Woo Ju-kang)
1962a The mandibles and dentition of *Gigantopithecus. Palaeontologia Sinica*, New Series D 11:1–62.
1962b *Gigantopithecus* and its phylogenetic significance. *Scientia Sinica* 11(3):391–396.
Wu Rukang (Woo Ju-kang) and Dong Xingren
1980 The fossil human teeth from Yunxian, Hubei. *Vertebrata PalAsiatica* 18(2):142–149.
1982 Preliminary study of *Homo erectus* remains from Hexian, Anhui. *Acta Anthropologica Sinica* 1(1):2–13.

Xu Chunhua, Han Kangxin, and Wang Linghong
1974 Discovery of *Gigantopithecus* teeth and associated fauna in western Hubei. *Vertebrata PalAsiatica* 12(4):293–309.

Zhang Yinyun
1982 Variability and evolutionary trends in tooth size of *Gigantopithecus blacki*. *American Journal of Physical Anthropology* 59:21–22.
1983 Variability in tooth size of *Gigantopithecus blacki* and the dietary hypothesis for australopithecines. *Acta Anthropologica Sinica* 2(3):205–217.
n.d. "*Australopithecus*" of west Hubei and some early Pleistocene hominids of Indonesia. *Acta Anthropologica Sinica*, in press.

Zhang Yinyun, Wang Linghong, Dong Xingren, and Chen Wenjun
1975 Discovery of a *Gigantopithecus* tooth from Bama district in Kwangsi. *Vertebrata PalAsiatica* 13(3):148–153.

Zhang Yinyun, Wu Maolin, and Liu Jinrong
1973 New discovery of *Gigantopithecus* teeth from Wuming, Kwangsi. *Kexue Tongbao* 18(3):130–133.

Zhou Mingzhen (Chow Min-chen)
1957 Mammalian faunas and the correlation of Tertiary and early Pleistocene of South China. *Kexue Tongbao* 13:394–399.

5

Homo erectus in China

WU RUKANG AND DONG XINGREN

The remains of *Homo erectus*, the direct ancestor of *H. sapiens*, are distributed throughout a large part of China in geological deposits ranging from nearly 1 million to 200,000 years old. To date, localities such as Yuanmou, Yunnan; Lantian, Shaanxi; Zhoukoudian, Beijing; and Hexian, Anhui, among others, have yielded a long and abundant record of the evolution and behavior of *H. erectus* in China.

This essay summarizes the principal discoveries and current interpretations of *H. erectus* fossils from China's most important Pleistocene hominid localities. Although the history of research on *H. erectus* in China extends back over 50 years, discoveries made in the past decade alone have amplified our understanding of this critical phase of hominid evolution manyfold.

Yuanmou, Yunnan

The Yuanmou *H. erectus* is at present represented by only two teeth: the upper right and left central incisors of a single individual (Figure 5.1). In 1965 Qian Fang of the Chinese Academy of Geological Sciences discovered these two incisors in the brownish-clay beds of the Yuanmou Formation at Shangnabang, Yuanmou County, northern Yunnan. Morphologically, these teeth resemble those of the Zhoukoudian Locality 1 *H. erectus* in their size, the presence of shovel-shaped lingual surfaces, well-developed basal tubercles and fingerlike projections. However, certain features of the teeth suggest some differences exist. For example, the distal portion of the crown of the Yuanmou incisors is

ISBN 0-12-601720-4

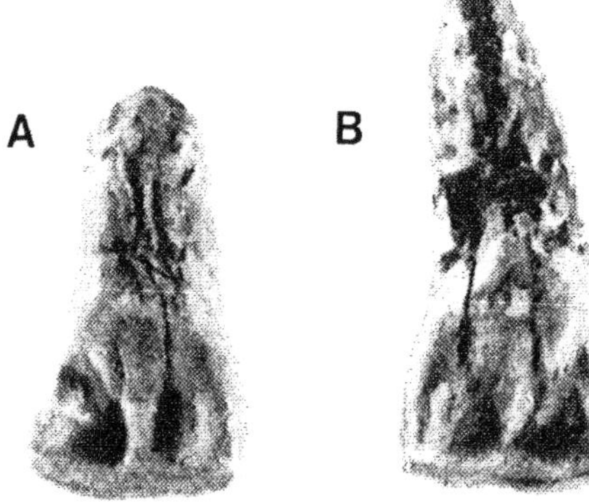

Figure 5.1 Lingual view of (A) upper left and (b) right central incisors from Shangnabang, Yuanmou County, Yunnan (casts).

more expanded than that of Beijing Man. The fingerlike projections are situated on the lateral half of the lingual surface with one ridge in the middle being particularly well developed and extending almost to the cutting edge of the tooth. In the Zhoukoudian hominids, these fingerlike projections are shorter and are situated in the center of the lingual surface.

Taking into consideration these morphological differences, Hu (1973) proposed a new subspecies, *H. erectus yuanmouensis,* for the Yuanmou specimens. Zhou and Hu (1979) further stressed the primitiveness of the Yuanmou morphological characters and regarded these incisors as indicating an early stage in the evolutionary development of *H. erectus.* The present authors consider these specimens to belong to the same subspecies as other *H. erectus* fossils found elsewhere in China.

The age of the Yuanmou specimens is still uncertain (see Chapter 2, this volume). Several years ago, the teeth were attributed to the early Pleistocene principally on the basis of biostratigraphy and faunal correlation. Palaeomagnetic data for Yuanmou originally suggested an extremely early age of 1.7 million years BP (Cheng *et al.* 1977; Li *et al.* 1976). However, recently accumulated biostratigraphic, lithostratigraphic, and magnetostratigraphic data suggest the fossils may be no older than the Brunhes–Matuyama boundary (i.e., circa 0.73 million years old) and may possibly be only 500,000–600,000 years old (Liu and Ding 1983; and Chapter 2, this volume). Of course, this is still a controversial issue. If the revised dates ultimately prove correct, the Yuanmou incisors may not constitute the earliest remains of *Homo erectus* yet discovered in China.

Lantian, Shaanxi

The remains of *H. erectus* from Lantian County in east-central Shaanxi derive from two distinct localities. In 1963 a well-preserved mandible was recovered near the village of Chenjiawo, about 10 km northwest of Lantian. The following year, a field team from the Institute of Vertebrate Palaeontology and Palaeoanthropology in Beijing discovered a cranium in reddish Middle Pleistocene clays at Gongwangling in the northern foothills of the Qinling Mountians, about 10 km east of Lantian.

The cranium, consisting of a calvarium, nasal bones, maxillae, and dentition, is that of a female individual over 30 years of age (Figure 5.2). The morphology of the Lantian cranium is more primitive than *H. erectus* fossils from both Zhoukoudian and the Kabuh Formation of Sangiran in Java. For example, the Lantian specimen's supraorbital tori are massive and heavy, and extend laterally much farther than those of *H. erectus* from Zhoukoudian. The postorbital constriction is also more pronounced and both the frontal squama and cranial vault are very low. The cranial bones are extraordinarily thick and the calculated cranial capacity of only 780 cc is smaller than that of either the Zhoukoudian or Java specimens (Wu 1966).

The Chenjiawo mandible is that of an old female, and is complete except for small portions of the rami (Figure 5.3). The morphology of the specimen is

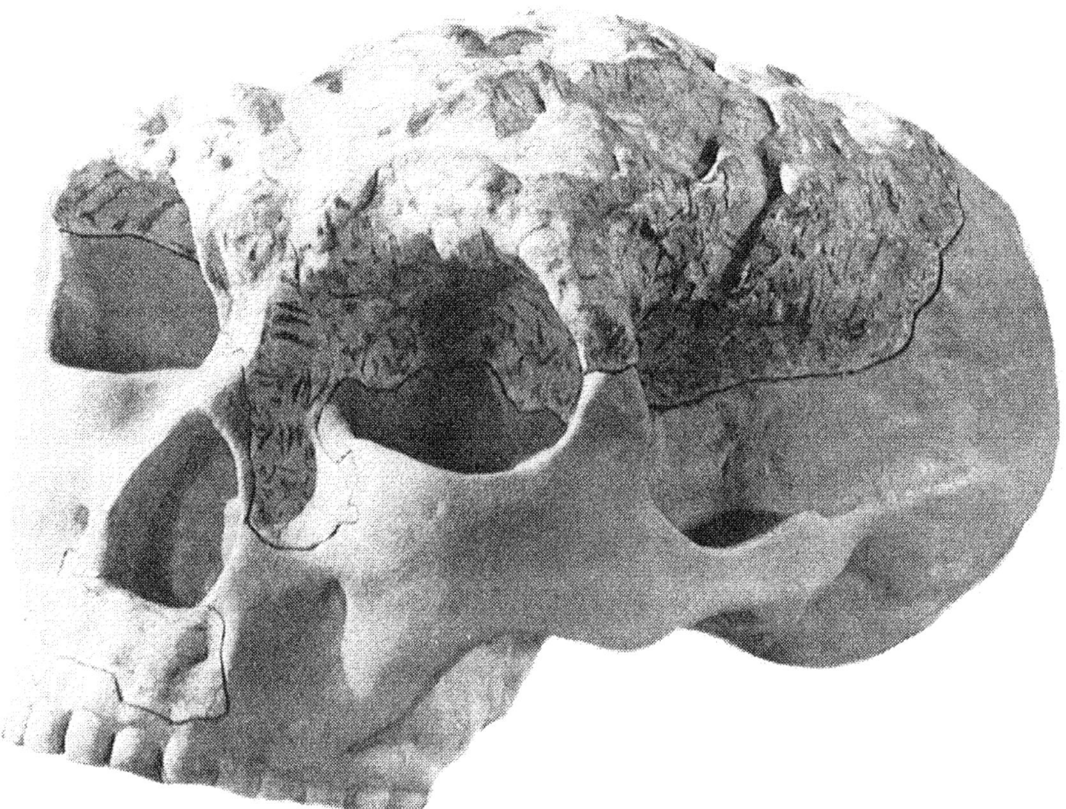

Figure 5.2 Reconstruction of the Gongwangling, Lantian, Shaanxi, cranium (cast).

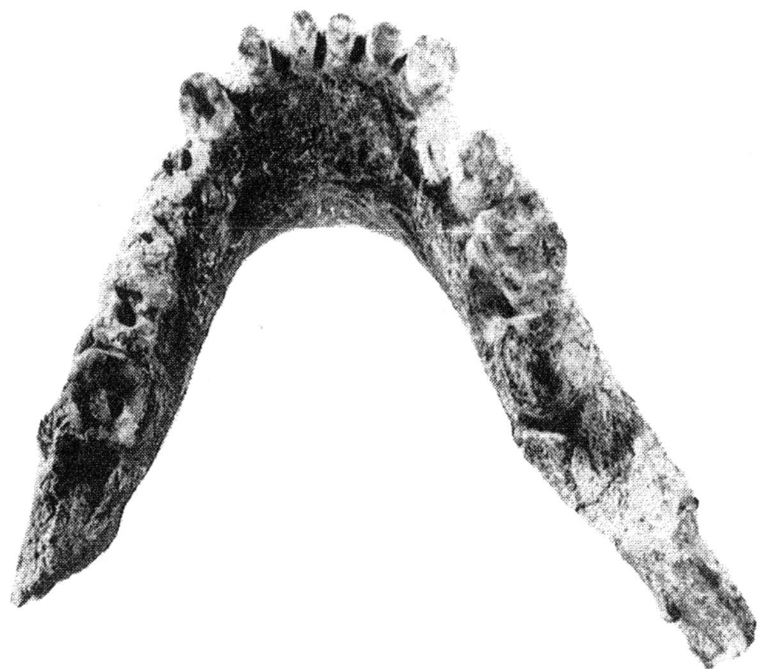

Figure 5.3 Mandible from Chenjiawo, Lantian, Shaanxi.

similar in many respects to mandibles of *H. erectus* from Zhoukoudian Locality 1. The robustness of the mandibular body, the form of the alveolar arch, and the multiplicity of the mental foramen all suggest close affinities. There are, nonetheless, additional features that distinguish the Lantian and Zhoukoudian mandibular remains. For example, the Lantian specimen is characterized by a smaller angle of inclination at the anterior end, as well as a marked difference in the height of the mandibular body at the symphysis compared to the level of the mental foramen. The Lantian jaw also exhibits a larger angle of divergence in the molar rows and less-developed bony prominences (Wu 1964).

Several lines of evidence suggest both the Chenjiawo and Gongwangling localities may be attributed to the Middle Pleistocene, although the latter is thought to be somewhat earlier. It seems clear based on presently available information that the Lantian hominid predates the *H. erectus* occupation at Zhoukoudian.

Zhoukoudian, Beijing

A large sample of *H. erectus* fossils have been discovered in the famous Locality 1 Beijing Man (or Peking Man) deposits at Zhoukoudian in Fangshan County, about 50 km southwest of Beijing's city center (Wu and Lin 1983).

Although the site has been known archaeologically since 1921, excavations conducted between 1927 and 1937 by the Geological Survey of China and the Cenozoic Research Laboratory in Beijing yielded an abundant array of fossils and artifacts. Among the most important finds produced during this decade of investigation were the remains of more than 40 *H. erectus* individuals including males, females, adults, and juveniles. The material comprises 5 fairly complete calvaria (Figures 5.4 and 5.5), 13 skull fragments including 6 facial bones, 14 mandibular fragments (Figure 5.6), and 147 teeth. In addition, many pieces of postcranial bones were also recovered including 7 femora, 2 humeri, 1 clavicle, and 1 os lunatum. Weidenreich (1936, 1937, 1941, 1943) studied these fossils in great detail before their loss during the Sino–Japanese War in 1941.

Since the liberation of Beijing in 1949, scientists from the Chinese Academy of Sciences' Institute of Vertebrate Palaeontology and Palaeoanthropology (IVPP) have resumed excavations at Zhoukoudian and several important new finds have been added to the assemblage of Beijing Man fossils. These discoveries include five teeth, a fragmentary humerus, and a tibia found in 1949 and 1951 (Wu and Jia 1954); the mandible of an old female unearthed in 1959 (Wu and Zhao 1959); and frontal and occipital bones as well as an isolated tooth recovered in 1966 (Qiu *et al.* 1973).

Initially classified as *Sinanthropus pekinensis* (Black 1927), the Zhoukoudian Locality 1 specimens have now all been subsumed under the taxonomic designa-

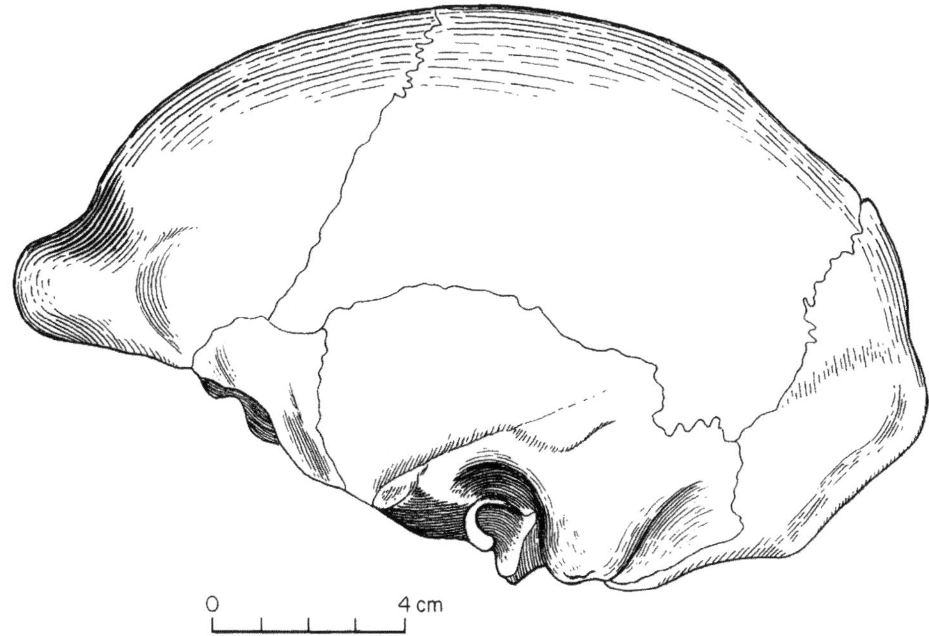

Figure 5.4 Left lateral view of Skull III from Zhoukoudian Locality 1, Beijing.

tion *Homo erectus pekinensis*. The overall character of the Zhoukoudian *H. erectus* fossils suggests they derive from a more progressive group of individuals than do the Lantian specimens; however, certain morphological characters are common to both. In contrast to the Lantian fossils, the Zhoukoudian specimens exhibit a less-pronounced lateral extension of the supraorbital tori. In addition, there is a broad and distinct supraorbital sulcus between the supraorbitals and the frontal squama, and the postorbital constriction is less pronounced than in Lantian Man. The thickness of the cranial walls of the Zhoukoudian individuals is not as great as that of the Lantian calvarium, but much thicker than that of modern *H. sapiens*. Although the cranial vault is flattened and the forehead receding, it is more expanded than the Lantian fossil. The cranial capacity of the Zhoukoudian *H. erectus* population ranges from 1015 to 1225 cc, with an average of 1088 cc for the five adult crania (Skulls II, V, X, XI, and XII).

Like the Lantian calvarium, the crania from Zhoukoudian exhibit a distinct sagittal keel. The nasofrontal, together with the frontomaxillary suture, follows an unbroken horizontal course. The nasal bones of the Zhoukoudian specimens are distinctly wide.

The zygomatic bone of Beijing Man is very high and the facies malaris is

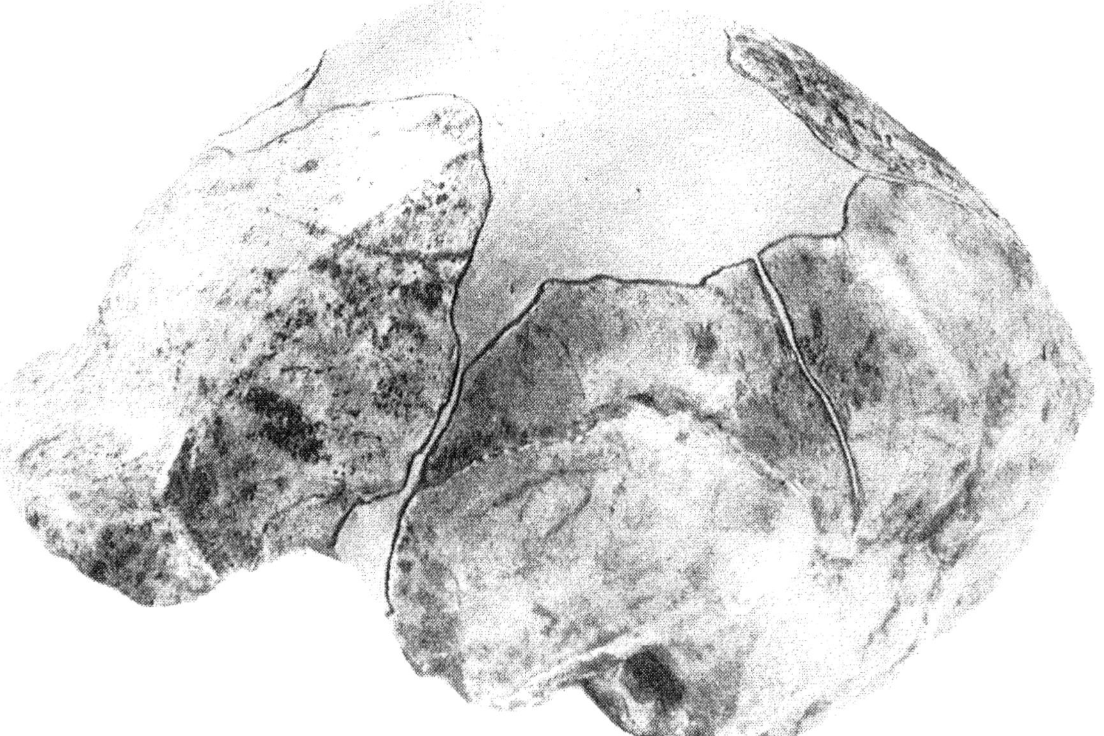

Figure 5.5 Reconstruction of Skull V from Zhoukoudian Locality 1, Beijing (cast).

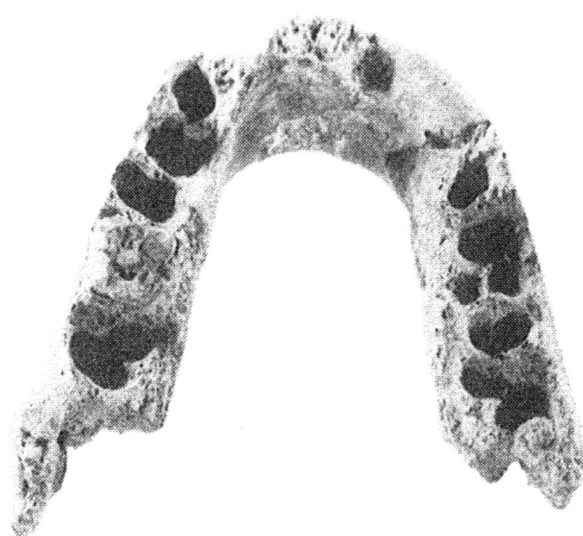

Figure 5.6 The 1959 mandible from Zhoukoudian Locality 1, Beijing.

oriented anteriorly. The mandible is very robust with a prominent mandibular torus. The teeth are also relatively large and the lingual surfaces of the upper incisors are typically shovel-shaped.

The appendicular skeleton of *H. erectus* from Zhoukoudian is similar to that of modern *H. sapiens* except that the limb bones possess thicker walls and the medullary cavity is therefore significantly reduced.

Thus, the skull of Beijing Man appears to retain many more primitive features than do its limb bones. Wu Rukang (1960) interpreted this allometric phenomenon as a result of differentiation of the extremities prior to the development of the large brain and cranium of modern humans through the protracted process of tool manufacture and use. The stature of the Zhoukoudian *H. erectus* was estimated to be 156 cm for the male and 144 cm for the female based on a single reconstructed femur by Weidenreich (1941). Judging from general tendencies in the evolution of human stature based on a wide variety of analyses, this value seems rather low.

Chronometric dating of the Zhoukoudian Locality 1 Middle Pleistocene deposits indicates this population continuously inhabited the vicinity from roughly 460,000 to 230,000 BP (see Chapter 2, this volume). Of interest is the fact that *H. erectus* Skull V was found in Layer 3, dated to 0.23 mya, and exhibits a series of morphological features that are much more progressive than those of the other *H. erectus* crania (Skulls II, III, X, XI, and XII) from the earlier Middle Pleistocene deposits in Layers 8–10, which are thought to be between 400,000 and 460,000 years old. For example, Skull V possesses slender supraorbital tori, a reduced occipital torus, thinner cranial walls, an arched parietal margin on the temporal bone, and a marked foreshortening of the distance between external and internal protuberances. Thus, at Zhoukoudian it is possible to witness morphological change within a single population of *H. erectus* (Qiu *et al.* 1973).

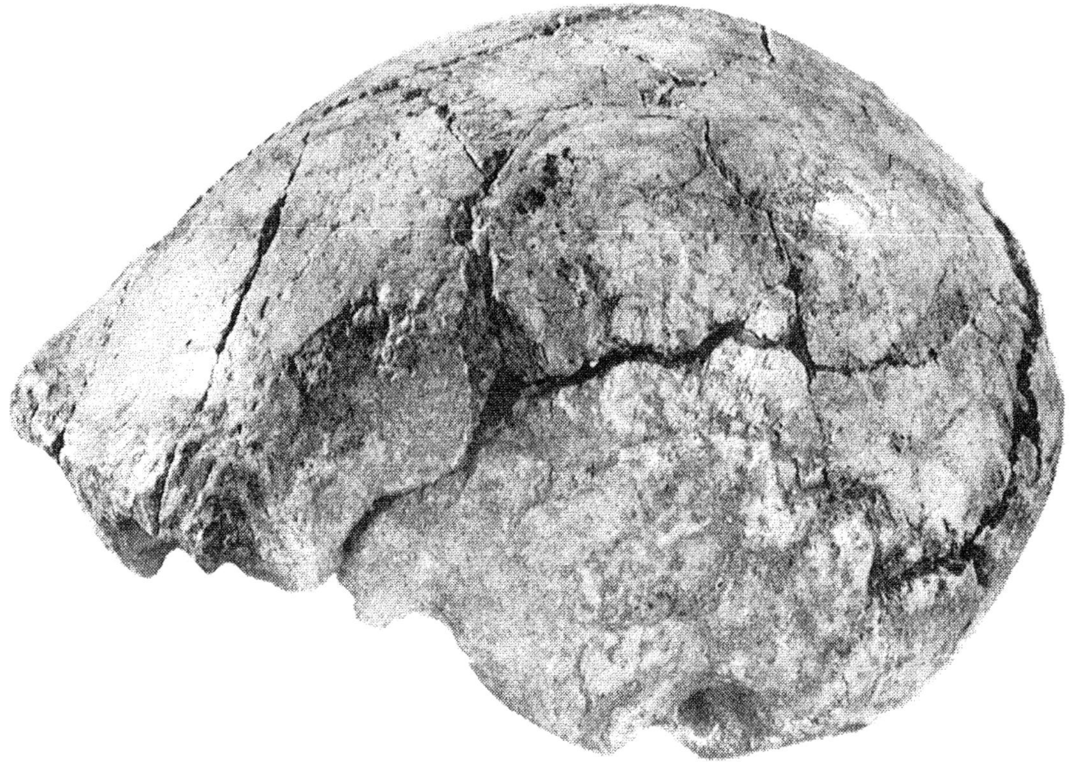

Figure 5.7 *Homo erectus* cranium from Hexian, Anhui.

Hexian, Anhui

The fossils of *H. erectus* from the Hexian locality at Longtandong Cave in Anhui Province represent several individuals. The specimens include a well-preserved cranium lacking the greater part of the basicranium (Figure 5.7), a fragmentary mandibular body, and four isolated teeth, all of which were found in 1980 by the IVPP palaeontologist Huang Wanbo and others (Wu and Dong 1982). In 1981, the sand–clay deposits of the Longtandong yielded additional *H. erectus* fossils including a frontal with partial supraorbital, a parietal fragment, and five isolated teeth (Wu 1983). An assemblage of mammalian fossils recovered in association with those of *H. erectus* allows the site to be dated to the Middle Pleistocene based on biostratigraphic evidence (Huang *et al.* 1982).

The skull of Hexian Man is that of a young male. Many morphological details of the Hexian cranium resemble those from the Middle Pleistocene deposits at Zhoukoudian Locality 1. For example, fossils from both sites exhibit a low cranial vault, flattened frontal bones, developed supraorbital tori and occipital torus, relatively thick cranial bones, a sagittal crest, a well-defined angle distinguishing the occipital and nuchal planes, and a maximum cranial breadth located at a relatively low point on the skull.

The cranial measurements of the Hexian specimen indicate that the size of the braincase and the cranial capacity (circa 1025 cc) are also close to those of Beijing Man. Based on these data, Wu Rukang and Dong Xingren (1982) have suggested a close relationship between the *H. erectus* specimens from Hexian and those from Zhoukoudian Locality 1. Nevertheless, certain progressive features may be noted in the Hexian individual. For example, the postorbital constriction is not as pronounced as in Beijing Man and is, in fact, less marked than in the Dali hominid from Shaanxi Province, which is thought to be an archaic *H. sapiens*. The temporal squama of the Hexian specimen is high with an arched parietal margin similar to Skull V from Zhoukoudian (Figure 5.5). The distance between the external and internal protuberances of the occipital is relatively short, shorter in fact than that of any of the Zhoukoudian crania. These combined data give us the impression that the Hexian *H. erectus* is somewhat advanced, and is perhaps best compared with the later forms of *H. erectus* at Zhoukoudian such as are exemplified by Skull V from Locality 1.

Homo erectus from Other Localities

Although Middle Pleistocene strata in the following localities have thus far yielded only a few isolated teeth attributed to *H. erectus*, they nonetheless provide us with an expanded data base for the discussion of hominid phylogeny in China.

Two localities in Hubei Province have yielded *H. erectus* teeth. Four left teeth (I^1, I_2, P^2, and M^1) were collected in 1975 from Longgudong Cave in Yunxian County (Wu and Dong 1980), and the Bailongdong Cave in Yunxi County yielded an additional seven teeth between 1976 and 1982 (Qunli 1983).

To the north, in Henan Province, a right lower second premolar was collected in the Xinghua foothills of Nanzhao County in 1978 (Qiu *et al.* 1982). A total of 13 human teeth were collected from the warehouses of traditional Chinese medicine and apothecary shops in Nanyang and Xisha, Henan, in 1973. Although exact provenances for these latter specimens are unknown, the teeth were all discovered in Xichuan County in southwest Henan (Wu and Wu 1982).

Conclusions

The fossils of *H. erectus* discovered thus far in China derive from eight localities that are widely distributed throughout North and South China, attesting to the diverse geographic range of Middle Pleistocene hominids in East Asia. In addition, evidence suggests that while the bulk of *H. erectus* fossils in China are clearly attributable to the Middle Pleistocene, it is possible some derive from late Lower Pleistocene contexts as well.

Among China's *H. erectus* fossils, those from Lantian exhibit more primitive morphological characteristics than do those from Zhoukoudian and Hexian. We believe these differences are a reflection of both spatial and temporal evolutionary diversification. Moreover, it is of interest to note that in certain morphological details *H. erectus* in China is distinguishable from Middle Pleistocene hominids in other parts of the world. Some of these features are suggestive of Mongoloid racial affinities and include the shovel-shaped upper incisors of all the specimens from Yuanmou, Zhoukoudian, Yunxian, and Hexian; the high malar bone and its forward projection; wide nasal bones; and the occurrence of a sagittal crest and mandibular torus. These morphological features continue to be found in both early and late *H. sapiens* fossils in China such as those from Maba, Tongzi, Dingcun, Zhoukoudian's Upper Cave, Liujiang, and Ordos (Hetao) (Wu and Zhang 1978; and Chapter 6, this volume). Thus, it seems that morphological continuity is a feature of human evolution in China.

References

Black, Davidson
1927 On a lower molar hominid tooth from the Choukoutien deposit. *Palaeontologia Sinica*, Series D 7(1):1–28.

Cheng Guoliang, Li Suling, and Lin Jinlu
1977 Discussion on the age of *Homo erectus yuanmouensis* and the event of early Matuyama. *Scientia Geologica Sinica* 1:34–43.

Hu Chengzhi
1973 Ape-man teeth from Yuanmou, Yunnan. *Acta Geologica Sinica* 1:65–71.

Huang Wanbo, Fang Dusheng, and Ye Yongxiang
1982 Preliminary study of the fossil hominid skull and fauna from Hexian, Anhui. *Vertebrata PalAsiatica* 20(3):248–256.

Li Pu, Qian Fang, Ma Xinghua, Pu Qingyu, Xing Lisheng, and Ju Shiqiang
1976 Preliminary study of the age of Yuanmou Man by palaeomagnetic techniques. *Scientia Sinica* 6:579–591.

Liu Dongsheng and Ding Menglin
1983 Discussion on the age of "Yuanmou Man". *Acta Anthropologica Sinica* 2(1):40–48.

Qiu Zhonglang, Gu Yumin, Zhang Yinyun, and Zhang Senshui
1973 Newly discovered *Sinathropus* remains and stone artifacts at Choukoutien. *Vertebrata PalAsiatica* 11(2):109–131.

Qiu Zhonglang, Xu Chunhua, Zhang Weihua, Wang Rulin, Wang Jianzhong, and Zhao Chengfu
1982 A human fossil tooth and fossil mammals from Nanzhao, Henan. *Acta Anthropologica Sinica* 1(2):109–117.

Qunli
1983 Discovery of additional *Homo erectus* teeth in Bailongdong, Yunxi county, Hubei. *Acta Anthropologica Sinica* 2(2):203.

Weidenreich, Franz
1936 The mandibles of *Sinanthropus pekinensis:* a comparative study. *Palaeontologia Sinica*, Series D 7(3):1–162.
1937 The dentition of *Sinanthropus pekinensis*: a comparative odontography of the hominids. *Palaeontologia Sinica*, New Series D 1:1–180.
1941 The extremity bones of *Sinanthropus pekinensis*. *Palaeontologia Sinica*, New Series D 5:1–150.

1943 The skull of *Sinanthropus pekinensis*: a comparative study on a primitive hominid skull. *Palaeontologia Sinica*, New Series D 10:1–485.

Wu Maolin

1983 *Homo erectus* from Hexian, Anhui found in 1981. *Acta Anthropologica Sinica* 2(2):109–115.

Wu Rukang (Woo Ju-kang)

1960 The unbalanced development of the physical features of *Sinanthropus pekinensis* and its interpretation. *Gu Jizhuidongwu Xuebao (Vertebrata PalAsiatica)* 4(1):17–26.

1964 Mandible of the *Sinanthropus*-type discovered at Lantian, Shensi—*Sinanthropus lantianensis*. *Vertebrata PalAsiatica* 8(1):1–17.

1966 The hominid skull of Lantian, Shensi. *Vertebrata PalAsiatica* 10(1):1–22.

Wu Rukang (Woo Ju-kang) and Dong Xingren

1980 The fossil human teeth from Yunxian, Hubei. *Vertebrata PalAsiatica* 18(2):142–149.

1982 Preliminary study of *Homo erectus* remains from Hexian, Anhui. *Acta Anthropologica Sinica* 1(1):2–13.

Wu Rukang (Woo Ju-kang) and Jia Lanpo (Chia Lan-po)

1954 New discoveries about *Sinanthropus pekinensis* in Choukoutien. *Gushengwu Xuebao (Acta Palaeontologica Sinica)* 2(3):267–288.

Wu Rukang (Woo Ju-kang) and Lin Shenglong

1983 Peking Man. *Scientific American* 248(6):78–86.

Wu Rukang (Woo Ju-kang) and Wu Xinzhi

1982 Human fossil teeth from Xichuan, Henan. *Vertebrata PalAsiatica* 20(1):1–9.

Wu Rukang (Woo Ju-kang) and Zhao Zikuei

1959 New discovery of *Sinanthropus* mandible from Choukoutien. *Gu Jizhuidongwu Xuebao (Vertebrata PalAsiatica)* 3(4):169–172.

Wu Xinzhi and Zhang Yinyun

1978 Chinese palaeoanthropological multidisciplinary studies. In *Gurenlei Lunwenji (Collected Papers of Palaeoanthropology)*, edited by the Institute of Vertebrate Palaeontology and Palaeoanthropology, Chinese Academy of Sciences. Beijing: Science Press. Pp. 28–42.

Zhou Guoxing and Hu Chengzhi

1979 Supplementary notes on the teeth of Yuanmou Man with a discussion on morphological evolution of mesial upper incisors in hominoids. *Vertebrata PalAsiatica* 17(2):149–162.

6

Early *Homo sapiens* in China

WU XINZHI AND WU MAOLIN

Introduction

The assemblage of pre–Late Palaeolithic *Homo sapiens* fossils known from China is entirely the result of discoveries made after the Liberation in 1949. Sixty years ago Emile Licent and Pierre Teilhard de Chardin recovered an isolated human tooth in association with what was thought at the time to be a Middle Palaeolithic archaeological assemblage at Dagouwan in the Ordos Region of southern Inner Mongolia (Licent *et al.* 1926; Teilhard and Licent 1924; Terra 1941). Subsequent investigations have proven the Dagouwan sequence is actually of late Upper Pleistocene antiquity.

Since the discovery of numerous early Upper Pleistocene human fossils at Dingcun, Xiangfen County, Shanxi, in 1954 (Pei *et al.* 1958; Wu 1976), five additional major localities have yielded early *H. sapiens* remains including Changyang, Hubei (Jia 1957); Maba, Guangdong (Wu and Peng 1959); Tongzi, Guizhou (Wu *et al.* 1975); Xujiayao, Shanxi (Jia *et al.* 1979; Wu 1980); and Dali, Shaanxi (Wang *et al.* 1979; Wu 1981).

Dali, Shaanxi

The well-preserved Dali cranium was discovered in 1978 in the lower gravels of the third terrace of the Luo River near Jiefang Village on Duanjia Commune, Dali County, Shaanxi. These gravels, and a sand stratum above it, yielded a number of stone artifacts and more than 10 species of fossil vertebrates including

Palaeoanthropology and
Palaeolithic Archaeology in the
People's Republic of China

ISBN 0-12-601720-4

Megaloceros pachyosteus, *Equus* sp. indet., and *Palaeoloxodon* sp. indet., which suggest a late Middle Pleistocene antiquity for the deposit (Wu 1981; Wu and You 1979; Zhang and Zhou 1984).

The Dali cranium is quite well preserved; only the right posterior portion of the braincase and the left zygomatic arch are missing. The inferior portion of the face has been pressed upward and is slightly distorted (Figure 6.1).

The cranium is rather large with robust supraorbital ridges and prominent temporal lines and other muscular markings. With the exception of the suture between the upper border of the left greater wing of the sphenoid and the frontal squama, all the sutures can be seen on the exterior surface of the cranial vault. The sutures are also visible on the endocranial surface.

Our data suggest that the Dali cranium is of a male less than 30 years of age. The cranium's maximum length and breadth, the median sagittal arc, the auriculobregmatic arc, the auriculobregmatic height, and overall height (ba-b) are all within the morphometric parameters of Western early *H. sapiens* individuals and are greater than the average of the population of *H. erectus* from Zhoukoudian, near Beijing. The maximum length and breadth of the Dali cranium and its median sagittal arc all closely approximate similar measurements taken on Western early *H. sapiens*, while the specimen's auriculobregmatic arc and height and overall height (ba-b) are all smaller than the average of these measurements for early Upper Pleistocene hominids of the West (Tables 6.1 and 6.2).

The transverse curvature and the relative skull height indicate that the Dali hominid occupies an intermediate position between *H. erectus pekinensis* and

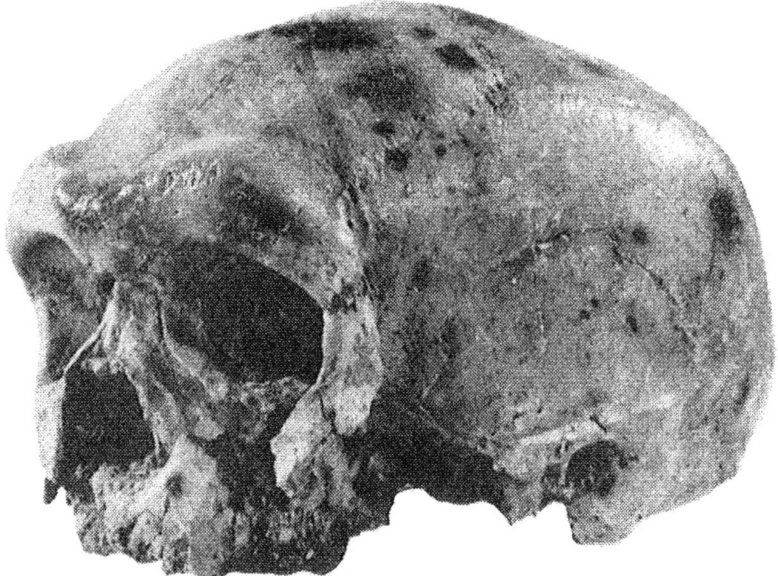

Figure 6.1 The Dali, Shaanxi, *Homo sapiens* cranium.

Table 6.1
MEASUREMENTS OF THE DALI CRANIUM[a]

Maximum length (g-op)	207
Maximum breadth (eu-eu)	149
Basibregmatic height (ba-b)	118
Auriculobregmatic height (po-b)	102.5
Median sagittal arc (n-o)	379
Auriculobregmatic arc (po-b-po)	299
Interparietal distance	136
Orbital height (right)	34
Orbital width (mf-ek) (right)	45
Zygomatic height	52.6
Height of temporal squama	46.5
Length of temporal squama	72
Nasozygomatic angle (fmo-n-fmo)	143°
Frontal inclination I (b-n-i)	54°
Frontal inclination II (b-n-o)	49°
Inclination of frontal squama I (b-g-i)	50°
Inclination of frontal squama II (b-g-o)	45°
Frontal profile I (m-g-i)	72°
Frontal profile II (m-g-o)	67°
Thickness (center of frontal squama)	9.0
Thickness (parietal eminence)	11.2
Thickness (cerebellar fossa)	3.9
Thickness (center of temporal squama)	7.0

[a]In millimeters. (After Wu 1981.)

Western early *H. sapiens*. Viewed laterally, the Dali cranial vault is low. The frontal inclination (b-n-i), the inclination of the frontal squama (b-g-i), and the frontal profile (m-g-i) are much larger than in Beijing Man and also exceed similar average measurements compiled from fossils of early *H. sapiens* from other areas of the world.

The morphology of the Dali cranium differs markedly from that of *H. erectus* from Zhoukoudian. The broadest part of the cranial vault is near the supero-posterior border of the temporal squama rather than near the base of the skull. The interparietal distance is 136 mm and the parietobasal index is 91.3, which makes the Dali hominid similar to many other early *H. sapiens* in these respects. The thickness of the cranial walls is slightly less than the average for Beijing Man but exceeds that of most Western early *H. sapiens*.

The cranium exhibits sagittal keeling that is particularly apparent in the center of the frontal squama and the sagittal suture. The suture pattern at pterion on both sides is of the frontotemporal type. A rectangular process projecting from the anterosuperior border of the temporal squama separates the parietal and sphenoid bones and joins the frontal. This type of pterion appears in all the Ngandong skulls from Java (Weidenreich 1951).

The superior border of the temporal squama is arc-shaped, the length and

Table 6.2
MORPHOMETRIC INDICES OF THE DALI CRANIUM[a]

Length–breadth	72.0
Length–height	57.0
Breadth–height	79.2
Transverse curvature	47.5
Orbital	75.6
Length–height of temporal squama	64.6
Cranial capacity	1120 cc

[a]After Wang *et al.* 1979; Wu 1981.

height measuring 72 and 46.5 mm, respectively. The index (64.6) approaches that of Western early *H. sapiens* and modern humans. The parietal notch between the superior border of the squamal and mastoid portions of the temporal bone is rather deep as in modern humans. An angular torus unites the ends of the temporal lines on the posteroinferior angle of the parietal bones. The contour of this angular torus is irregular.

The occipital bone forms an angle rather than a curve between the occipital and nuchal planes. The occipital torus occupies only half the width of the occipital bone. It is thickest at the center and gradually thins toward both ends joining the occipitomastoid ridge. Above the torus a shallow transverse groove separates the torus from the occipital plane of the occipital bone. The upper right margin of the occipital bone is missing but, judging from the sutures on the preserved left side, the Dali cranium probably originally possessed an Inca bone.

The supraorbital ridges are very robust and are even greater in height than those of *H. erectus pekinensis*. These ridges are thickest at their centers and gradually thin toward their margins. Both extend from the anteromedial side of the cranium to the posterolateral side forming a curved bony bar rather than a transverse one. The glabellar prominence is slightly depressed on the anterior surface so the supraorbital tori are more similar to those of the Ngandong hominid than they are to Western early *H. sapiens*. A groove runs behind the supraorbital tori, its lateral segment being shallower than the medial one.

The Dali cranium exhibits a pronounced postorbital constriction; the minimum width here is 106.4 mm while the distance between the lateral margins of the supraorbital ridges measures 125 mm. The postorbital constriction index is 85.1. These measurements fall within the range of 11 early European *H. sapiens* skulls available for comparison and fall below the average of the whole collection.

The suture joining the frontal bone, the nasal bones, and the frontal processes of the maxilla is arc-shaped. The nasozygomatic angle is 143°. The nasal bones are narrow and flat and are oriented nearly vertically, while the nasal profile angle approaches 90°. Where the zygomatic process of the maxilla contacts zygomatic bone there is an abrupt curve instead of a gradual one. Although the lower facial bones are somewhat distorted, the Dali cranium does not appear prognathic. The anterolateral surfaces of the frontosphenoidal processes of the zygomatic bone face more anteriorly than those of *H. sapiens neanderthalensis*. The orbital contour is not circular, the inferolateral angle in particular being very acute. These characters distinguish the Dali cranium from *H. sapiens neanderthalensis*.

The superior orbital margin is evenly curved and no supraorbital foramen or tubercle are present. The roof of the orbit is flat with only a shallow depression. The right zygomatic arch is complete and rather slender with a minimum height of 7 mm and a minimum width of 4.3 mm. The arch is essentially parallel to the Frankfurt plane, but even the superior margin of the arch falls below this plane.

On the base of the cranium, no infratemporal ridge can be seen on the greater wing of the sphenoid bone, but a definite demarcation exists between the temporal and infratemporal surfaces. The postglenoid process is rather well developed. Both the thickness and concavity of the tympanic plate are intermediate between those exhibited by Beijing Man and modern humans. The long axis of the petrous portion of the temporal bone intersects the sagittal plane to form an angle of 40°. On the endocranial surface there is a crista galli in the anterior cranial fossa. The complete branching system of the middle meningeal artery can be observed on the left side; the frontoparietal branch that terminates at the bregma and obelion regions is slightly larger in diameter than the superotemporal one, although the latter is longer. The inferior temporal branch is almost parallel with its superior counterpart and is slightly more slender. Although this pattern closely resembles that observed in Zhoukoudian Skull V, the branching of the meningeal arteries is much more complex in the Dali cranium.

The ratio of the dimensions of the cerebral and cerebellar fossae of the occipital bone in the Dali hominid is about 3:2, while the distance between the inion and the internal occipital protuberance is 11 mm (Wu 1981).

Tongzi, Guizhou

The Tongzi human fossils were discovered in the karstic Yanhui Cave about 10 km northwest of Tongzi, Guizhou, in 1972. The hominid remains comprise two isolated teeth: a right central upper incisor and a right first upper premolar (Table 6.3).

The incisor is quite robust. Although part of the lingual fossa is worn, the shovel-shaped structure of the surface can still be clearly seen. The lingual surface also bears a well-developed lingual tubercle divided into several fingerlike projections. The buccolingual diameter is larger than the mesiodistal diameter. The buccal surface of the crown is markedly convex in the transverse direction. The longitudinal axis of the crown almost parallels that of the root. The apex of the root is obtuse and bends distally, which distinguishes this specimen from the teeth of *H. erectus pekinensis*.

Table 6.3
MEASUREMENTS OF THE TONGZI RIGHT UPPER CENTRAL INCISOR AND RIGHT UPPER FIRST PREMOLAR

	Crown			Root		
	Length	Breadth	Height	Length	Breadth	Height
Incisor	(10.3)	8.3	—	—	—	17.9
Premolar	9.0	(12.8)	—	—	—	—

[a]In millimeters. (After Wu *et al.* 1975.)

The Tongzi premolar is incomplete. The buccal surface of the crown and the buccal root are missing. The buccolingual and mesiodistal diameters are both large and the mesiodistal diameter of the buccal surface is greater than that of the lingual surface. The lingual surface is hemispherical and is more curved transversely than longitudinally. The lingual surface is therefore very precipitous and there is no depression or bordering ridge. The size of the crown slightly exceeds those of the Changyang hominid and the crenulations of the occlusal surface are also more complex, closely resembling those of Beijing Man (Wu *et al.* 1975).

These morphological features lead us to believe that the Tongzi dentition is morphologically more primitive than those of the roughly contemporaneous Dingcun and Changyang humans, suggesting an appropriate systematic position between *H. erectus pekinensis* and the Dingcun and Changyang *H. sapiens*. The stone artifacts and mammalian fossils associated with the Tongzi teeth corroborate a late Middle Pleistocene or early Upper Pleistocene antiquity for the site.

Maba, Guangdong

In June 1958, a fossil human skull and many mammalian fossils were found in a limestone cave on Shizi Hill about 1.5 km southwest of Maba Village in Shaoguan County, Guangdong. Although no artifacts were found in direct association, the cave's *Ailuropoda–Stegodon* fauna indicates an early Upper Pleistocene antiquity for the deposit (see Chapter 15, this volume). The preserved material is a calotte comprising the two parietal bones and the frontal bone with fairly complete nasals and the right orbit (Table 6.4).

Judging from the indistinct appearance of the sutures and the fairly rugose external surface of the skull, this specimen is thought to be that of a male individual of middle age. The sutures on the Maba skull are obliterated with the exception of the coronal suture and the anterior part of the sagittal suture.

The cranium is ovoid in vertical aspect and the temporal lines are indistinct.

Table 6.4
MEASUREMENTS AND INDICES OF THE MABA CRANIUM

Orbital breadth (mf-ek)	44.3
Orbital height	39.0
Orbital index	88.0
Interoribtal breadth	20.8
Subtense, nasal bridge to breadth	5.8
Maxillofrontal index	27.9
Simotic chord	13.3
Simotic subtense	4.3
Simotic index	32.3
Frontal chord	115.6
Frontal arc	134.0
Frontal chord–arc index	86.3
Parietal chord	107.0
Parietal arc	114.0
Parietal chord–arc index	93.9
Calvarial height index	41.6
Bregma position index	40.6
Nasozygomatic angle (fmo-n-fmo)	152°
Bregma angle (b-g-o)	45°
Frontal profile II (m-g-o)	70°
Thickness at bregma	7.0

[a]In millimeters. (After Wu and Peng 1959; Wu and Zhang 1978.)

The cranial wall is thick but does not equal that of *H. erectus pekinensis*. No parietal foramen is recognizable on either side. The broadest part of the skull is just above the supramastoid crest and indistinct sagittal keeling is present near the center of the frontal squama (Figure 6.2). Measurements indicate that although the Maba calvarium is rather flat it is higher than that of Beijing Man. That is to say, the frontal and parietal bones are more rounded in the Maba specimen.

The frontal squama displays a distinct bulge that is separated from the glabellar part of the supraorbital torus by a very distinct supratoral groove. The glabella is a most distinctive landmark in both lateral and vertical views (Wu and Peng 1959).

The medial parts of the supraorbital tori project anteriorly more than their lateral margins and the ridges are thickest at the medial ends as well. When viewed vertically the supraorbital tori form a curved bony bar instead of a transverse one, a feature that is quite similar to the Ngandong hominids and rather different from those of Beijing Man. The lateral margins of the supraorbital tori clearly project posterolaterally to make the postorbital constriction very marked. Due to this projection, the temporal fossae below the postorbital constriction appear very deep. The frontal sinuses are very large, extending laterally well into the supraorbitals, and are separated by a thick bony partition. The frontal sinuses of the Maba cranium are larger than those of *H. erectus pekinensis*.

The contours of the right orbit are mostly intact with the exception of the inferior margin. The orbit is rounded and has no frontal notch. These particular characters are similar to those of Western Neanderthals and quite different from either the Ngandong, Java, or Zhoukoudian Locality 1 hominids. The orbital index of the Maba cranium places it in the hypsiconchic range and there is no trace of a deep fossa lacrimalis.

Based on the measurements of the reconstructed Maba cranium, the nasomalar angle indicates that the upper face is rather flat and, further, the lateral surface of the frontosphenoidal process of the zygomatic bone projected relatively far anteriorly.

All the sutures that separate the nasal portion of the frontal bone from the nasal, maxillary, and lacrimal bones lie at nearly the same level, a structure very similar to that of Beijing Man. The profile of the nasal bridge in the Maba cranium is slightly concave and, like the Zhoukoudian *H. erectus* individuals, the nasal breadth is rather wide. The frontal arc of the Maba specimen reflects a cranial vault more elevated than that of Beijing Man but less than that of modern *H. sapiens sapiens*.

From these descriptions it may be seen that although the Maba cranium shares

Figure 6.2 Right lateral view of the Maba, Guangdong, *Homo sapiens* cranium.

Table 6.5
MEASUREMENTS OF THE DINGCUN DENTITION

	Crown			Root		
	Length	Breadth	Height	Length	Breadth	Height
Right I^1	8.3	6.4	11.6	5.6	5.5	11.0
Right I^2	7.0	6.0	10.6	4.4	5.5	—
Right M_2	11.2	10.1	8.0	—	—	—

[a]In millimeters. (After Wu 1958.)

a number of morphological features in common with *H. erectus,* it is on the whole a more advanced physical type. The Maba skull and the crania of European Neanderthals also possess a number of common traits, although the differences between them are much greater. Some morphological features of the Maba cranium may be regarded as Mongoloid.

Dingcun, Shanxi

While digging sand for construction at Dingcun, Xiangfen County, Shanxi, during the spring of 1953 local laborers discovered large numbers of animal fossils.

From September to November 1954 a combined field team of the Institute of Vertebrate Palaeontology, Chinese Academy of Sciences, and the Shanxi Provincial Commission for the Preservation of Cultural Relics carried out large-scale excavations at 14 localities in the Dingcun area. At 10 of these sites Palaeolithic stone implements were recovered from Upper Pleistocene deposits (see Chapter 15, this volume). Locality 54.100 yielded three fossilized human teeth: one right upper central incisor, one right upper lateral incisor, and one right lower second molar (Table 6.5). Provenance data and the morphology of the teeth themselves suggest they all derive from a single individual estimated to be 12–13 years of age (Wu 1958).

The buccal surface of the central incisor is markedly convex in both sagittal and transverse planes. The lingual fossa is shovel-shaped, exhibiting a small depression in the center formed by borders of thickened, folded enamel. Although in this respect the Dingcun central incisor resembles those of the Zhoukoudian Locality 1 hominids, the Dingcun specimen's basal tubercle and fingerlike projections are not as well developed or complex as those of Beijing Man. The apex of the root of the Dingcun specimen is blunt while those of *H. erectus pekinensis* are relatively sharp, and the Dingcun central incisor is smaller overall than those of Western European *H. sapiens neanderthalensis,* but its shovel-shaped lingual surface is much more pronounced. The basal tubercle and fingerlike projections of the Dingcun tooth are not as highly developed as those of the Western Neanderthal group.

The upper lateral incisor also possesses a swollen basal tubercle and shovel-shaped lingual fossa. Its crown and root are all thinner and smaller than those of Beijing Man. Morphologically speaking, the upper lateral incisor from Dingcun seems intermediate between *H. erectus* and *H. sapiens sapiens.*

The occlusal surface of the lower second molar has five cusps. The mesial buccal cusp is larger than the mesial lingual cusp. The furrows that separate the cusps are in the form of a cross and a small but distinct additional tubercle is present on the lateral surface of the distal cusp, which may be regarded as a faint trace of a sixth cusp. The mesial and distal widths of the tooth are nearly equal, but the anterior part of the crown is longer than the posterior.

In addition to the main ridges extending along the central axis of the occlusal surface, an accessory ridge runs along both sides. The middle of the buccal surface of the crown is swollen in the Dingcun tooth as opposed to the base of the crown, which is swollen in *H. erectus pekinensis.* The mesiolingual cusp is larger than the mesiobuccal cusp in Beijing Man, therefore the furrows between the cusps are of the *Dryopithecus* (Y-5) pattern. When a sixth tubercle is present in the dentition of *H. erectus pekinensis,* it occurs on the lingual rather than the buccal side. Although the mesiolingual cusp is equal to the mesiobuccal cusp in the Neanderthals, a low ridge extends from the mesiolingual to the distobuccal cusp. The Dingcun dentition does not exhibit this structure. However, it does exhibit a number of characters that parallel those of Western European *H. sapiens neanderthalensis.* For example, the Spy hominid is similar to the Dingcun individual in that the dentition of neither exhibits the *Dryopithecus* pattern of cusp arrangement. According to Hellman (1928), lower second molars that exhibit an alternative cusp arrangement, the "plus pattern," approach 81% in modern Chinese populations (Wu 1958).

Although the morphological features of the Dingcun hominid bear certain resemblances to those of European Neanderthals, marked differences between the two are also apparent. In comparison with Beijing Man, although the Dingcun teeth were clearly derived from a more progressive hominid, strong parallels between the two nonetheless exist and some of the morphological features of the Dingcun dentition reflect close affinities with those of modern Mongoloids. The right parietal of a small child was also discovered at Locality 54.100 in 1976. Although too immature for detailed analysis, the remaining sutures suggest the specimen probably originally possessed an Inca bone (Wu 1976).

A total of 171 stone artifacts and 15 species of fossil vertebrates were also collected at Locality 54.100, all of which indicate an early Upper Pleistocene antiquity for the site (Wu 1958; and Chapter 15, this volume).

Xindong, Zhoukoudian, Beijing

The Xindong, or New Cave, hominid was recovered from Locality 4 on Longgushan at Zhoukoudian, Beijing, in 1973. The human fossil remains comprise only a single tooth, thought to be a left upper first premolar (Table 6.6).

Table 6.6
MEASUREMENTS OF THE XINDONG, ZHOUKOUDIAN, PREMOLAR

	Crown			Root		
	Length	Breadth	Height	Length	Breadth	Height
Left P^1	8.5	11	6.1	5.1	9.3	18.8

[a]In millimeters. (After Gu 1978.)

The specimen is nearly complete with only the apex of the root missing. The crown carries two cusps and its buccolingual diameter is greater than the mesiodistal. The mesiobuccal angle is closer to the longitudinal axis of the tooth than is the distobuccal angle. The occlusal surface of the crown is worn and divided by a short longitudinal furrow into a larger buccal cusp and a smaller lingual cusp. The distal side of the buccal cusp exhibits a small groove that connects to the main longitudinal furrow of the tooth. The buccal surface is relatively flat and the lingual surface is more rounded. The distal surface is more markedly curved than the mesial.

Both mesial and distal sides have shallow, narrow furrows coursing along the middle of the root; the mesial one is wide and flat, the distal deeper. The apex of the root is not divided. The Xindong premolar is smaller than those of Beijing Man and the triangular prominence on the buccal side is absent. The crenulations of the occlusal surface are less complex than those of *H. erectus pekinensis* and the cingulum is rather indistinct. The root of the Xindong tooth is much less robust than those of Beijing Man, which are divided into two branches at the apex.

The Xindong specimen also diverges significantly from the premolars of modern *H. sapiens sapiens* and the data suggest an intermediary position between *H. erectus pekinensis* and modern Chinese populations for this tooth (Gu 1978).

The large sample of vertebrate fossils found in association with the Xindong premolar indicates an early Upper Pleistocene antiquity for the deposit.

Changyang, Hubei

In 1956 human fossils were found in a cave deposit near Xiazhongjiawan Village, about 45 km southwest of Changyang, Hubei. The hominid fossils recovered thus far include a left maxilla fragment with the first premolar and first molar intact, and an isolated left lower second premolar (Table 6.7).

The maxilla comprises the greater part of the body although the posterior margin of the alveolus for the first molar and the base of the zygomatic arch are missing. The left lower second premolar is complete. Enough of the anterior nasal spine is preserved to indicate that it was weak. The alveolar portion of the maxilla is almost orthognathous while the palatal surface is quite rugose. The

Table 6.7
MEASUREMENTS OF THE CHANGYANG DENTITION

	Crown			Root		
	Length	Breadth	Height	Length	Breadth	Height
Left P^1	7.4	10.6	—	—	—	—
Left M^1	10.8	12.8	—	—	—	—
Left P_2	8.3	10.6	4.8	7.2	9.8	20.5

[a]In millimeters. (After Jia 1957.)

incisive foramen lies very close to the alveolar margin. The anterior wall of the maxillary sinus extends forward to a point anterior to the first premolar.

Although these characters are similar to those found in modern *H. sapiens sapiens,* the Changyang hominid also possesses the following rather primitive morphological features. The inferior margin of the nasal aperture is relatively wide and its lateral wall is less curved than in modern humans. The canine eminence is very pronounced and extends upward beyond the nasal floor indicating that the root of the canine was well developed.

Both the upper first premolar and first molar are quite large and the crenulations of their occlusal surfaces are complex (Jia 1957). The chewing surface of the left lower second premolar is slightly worn. The rectangular crown is characterized by its lowness in relation to its length and breadth.

Eighteen fossil vertebrate species were recovered in association with the Changyang hominid remains, which were originally thought to be of Middle Pleistocene antiquity (Jia 1957). Biostratigraphic analyses that have been conducted since the original discovery of the fossils, however, indicate a later, Upper Pleistocene age for the site (see Chapter 15, this volume).

Xujiayao, Shanxi

The Xujiayao site is on the west bank of the Liyikou, a small tributary of the Sangan River about 1 km southeast of Xujiayao Village in Yanggao County, Shanxi, on the border of Yangyuan County, Hebei. The site was discovered in 1974. Excavations at Xujiayao in 1976 and 1977 yielded 17 human fossils, including 11 parietal fragments, 2 occipitals, 1 fragmentary left maxilla, 1 fragmentary right mandibular ramus, and 2 isolated teeth (Tables 6.8–6.10).

In addition, nearly 20,000 stone and bone artifacts and a large assemblage of vertebrate fossils were unearthed at Xujiayao. Although the hominid remains are quite abundant, a complete cranium has yet to be discovered. Among the 11 parietal fragments, only 2 specimens are nearly complete. Both occipital bones are well preserved but the remaining Xujiayao hominid material is all fragmentary.

Table 6.8
THICKNESS OF THE XUJIAYAO PARIETAL BONES

Location	Specimen number 6	4.5	10	Average
Bregma	6.5	9	8.5	8
Eminence	7	10.8	12.6	10.1
Mastoid angle	7.2	—	13.0	10.1

[a]In millimeters. (After Jia *et al.* 1979; Wu 1980.)

The Xujiayao hominid possesses a rather thick cranial vault, falling toward the upper limit of, and sometimes exceeding, the range of variation of this character in *H. erectus pekinensis.* The coronal and lambdoidal margins of the parietal are not as curved as those of Beijing Man, but are more curved than in modern *H. sapiens sapiens.* The curved contours of the sagittal and temporal margins are very similar to those of the Zhoukoudian *H. erectus.*

On the endocranial surface of the parietal bones, the branching of the middle meningeal artery is more complex than that of Beijing Man but simpler than in modern *H. sapiens.* The vessel diameter of the Xujiayao specimen is smaller than those of the Zhoukoudian Middle Pleistocene population and, like the Maba hominid, the posterior branch is longer than the anterior.

The occipital torus of the Xujiayao hominid exhibits a long, narrow swelling, being thick and broad in the center and gradually thinning toward the margins. The occipital angle is 116°, which exceeds the maximum value for *H. erectus pekinensis* but is more acute than that of modern *H. sapiens sapiens.*

The cerebral fossae are much larger than their cerebellar counterparts. The average distance between the cruciate eminence and the inion is 13 mm, which is shorter than that of Beijing Man.

The maxilla fragment is derived from an immature individual of perhaps 7–9 years of age, and exhibits a deeply hidden canine and erupted first and second molars. The bone is comparatively massive and the anterior end is constricted as

Table 6.9
CHORD–ARC INDICES OF PARIETAL BONE NO. 10 FROM XUJIAYAO

Margin	Chord	Arc	Index
Sagittal	114.2	121	94.4
Coronal	102.5	122	84.1
Lambdoidal	105	120	87.5
Temporal	104.8	111	94.4

[a]In millimeters. (After Wu 1980.)

Table 6.10
MEASUREMENTS OF THE XUJIAYAO DENTITION

	Crown			Root		
	Length	Breadth	Height	Length	Breadth	Height
Left I^1	10.0	8.4	11.0	—	—	—
Left C^1	10.8	10.4	13.2	—	—	—
Left M^1	13.4	14.0	7.4	—	—	—
Left M^2	11.4	13.8	6.2	—	—	17.3
Left M^{1-2}	12.0	13.7	—	9.5	13.1	buccal: 16.0 (mes.) 15.5 (dis.)

[a]In millimeters. (After Jia *et al.* 1979; Wu 1980.)

in *H. erectus pekinensis*. The anterior nasal spine is very clear and prosthion exceeds the posterior border of the spine. The facial region of the maxilla projects slightly, being intermediate between Beijing Man and modern humans (Jia *et al.* 1979).

The Xujiayao upper central incisor closely resembles those of the Zhoukoudian *H. erectus* in its shovel-shaped lingual morphology. The fingerlike projections end abruptly at the center of the tooth and do not extend to the cutting edge. A basal tubercle is present, but is smaller than those of the Zhoukoudian Middle Pleistocene population. In overall size, the presence of a clear cingulum, and the complexity of the crenulations on their occlusal surfaces, the Xujiayao dentition bears definite affinities with that of Beijing Man.

We believe the Xujiayao hominid may be considered intermediate between North China's *H. erectus* and modern *H. sapiens sapiens* populations and that some evidence of Mongoloid affinity is also present. Although the absolute age of the Xujiayao deposit is still in question (see Chapter 2, this volume), biostratigraphic and lithostratigraphic data indicate an Upper Pleistocene antiquity.

Discussion

The relationships among early *H. sapiens* in China and both earlier and later fossil humans in China and elsewhere are matters of great interest to us. In China, early *H. sapiens* shares a number of morphological traits in common with *H. erectus,* such as the presence of weak sagittal keeling; the contact of the frontonasal and frontomaxillary sutures, which are on almost the same level and form an arc; the flattened nasal bones; the anterior-facing malar surface of the frontosphenoidal process of the zygomatic bone; and the angular rather than rounded junction of the zygomatic bone and the zygomatic process of the maxilla. In addition, the frequent presence of an Inca bone and the shovel-shaped morphology of the lingual fossae of the incisors are also characteristically primitive features found in both Chinese *H. erectus* and early *H. sapiens*.

Most of these features may also be observed in later fossil and modern *H. sapiens* in China (see Chapter 7, this volume) indicating substantial phylogenetic continuity. These morphological characters also distinguish China's early *H. sapiens* from populations of *H. sapiens neanderthalensis* in the West.

Such Neanderthaloid features as the large, prognathic face, the lack of canine fossae, the nearly circular orbital contours, and the bun-shaped supraoccipital region are not found in Chinese early *H. sapiens*. The fact that Chinese early *H. sapiens* seem to appear in the fossil record somewhat earlier than their European counterparts may partially account for this lack of congruence in specific morphological features. However, it is our opinion that, considering the marked continuity among Chinese Pleistocene fossil hominids, geographical phylogenetic variation is sufficient to warrant the inclusion of Chinese, and perhaps other East Asian, early *H. sapiens* in a subspecies distinct from *H. sapiens neanderthalensis*. For these Pleistocene hominids, the senior author has proposed the name *Homo sapiens daliensis*.

References

Black, Davidson

1928 A study of Kansu and Honan Aeneolithic skulls from later prehistoric sites in comparison with North China and other recent crania. *Palaeontologia Sinica*, Series D 6(1).

Gu Yumin

1978 New Cave Man of Zhoukoudian and his living environments. In *Gurenlei Lunwenji (Collected Papers of Palaeonathropology)*, edited by the Institute of Vertebrate Palaeontology and Palaeoanthropology, Chinese Academy of Sciences. Beijing: Science Press, Pp. 158–174.

Hellman, Milo

1928 Racial characters in human dentition. *Proceedings of the American Philosophical Society* 68:157–174.

Jia Lanpo (Chia Lan-po)

1957 Notes on the human and some other mammalian remains from Changyang, Hupei. *Gu Jizhuidongwu Xuebao (Vertebrata PalAsiatica)* 1(3):247–258.

Jia Lanpo (Chia Lan-po), Wei Qi, and Li Chaorong

1979 Report on the excavation of Hsuchiayao Man site in 1976. *Vertebrata PalAsiatica* 17(4):277–293.

Licent, E., P. Teilhard de Chardin, and D. Black

1926 On a presumably Pleistocene human tooth from the Sjara-osso-gol deposits. *Bulletin of the Geological Society of China* 5(3–4):285–290.

Pei Wenzhong (Pei Wen-chung), Wu Rukang (Woo Ju-kang), Jia Lanpo (Chia Lan-po), Zhou Mingzhen (Chow Min-chen), Liu Xianting, and Wang Zeyi

1958 Report on the excavation of Palaeolithic sites at Tingtsun, Hsiangfenhsien, Shansi province, China. *Memoirs of the Institute of Vertebrate Palaeontology and Palaeoanthropology*, Series A 2:1–111.

Teilhard de Chardin, Pierre and Emile Licent

1924 On the discovery of a Palaeolithic industry in northern China. *Bulletin of the Geological Society of China* 3(1):45–50.

Terra, Helmut de
1941 Pleistocene formations and Stone Age man in China. *Institut de Géo-Biologie Publication 6*, Pp. 1–54.
Wang Yongyan, Xue Xiangxu, Yue Leping, Zhao Jufa, and Liu Shuntang
1979 Discovery of Dali fossil man and its preliminary study. *Kexue Tongbao* 24(7):303–306.
Weidenreich, Franz
1951 Morphology of Solo Man. *Memoirs of the American Museum of Natural History* 43(3):205–290.
Wu Maolin
1980 Human fossils discovered at Xujiayao site in 1977. *Vertebrata PalAsiatica* 18(3):229–238.
Wu Maolin, Wang Linghong, Zhang Yinyun, and Zhang Senshui
1975 Fossil human teeth and associated fauna from northern Guizhou. *Vertebrata PalAsiatica* 13(1):14–23.
Wu Rukang (Woo Ju-kang) and Peng Ruce
1959 Fossil human skull of early Palaeoanthropic stage found at Mapa, Shaokuan, Kwangtung province. *Gu Jizhuidongwu yu Gu Renlei* (*Palaeovertebrata et Palaeoanthropologia*) 1(4):159–164.
Wu Xinzhi
1976 Turning grief into strength: excavating Neoanthropus fossils at Dingcun. *Vertebrata PalAsiatica* 14(4):270.
1981 The well preserved cranium of an early *Homo sapiens* from Dali, Shaanxi. *Scientia Sinica* 2:200–206.
Wu Xinzhi and You Yuzhu
1979 A preliminary observation of Dali Man site. *Vertebrata PalAsiatica* 17(4):294–303.
Wu Xinzhi and Zhang Yinyun
1978 Chinese palaeoanthropological multidisciplinary studies. In *Gurenlei Lunwenji* (*Collected Papers of Palaeoanthropology*), edited by the Institute of Vertebrate Palaeontology and Palaeoanthropology, Chinese Academy of Sciences. Beijing: Science Press. Pp. 28–42.
Zhang Senshui and Zhou Chunmao
1984 A preliminary study of the second excavation of Dali Man locality. *Acta Anthropologica Sinica* 3(1):19–29.

7

Homo sapiens Remains from Late Palaeolithic and Neolithic China

WU XINZHI AND ZHANG ZHENBIAO

Introduction

Fossilized remains of *Homo sapiens sapiens* have been recovered from relatively few late Pleistocene contexts in China. Principal localities where such remains have been found include the Upper Cave (Shandingdong) at Zhoukoudian, Beijing; Tongtianyan, Liujiang County, Guangxi Zhuang Autonomous Region; and Huangshanxi, Ziyang County, Sichuan. In addition, a number of fragmentary late *H. sapiens* remains have been discovered including those of "Ordos Man" from the southern Inner Mongolia Autonomous Region; Maomaodong, Xingyi County, Guizhou; Zuozhen, Tainan County, Taiwan; Shiyu, Suoxian, Shanxi; Xintai, Shandong; Lipu and Laibin, Guangxi; Jiande, Zhejiang; and Changwu, Shaanxi (Figure 7.1). Collectively, these discoveries have provided Chinese physical anthropologists with the material resources upon which interpretations about the origins of China's unique racial composition and later Pleistocene evolutionary trends may be based. Following is a discussion of China's most important late Upper Pleistocene and Holocene *H. sapiens sapiens* remains and their significance in the study of China's modern racial milieu.

Palaeoanthropology and
Palaeolithic Archaeology in the
People's Republic of China

ISBN 0-12-601720-4

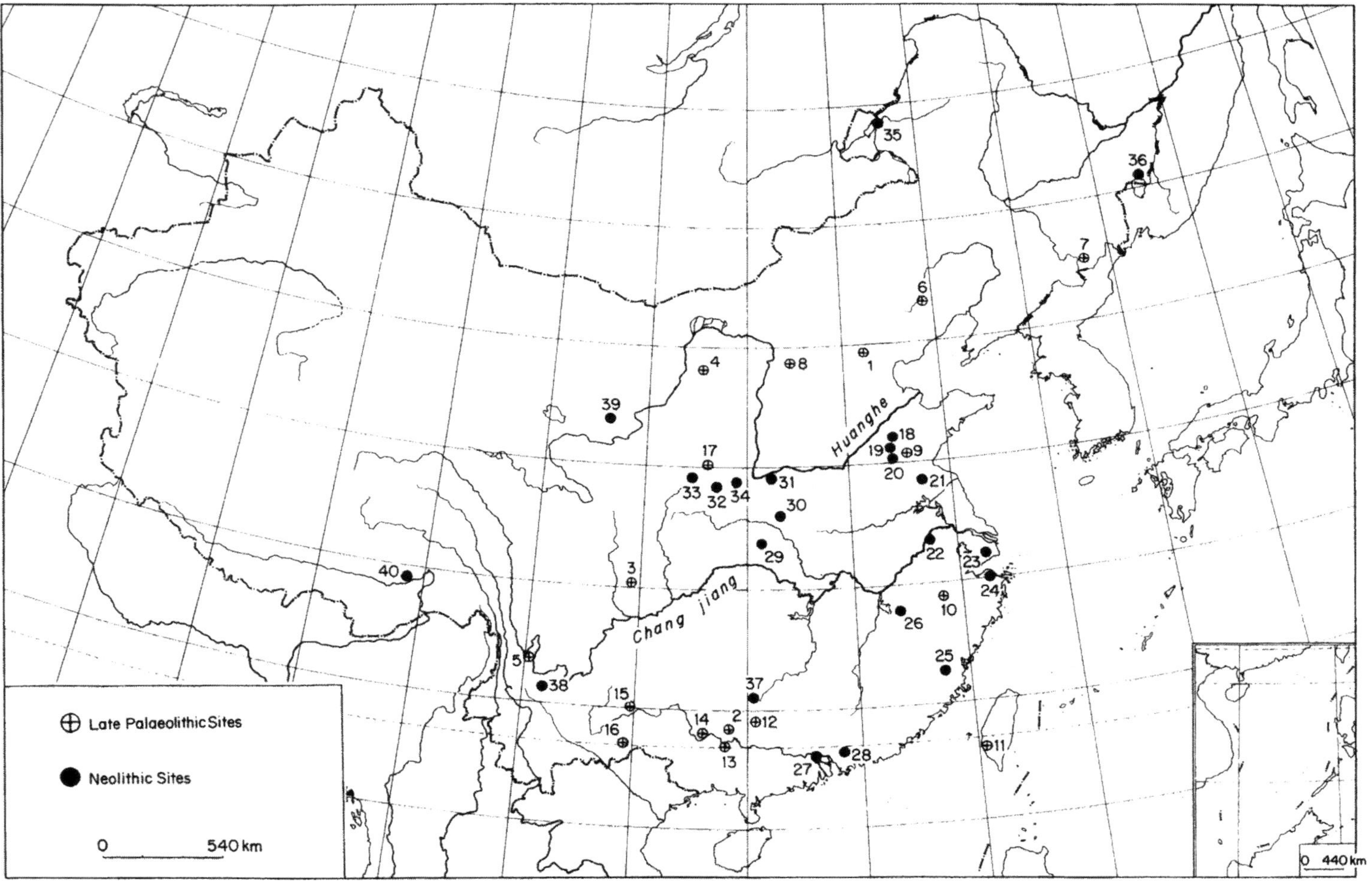

Figure 7.1 Selected Late Palaeolithic and Neolithic sites in China. 1, Upper Cave, Zhoukoudian, Beijing; 2, Liujiang, Guangxi; 3, Ziyang, Sichuan; 4, Ordos, Inner Mongolia; 5, Lijiang, Yunnan; 6, Jianping, Liaoning; 7, An'tu, Jilin; 8, Shiyu, Shanxi; 9, Xintai, Shandong; 10, Jiande, Zhejiang; 11, Zuozhen, Taiwan; 12, Lipu, Guangxi; 13, Qilinshan, Guizhou; 14, Du'an, Guangxi; 15, Maomaodong, Guizhou; 16, Xichou, Yunnan; 17, Changwu, Shaanxi; 18, Dawenkou, Shandong; 19, Xixiahou, Shandong; 20, Yedian, Shandong; 21, Dadunzi, Pi County, Jiangsu; 22, Beiyinyangying, Nanjing; 23, Songze, Shanghai; 24, Hemudu, Zhejiang; 25, Tanshishan, Fujian; 26, Xianrendong, Jiangxi; 27, Hedang, Guangdong; 28, Zengcheng, Guangdong; 29, Qilihe, Hubei; 30, Xichuan, Henan; 31, Miaodigou, Henan; 32, Banpo, Shaanxi; 33, Baoji, Shaanxi; 34, Huaxian, Shaanxi; 35, Zharen Nur, Inner Mongolia; 36, Xinkaihu, Heilongjiang; 37, Zhenpiyan, Guangxi; 38, Dadunzi, Yuanmou County, Yunnan; 39, Machang, Gansu; 40, Lingzhi, Xizang (Tibet).

The Pleistocene Record

Liujiang, Guangxi

The Liujiang hominid was discovered in 1958 in a small cave at Tongtianyan, about 16 km southwest of Liuzhou in the Guangxi Zhuang Autonomous Region (Wu 1959). The *Ailuropoda–Stegodon* fauna found in association with the Liujiang hominid includes *Rhinoceros sinensis, Megatapirus* sp. indet., *Sus* sp. indet., and *Ursus* sp. indet., and although in 1958 most of the representatives of the fauna were thought to have been deposited during the Middle Pleistocene, Wu Rukang (1959) believes the hominid remains postdate this epoch.

The fossil *H. sapiens* materials from Liujiang consist of a well-preserved cranium, the lower four thoracic vertebrae, all five lumbar vertebrae with articulated ribs, the sacrum, the right innominate, and two femur fragments (Figure 7.2b–d).

Wu (1959) has determined the Liujiang cranium to be that of a middle-age male exhibiting morphological features more primitive than either the Upper Cave or Ziyang hominids (Table 7.1).

Morphometric characters in the Liujiang cranium reflect both Mongoloid and Australoid racial affinities. The skull has well-developed superciliary arches, although both the temporal and parietal eminences are not marked. The supraoccipital region is slightly bulged in the "bunlike" structure similar to that of Western European Neanderthals. The mastoid process is diminutive but the supramastoid crest is well developed. The pterion region is H-shaped and the boundary between the temporal and inferior temporal surfaces forms a clear ridge.

The mandibular fossae are shallow and the foramen magnum is small, but the Liujiang cranium's occipital condyles are relatively massive. The palate is moderate in size as is the dentition. The maxillary third molars have not erupted, which is of special interest in view of the hominid's estimated age of 40 years. The cranial height is moderate with a relatively low height–length index of 42.9. The bregma index however, is very high (44.2), falling within the range of other Chinese fossil *H. sapiens*, but lying relatively far posteriorly in comparison to most modern humans.

The position of the frontonasal suture is higher than the frontomaxillary suture and the face in general is broad and short. The orbits are wide and low, being of the chamaeconchic type. The nasals are also wide and the lower margin of the nasal aperture is especially broad. The anterolateral surface of the frontal process of the malar is rotated forward, as in Mongoloids. The prenasal fossa is shallow and the anterior nasal spine is small. The canine fossae are not marked and, while the upper right lateral incisor is shovel-shaped, one central incisor was missing and the other one is too worn to allow accurate assessment of this point.

The Liujiang cranium's nasomalar angle (fmo-n-fmo) of 143.5 and its low

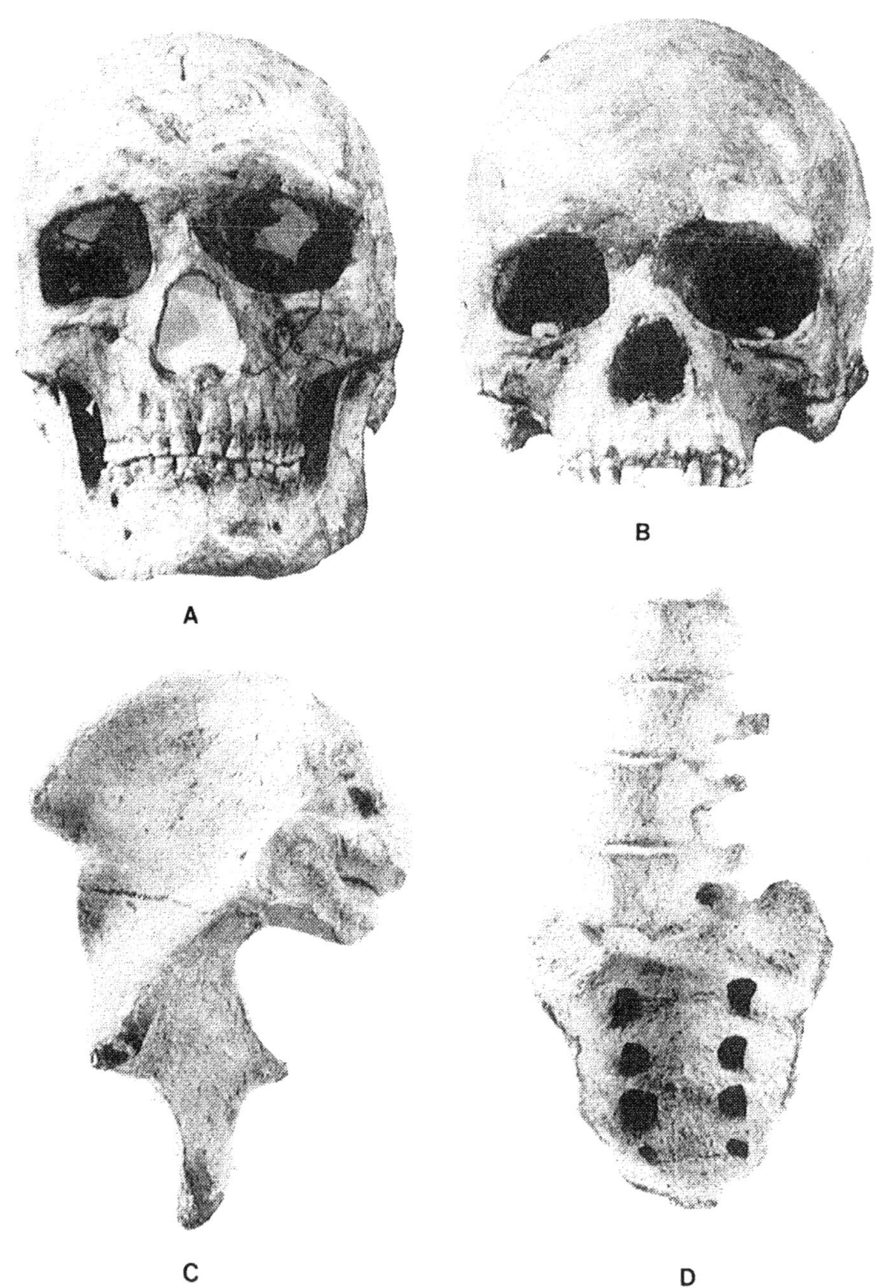

Figure 7.2 A, Skull No. 101 from the Upper Cave (Shandingdong) at Zhoukoudian, Beijing; B, cranium from Liujiang, Guangxi; C, ilium from Liujiang, Guangxi; D, sacrum and lumbar vertebrae from Liujiang, Guangxi.

Table 7.1
MEASUREMENTS AND INDICES OF THE LIUJIANG AND ZHOUKOUDIAN UPPER CAVE CRANIA[a]

	Liujiang, Guangxi cranium	Zhoukoudian Upper Cave skull		
		No. 101	No. 102	No. 103
Maximum cranial length (g-op)	189.3	204.0	196.0	184.0
Glabella–inion (g-i)	172.0	198.0	185.0	180.0
Maximum cranial breadth (eu-eu)	142.2	143.0	136.0	131.0
Minimum frontal breadth (ft-ft)	95.2	107.0	102.5	101.0
Maximum bizygomatic breadth (zy-zy)	136.0	143.0	131.0	137.0
Upper facial height (n-pr)	65.9	77.0	69.0	68.5
Nasal height (n-ns)	45.8	58.0	46.5	51.0
Nasal breadth	26.8	32.0	26.0	25.5
Orbital breadth (mf-ek)				
(Left)	42.0	48.5	40.5	45.0
(Right)	43.1	48.0	45.0	45.0
Orbital height				
(Left)	28.7	31.5	29.3	31.0
(Right)	29.0	33.2	31.5	32.0
Bimalar breadth (zm-zm)	97.1	106.2	106.4	101.0
Subtense GB	31.5	35.1	36.5	33.5
Internal biorbital breadth (fmo-fmo)	98.8	110.0	104.1	106.0
Subtense IOW (fmo-fmo)	15.5	21.4	23.5	13.5
Interorbital breadth (mf-mf)	21.2	19.1	21.0	20.5
Subtense mf-mf	6.2	9.2	7.7	7.5
Simotic breadth (sc)	10.6	7.0	9.1	9.0
Simotic subtense (ss)	3.0	4.0	4.5	3.1
Palatal length (ol-sta)	45.0	52.0	47.0	48.0
Palatal breadth (enm-enm)	36.0	43.0	40.0	38.0
Palatal height	9.5	13.8	10.5	8.5
Foramen magnum length (ba-o)	36.9	39.2	44.0	40.5
Foramen magnum breadth (fmb)	30.5	35.0	32.3	32.8
Profile length (ba-pr)	100.0	106.2	113.6	109.3
Midprofile length (ba-ss)	95.0	103.0	109.6	104.0
Basicranial length (ba-n)	103.5	111.0	116.0	108.5
Basibregmatic height (ba-b)	134.8	136.0	150.0	143.0
Basivertex height (ba-v)	134.0	137.5	154.5	144.5
Auricular height (OH)	114.5	113.0	119.0	118.0
Porion–bregma height (po-b)	114.8	148.0	120.0	118.5
Alveolar length	—	57.0	57.5	58.3
Alveolar breadth	—	69.2	72.6	66.0
Sagittal arc (n-o)	374.0	388.5	348.5	363.0
Frontal arc (n-b)	136.5	132.0	126.0	121.0
Parietal arc (b-l)	132.0	132.0	135.5	132.5
Occipital arc (l-o)	105.5	124.5	123.0	110.0
Frontal chord (n-b)	117.2	115.5	116.2	107.0
Parietal chord (b-l)	119.2	120.8	120.4	120.0

(continued)

Table 7.1 (*Continued*)

	Liujiang, Guangxi cranium	Zhoukoudian Upper Cave skull		
		No. 101	No. 102	No. 103
Occipital chord (l-o)	91.5	97.6	106.0	93.0
Facial profile angle (n-pr-FH)	86.0°	84.0°	80.0°	79.0°
Nasal profile angle (n-ns-FH)	89.0°	90.0°	82.0°	80.0°
Alveolar profile angle (ns-pr-FH)	79.0°	80.0°	75.0°	73.0°
Glabella-bregma angle (g-b-FH)	46.0°	45.0°	48.0°	46.0°
Frontal angle (b-g-i)	—	52.0°	59.0°	57.0°
Frontal profile angle (m-g-FH)	74.0°	65.5°	65.0°	76.5°
Nasomalar angle (fmo-n-fmo)	143.5°	135.0°	130.0°	148.0°
Zygomaxillary angle (zm-ss-zm)	138.0°	128.0°	125.0°	131.0°
Cranial index (eu-eu × 100/g-op)	75.1	70.1	69.4	71.2
Length–height index I (ba-b × 100/g-op)	71.2	66.7	76.5	77.7
Length–height index II (OH × 100/g-op)	60.5	55.4	60.7	64.1
Breadth–height index (ba-b × 100/eu-eu)	94.8	95.1	110.3	109.2
Breadth–height index (OH × 100/eu-eu)	80.5	79.0	87.5	90.1
Craniofacial index (n-sd × 100/OH)	48.9	56.6	46.0	47.9
Craniofacial breadth index (zy-zy × 100/eu-eu)	95.6	100.0	96.3	104.6
Upper facial index (n-sd × 100/zy-zy)	48.5	53.8	52.7	50.0
Facial projection index (ba-pr × 100/ba-n)	96.6	95.7	97.9	100.7
Orbital index (Left)	68.3	64.9	72.3	68.9
Nasal index	58.5	55.2	55.9	50.0
Palatal index	80.0	82.7	85.1	79.2
Frontal index (Sub fmo-fmo × 100/fmo-fmo)	15.7	19.5	22.6	12.7
Simotic index (SS × 100/SC)	28.3	57.1	49.5	34.1
Premaxillary index (Sub zm-zm × 100/zm-zm)	32.4	33.1	34.3	33.2
Maxillary frontal index	29.2	48.2	36.7	36.6
Frontal chord–arc index	85.9	87.5	92.2	88.4
Parietal chord–arc index	90.3	91.5	88.9	90.6
Occipital chord–arc index	86.7	78.4	86.2	84.5

[a]In millimeters.

simotic index (23.9) clearly fall within the range of the modern Mongoloids. The bregmatic position and moderate lambdoidal flattening are interpreted as primitive features.

The postcranial remains of the Liujiang *H. sapiens* have been the cause of some controversy as regards their racial affinity. Coon (1969) emphasized the Australoid character of these remains based on his interpretation of Wu's original data (1959). Howells (1977) however, based on his own examination of the fossils, disagrees with this.

The lower four thoracic vertebrae and the first lumbar vertebra were found in an articulated state. The heights of the ventral sides of the vertebral bodies of the lower four thoracics and first lumbar vertebra are as follows: 20.0, 20.5, 21.0, 22.5, and 23.6 mm.

The lower four lumbar vertebrae and the sacrum were also found as a separate articulated unit. Beginning at the proximal end of the column, the heights of the vertebral bodies on their ventral sides are 24.5, 21.0, 25.0, and 25.0 mm. The upper two-thirds of the ventral surface of the sacrum is fairly flat, although the caudal region is markedly curved. The ventral length of the sacrum is 92.2 mm, while the upper ventral breadth is 86.5 mm, yielding a small, flattish sacrum of dolichohieric type. The sacral hiatus extends upward to the middle of the third sacral vertebra. The length and breadth of the two sacroiliac surfaces are as follows: 56 and 32 mm on the left side, 54 and 31 mm on the right. The Liujiang pattern of large cranium and small sacrum is similar to that of the Broken Hill hominid, although no affinity is implied. The Liujiang right innominate is fairly well preserved, although the superior and inferior rami of the pubis and the inferior ramus of the ischium are broken off.

Two femoral diaphysis fragments are preserved, one left and one right. At the subtrochanteric level of the right femur, its transverse diameter is 28.5 mm while its sagittal diameter is 21.0 mm. Its platymeric index (73.7) is great, placing it within the hyperplatymeric range. The circumference of this bone is 83.0 mm. At middiaphysis the transverse diameter of the right femur is 22.5 mm, the sagittal diameter is 27.0 mm, and the pilastric index is 83.3 with a circumference of 82.0 mm.

The left femur's middiaphysis transverse diameter is 22.0 mm, its sagittal diameter is 26.2 mm, its pilastric index is 84.0, and its circumference is 80.0 mm. The left femoral fragments' broken margins allow measurements of the interior to be taken resulting in the following metrical data: transverse diameter of medullary canal, 8.0 mm; sagittal diameter, 10.0 mm. The linea aspera of both femora are marked and the femoral shafts bend forward at middiaphysis. Below the lesser trochanter the femoral shafts are flattened, producing prominent medial and lateral bulges. The thick walls and narrow medullary cavities of the Liujiang femora are very similar to Western Neanderthals in this regard and diverge significantly from those of modern *H. sapiens sapiens*.

Upper Cave, Zhoukoudian, Beijing

The lower chamber of the Upper Cave (or Shandingdong) at Zhoukoudian, outside Beijing, yielded in 1933 and 1934 a series of human fossils and archaeological remains in an apparently ritual context (Pei 1934, 1939a,b). The discovery of finely crafted ornaments and a bone needle in association with the remains of at least eight human individuals and an abundant faunal assemblage—

including *Crocuta crocuta ultima*, *Acinonyx* cf. *jubatus*, *Panthera tigris*, *P. pardus*, *Equus hemionus*, and *Struthio anderssoni*—all immediately suggested an Upper Pleistocene antiquity to the site's original investigators. Recently, two radiocarbon dates have been generated that are thought to bracket the episode of archaeological deposition in the cave. The sample from the lower chamber has an associated date of 10,470 ± 360 BP (ZK-136-0-3), while that from the lower recess has been dated to 18,865 ± 420 BP (ZK-136-0-1). Given the stratigraphic circumstances in which the hominid materials occurred, it is suggested that the former of these two determinations probably more closely approximates the time of interment.

The human fossils found in the Upper Cave include three relatively complete crania (Nos. 101, 102, and 103); a maxilla fragment (No. 110); four mandibles (Nos. 101, 104, 108, and 109), two of which are complete; and fragments of radius, femur, and patella.

Franz Weidenreich (1939a,b) suggested that skull No. 101 (Figure 7.1a) was that of an elderly male that exhibited morphological characters of both Western European *H. sapiens sapiens* and those of the Mongoloid race. The cranium and mandible are both nearly complete, the left temporal region being slightly fractured. The cranium is quite large with a capacity of about 1500 cc. The vault is low and the forehead moderately receding. A poorly developed sagittal prominence is present in the posterior two-thirds of the frontal squama. The parietal tuberosities are not marked and they are situated posteriorly and dorsally to the mastoid processes. The superior margin of the temporal squama is relatively flat. The superciliary arches are prominent and their medial ends are joined in the glabellar region.

The superior facial height is low in comparison to that of modern Mongoloids. The orbits are low and rectangular. The nasal bridge is high and a broad nasal aperture is present. The upper face is not prominent, exhibiting a nasomalar angle of 135°, but both malar bones are perpendicular and their anterolateral surfaces are rotated forward. The inferior margin of the nasal aperture grades into the prenasal fossa while the sagittal contour of the alveolar process is rather convex.

Skull No. 102 is also well preserved in spite of numerous cracks and fissures that penetrate the specimen. This cranium is thought to be that of a young female and exhibits what is apparently intentional deformation of the frontal region, producing a high vault, flat forehead, and shallow supraorbital groove. The cranial capacity is moderate at about 1380 cc.

Judging from such morphological characters as the small cranial index, the large breadth–height index, the nearly vertical craniofacial index, the low position of the orbits, and the broad nose, Weidenreich (1939a,b) considered this specimen to be of a Melanesoid type and pointed out that the total facial index is closest to the average of modern New Caledonians. Subsequently, Wu Xinzhi (1960, 1961) reanalyzed casts of the Upper Cave material and concluded that cranium No. 102 and mandible No. 104 were actually derived from two individuals, thus calling into question Weidenreich's original total facial height index, which is based on the supposition that these two specimens are representative of a single individual. Many important measurements and indices of skull No. 102 fall within the range of other fossil *H. sapiens sapiens* in China. Its cranial height (ba-b) is slightly higher than normal, but this parameter could easily have been affected by the artificial deformation of the skull. The relatively long, narrow character of the cranium when viewed vertically, the low orbits, and the broad nasal aperture are all found in other fossil Chinese *H. sapiens* in addition to modern Melanesians.

Skull No. 103 is that of a middle-age female, which, with the exception of the zygomatic arches, is in a good state of preservation. The cranium is very high and a sagittal keel is apparent along with flattened areas on both sides. The parietal eminences are not marked and are situated on the superoanterior portion of the mastoid process. The transverse craniofacial index is large. The superior margin of the temporal squama almost forms a segment at right angles to its anterior margin. These combined features led Weidenreich (1939a,b) to conclude that Upper Cave skull No. 103 closely resembles modern Eskimoid individuals. However, these characters are also found in modern Chinese populations and some features, such as the broad nasal aperture, are not associated with the Eskimoid phenotype.

The alveolar process and a small part of the palate are preserved in the maxilla No. 110. The inferior margin of the nasal aperture forms a low ridge that distinguishes it from the other three Upper Cave crania, which all display a prenasal fossa. Maxilla No. 110 is the only fossil of a later *H. sapiens* yet known in China that exhibits a maxillary torus, although this is a feature found in all three of the known *H. erectus pekinensis* maxillae from Locality 1 at Zhoukoudian. Although half the dental arcade of No. 110 is missing, the remaining portion is parabolic as in modern *H. sapiens sapiens*.

In spite of some interindividual variation, the Upper Cave crania nonetheless exhibit a series of shared morphological traits:

1. the cranial indices are all relatively low;
2. the maximum width of the skulls lies near the temporal squama;
3. the frontal and parietal eminences are poorly developed;
4. the superciliary arches are marked;
5. the upper facial indices classify the crania as mesene;
6. the orbits are rectangular;
7. the orbital indices categorize the specimens as chamaeconchic;
8. the lachrymal fossae are shallow;
9. the degrees of facial projection are all similar;
10. the internal biorbital diameters are large;
11. the inferior margins of the nasal apertures exhibit prenasal fossae; and

12. the premaxillary index and the zygomaxillary angle, which indicate the degree of facial projection in the horizontal plane, are similar in all specimens.

There is a shallow rhombic depression in the obelion region of skulls Nos. 101 and 103, and a depression is also visible near the posterior limit of the sagittal suture of skull No. 102. In all three specimens the junction between the temporal surface and the inferior margin of the greater wing of the sphenoid forms a rounded obtuse angle. In skulls Nos. 101 and 102, the angle of the intersection between the tympanic plate and median sagittal plane exceeds 80°. The foramina magna face slightly backward.

Four mandibles are preserved in the Upper Cave. Numbers 101 and 108 are classified as male, while Nos. 104 and 109 are thought to be female. The mandibular body is only preserved in mandibles 108 and 109. The gonial angles of mandibles Nos. 101 and 104 show slight eversion and a roughened surface. The Upper Cave male mandible No. 101 exhibits a bicondylar breadth of 130 mm while the female mandible No. 104 measures 126 mm; the bigonial breadth is 116 mm in No. 101; while the minimum breadth of the ascending ramus measures 41.3 mm in the male and 40.5 mm in the female.

With all specimens considered, the average-height index of the mental foramina is 44.5, which is close to that of other Upper Pleistocene *H. sapiens* (averaging 46.3 on the basis of a sample of 20 individuals), but its position is lower than in modern humans, which exhibit an index of 51.1. The mental foramen is situated on the mandibular body beneath the second premolar or between the second premolar and the first molar, which is a position posterior to that of most modern Chinese but anterior to that of *H. erectus*. The internal surface of mandible No. 101 (male) possesses a mandibular torus that falls near the second premolar on the right side. Mandibular tori are not apparent on the other Upper Cave specimens. The occurrence of a mandibular torus is a common feature in Mongoloid populations. It is present in *H. erectus pekinensis* and in historic populations such as the Shang period Houjiazhuang group, where this trait occurs in 78% of the population, and the Sui and Tang dynasty populations from Xiaotun, in which 73% of the specimens examined possess a mandibular torus.

The breadth–height index of the mandibular body in the Upper Cave female (Table 7.2) is similar to that of modern Chinese, but this index is less than that of present Mongoloid populations for the males. In general, the mandibles exhibit clearer sexual dimorphism than in modern osteological collections.

The platymeric index of the Upper Cave femur is 86.1 (81.3–104.8) and its pilastric index is 125.6 (112.0–139.5). These measurements are much greater than those of any Neolithic or modern Chinese groups. The popliteal index is 76.9 (74.7–81.4), which is closer to similar measurements taken on Chinese Neolithic populations.

It should be noted that due to the loss of the original Upper Cave fossil

Table 7.2
BREADTH–HEIGHT INDEX OF THE MANDIBULAR BODY IN THE UPPER CAVE *HOMO SAPIENS SAPIENS*

	Point of measurement	
Specimen	Mental foramen	M_1–M_2
No. 101 (male)	34.2	42.0
No. 108 (male)	35.8	40.6
No. 104 (female)	42.1	56.7
No. 109 (female)	—	—

specimens in 1941, all the measurements reported here and by Wu Xinzhi (1960, 1961) are based on a series of accurate casts.

Wu (1960, 1961) reanalyzed casts of the Upper Cave materials and concluded that all of them are consistent with an essentially homogeneous Mongoloid population. The broad spectrum of age classes represented in the Upper Cave collection, from foetal to elderly, suggested to Weidenreich the sudden, calamitous demise of a family group. Further, marks on the crania were interpreted as evidence of cannibalism. Pei Wenzhong and others have refuted Weidenreich's claims stressing that taphonomic factors such as exfoliation of the cave's roof could easily account for the damaged crania, while bioturbation and carnivore activity provide an alternative explanation for the apparent disarray of some of these human remains.

That the Upper Cave at Zhoukoudian was a focus of human activity between 20,000 and 10,000 years ago is unquestionable. What remains to be determined is whether the intentional human burials discovered there represent a single occurrence or whether they accumulated as a result of repeated ritual activity. The discovery of concentrations of stone tools and ash, albeit very few, suggests the Upper Cave may have been the scene of human occupation from time to time as well.

Of greatest importance is the fact that the morphometric studies of Wu (1960, 1961) indicate there is no reason to consider the Upper Cave fossils as representing anything other than a Mongoloid population entirely consistent with what is known about the development of modern *H. sapiens sapiens* in North China.

Laibin, Guangxi

In 1956 human remains consisting of a cranial fragment (palate, right malar, and partial occipital), a right maxilla with partial dentition, and an isolated upper molar were found in a yellowish-grey breccia deposit in a cave at Qilinshan, Laibin, in the Guangxi Zhuang Autonomous Region. Remains of *Cervus* sp.

indet., *Sus* sp. indet., and a large quantity of mollusk shells were found in association with the hominid fossils. Artifacts from Qilinshan consist of a split pebble and traces of ash and burned bone.

The Laibin fossils are thought to be those of an elderly male (Jia and Wu 1959). The palate is high and the bottom of the maxillary sinus is lower than the floor of the nasal cavity. The inferior margin of the nasal cavity exhibits a low transverse ridge and the aperture itself is comparatively wide. The alveolar profile is mesognathous and the maxillary dental arcade is parabolic with heavy wear apparent on the third molar. The upper left second and third molars, though erupted, are not preserved in the Laibin specimen. Four molars remain in the maxilla, their buccolingual diameters exceeding their anteroposterior diameters. The alveolar juga is well developed but the canine fossa is very shallow.

The right malar is rather small and has been distorted during interment. The right occipital squama and part of the left occipital bone are preserved. The occipital chord is about 101 mm and the occipital arc is estimated at 121 mm based on the preserved portions. The resulting occipital chord–arc index of 83.5 is large. The superior nuchal line is well developed but the external occipital protuberance is weak. The heights of the external and internal occipital protuberances are not equal and the right branch of the cruciate eminence is higher than that of the left branch.

The combined morphological features have led Jia and Wu (1959) to conclude that the Laibin hominid falls within the range of modern *H. sapiens* and exhibits some characters that are non-Mongoloid traits, although this interpretation is not universally held (e.g., Coon 1969; Thoma 1964). The very scant evidence available suggests a late Upper Pleistocene antiquity for the Laibin assemblage.

Lijiang, Yunnan

The hominid remains from Lijiang County, Yunnan, comprise a nearly complete cranium of an adolescent individual of uncertain sex. The exact location of the site that yielded this cranium is not known. The authors of the preliminary report consider that matrix adhering to the skull corresponds to that from Locality 6003 in Lijiang County, a site that has yielded mammalian fossils and is thought to be of late Pleistocene age (Yunnan Provincial Museum 1977).

The Lijiang cranium shares many features in common with those of fully modern *H. sapiens sapiens*, of which the following warrant special mention:

1. a poorly developed sagittal keel;
2. a nasomalar angle of 146.5°;
3. a simotic index of 37.6;
4. orbital indices within the mesoconchic range (77.8, left; 79.2, right);
5. a poorly developed palatal torus;
6. a bun-shaped prominence in the occipital region; and
7. Carabelli's tubercle is preserved on the buccal surface of the right upper second molar.

Ziyang, Sichuan

During construction of the Chengdu to Chongqing railway in 1951, a fossil human skull was discovered during the erection of a trestle over the Huangshanxi River in Ziyang County, western Sichuan, about 80 km southeast of Chengdu (Pei 1952; Pei and Wu 1957).

The Ziyang specimen consists of the palate and partial maxilla along with small fragments of the nasals that are attached to a nearly complete calvarium. The basicranium and most of the facial bones are missing. The skull is thought to be that of an old female. The cranium is small and smooth and all its principal morphometric indices fall within the range of modern *H. sapiens*. Viewed vertically, the cranium is ovoid and the frontal and parietal tuberosities are very prominent.

The superciliary arches are well developed and their medial ends unite over the nasal root to form a transverse ridge. The cranium is slightly gabled; a distinguishable eminence runs from the level of frontal bosses posteriorly to the vicinity of the parietal foramina where it enters the rhombic depression in the obelion region. The keel is widest at bregma and forms a prominent structure somewhat similar to the cruciate eminence. Both mastoid angles of the parietal bones possess a relatively wide and low torus angularis.

The Ziyang cranium's occiput is rounded, the lambda and inion lie almost in a perpendicular plane. The mastoid processes are very heavy and lie just below the parietal tuberosities. The apex of the mastoid process curves slightly inward and the superior margin of the temporal squama is slightly convex. The supramastoid crest is oblique and forms an angle of 45° in relation to the eye–ear plane. The superior part of the occipital squama has a small bun-shaped prominence.

The exact depositional circumstances in which the Ziyang cranium was originally found are unclear since the fossil was removed by railway workers before accurate provenance data could be gathered. Thus our ability to judge the geological age of this hominid on other than morphological grounds is limited.

Fluorine and specific-gravity tests (Qiu 1955) conducted on both hominid and other mammalian remains from Ziyang suggest two distinct periods of deposition account for the Huangshanxi sequence and the character and condition of the faunal assemblage recovered also supports such a division.

The radiocarbon dates on wood gathered from sites nearby and thought to correlate with the Ziyang cranium's horizon have yielded a broad temporal range for the fossil from roughly 7000 to 37,500 BP (see Chapter 2, this volume).

That the Ziyang hominid is somewhat more primitive than those discovered in the Upper Cave at Zhoukoudian is demonstrated by such morphological characters as the height of the calvarium, the position of bregma, and the bregma and frontal angles. As no artifacts have yet been found in unquestionable association with either of the Ziyang faunal components, archaeological corroboration of the radiocarbon or morphological chronologies is not possible.

Table 7.3
PRINCIPAL ANALYSES OF NEOLITHIC HUMAN SKELETAL REMAINS IN CHINA

Site	Age (years BP)	Associated culture	Reference
Yongdengxian, Gansu	3570–3670	Machang	Black 1928
Banpo, Shaanxi	6140–6720	Yangshao	Yan *et al.* 1960b
Baoji, Shaanxi	5745–7100	Yangshao	Yan *et al.* 1960a
Huaxian, Shaanxi	5745–7100	Yangshao	Yan 1962
Hengzhen, Shaanxi	6140–6720	Yangshao	Institute of Archaeology, Lab. of Phys. Anth. 1977
Miaodigou, Henan	4140–5080	Late Yangshao–Early Longshan	Han and Pan 1979
Xiawanggang, Henan	4500–5200	Qujialing	Zhang and Chen n.d.
Dawenkou, Shandong	4300–6500	Dawenkou	Yan 1972
Xixiahou, Shandong	4300–6500	Dawenkou	Yan 1973
Fangxian, Hubei	4500–5200	Qujialing	Zhang *et al.* 1982
Tanshishan, Fujian	ca. 3000	Late Neolithic	Han *et al.* 1976
Hedang, Guangdong	ca. 3500	Late Neolithic	Han and Pan 1982
Zhenpiyan, Guangxi	ca. 6600	Early Neolithic	Zhang *et al.* 1977
Beiyinyangying, Nanjing	4500–5200	Beiyinyangying	Wu 1961

The Holocene Record

Many Neolithic archaeological sites in China have yielded substantial quantities of human skeletal remains that have become the subject of intensive analysis. Table 7.3 summarizes the principal analyses of Neolithic human skeletal material that have been conducted thus far in China.

Recently, cluster analyses performed by Zhang Zhenbiao, Wang Linghong, and Ouyang Lian (1982) have revealed the interrelationships among the major Neolithic human populations of China (Figure 7.1). For their study, the following points were chosen for quantification and comparison:

1. cranial length, breadth, and height;
2. least frontal breadth and bizygomatic breadth;
3. superior facial height;
4. orbital height and breadth;
5. nasal height and breadth;
6. total facial angles and alveolar prognathism;
7. bicondylar breadth of the mandible;
8. bigonial breadth of the mandible;
9. symphyseal height of mandible;
10. mandibular height at mental foramen and the point between the first and second molars;
11. mandibular thickness; and
12. minimum breadth of ascending ramus.

Figure 7.3 indicates that these Neolithic human crania and mandibles may be distinguished on the basis of geographically discrete physical characters (Figure 7.4). Not only can southern and northern Neolithic populations be separated, but the North China group alone can be further subdivided into eastern and western subgroups. There are a number of common features among these Neolithic samples that bear enumeration:

1. The most common cranial shape, with the exception of the eastern subgroup, is ovoid.
2. The sagittal suture is simple or sinusoidal rather than saw-toothed.
3. The pterygoid region of most individuals is of the H-type (i.e., the juncture of the four bones in the pteric region is achieved by sphenoparietal contact, isolating the frontal from the temporal).
4. The arcus superciliaris is slender, but stronger in the southern Chinese individuals.
5. A prenasal fossa is present in most cases; the infantile type of lower margin of the nasal aperture occurs more frequently in the South Chinese samples.
6. The orbital margins are rounded.
7. The zygomatic bone tends to be high and relatively forward.
8. The canine fossae are shallow.
9. In basal view, the anterior portion of the zygomatic arch forms an angled transition.
10. Shovel-shaped lingual surfaces on upper incisors are a common feature.
11. The averages of total facial angles of specimens from different sites are almost always less than 85°.

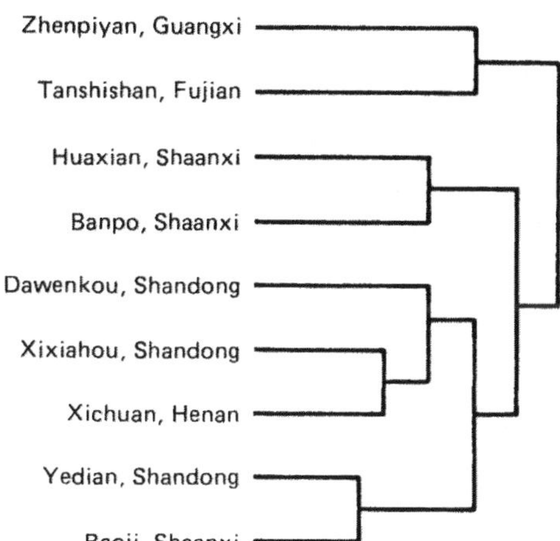

Figure 7.3 Cluster diagram indicating relationships among populations of Neolithic humans in China.

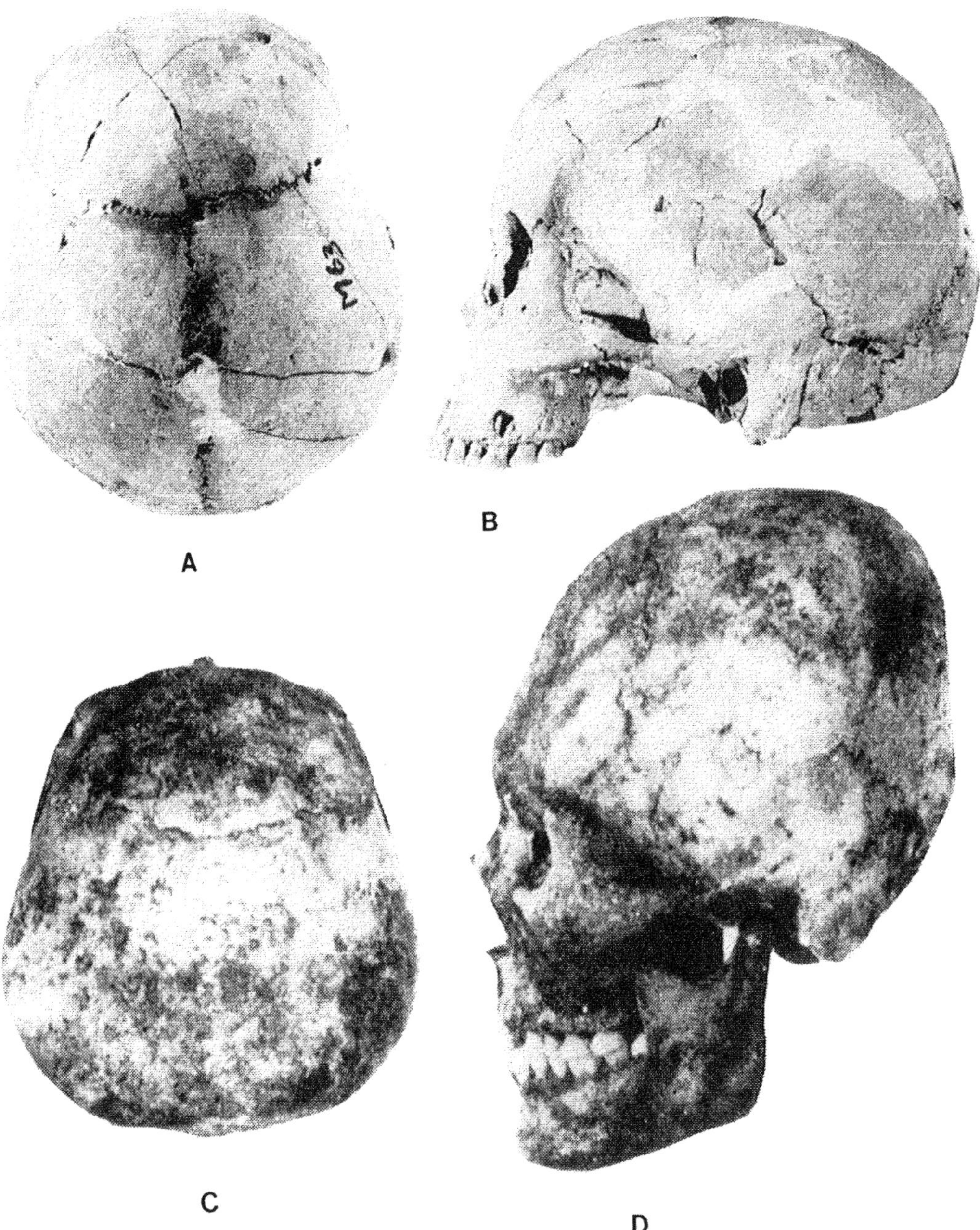

Figure 7.4 A, Skull from the Neolithic site at Xichuan, Henan; superior view. B, Same specimen, lateral view. C, Artificially deformed Neolithic skull from the Dawenkou site, Shandong; superior view. D, Same specimen, lateral view.

In both major geographic regions the nasozygomatic angle is large, but quantitative data indicate the northern Neolithic populations are characterized by flatter faces than those in the south. In males of every group except the Hedang, Guangdong, series, this angle falls between 144 and 150° (Table 7.4). In females, the range of variation is somewhat greater, running from 139.8 to 153.5° (Table 7.5). Most of the cranial indices of the North Chinese groups are over 77, while those of the southern populations universally fall under 75.

The upper facial height index of the populations may be classified as mesene. The vertical craniofacial index from the western part of North China is slightly higher than those found in the eastern and southern regions. With the exception of only a few individuals, the orbital indices of all the samples place them within the mesoconchic range.

The nasal index shows substantial variation between the northern and southern groups, the nasal aperture of the southern Chinese population being generally wider than in the north.

When eastern and western geographic distinctions are taken into consideration an interesting pattern emerges. The vertical craniofacial index of the eastern subgroup is lower, but their total facial angle is greater. The zygomaxillary angle is smaller, the nasal index lower, the basicranium longer, and the facial bones wider in men of the eastern region.

It is important to note that the custom of tooth extraction in Neolithic groups in both East and South China has been demonstrated.

It should be remembered that the morphological variation apparent in different geographic regions are based on relatively small samples and that there are exceptions. It is hoped that continued research will clarify the interrelationships among China's Neolithic populations.

Discussion and Conclusion

During the Late Palaeolithic and Neolithic in China some morphological features of the human cranium remained constant. These characters include:

1. relatively simple suture morphology;
2. H-shaped pterygoid region;
3. flattened nasal saddle;
4. weak subnasal spine;
5. obtuse angle formed by the zygomatic and maxillary bones;
6. shallow canine fossae; and
7. shovel-shaped incisors.

Certainly, morphological developmental trends are still visible between these temporally discrete populations, including a general reduction in overall cranial size and cranial index in the Holocene and a gradual increase in cranial height.

Table 7.4

MEAN VALUES OF MEASUREMENTS AND INDICES OF CHINESE NEOLITHIC CRANIAL SERIES (MALE)[a]

	Banpo, Shaanxi (Yan *et al.* 1960b)	Huaxian, Shaanxi (Yan 1962)	Baoji, Shaanxi (Yan *et al.* 1960a)
Cranial length (g-op)	180.84 (11)	178.84 (9)	180.22 (26)
Cranial breadth (eu-eu)	138.93 (9)	140.69 (8)	142.25 (24)
Cranial height (ba-b)	138.80 (3)	144.30 (8)	141.55 (14)
Basi-cranial length (ba-n)	93.85 (2)	105.65 (8)	102.63 (12)
Min. frontal length (ft-ft)	93.10 (11)	94.25 (12)	93.29 (21)
Bizygomatic breadth (zy-zy)	130.50 (2)	133.86 (5)	137.13 (8)
Basi-facial length (ba-pr)	102.20 (1)	103.44 (7)	102.02 (9)
Upper facial height			
(n-pr)	75.96 (5)	75.23 (13)	72.66 (11)
(n-sd)	—	—	—
Nasal height (n-ns)	55.50 (7)	53.51 (14)	52.13 (15)
Nasal breadth	27.05 (7)	28.52 (13)	27.29 (15)
Orbital height			
right	34.20 (2)	33.05 (11)	33.90 (13)
left	33.68 (4)	33.50 (11)	34.02 (17)
Orbital breadth (mf-ek)			
right	42.75 (2)	42.99 (12)	43.60 (14)
left	42.38 (4)	42.88 (12)	43.50 (13)
Orbital breadth (d-ek)			
right	39.95 (2)	39.14 (7)	40.47 (11)
left	38.00 (1)	39.57 (9)	40.70 (11)
Cranial index	78.38 (7)	78.50 (8)	79.34 (24)
Cranial length–height index	77.27 (3)	80.43 (8)	78.73 (14)
Cranial breadth–height index	97.37 (3)	103.90 (7)	98.80 (14)
Vertical craniofacial index	—	53.06 (8)	52.10 (11)
Upper facial index	51.28 (2)	57.79 (5)	53.49 (6)
Nasal index	50.00 (5)	53.40 (13)	52.50 (15)
Orbital index (mf-ek)			
right	82.14 (1)	77.02 (11)	77.98 (12)
left	82.11 (4)	77.96 (11)	78.30 (13)
Orbital index (d-ek)			
right	85.18 (1)	84.06 (7)	84.41 (10)
left	86.32 (1)	83.89 (9)	85.58 (11)
Simotic breadth (sc)	—	—	—
Simotic height (ss)	—	—	2.28 (16)
Simotic index	29.24 (8)	—	28.09 (15)
Palatal length (ol-sta)	48.22 (6)	49.76 (11)	—
Palatal breadth (enm-enm)	42.17 (11)	40.09 (11)	—
Palatal index	—	—	—
Facial profile angle (n-pr-FH)	81.0° (3)	83.61° (9)	82.35° (16)
Nasal profile angle (n-ns-FH)	—	85.77° (11)	86.06° (16)
Alveolar angle (ns-pr-FH)	78.5° (4)	77.57° (7)	70.73° (14)
Nasomalar angle (fmo-n-fmo)	146.7° (5)	145.18° (6)	144.13° (12)
Zygomaxillary angle (zm-ss-zm)	136.7° (3)	—	137.38° (12)
Bicondylar breadth (cdl-cdl)	121.53 (15)	118.50 (2)	127.38 (12)
Bigonial breadth (go-go)	106.15 (16)	96.50 (4)	102.92 (18)
Symphyseal height (id-gn)	34.00 (26)	31.90 (5)	34.17 (20)
Height of mandibular body (M_1M_2)			
right / left	29.90 (31)	30.92 (6)	30.89 (20)
Thickness of mandibular body (M_1M_2)			
right / left	17.90 (28)	18.50 (6)	18.01 (23)
Minimum breadth of asc. ramus	36.58 (27)	37.04 (5)	38.95 (23)
Maximum proj. mandibular length	111.90 (9)	101.50 (2)	—

Hengzhen, Shaanxi (Institute of Archaeology 1977)	Yongdengxian, Gansu (Black 1928)	Miaodigou, Henan (Han and Pan 1979)	Xiawanggang, Henan (Zhang and Chen n.d.)
180.40 (15)	181.65 (25)	179.43 (12)	175.75 (40)
144.80 (14)	137.00 (26)	143.75 (10)	146.38 (39)
141.40 (9)	136.80 (23)	143.17 (3)	147.08 (8)
—	102.10 (23)	108.13 (4)	105.27 (7)
93.10 (14)	92.30 (24)	93.69 (13)	94.81 (39)
138.70 (3)	130.70 (19)	140.83 (6)	137.85 (15)
—	97.30 (14)	104.50 (2)	107.30 (5)
69.50 (8)	74.80 (16)	—	—
—	—	73.48 (6)	71.06 (21)
53.60 (8)	55.00 (20)	53.99 (7)	53.68 (21)
27.50 (9)	25.60 (17)	27.31 (8)	27.20 (20)
32.90 (9)	33.80 (16)	32.42 (6)	—
—	—	—	32.93 (25)
43.40 (9)	45.00 (18)	41.75 (6)	—
—	—	—	41.38 (24)
—	42.00 (18)	41.00 (1)	—
—	—	—	—
80.50 (13)	74.96 (25)	80.31 (11)	83.24 (39)
77.90 (9)	75.65 (23)	77.64 (3)	84.59 (8)
96.10 (8)	100.45 (22)	99.47 (2)	101.02 (8)
—	—	54.06 (2)	48.50 (7)
52.20 (3)	56.48 (15)	51.86 (5)	51.80 (15)
49.90 (7)	47.33 (18)	50.15 (7)	50.05 (18)
76.10 (9)	75.02 (19)	77.71 (6)	—
—	—	—	79.26 (25)
—	80.48 (6)	78.05 (1)	—
—	—	—	—
—	—	—	8.34 (5)
—	—	—	2.60 (5)
27.20 (7)	—	—	—
—	46.50 (15)	45.60 (10)	45.35 (12)
—	43.80 (13)	42.44 (9)	—
—	94.28 (12)	92.55 (9)	—
80.40° (8)	84.96° (17)	85.75° (6)	84.90° (12)
—	91.11° (18)	88.60° (6)	86.50° (13)
—	71.67° (18)	71.50° (6)	74.10° (14)
149.60° (10)	—	147.56° (10)	—
—	—	131.90° (7)	—
126.60 (4)	—	124.93 (4)	132.78 (58)
101.50 (8)	—	106.14 (7)	105.52 (79)
38.10 (13)	—	36.13 (7)	35.44 (63)
—	—	—	—
32.40 (14)	—	31.96 (8)	31.44 (67)
—	—	—	—
17.30 (14)	—	17.69 (8)	17.66 (83)
38.00 (10)	—	37.31 (8)	37.40 (86)
108.50 (4)	—	106.00 (4)	108.42 (51)

(*continued*)

Table 7.4 (*Continued*)

	Dawenkou, Shandong (Yan 1972)	Xixiahou, Shandong (Yan 1973)	Fangxian, Hubei (Zhang *et al.* 1982)
Cranial length (g-op)	[b]168.71 (12) 181.11	[b]176.22 (9) 180.30	176.20 (4)
Cranial breadth (eu-eu)	[b]150.08 (12) 145.70	[b]143.94 (4) 140.90	152.00 (4)
Cranial height (ba-b)	[b]147.68 (11) 142.89	[b]147.72 (9) 148.30	145.40 (3)
Basi-cranial length (ba-n)	104.95 (11)	106.00 (9)	—
Min. frontal length (ft-ft)	91.64 (14)	93.94 (9)	95.40 (6)
Bizygomatic breadth (zy-zy)	140.56 (8)	139.43 (7)	138.90 (3)
Basi-facial length (ba-pr)	98.28 (9)	101.69 (9)	—
Upper facial height			
(n-pr)	74.84 (10)	72.03 (9)	—
(n-sd)	—	—	69.72 (4)
Nasal height (n-ns)	54.72 (9)	57.12 (9)	50.78 (4)
Nasal breadth	27.45 (10)	27.66 (9)	27.00 (4)
Orbital height			
right	35.05 (11)	34.34 (8)	31.90 (3)
left	35.23 (12)	34.19 (8)	32.00 (3)
Orbital breadth (mf-ek)			
right	42.82 (11)	44.22 (9)	42.00 (3)
left	43.07 (12)	44.04 (8)	42.50 (3)
Orbital breadth (d-ek)			
right	40.19 (8)	40.98 (8)	—
left	40.49 (9)	40.72 (6)	—
Cranial index	[b]90.46 (12) 78.71	[b]81.70 (9) 78.20	86.70 (4)
Cranial length–height index	88.24 (10)	83.91 (9)	82.52 (3)
Cranial breadth–height index	97.46 (11)	105.07 (8)	95.66 (3)
Vertical craniofacial index	51.37 (8)	48.92 (6)	48.05 (3)
Upper facial index	54.31 (7)	52.26 (7)	50.20 (3)
Nasal index	49.45 (8)	48.46 (9)	53.17 (4)
Orbital index (mf-ek)			
right	81.94 (11)	77.97 (8)	75.95 (3)
left	81.83 (12)	77.97 (8)	75.30 (3)
Orbital index (d-ek)			
right	86.18 (8)	84.61 (7)	—
left	86.55 (9)	84.88 (7)	—
Simotic breadth (sc)	7.29 (10)	7.56 (9)	—
Simotic height (ss)	2.47 (9)	2.31 (8)	—
Simotic index	33.60 (9)	31.05 (8)	—
Palatal length (ol-sta)	44.95 (11)	48.50 (9)	—
Palatal breadth (enm-enm)	41.85 (11)	40.17 (5)	—
Palatal index	92.72 (11)	82.99 (5)	—
Facial profile angle (n-pr-FH)	83.61° (9)	84.38° (8)	84.10° (3)
Nasal profile angle (n-ns-FH)	85.50° (10)	86.94° (8)	—
Alveolar angle (ns-pr-FH)	77.56° (9)	60.38° (8)	73.98° (3)
Nasomalar angle (fmo-n-fmo)	149.76° (11)	145.03° (8)	—
Zygomaxillary angle (zm-ss-zm)	134.68° (11)	131.70° (8)	—
Bicondylar breadth (odl-odl)	132.42 (14)	133.24 (7)	124.50 (7)
Bigonial breadth (go-go)	107.75 (14)	107.44 (9)	108.41 (7)
Symphyseal height (id-gn)	36.28 (12)	36.60 (10)	33.80 (5)
Height of mandibular body (M_1M_2)			
right	32.41 (14)	30.45 (10)	—
left			31.00 (7)
Thickness of mandibular body (M_1M_2)			
right	17.09 (14)	16.10 (10)	—
left			17.30 (7)
Minimum breadth of asc. ramus	37.64 (14)	37.30 (9)	36.20 (7)
Maximum proj. mandibular length	110.46 (13)	110.40 (8)	108.60 (5)

Tanshishan, Fujian (Han *et al.* 1976)	Hedang, Guangdong (Han and Pan 1982)	Zhenpiyan, Guangxi (Zhang *et al.* 1977)
189.70 (3)	181.40 (4)	193.30 (6)
139.20 (3)	132.50 (4)	143.20 (6)
141.30 (2)	142.50 (2)	140.90 (2)
101.10 (2)	104.50 (2)	—
91.00 (3)	91.50 (5)	93.50 (6)
135.60 (3)	130.50 (3)	138.00 (3)
103.50 (2)	103.20 (2)	—
68.00 (3)	—	—
71.10 (3)	67.90 (4)	70.50 (3)
51.90 (3)	51.90 (4)	53.10 (3)
29.50 (3)	26.70 (4)	28.30 (3)
33.80 (3)	33.00 (3)	34.40 (4)
33.40 (3)	31.90 (4)	—
42.20 (3)	41.10 (3)	42.60 (4)
43.30 (3)	42.50 (4)	—
39.90 (3)	38.80 (3)	—
39.60 (3)	39.10 (2)	—
73.40 (3)	73.10 (4)	74.10 (6)
73.80 (2)	78.40 (2)	70.50 (2)
99.50 (2)	106.20 (2)	97.90 (2)
48.10 (2)	45.70 (2)	—
52.50 (3)	51.30 (3)	51.02 (3)
57.00 (3)	51.60 (4)	53.30 (3)
80.00 (3)	80.30 (3)	80.40 (4)
77.10 (3)	75.60 (3)	—
84.70 (3)	85.10 (2)	—
84.40 (3)	81.10 (3)	—
—	9.40 (2)	—
—	2.40 (2)	—
—	26.30 (2)	30.00 (3)
—	44.60 (2)	—
—	40.70 (2)	—
—	91.60 (2)	—
81.00° (3)	82.30° (3)	84.00° (1)
85.00° (3)	85.00° (3)	85.50° (2)
71.70° (3)	65.30° (3)	79.00° (1)
143.80° (3)	142.60° (4)	144.80° (3)
137.00° (3)	127.30° (4)	138.00° (4)
123.00 (3)	—	127.80 (4)
107.90 (3)	—	105.10 (5)
34.90 (3)	—	31.50 (6)
—	—	31.60 (5)
32.50 (2)	—	29.80 (4)
—	—	16.70 (5)
17.80 (3)	—	15.60 (4)
36.60 (3)	—	35.60 (5)
107.40 (3)	—	108.50 (4)

[a]In millimeters. Numbers of individual specimens are in parentheses. (Biometric characters after Black 1928.)

[b]Intentionally deformed specimens. Figure immediately below value marked by superscript is mean of measurements taken on unmodified individuals.

Table 7.5

MEAN VALUES OF MEASUREMENTS AND INDICES OF CHINESE NEOLITHIC CRANIAL SERIES (FEMALE)[a]

	Banpo, Shaanxi (Yan *et al.* 1960b)	Huaxian, Shaanxi (Yan 1962)	Baoji, Shaanxi (Yan *et al.* 1960a)
Cranial length (g-op)	178.12 (4)	174.25 (4)	175.30 (10)
Cranial breadth (eu-eu)	141.13 (4)	140.67 (3)	138.56 (9)
Cranial height (ba-b)	—	136.17 (3)	135.94 (8)
Basicranial length (ba-n)	—	97.50 (2)	96.57 (7)
Min. frontal length (ft-ft)	89.33 (6)	94.00 (1)	91.96 (12)
Bizygomatic breadth (zy-zy)	105.10 (1)	—	128.25 (4)
Basifacial length (ba-pr)	—	97.25 (2)	96.58 (6)
Upper facial height			
(n-pr)	69.00 (2)	70.50 (2)	68.26 (7)
(n-sd)	—	—	—
Nasal height (n-ns)	51.10 (2)	51.00 (1)	49.12 (9)
Nasal breadth	26.10 (1)	23.25 (2)	25.86 (8)
Orbital height			
right	34.00 (1)	33.00 (2)	33.23 (7)
left	33.10 (1)	33.60 (2)	33.02 (9)
Orbital breadth (mf-ek)			
right	40.00 (1)	41.25 (2)	41.64 (7)
left	—	42.17 (2)	41.34 (8)
Orbital breadth (d-ek)			
right	38.90 (1)	37.00 (2)	38.53 (6)
left	—	38.25 (1)	38.60 (5)
Cranial index	79.41 (4)	80.24 (3)	78.59 (9)
Cranial length–height index	—	77.67 (3)	78.68 (8)
Cranial breadth–height index	—	96.80 (3)	97.91 (7)
Vertical craniofacial index	—	—	—
Upper facial index	—	—	52.39 (3)
Nasal index	50.19 (1)	—	52.43 (8)
Orbital index (mf-ek)			
right	—	79.98 (2)	79.85 (7)
left	—	79.57 (2)	79.91 (7)
Orbital index (d-ek)			
right	—	83.78 (1)	86.07 (6)
left	—	86.23 (1)	83.38 (5)
Simotic breadth (sc)	—	6.00 (1)	—
Simotic height (ss)	—	2.00 (1)	—
Simotic index	—	33.33 (1)	24.27 (8)
Palatal length (ol-sta)	50.40 (2)	47.00 (3)	—
Palatal breadth (enm-enm)	41.20 (3)	41.00 (3)	—
Palatal index	—	—	—
Facial profile angle (n-pr-FH)	—	87.00° (1)	83.22° (9)
Nasal profile angle (n-ns-FH)	—	92.00° (1)	86.67° (9)
Alveolar angle (ns-pr-FH)	—	79.00° (2)	74.44° (9)
Nasomalar angle (fmo-n-fmo)	—	—	143.50° (9)
Zygomaxillary angle (zm-ss-zm)	—	129.50° (1)	138.92° (6)
Bicondylar breadth (odl-odl)	117.16 (5)	—	—
Bigonial breadth (go-go)	92.20 (3)	—	—
Symphyseal height (id-gn)	31.81 (8)	—	—
Height of mandibular body (M_1M_2)			
right	—	—	—
left	—	—	—
Thickness of mandibular body (M_1M_2)			
right	—	} 19.00 (1)	—
left	—		—
Minimum breadth of asc. ramus	30.03 (8)	40.00 (1)	—
Maximum proj. mandibular length	107.73 (3)	102.00 (1)	—

Xixiahou, Shandong (Yan 1973)	Dawenkou, Shandong (Yan 1972)	Xiawanggang, Henan (Zhang and Chen n.d.)	Hedang, Guangdong (Han and Pan 1982)
169.30 (8)	160.45 (11)	166.17 (15)	183.90 (5)
144.25 (8)	145.21 (14)	138.34 (14)	136.10 (5)
142.60 (5)	142.96 (8)	132.25 (2)	149.00 (1)
99.00 (4)	101.44 (8)	97.40 (3)	104.00 (1)
91.33 (6)	90.17 (12)	89.00 (13)	91.10 (5)
133.40 (5)	129.06 (8)	129.50 (18)	134.10 (3)
96.38 (4)	94.44 (8)	90.10 (2)	99.00 (1)
67.20 (6)	69.02 (10)	—	—
—	—	65.45 (4)	70.60 (4)
53.87 (6)	51.68 (11)	48.25 (9)	50.60 (4)
25.58 (6)	25.71 (12)	24.47 (7)	27.80 (4)
32.58 (5)	34.50 (13)	—	33.40 (4)
33.38 (6)	34.31 (13)	32.92 (8)	33.40 (3)
63.90 (6)	42.52 (11)	—	42.20 (4)
42.50 (6)	41.73 (11)	38.76 (9)	41.60 (4)
39.20 (6)	38.88 (8)	—	38.00 (2)
33.47 (6)	38.69 (8)	—	38.70 (2)
85.22 (8)	91.00 (11)	84.25 (12)	74.00 (5)
84.98 (5)	88.79 (8)	83.61 (3)	81.00 (1)
99.52 (5)	98.00 (8)	102.34 (3)	112.90 (1)
—	47.88 (8)	48.87 (3)	49.70 (1)
49.99 (4)	53.26 (8)	50.29 (7)	52.60 (3)
47.46 (6)	50.84 (10)	50.12 (8)	55.00 (4)
76.35 (6)	81.35 (11)	—	79.10 (4)
78.78 (5)	82.31 (11)	81.46 (8)	79.10 (3)
83.24 (5)	87.45 (8)	—	88.40 (2)
86.71 (6)	86.65 (8)	—	86.50 (3)
4.96 (5)	7.43 (11)	9.00 (1)	6.60 (3)
1.14 (5)	2.17 (9)	2.80 (1)	1.30 (1)
24.53 (5)	26.33 (9)	31.11 (1)	17.40 (1)
47.88 (6)	43.09 (13)	49.11 (4)	45.50 (2)
40.42 (6)	42.16 (14)	—	41.00 (1)
86.00 (6)	92.96 (12)	—	94.30 (1)
84.63° (4)	84.40° (10)	79.87° (8)	85.70° (3)
87.50° (4)	85.45° (10)	84.50° (8)	90.00° (3)
61.63° (4)	77.09° (11)	64.71° (7)	78.00° (3)
146.78° (5)	148.44° (12)	—	144.90° (4)
131.98° (5)	136.40° (10)	—	131.80° (3)
125.96 (8)	126.46 (13)	124.52 (19)	—
100.96 (8)	98.63 (13)	95.74 (31)	—
35.22 (8)	33.79 (14)	33.06 (25)	—
28.19 (8)	27.84 (14)	—	—
		30.00 (25)	—
16.80 (8)	16.94 (14)	—	—
		16.65 (29)	—
36.66 (8)	35.62 (13)	36.68 (32)	—
105.60 (8)	103.31 (13)	103.72 (20)	—

(continued)

Table 7.5 *(Continued)*

	Tanshishan, Fujian (Han et al. 1976)	Zhenpiyan, Guangxi (Zhang et al. 1977)
Cranial length (g-op)	187.00 (5)	184.30 (5)
Cranial breadth (eu-eu)	135.50 (4)	137.50 (4)
Cranial height (ba-b)	—	136.10 (4)
Basicranial length (ba-n)	—	—
Min. frontal length (ft-ft)	93.50 (5)	91.90 (5)
Bizygomatic breadth (zy-zy)	—	127.80 (2)
Basifacial length (ba-pr)	—	—
Upper facial height		
(n-pr)	67.30 (6)	—
(n-sd)	68.70 (6)	63.80 (4)
Nasal height (n-ns)	49.30 (6)	45.80 (4)
Nasal breadth	25.80 (5)	27.30 (3)
Orbital height		
right	32.30 (4)	30.40 (4)
left	33.00 (5)	—
Orbital breadth (mf-ek)		
right	41.60 (4)	42.30 (4)
left	42.60 (5)	—
Orbital breadth (d-ek)		
right	37.90 (4)	—
left	39.40 (5)	—
Cranial index	72.80 (4)	73.90 (5)
Cranial length–height index	—	74.30 (4)
Cranial breadth–height index	—	96.10 (3)
Vertical craniofacial index	—	—
Upper facial index	52.50 (3)	47.75 (4)
Nasal index	52.90 (5)	60.10 (3)
Orbital index (mf-ek)		
right	77.80 (4)	71.90 (4)
left	73.80 (5)	—
Orbital index (d-ek)		
right	85.10 (4)	—
left	83.40 (5)	—
Simotic breadth (sc)	7.60 (6)	—
Simotic height (ss)	2.10 (5)	—
Simotic index	30.35 (5)	—
Palatal length (ol-sta)	—	—
Palatal breadth (enm-enm)	—	—
Palatal index	—	—
Facial profile angle (n-pr-FH)	86.20° (6)	82.30° (4)
Nasal profile angle (n-ns-FH)	91.90 (3)	86.30° (4)
Alveolar angle (ns-pr-FH)	71.60° (5)	69.10° (4)
Nasomalar angle (fmo-n-fmo)	139.60° (4)	147.50° (4)
Zygomaxillary angle (zm-ss-zm)	133.00° (3)	139.50° (4)
Bicondylar breadth (odl-odl)	120.90 (4)	118.30 (4)
Bigonial breadth (go-go)	98.60 (5)	91.00 (5)
Symphyseal height (id-gn)	34.90 (5)	31.00 (5)
Height of mandibular body (M_1M_2)		
right	—	29.10 (4)
left	29.80 (5)	27.00 (4)
Thickness of mandibular body (M_1M_2)		
right	—	14.40 (5)
left	18.50 (5)	15.10 (4)
Minimum breadth of asc. ramus	36.20 (5)	36.40 (4)
Maximum proj. mandibular length	102.30 (4)	103.00 (5)

[a]In millimeters. (Biometric characters after Black 1928.)

Namely, the length–height index of both North and South Chinese Neolithic populations exceeds those of both the Liujiang and Zhoukoudian Upper Cave Pleistocene hominids. Additional Pleistocene–Holocene contrasts in Chinese *H. sapiens sapiens* populations include:

1. increase in orbital height;
2. narrowing of the nasal aperture;
3. separation of the superciliary arches and a reduction in their overall robustness;
4. the nasomalar and zygomaxillary angles observed in Neolithic groups are larger than those of the Upper Cave hominids, but similar to that of the Liujiang *H. sapiens;* and
5. in most of the Neolithic specimens observed, the frontal arc exceeds the parietal arc, in contrast to the Upper Cave, Liujiang, and Ziyang hominids.

An attempt to correlate Chinese Neolithic human skeletal remains with those of modern ethnic groups has yielded preliminary results. Their facial breadths are close to East Asians and South Asians, and the upper facial height and its index in North Chinese Neolithic populations are very similar to those of East Asians. South Chinese Neolithic remains resemble those of South Asians. Nasal heights of South Chinese Neolithic groups are similar to those in modern South Asians. In all observed Chinese Neolithic populations the nasal and orbital indices approximate those of modern South Asians and differ from extant East Asians. The vertical craniofacial index of the North Chinese Neolithic crania most closely resembles modern East Asians, and those of southern Chinese Neolithic skulls are even lower than South Asian populations.

Our research thus far on the Late Palaeolithic and Neolithic human populations of China has accomplished relatively little, considering the massive geographic area to be dealt with. Data on Bronze Age and later human skeletal remains in China are still very rare and we continue to face the problem of acquiring accurate chronometric determinations for many of our Pleistocene fossil materials (see Chapter 2, this volume).

We can at this point only illuminate what we perceive as evolutionary trends, but the specifics of the development of *H. sapiens sapiens* in China and the florescence of China's national minorities has yet to be fully understood. We hope that a combination of archaeological and physical anthropological approaches to these questions will ultimately yield fruitful results.

References

Black, Davidson

1928 A study of Kansu and Honan Aeneolithic skulls from later prehistoric sites in comparison with North China and other recent crania. *Palaeontologia Sinica,* Series D 6(1).

Coon, Carleton S.

1969 *Origin of races.* New York: Alfred Knopf.

Han Kangxin and Pan Qifeng
1979 A study of the human skeletal remains unearthed from tombs of the Miaodigou II culture in Shanxian, Henan. *Acta Archaeologica Sinica* 2:255–270.
1982 Late Neolithic human skeletons from the Hedang site, Foshan, Guangdong. *Acta Anthropologica Sinica* 1(1):42–52.

Han Kangxin, Zhang Zhenbiao, and Zeng Fan
1976 The Neolithic human skeletons unearthed at Tanshishan, Minhou county, Fujian. *Acta Archaeologica Sinica* 1:121–129.

Howells, William W.
1977 Hominid fossils. In *Palaeoanthropology in the People's Republic of China*, edited by W. W. Howells and P. J. Tsuchitani, CSCPRC Report No. 4. Washington: National Academy of Sciences. Pp. 66–78.

Institute of Archaeology, Laboratory of Physical Anthropology
1977 The Yangshao Culture human remains from Hengzhen, Huayinxian, Shaanxi. *Kaogu* 4:247–250.

Jia Lanpo (Chia Lan-po) and Wu Rukang (Woo Ju-kang)
1959 Fossil human skull base of Late Palaeolithic stage from Ch'ilinshan, Leibin district, Kwangsi, China. *Gu Jizhuidongwu yu Gu Renlei (Palaeovertebrata et Palaeoanthropologia)* 1(1):16–18.

Pei Wenzhong (Pei Wen-chung)
1934 A preliminary report on the Late Palaeolithic cave of Choukoutien. *Bulletin of the Geological Society of China* 13(3):327–358.
1939a The Upper Cave Industry of Choukoutien. *Palaeontologia Sinica,* New Series D 9:1–41.
1939b On the Upper Cave Industry. *Bulletin of the Natural History Society of Peking* 13:175–179.
1952 Report on the excavation of Tzeyang Man remains and associated faunal remains from the Huangshanhsi in Szechuan. *Kexue Tongbao* 3(10):7–13.

Pei Wenzhong (Pei Wen-chung) and Wu Rukang (Woo Ju-kang)
1957 Tzeyang Man. *Memoirs of the Institute of Vertebrate Palaeontology and Palaeoanthropology,* Series A 1:1–71.

Qiu Zhonglang
1955 Notes on the application of the fluorine dating method to the dating of some fossil human remains from China. *Gushengwu Xuebao (Acta Palaeontologica Sinica)* 3(4):323–329.

Thoma, A.
1964 Die entstehung der Mongoliden. *Homo* 15(1):1–22.

Weidenreich, Franz
1939a On the earliest representatives of modern mankind recovered on the soil of East Asia. *Bulletin of the Natural History Society of Peking* 13(3):161–174.
1939b The duration of life of fossil man in China and the pathological lesions found in his skeleton. *Chinese Medical Journal* 45:33–44.

Wu Dingliang
1961 A study of the late Neolithic human mandibles from the Beiyinyangying site, Nanjing. *Vertebrata PalAsiatica* 4:49–54.

Wu Rukang (Woo Ju-kang)
1959 Human fossils found in Liukiang, Kwangsi, China. *Gu Jizhuidongwu yu Gu Renlei (Palaeovertebrata et Palaeoanthropologia)* 1(3):97–104.

Wu Xinzhi
1960 On the racial type of Upper Cave Man of Choukoutien. *Gu Jizhuidongwu yu Gu Renlei (Palaeovertebrata et Palaeoanthropologia)* 2(2):141–149.
1961 Study of the Upper Cave Man of Choukoutien. *Vertebrata PalAsiatica* 3:181–211.

Yan Yan
1962 A study of the Neolithic human skeletons from Huaxian, Shaanxi. *Acta Archaeologica Sinica* 2:85–104.

1972 The Neolithic human skeletons from the Dawenkou site, Shandong. *Acta Archaeologica Sinica* 1:91–122.

1973 The Neolithic human skeletal remains from Xixiahou. *Acta Archaeologica Sinica* 2:91–126.

Yan Yan, Liu Changzhi, and Gu Yumin

1960a Study of the Neolithic human skeletons from the Baoji site, Shaanxi. *Gu Jizhuidongwu yu Gu Renlei* (*Palaeovertebrata et Palaeoanthropologia*) 2(1):33–43.

Yan Yan, Wu Xinzhi, Liu Changzhi, and Gu Yumin

1960b A study of human skeletons from Banpo, Xi'an, Shaanxi. *Kaogu* 9:36–47.

Yunnan Provincial Museum

1977 Note on Lijiang Man's skull from Yunnan. *Vertebrata PalAsiatica* 15(2):157–161.

Zhang Yinyun, Wang Linghong, and Dong Xingren

1977 The human skulls from the Zhenpiyan Neolithic site at Guilin, Guangxi. *Vertebrata PalAsiatica* 15(1):4–13.

Zhang Zhenbiao and Chen Dezhen

n.d. The study of the human remains from the Xiawanggang Neolithic site, Xichuan, Henan. *Shiqian Yanjiu (Prehistory).* In press.

Zhang Zhenbiao, Wang Linghong, and Ouyang Lian

1982 Physical patterns of Neolithic skulls in China in view of cluster analysis. *Vertebrata PalAsiatica* 20(1):72–80.

8

China's Earliest Palaeolithic Assemblages

JIA LANPO

Since the founding of the People's Republic of China in 1949 a number of important Lower Palaeolithic localities have yielded what are now considered by many to be China's earliest archaeological assemblages. Consisting of stone artifacts and other cultural remains, evidence has been gathered from both North and South China reflecting a diversity of palaeoenvironmental regimes and depositional contexts.

This essay summarizes the findings of investigations conducted at four such localities: Xihoudu, Shanxi; Shangnabang, Yunnan; and the related sites of Xiaochangliang and Donggutuo, Hebei.

Xihoudu, Shanxi

The lithic implements from the Xihoudu site constitute, as far as we know, the earliest archaeological assemblage in China (Jia and Wang 1978). Discovered in 1959 near Xihoudu Village in Ruicheng County, Shanxi (34°41′05″N, 110°17′30″E), this site is part of a complex of Palaeolithic localities in the vicinity of Kehe near the east bank of the Huanghe (Yellow River). Excavations conducted in 1961 and 1962 yielded more than 30 stone artifacts and an abundant fossil-vertebrate assemblage including burned mammalian ribs, deer antlers, and horse dentition. The fossil and archaeological remains were concentrated in cross-bedded sands within a gravel bed beneath a 50 m deposit of Middle Pleistocene clay. The cross-bedded

Palaeoanthropology and Palaeolithic Archaeology in the People's Republic of China

ISBN 0-12-601720-4

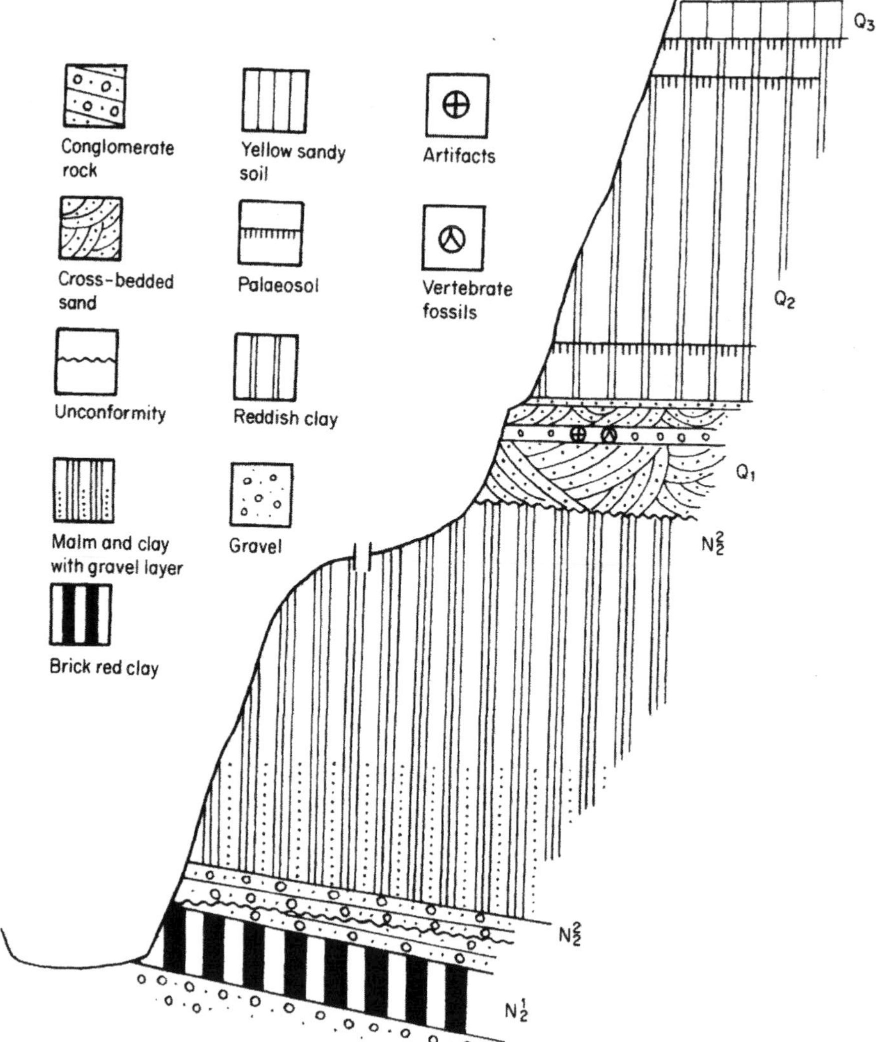

Figure 8.1 Geological section, Xihoudu, Shanxi.

sands rest on top of an unconformity that is in turn underlain by a 65-m-thick layer of Upper Pliocene calcareous sands and clay. At the bottom of this stratigraphic sequence a terrace, possibly composed of Pliocene conglomerates and brick-red clay, was exposed. This long cycle of sedimentation is so clearly preserved in the geological section at Xihoudu that the approximate antiquity of the site could be determined on geological evidence alone.

The relevant fossiliferous remains and stone artifacts were found distributed throughout a stratum averaging about 1 m in thickness (Figure 8.1). The lithic assemblage itself is not directly comparable to any other Palaeolithic materials yet reported in China. Artifacts include cores, flakes, chopper–chopping tools, and heavy triangular points. Of particular interest is the fact that differentiated techniques of stone-implement manufacture and secondary retouch are apparent in the Xihoudu assemblage. Flakes were removed from rounded pebbles and nuclei fashioned on very thick flakes. Some of the cores recovered seem to have been produced by the bipolar technique through anvil-supported direct percussion. Although most flakes appear to have been detached by simple direct percussion with a hard hammer, a few were also struck by the anvil or block-on-block technique.

Finished tools include concave and straight side scrapers made on flakes, in addition to many flakes that bear signs of either minimal retouch or simple use damage (Figures 8.2 and 8.3). Unifacial choppers and bifacial chopping tools have also been discovered, while some of the largest flakes recovered at the site exhibit no signs of further intentional modification at all (Figure 8.4).

One of the most important of the Xihoudu artifacts is a heavy triangular point (Figure 8.5) which bears striking similarities to heavy points from later Palaeolithic localities elsewhere in China. Unfortunately, this particular implement was recovered in a shallow depression in an unclear stratigraphic relationship with the rest of the site's cultural remains.

A number of deer antlers bearing signs of chopping and scraping were also

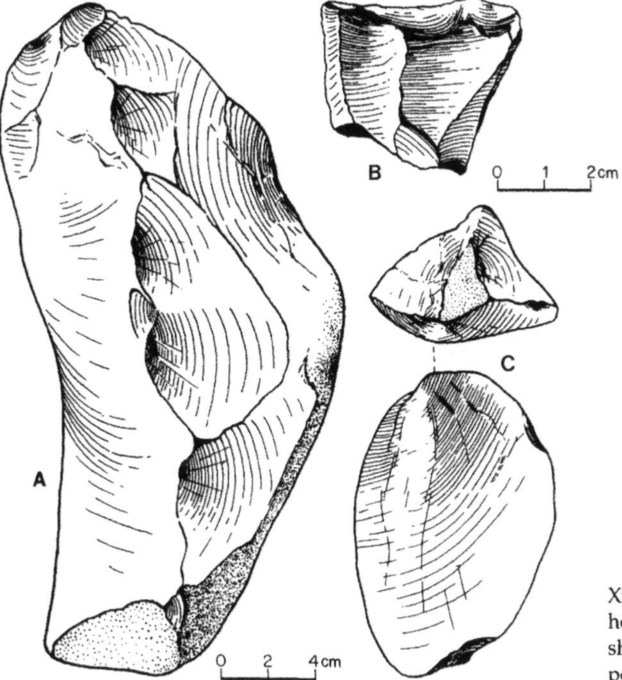

Figure 8.2 Artifacts from the Xihoudu site, Shanxi: A, core on a heavy quartzite flake; B, funnel-shaped core in vein quartz; C, bipolar core in quartzite.

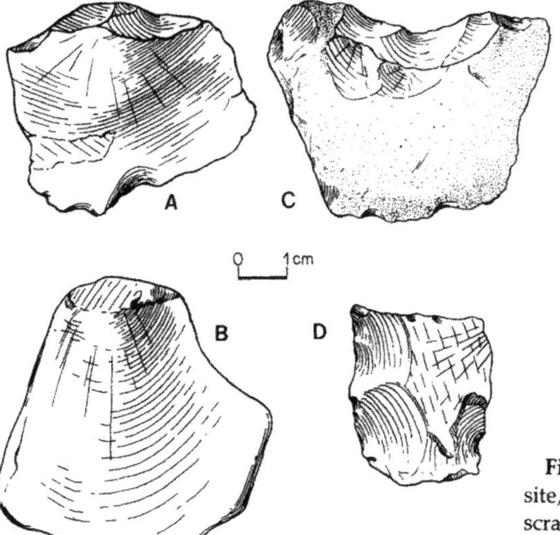

Figure 8.3 Artifacts from the Xihoudu site, Shanxi: A,B, quartzite flakes; C, concave scraper in quartzite; D, straight scraper in quartzite.

discovered, although no complete, unequivocal antler or bone tools have yet been recovered at Xihoudu. Also of interest are a series of grey, greyish-green, and black mammalian ribs, deer calvaria, and horse teeth that laboratory tests prove have been burned (Jia and Wang 1978:68). The fact that these traces of fire were found in areas clearly preserving a record of human activity suggests this was not an accidental phenomenon such as charring as a result of natural wild fire (Jia 1980:11–12; Jia and Wang 1978:68–69). What is particularly noteworthy is that this evidence of fire utilization at Xihoudu significantly antedates that dis-

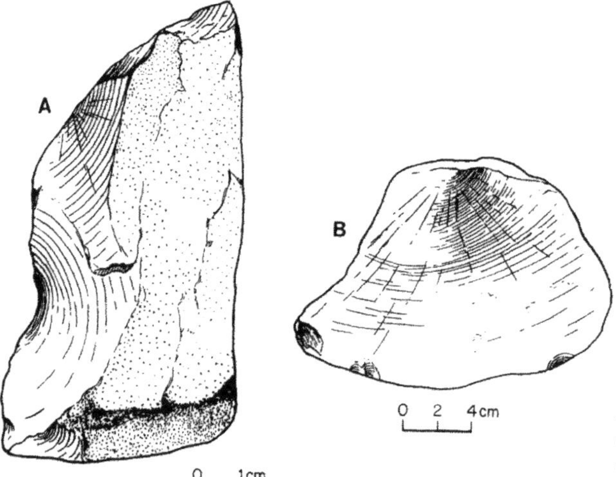

Figure 8.4 Artifacts from the Xihoudu site, Shanxi: A, light-duty unifacial chopper in quartzite; B, large quartzite flake with utilized edge.

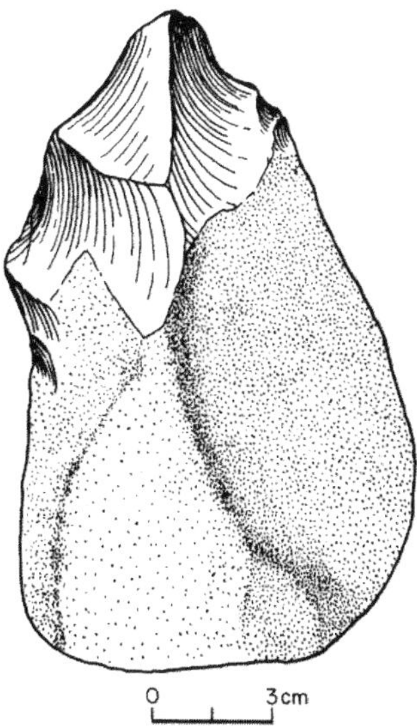

Figure 8.5 Heavy triangular point in quartzite, Xihoudu, Shanxi.

covered at such sites as Zhoukoudian Localities 1 and 13, Beijing; Shangnabang, Yunnan; Gongwangling, Shaanxi; and Kehe, Shanxi.

Remains of more than 20 vertebrate species have been discovered at Xihoudu, including *Trogontherium* sp. indet., *Archidiskodon planifrons, Palaeoloxodon* cf. *namadicus, Cervus bifurcatus, C. chinnaniensis, Coelodonta antiquitatis shansius, Elasmotherium* cf. *inexpectatum, Proboscidipparion* (*Hipparion*) *sinense, Equus sanmeniensis, Axis rugosus, A. shansius, Gazella* cf. *blacki*, and *Bison palaeosinensis* among others (see Chapter 15, this volume).

The faunal remains indicate a Lower Pleistocene antiquity for the site—at least 1 million years old by conservative estimate. Of the taxa thus far identified, 47% of the genera and 100% of the species are extinct forms, suggesting rough contemporaneity with the Yuanmou *Homo erectus* assemblage of Yunnan. These species seem to indicate a mixed steppe and thin woodland environment prevailed in the Xihoudu region during the period of the site's occupation. We believe the Lower Pleistocene of North China was characterized by a cooler, somewhat drier climate than at present.

Preliminary palaeomagnetic data indicate an absolute age for the Xihoudu site of about 1.8 million years BP. Clearly, if these provisional chronometric determinations are corroborated by additional data, the Xihoudu site may prove to be one of the most significant archaeological localities in East Asia. Unfortunately, the site has not yet produced hominid fossils and the sample of cultural remains thus far discovered is rather small. In addition, nearly all the Xihoudu artifacts found *in situ* nonetheless exhibit indications of having been transported some distance by water, leading some archaeologists to question the stratigraphic provenance of these materials. The evidence accumulated to the present moment is tantalizing, suggesting hominid occupation of North China during the

Lower Pleistocene. Until more cultural and fossil remains are collected *in situ* at Xihoudu and additional chronometric dates are forthcoming, we can only speculate on the true antiquity and archaeological significance of this site.

Shangnabang, Yuanmou, Yunnan

The age of the geological strata that yielded the remains of the Yuanmou *Homo erectus* is currently a subject of intense debate, although they are certainly younger than the deposits at Xihoudu. Archaeomagnetic dates originally generated for the Yuanmou locality near Shangnabang, Yunnan, suggested an antiquity of 1.7 ± 0.1 million years BP, which some scholars refined to an "absolute" age of 1.64 million years. Today, although the Lower Pleistocene age of the Yuanmou deposits has been called into question (Liu and Ding 1983), the associated fauna still reflects a Lower Pleistocene antiquity (see Chapter 15, this volume).

In 1965, several geologists discovered two human central incisors at Shangnabang Village in the Yuanmou Basin of Yunnan. These teeth, subsequently referred to the taxon *H. erectus yuanmouensis*, are still the only hominid fossils to be discovered at Yuanmou. Continuing excavations in the Shangnabang vicinity have led to the discovery of scraps of charcoal, several stone artifacts, and additional nonhominid vertebrate fossils.

The Yuanmou Basin preserves a section of fluviolacustrine sediments up to 695 m in thickness, which is divided from bottom to top into a series of four members containing a total of 28 layers. The fourth, or uppermost, member is a 122-m-thick sequence of brown and yellow-brown sands and gravels with interbedded silt and clay laminae. The teeth of *H. erectus*, charcoal scraps, and other cultural remains all derive from Member 4, Layer 25.

The brown-clay deposit containing the human fossils also yielded three clearly retouched stone implements, although none was derived from the same stratum as the Yuanmou incisors. Two were collected one-half meter below the incisors and one was derived from a stratigraphic context about 1 m above the dentition. All three specimens were found within a 5–20-m radius of the fossils' findspot. In addition to these implements, three stone artifacts collected from the surface at Shangnabang are thought on typological grounds to have also been fashioned by *H. erectus yuanmouensis*.

These artifacts are all made of vein quartz and, although very small, exhibit distinct retouching. All are classified as cores or scrapers, the typological distinction between them being indefinite (Figure 8.6). Although few in number, the human fossils and artifacts from Shangnabang are of great importance as they testify to hominid activity in the region as early as 1.6–1.7 million years ago.

In 1973, large quantities of charcoal—individual pieces ranging in size from that of soya beans to sesame seeds—were excavated from the bed that contained the fossils of *H. erectus yuanmouensis*. In all, three layers totaling about 3 m were found to contain charcoal traces. Distribution analyses demonstrated that one horizon in a 4 × 4-m excavation unit contained as many as 16 charcoal fragments per square millimeter. In 1975 two additional mammalian bones, almost certainly blackened by burning, were recovered, which, when taken in conjunction with the other traces of fire utilization at Yuanmou, provides powerful evidence for human manipulation of fire in South China more than 1.5 million years ago.

The fourth member of the Yuanmou Formation has produced 29 varieties of mammalian fossils of which 18 species are extinct, suggesting a Lower Pleistocene life assemblage.

At present, considerable controversy surrounds the chronometric dating of the sedimentary beds containing the fossils of *H. erectus* at Yuanmou. According to Liu and Ding (1983:46), the fourth member at Yuanmou is actually Middle Pleistocene in age and these authors suggest revising the area's geological nomenclature by removing the fourth member from the Yuanmou Formation and renaming it the Shangnabang Formation. Furthermore, Liu and Ding's magnetostratigraphic data indicate the layers that produced the hominid incisors and artifacts occur at a point in the sequence *above* the Matuyama–Brunhes horizon, a fact that has led those scholars to conclude the relevant strata are certainly less than 730,000 and probably only 500,000 to 600,000 years old or even later.

Because of the apparent contradiction between these data and the extremely archaic mammalian fossil assemblage associated with the Yuanmou incisors, and due to the primitive morphological features of the teeth themselves, I do not currently share the opinions of Liu and Ding in this matter. Until more evidence to the contrary is accumulated, I believe the archaeological and fossil materials from Shangnabang are among China's earliest evidence of human activity.

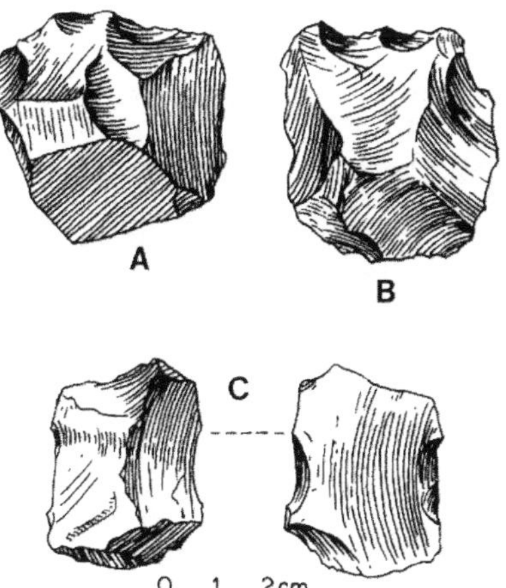

Figure 8.6 Thick quartzite scrapers from Yuanmou, Yunnan.

Xiaochangliang, Hebei

The Xiaochangliang site is 500 m northwest of Guanting Village in Yangyuan County, Hebei (41°13′N, 114°40′E). During investigations in 1978, the geological section at Xiaochangliang was found to consist of a bedrock base overlain by a thick deposit of interbedded sands and clays of the Nihewan Formation (You *et al.* 1980). The sequence is capped by an 8–15-m thick bed of loess. A layer of sand and concretions some 40 m below present ground surface was found to contain remains of extinct horses and deer. In a reddish-yellow sand lense an additional 20 m deeper, more mammalian fossils and stone artifacts were discovered (Figure 8.7).

The preliminary investigations at Xiaochangliang yielded 84 cores, flakes, and implements, in addition to lithic-waste material. Six bone splinters, tentatively thought to have been the product of human activity, were also discovered. The lithic raw material most commonly used was flint. Flakes are relatively thin with sharp edges, some apparently having been utilized without any prior retouching. Of particular interest is the fact that bipolar flakes are present in the Xiaochangliang assemblage, perhaps establishing it as an early member of a generalized North Chinese Palaeolithic tradition that has as one of its dis-

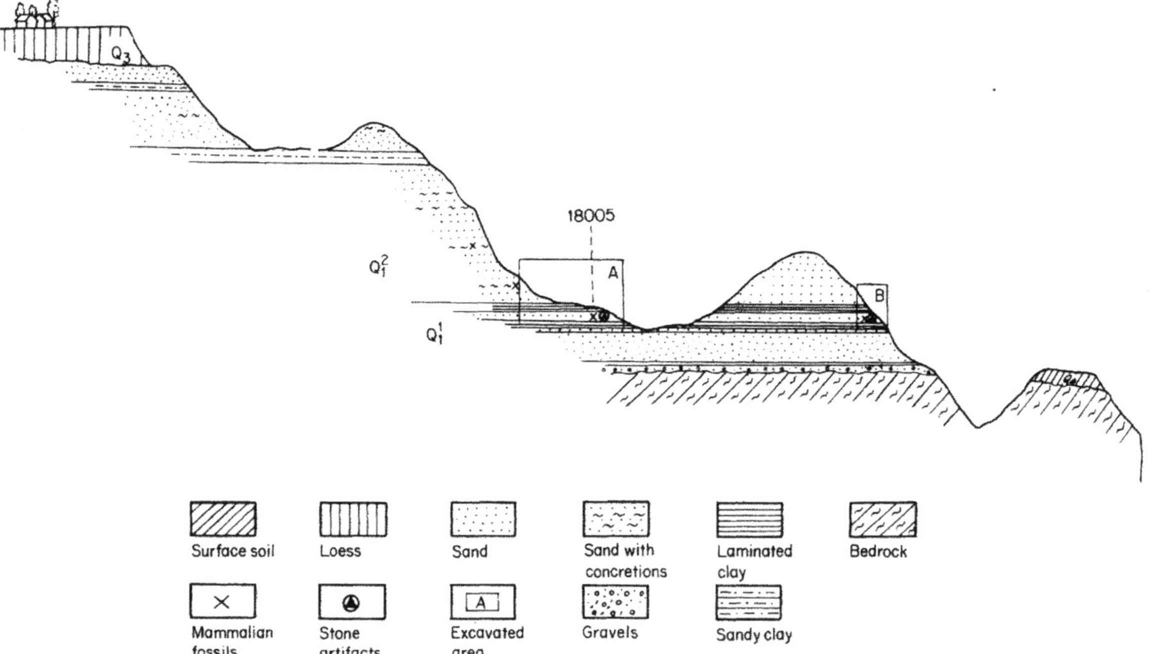

Figure 8.7 Geological section, Xiaochangliang, Nihewan, Hebei.

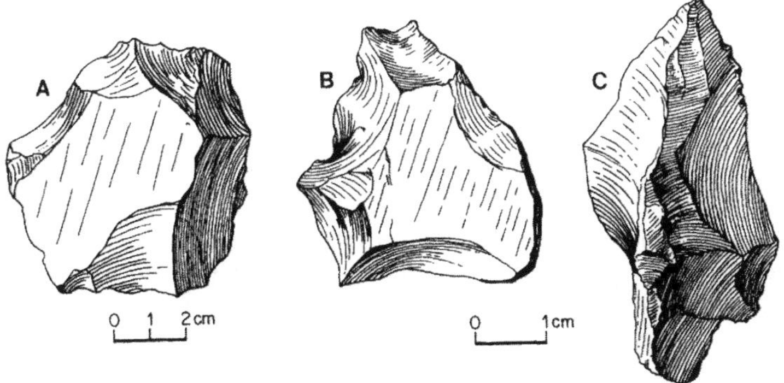

Figure 8.8 Artifacts from Xiaochangliang, Nihewan, Hebei: A, chopper; B,C, scrapers.

tinguishing characteristics the pervasive use of anvil-supported direct percussion to produce bipolar flakes. The small scrapers and choppers that are also typical of the Xiaochangliang collection were retouched onto their dorsal surfaces (Figures 8.8 and 8.9).

Archaeomagnetic dates originally suggested an age for the Nihewan Formation of 3.0 to 1.52 million years based on geological investigations conducted at Xiaodukou, about 2 km northwest of the Xiaochangliang site. Geological correlation led scholars to conclude that the Xiaochangliang cultural remains also dated to this range. Recent recalculations of the age of the Nihewan Formation indicate an age of roughly 1 million years for the Xiaochangliang archaeological assemblage. Nonetheless, these artifacts constitute some of North China's earliest Palaeolithic remains.

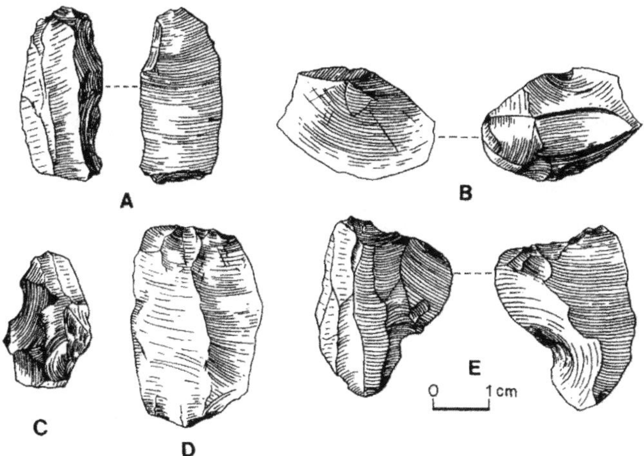

Figure 8.9 Artifacts from Xiaochangliang, Nihewan, Hebei: A,B, flint flakes; C–E, flint scrapers.

Donggutuo, Hebei

Located only 1 km from Xiaochangliang, the Donggutuo site occupies a large area and has produced abundant archaeological materials (Jia *et al.* 1982). A 2-week excavation yielded over 2000 artifacts including points and scrapers of various forms. Interestingly, retouching techniques apparent in the Donggutuo assemblage share similarities with the Zhoukoudian Locality 1 Early Palaeolithic and Xujiayao Middle Palaeolithic industries (the latter site is only 70 km west of Donggutuo). Although archaeomagnetic dates suggest a 1-million-year antiquity for the Donggutuo site, it is clearly part of a Palaeolithic tradition in North China, characteristic elements of which can be traced in archaeological collections throughout the Pleistocene.

Many of the retouching techniques and even specific tool types typical of the Zhoukoudian Locality 1 collections are found in the earlier deposits at Donggutuo. The investigation of this site and its contemporary at Xiaochangliang has produced important new data of concern to Chinese prehistorians interested in the emergence and subsequent development of East Asia's Palaeolithic cultural traditions (Jia *et al.* 1982).

It now seems clear that several Lower Pleistocene archaeological sites in China have a history of over 1 million years. These assemblages exhibit rather crude retouching and nearly amorphous or highly opportunistic tool types. Nonetheless, it is clear from the careful selection of raw materials and the development of specialized flaking techniques capable of dealing with such intractable lithic sources as flint and vein quartz pebbles that the hominids responsible for these toolkits had already developed many of the principal techniques that facilitated adaptation to the rigors of East Asia's Pleistocene environment.

Early Palaeolithic localities such as Xihoudu, Shangnabang, Xiaochangliang, and Donggutuo have yielded China's earliest known archaeological assemblages, yet the relatively developed character of many of these artifacts suggests even earlier cultural remains may be expected to be encountered. It is not impossible, based on what we know of the prehistory of both East Africa and China, that the earliest archaeological assemblages of East Asia may yet be found in late Pliocene strata (Jia and Wang 1982).

References

Hu Chengzhi
1973 Ape-man teeth from Yuanmou, Yunnan. *Acta Geologica Sinica* 1:65–69.

Jia Lanpo (Chia Lan-po)
1980 *Early man in China.* Beijing: Foreign Languages Press.

Jia Lanpo (Chia Lan-po) and Wang Jian (Wang Chien)
1978 *Hsihoutu—A culture site of early Pleistocene in Shansi province.* Beijing: Cultural Relics Press.
1982 Earliest human skeletal remains and cultural relics estimated to have existed in Pliocene Epoch strata. *Wenwu* 2:67–68.

Jia Lanpo (Chia Lan-po), Wei Qi, and Chen Chun
1982 The Lower Palaeolithic of China. *Kokogaku Zasshi* 206:36–41.
Liu Dongsheng and Ding Menglin
1983 Discussion on the age of "Yuanmou Man." *Acta Anthropologica Sinica* 2(1):40–48.
You Yuzhu, Tang Yingjun, and Li Yi
1980 New discovery of palaeoliths in the Nihewan Formation. *Quaternaria Sinica* 5(1):1–13.

9

The Early Palaeolithic of China

ZHANG SENSHUI

Introduction

China is a country with abundant Early Palaeolithic cultural remains. Thus far dozens of sites have been found, of which one of the most important is the famous fossiliferous cavern of Locality 1 at Zhoukoudian near Beijing.

China's known Early Palaeolithic sites cover a broad area from roughly 26°55′N to 40°40′N and 105°55′E to 122°10′E incorporating the administrative districts of Shanxi, Shaanxi, Liaoning, Henan, Hubei, Guizhou, and Beijing Municipality. In addition, fossils of *Homo erectus* have recently been discovered in Anhui and Shandong provinces; however, no unequivocal Palaeolithic artifacts have been found in these localities as yet.

Cultural development during the Early Palaeolithic in China was a slow, gradual process beginning perhaps as early as 1 million years BP and persisting until at least 200,000 BP, although individual localities yielding Early Palaeolithic materials may be as young as 100,000 years BP.

The cores, flakes, and tools of the Chinese Early Palaeolithic vary greatly in morphology, and typologically classifiable tools are relatively scarce. Tools that seem to be multifunctional occur frequently and techniques of production are relatively simple.

Flakes were made by four principal methods: simple direct percussion, anvil-supported direct percussion or "crushing" (i.e., bipolar technique), anvil or block-on-block, and throwing. Three major retouching techniques were employed during the Chinese Early Palaeolithic, the most common being simple direct percussion. The bipolar and block-on-block methods were also occasion-

Palaeoanthropology and
Palaeolithic Archaeology in the
People's Republic of China

ISBN 0-12-601720-4

ally utilized in the production of implements; however, these fabrication techniques never account for more than a small percentage of the total artifacts in any given assemblage.

Early Palaeolithic tools may be subdivided into two discrete categories. The first group includes tools used in the production of primary flakes and for retouching—principally hammerstones of several types and anvils. Almost all such implements are fashioned from pebbles or large cobbles that bear traces of battering and other use damage. The second category comprises finished tools such as scrapers, points, choppers, gravers, awls, and stone spheroids, among others.

Most of these artifacts were made on flakes of various sizes and shapes and far outnumber core tools in Early Palaeolithic assemblages. In most cases, choppers were made from exhausted cores or pebbles, choppers fashioned on large flakes being rather rare. Stone spheroids (bolas) are all core tools, while small implements such as scrapers and points are almost invariably chipped on flakes. We can therefore characterize the Early Palaeolithic traditions of China as flake industries.

Principal Early Palaeolithic Sites

In order to provide the reader with a more complete understanding of China's Early Palaeolithic, a series of particularly significant localities have been selected for detailed discussion.

Gongwangling, Shaanxi

The Gongwangling locality is some 20 km east of Lantian in central Shaanxi Province. Successive investigations at this site have yielded 20 stone artifacts including 11 cores, 5 flakes, and 4 scrapers in association with a hominid calvarium classified as *H. erectus lantienensis* (Dai 1966; Dai and Xu 1973). In addition, charcoal granules were collected from the fossiliferous stratum; however, it is not yet possible to determine with absolute certainty that these granules are evidence of intentional fire utilization on the part of *H. erectus*.

Quartzite is the principal raw material in the lithic industry, although a few pieces fashioned from quartz are also known. From the concentrated points of percussion visible on both the cores and flakes, it is apparent that the main fabrication technique employed at Gongwangling was simple direct percussion with a hard hammer. The cores are all made on pebbles and exceed 100 mm in length. The width of the cores generally exceeds their length, and most approximate 100 mm in thickness. Given the fact that each core only exhibits a few flake scars, it seems that the utilized proportion of the Gongwangling nuclei is relatively low. With the exception of one polyhedral core, all the Gongwangling specimens bear a single striking platform. The polyhedral nucleus is characterized by right angles between each of the striking platforms. The remaining

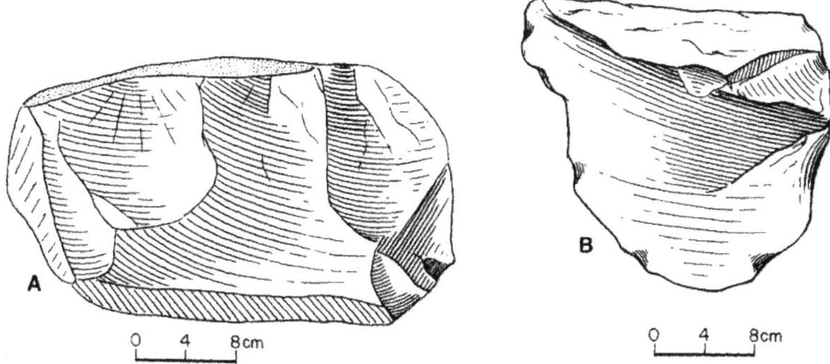

Figure 9.1 Quartzite artifacts from Gongwangling, Lantian, Shaanxi: A, tabular core with single striking platform; B, flake probably detached by the block-on-block or anvil technique.

core is both tabular and semicolumnar (Figure 9.1A). The striking platforms of all of the Gongwangling cores are on cortex and bear no indication of preparation. The angle between the striking platform and the flake removal surfaces ranges between 63 and 90°, but in most cases exceeds 80°.

The flakes, of various shapes, are all relatively large, exceeding 60 mm in length. Their striking platforms are either directly on pebble cortex or on unmodified previous flake scars. Bulbs of percussion are all rather shallow and twin bulbs of percussion have not yet been observed in our collections. All but one of these flakes were produced by simple direct percussion with a hammerstone. The exception is a very large specimen (120 mm long by 130 mm wide) with a broad, oblique striking platform that forms an obtuse angle in relation to the main flake surface. This flake is similar to those known to have been produced by the block-on-block technique (Figure 9.1B).

Only four finished tools, all scrapers, have been recovered from the Gongwangling locality, of which three are flake tools and one is fashioned on a core. One specimen is a straight side scraper that seems to have been produced by applying limited retouch to the ventral surface of a flake already nearly exhausted through use (Figure 9.2A). Another specimen is a convex side scraper fashioned by local retouch from the dorsal to the ventral surface. This specimen,

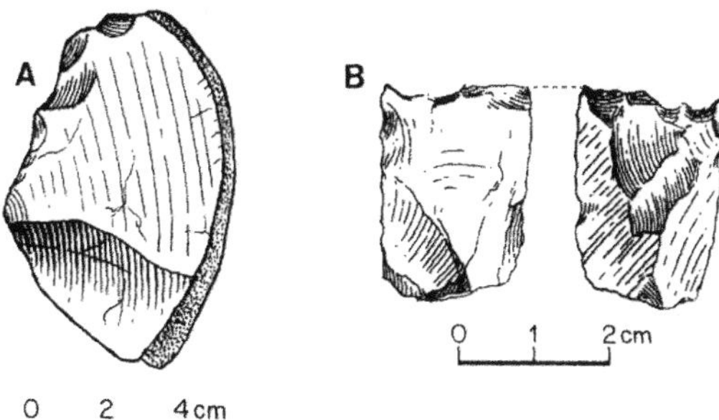

Figure 9.2 Quartzite implements from Gongwangling, Lantian, Shaanxi: A, straight scraper; B, end scraper.

originally classified as a utilized flake, is characterized by crude retouch that has produced a rather sinuous working edge. The third Gongwangling tool is an end scraper with a transverse edge made on a small rectangular quartz flake. The working margin, opposite the bulb of percussion, was roughly retouched from many directions, thus producing microscopic flake scars on both surfaces of the flake. Close examination indicates that careful secondary retouch is also apparent on the dorsal surface (Figure 9.2B). The final specimen, a convex end scraper made on a small core, measures 44 mm in length. Its edge is characterized by crude bifacial trimming.

As mentioned above, it can be demonstrated that with one exception the Gongwangling flakes were all produced by direct percussion and that retouching was accomplished by essentially the same technique. Secondary retouch, or trimming, although crude, seems to have been directed both from the ventral to the dorsal surface of the flakes and vice versa.

Although we consider these artifacts to be the products of toolmaking activities on the part of *H. erectus lantienensis,* such a small assemblage of finds does not allow a thorough reconstruction of behavior or technological processes involved in the production of these artifacts and their use.

According to biostratigraphic evidence, the Gongwangling site is slightly older than the Middle Pleistocene sequence at Zhoukoudian Locality 1 outside Beijing (see Chapter 15, this volume). Controversy still surrounds the chronometric age of the Lantian deposits; however, it is fairly certain that the palaeoenvironmental milieu in central Shaanxi during the period of the site's occupation was considerably warmer and moister than at present, possibly classifiable as a subtropical zone.

Chenjiawo, Shaanxi

The Chenjiawo (or Chenjiawozi) site is about 10 km northwest of Lantian. Principal discoveries include the mandible of *H. erectus lantienensis,* four artifacts (Jia *et al.* 1966), and an assemblage of mammalian fossils, all of which derive from the locality's reddish clay stratum.

The artifacts consist of a scraper and three flakes, one of which is broken. The flakes all appear to have been produced by simple direct percussion due to the morphology of their bulbs. Flakes with a cortex striking platform and those with the platform on a broken surface both occur at Chenjiawo. The scraper is characterized by alternating retouch that has resulted in a relatively blunt and sinuous working edge. Due to this peculiar edge morphology, this particular specimen was originally classified as a small chopper; however, because of its extremely small size we now consider it to be a variety of scraper.

Although the Chenjiawo and Gongwangling localities at Lantian share a number of fossil vertebrates in common, nine mammalian species from Chenjiawo are found in both Middle and Upper Pleistocene deposits, suggesting this locality may be somewhat younger than Gongwangling. Preliminary palaeomagnetic determinations indicate the Chenjiawo deposits may represent a cycle of deposition some 530,000 to 650,000 years old.

Localities in Shaanxi, Henan, and Shanxi Provinces

Early Palaeolithic artifacts have been discovered in the reddish clay deposits of several dozen localities in Shaanxi, Henan, and Shanxi provinces. Of these sites, only Kehe in the Fen River Valley of Shanxi has been subjected to excavation (Jia *et al.* 1962), but concentrations of Early Palaeolithic cultural materials are known to be distributed in Lantian, Lingdong, Weinan, and Tongguan counties, Shaanxi; Shan, Lingbao, and Sanmenxia counties, Henan; and Yuanqu, Ruicheng, and Wanrong counties, Shanxi. None of these isolated localities has produced more than 100 artifacts and in most cases only a few pieces have been collected from the surface.

The flaking techniques employed at these sites include the basic Chinese Early Palaeolithic repertoire of simple direct percussion, anvil-supported direct percussion (bipolar technique), anvil or block-on-block, and throwing. Of these techniques, simple direct percussion is the most common, with cores and flakes produced by this method occurring at many sites in the region. Most of these artifacts are relatively large, with cores in most cases measuring more than 100 mm in length and flakes more than 60 mm.

Most flakes are irregularly shaped but a few seem to conform to more patterned plan forms such as triangular, trapezoidal, and rectangular. As with the Lantian material, these flakes exhibit striking platforms on both cortex and broken surfaces. No specimens exhibiting prepared striking platforms have yet been observed in these localities, but a few pieces bear rudimentary faceting on their striking platforms. The cores from which flakes have been removed directly from the cortex exhibit no indications of preparation. A few flake scars remain on the worked surface and are both short and wide. The majority of the nuclei bear a single striking platform, only a few being classifiable as polyhedral or multifaceted cores.

Flakes struck by the anvil method are also rather common and have been found at a number of sites in Sanmenxia, Henan (Huang 1964); Ruicheng, Shanxi; and Lantian, Shaanxi. These flakes are characterized by large, oblique striking platforms; large, shallow bulbs of percussion, and an angle between the striking platform and the main flake surface that exceeds 120°. A few bipolar flakes have been gathered from three sites in China's reddish clay deposits: Kehe Locality 6055 in Shanxi, and the Hujiazigou and Wanjiagou sites in Lantian county, Shaanxi. In the latter two localities, the bipolar flakes were surface finds and their exact provenance is uncertain. However, at Kehe bipolar flakes have been excavated *in situ*. Unfortunately, only a single bipolar flake has thus far been recovered at each of these localities, so no meaningful interpretation is yet possible.

One large flake (235 × 315 × 75 mm) was discovered at Kehe Locality 6055.

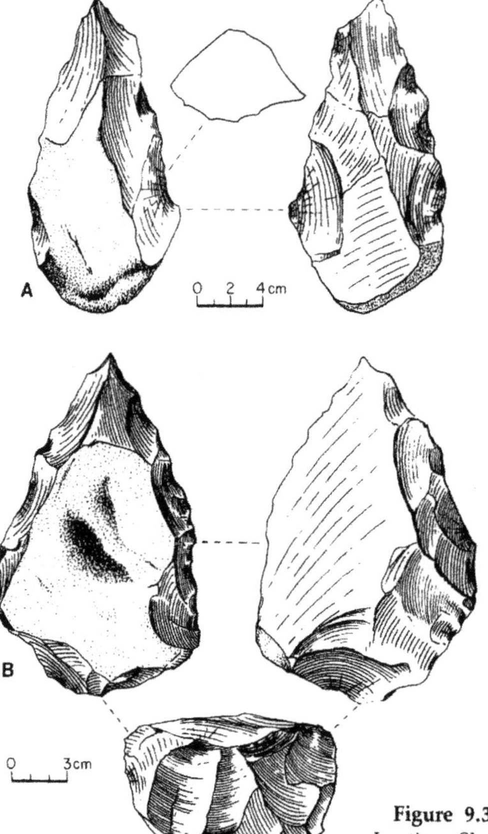

Figure 9.3 A, Quartzite protobiface from Pingliang, Lantian, Shaanxi; B, quartzite pointed chopper from the Shuigou site, Sanmenxia, Henan.

This fan-shaped piece was apparently produced by the throwing technique (Jia *et al.* 1962).

Finished tools recovered in these localities include scrapers, choppers, points, and spheroids. Generally speaking, core tools are more numerous than those made on flakes although a large number of taphonomic factors could account for this disparity. Choppers are by far the most numerous tool type. Most are rather large, exceeding 100 mm in length and 500 g in weight. Choppers themselves may be typologically subdivided into single straight, convex, double, end, discoidal, and pointed varieties. Tools in the latter category often resemble bifaces (Figure 9.3A), although the unifacial pieces that conform to the classical definition of *chopper* are more common (Figure 9.3B). The choppers were retouched by simple direct percussion and, although most exhibit rather rough retouch, a few were subjected to more careful trimming, producing a regularly shaped artifact with a relatively sharp edge. Examples of such artifacts include a complex, multiedged chopper from the Zhangjiawan site in Tongguan County, Shaanxi

(Figure 9.4A), and an end chopper collected in Henancun, Yuanqu County, Shanxi (Figure 9.4B). Both of these specimens were elaborately trimmed onto their dorsal surfaces by simple direct percussion; however, some choppers were manufactured by directing blows onto the ventral surface or by alternating percussion.

About 20 crudely retouched scrapers, mostly single edged, have been recovered from several Early Palaeolithic localities in Lantian County, Shaanxi, and Ruicheng County, Shanxi.

A single point made on a flake was discovered in Kehe Locality 6056 (Figure 9.5). This small specimen (34 × 27 × 13 mm) was formed by retouching the flake on its dorsal surface so that the oblique edges meet at a point directly opposite the striking platform. Unfortunately, the tip of this specimen is slightly broken.

Eight spheroids (sometimes referred to as *bolas*) have been recovered from Kehe Locality 6054; the Shuigou site in Sanmenxia County, Henan; and Choushuihegou in Lantian County, Shaanxi. These stone balls exhibit scarred sur-

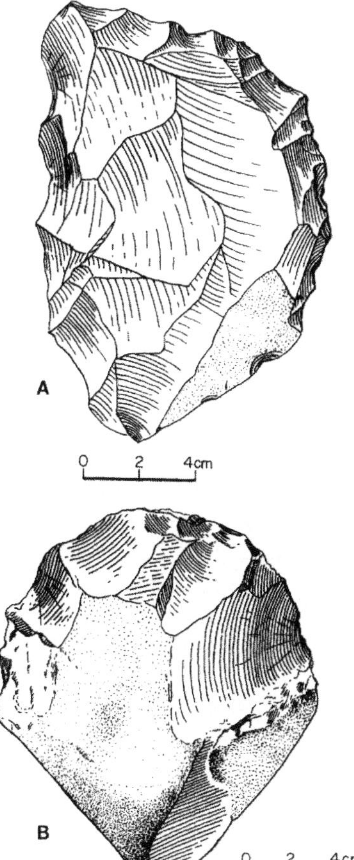

Figure 9.4 A, Quartzite multiple-edge chopper from Zhangjiawan, Shaanxi; B, quartzite end chopper from Yuanchu County, Shanxi.

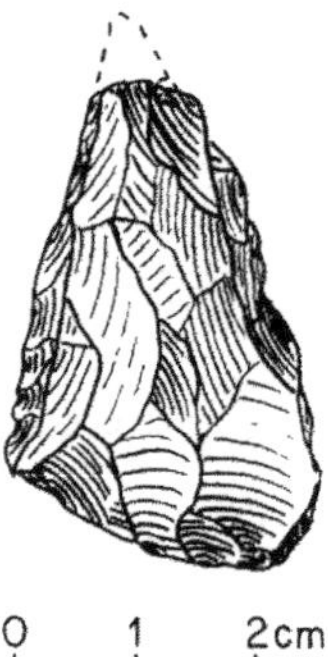

Figure 9.5 Quartzite point from Kehe Locality 6056, Shanxi.

faces as if they have been pecked into shape. Although their size and shape suggest use as missiles or hammerstones, this hypothesis has yet to be adequately tested.

Locality 1, Zhoukoudian, Beijing

Locality 1, the *Sinanthropus* site, is near the village of Zhoukoudian in Fangshan County, 48 km southwest of Guang'anmen in the city of Beijing. The site is on the boundary of the Huabei (North China) Plain and Beijing's Western Hills, a region characterized by many prominences of massive Ordovician limestone. The hills west of Zhoukoudian village possess numerous fissures and caverns that contain abundant vertebrate fossils, leading local inhabitants, who used the bones as an important ingredient in traditional medicines, to refer to this locality as Longgushan, or "Dragon Bone Hill."

Since the 1920s many seasons of excavation have been conducted in the fossiliferous limestone fissures of the Zhoukoudian vicinity, yielding abundant evidence of Middle Pleistocene occupation by *H. erectus pekinensis* (= *Sinanthropus*, or "Beijing Man").

The remains of Beijing Man's tools, fire utilization, and subsistence activities, as well as the fossil remains of *H. erectus* themselves, have rendered Locality 1 at Zhoukoudian one of the most important Middle Pleistocene archaeological sites in the world. The summit of the hill into which Locality 1 extends is approximately 145 m above sea level. The cavern in which *H. erectus* apparently lived is about 140 m long (east–west) and about 20 m wide at the middle of the cavern. In the western part of the cavern the deposits narrow down to only about 2 m and then seem to disappear completely.

The excavated deposit in Locality 1 is over 50 m deep and in many areas the deposits may be considerably deeper. The strata containing cultural remains vary in thickness throughout the site but are between 30 and 40 m deep (Black *et al.* 1933; Jia 1959).

The scientific significance of the Locality 1 deposits was recognized during the summer of 1921. However, a decade passed before Palaeolithic artifacts were reported from the site. During the original 2 years of investigation (1921 and 1923) and during the first period of systematic excavation (1927–1928), little attention was paid to artifactual remains including evidence of fire utilization. In 1929, when Pierre Teilhard de Chardin and Pei Wenzhong began conscientiously to survey the Locality 1 deposits, pigmented bones and antlers and a chipped-quartz block were almost immediately collected by Pei. By 1931 most scientists acknowledged the importance of Zhoukoudian as a repository of both fossil and archaeological data (Pei 1931). The investigations conducted at Locality 1 laid the foundation for Palaeolithic archaeology, palaeoanthropology, and Quaternary vertebrate palaeontology in China.

The deposits bearing Palaeolithic materials in Locality 1 are divided into 11 layers, numbered sequentially from the top. Fossil vertebrates have been recovered from Layers 12 and 13 (Jia 1959), but no unequivocal cultural remains have been discovered below Layer 11.

Beneath Layer 13 the excavated deposits have been further subdivided into four strata: Layers 14 and 15, reflecting early Middle Pleistocene depositional events, and Layers 16 and 17, which are thought to be of late Lower Pleistocene antiquity.

Following is a brief description of the principal strata in Locality 1 (Figure 9.6):

Layers 1 and 2: Fossiliferous, coarse breccia deposits with several lenses of strongly consolidated stalagmitic blocks. Thickness about 4 m. Few mammalian fossils and artifacts have been discovered in these layers. Often referred to as the Upper Breccia and Upper Travertine layers.

Layer 3: Fossiliferous, coarse breccia deposit. A large limestone block in the lower part of this layer is part of the collapsed roof of the original cave. Ash heaps scattered on the surface of this block are thought to reflect human activity. Large quantities of artifacts and a few human fossils have been found in this stratum, particularly at Locus B. Thickness is about 4 m.

Layer 4: Upper ash layer pushed into its present configuration by lithostatic pressure generated by a fallen block of limestone from the collapsed cavern roof. The deposits of the layer, about 6 m thick, have been subdivided into over 100 laminae from which a large number of microfaunal remains and *H. erectus* fossils have been recovered. Cultural remains are particularly abundant.

Layer 5: Strongly consolidated black and gray clay matrix often referred to as a *calcium slab*. Stalagmitic crust at bottom. Contains few artifacts. Thickness about 1 m.

Layer 6: Hard breccia level containing fossils of *H. erectus*, artifacts, and evidence of fire utilization. Stratum becomes progressively less consolidated from top to bottom. Thickness is approximately 5 m.

Layer 7: Deep gray, partly cross-bedded loose sands. Deposit thickest in west (ca. 6.5 m), thinning out to about 2 m in the east and eventually disappearing in the western Gezitang. Rich, well-preserved fossil assemblage, including skulls of *Bubalus*. Thickness averages 2 m.

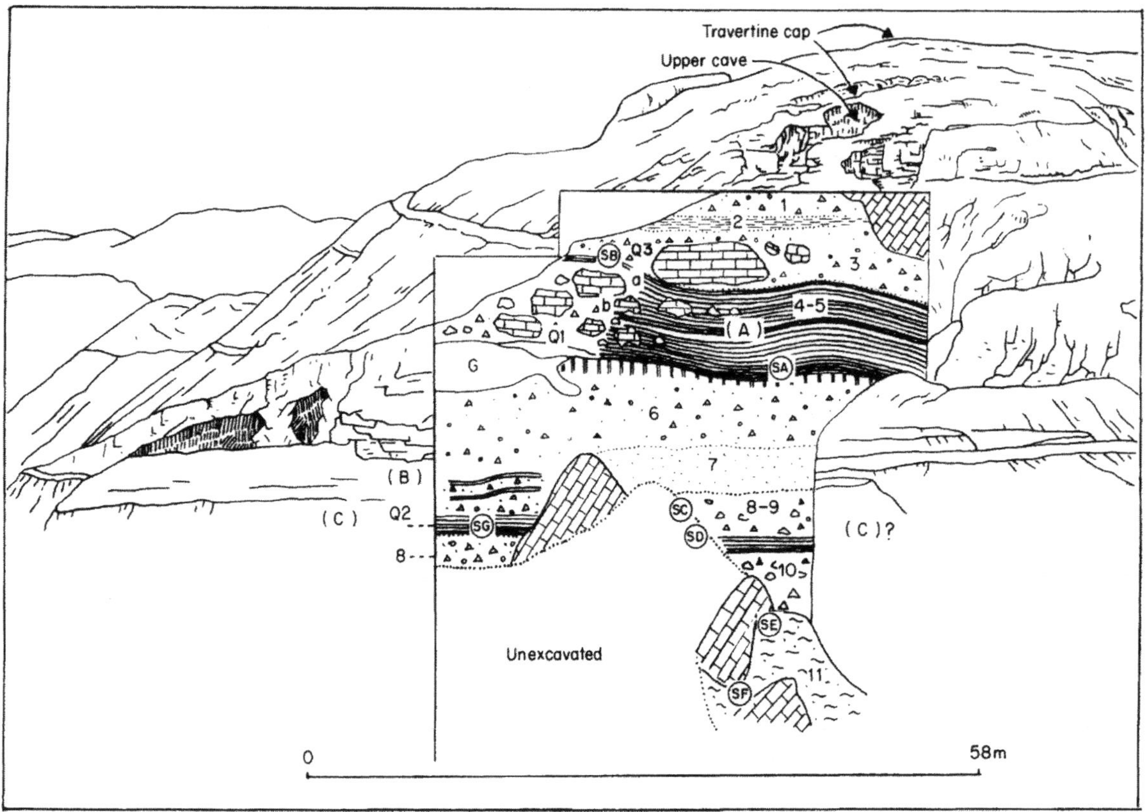

Figure 9.6 A partly diagrammatic longitudinal section through Zhoukoudian, Locality 1, Beijing. (A),(B),(C), and a,b, cultural layers; G, Gezitang; Q1–Q3, quartz horizons; SA–SG, *Homo erectus* fossil loci. Chief stratigraphic layers are numbered 1–11. (After Black *et al.* 1933.)

Layers 8 and 9: Fossiliferous, coarse breccia with several thin ash lenses present. In 1936 three *H. erectus* crania were discovered *in situ*. Thickness about 6 m.

Layer 10: Red clay deposit with weakly brecciated limestone blocks. A thin ash layer occurs at the bottom of this stratum. Few cultural and fossil remains have been recovered. Thickness about 2 m.

Layer 11: Fossiliferous, reddish breccia containing mammalian coprolites, artifacts, and fossils in the upper and middle units. The first cranium of *H. erectus pekinensis* was discovered in this layer in the Lower Cave. Thickness about 2 m.

In addition to lithic artifacts, abundant evidence of fire utilization has been discovered in Zhoukoudian Locality 1 (Black 1931). As mentioned above, two ash heaps were found on the surface of a large limestone block at the bottom of Layer 3, and concentrations of ash were also discovered in Quartz Horizon 2 in the Gezitang as well as in Layers 4 and 5. The thickness of these ash deposits varies from over 10 cm to several meters. Evidence of fire utilization, including scattered burned bones and stones, charcoal granules, and ash, have been discovered in every layer containing cultural remains. A few burned artifacts have also been recovered from several loci in Locality 1.

Large quantities of burned bone provide extensive evidence of fire utilization at Zhoukoudian. Most specimens are black, gray, blue, and blue-green in color, and some exhibit warping and minute cracks or crazing due to thermal stress. Charcoal from a presumed hearth feature in Quartz Horizon 2 in the Gezitang has been identified as redbud—*Cercis* sp. indet. (Chaney and Daugherty 1933)—close to the living *C. siliquastrum* or *C. chinensis*, the latter of which may be found growing today in the Western Hills near Beijing. In areas where extensive concentrations of ash occur, the original land surface often appears deep red in color and has clearly been hardened through close proximity to fire.

Based on our analyses of the stratigraphic occurrence of these features on the nature of the artifacts themselves, there is no doubt these remains are not the product of any natural process. Rather, the Zhoukoudian Locality 1 evidence establishes a clear case for the utilization of fire by *H. erectus* between 400,000 and 500,000 years ago. From these remains we may deduce that the fuel employed in the production of these fires consisted principally of a wide variety of herbaceous plants, although larger tree twigs and other vegetal fragments are also known to occur.

In our opinion, *H. erectus* at Zhoukoudian not only understood the use of fire but was capable of controlling and preserving it through the management of kindling. We do not believe, however, that the Middle Pleistocene inhabitants of Zhoukoudian had acquired the ability to *make* fire; it seems likely they could only collect and preserve naturally occurring fires. It is of great importance to note that, due to the abundance of evidence for fire utilization at Zhoukoudian, we do not believe *H. erectus pekinensis* was the earliest hominid to engage in such activities in China. Unfortunately, we have as yet no firm data to support an earlier occurrence of this phenomenon.

The presence or absence of bone artifacts in Early Palaeolithic localities is always a subject of considerable debate, and Zhoukoudian is no exception. Although controversy still exists, some Chinese prehistorians believe that *H. erectus* did indeed manufacture and use osseous artifacts at Zhoukoudian. Given the opportunistic nature of these tools, such vital questions as how they were manufactured and used have yet to be answered. A formal typology for these bone artifacts has not yet been devised. It is hoped that microscopic study of the traces of manufacture and use will facilitate our understanding of this assemblage.

Stone tools comprise the bulk of our data concerning the culture of *H. erectus pekinensis* (Pei 1931; Pei and Zhang n.d.; Teilhard and Pei 1932; Zhang 1962). On the basis of the analysis of tens of thousands of artifacts from Locality 1 (Zhang 1962), as well as from similar Early Palaeolithic sites such as Zhoukoudian Locality 13 (Teilhard and Pei 1941) and Nanhaiyu in Yuanqu County, Shanxi (Wang *et al.* 1959), it can be seen that these Middle Pleistocene industries possess distinctive characteristics that influenced the nature of later stone assemblages in North China.

Forty-four varieties of lithic raw material have been identified in the Zhoukoudian industry, of which vein quartz is the most common, accounting for 88.4% of the total artifacts. Rock crystal constitutes 4.7% of the raw material encountered, while sandstone and flint occupy lesser positions, representing 2.6 and 2.4% of the assemblage, respectively. The remaining 40 varieties of stone collectively account for only 1.9% of the raw material utilized at Zhoukoudian, so their influence on the character of the lithic assemblage is insignificant.

All known raw materials were collected in the immediate vicinity of Locality 1, pebbles and gravels of many kinds being readily available in the bed of the Zhoukou River near the site. The Lower Pebble Layer of the Locality 1 stratigraphic sequence is, in fact, a manifestation of the fluvial actions of the Zhoukouhe. Rock crystals and some other types of small, nodular raw material were apparently gathered from the surface of weathered granite exposures about 5 km from the site.

Flakes were produced by three principal methods at Zhoukoudian: anvil-supported direct percussion or crushing (i.e., bipolar technique), simple direct percussion, and anvil or block-on-block, the most common of which was anvil-supported direct percussion. Several thousand bipolar flakes have been recovered in the Locality 1 deposits (Figure 9.7A,B), in addition to several hundred nuclei. In most cases, the bipolar flakes are relatively small, measuring less than 40 mm in length and 10 mm in thickness. Most such flakes are longer than they are wide, although a broad spectrum of plan forms has been observed.

Products derived through the process of bipolar reduction may be subdivided into two categories: flakes with a crushed microscar of percussion on only one end, and those exhibiting crushed microbulbs on both ends, the latter of which

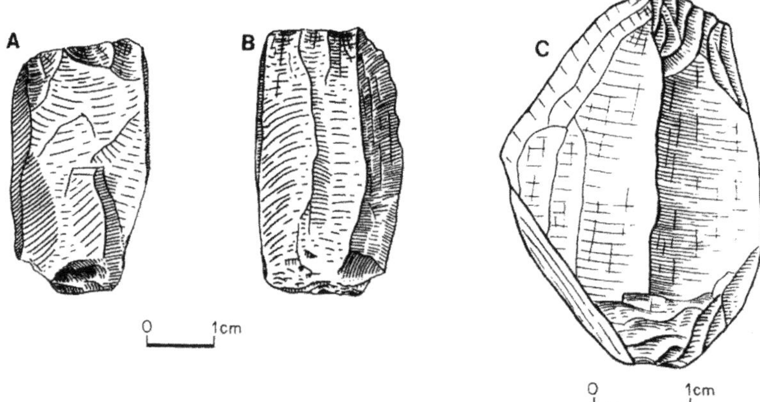

Figure 9.7 Quartz artifacts from Zhoukoudian Locality 1, Beijing: A,B, bipolar flakes; C, bipolar core.

are termed *bipolar flakes.* Replicative experimentation indicates that those flakes with a single crushed end—which were much more irregular in form, shorter, and thicker than their bipolar counterparts—were struck from the core in the initial stages of its use. The same bipolar technique of production seems to yield both varieties of crushed flakes.

In true bipolar flakes the length of the specimens exceeds twice their width, in most cases. Most are rectangular, trapezoidal, or are in the shape of a flat, pointed tablet (*guixing*). A few bipolar flakes are irregular in plan view. Our experimentation, consisting of both replication and the analysis of conjoining fragments, suggests that the bipolar flakes produced from any given nucleus become progressively longer, thinner, and more regular until the core is exhausted. The exhausted bipolar cores are readily distinguishable due to their relatively small size (ca. 20 to 40 mm in length) and the presence of crushed scars on opposite ends.

Regular bipolar cores are less common than are irregular examples and are classified as spindle-shaped (Figure 9.7C), prismatic, and conical. From the condition of the recovered cores, particularly the placement and magnitude of the flake scars present, it is possible to determine at what stage in the flake manufacturing process the nucleus ceased to be used.

A core used in the bipolar approach is generally very irregular in the initial stages of flake production, with deep, concave flake removal surfaces apparent. In the later stages of manufacture these bipolar cores assume a more regular form, exhibiting elongated flake scars on several surfaces.

Bipolar cores are generally fashioned of vein quartz, a highly intractable raw material from which it is difficult to obtain regular flakes through simple direct percussion. Because of the naturally small size of the available vein quartz nodules and due to its intractable nature, *H. erectus pekinensis* developed the anvil-supported direct percussion, or bipolar technique, as an approach to flake fabrication.

The simple direct percussion technique, in which the core is usually held directly in the hand, was also frequently utilized at Zhoukoudian, although most cores of this type are fashioned from relatively high-quality raw material such as hard sandstone, flint, milky quartz, and a variety of igneous rocks. Flakes produced by this method are typically irregular and fall naturally into a bimodal size distribution that seems, in most cases, to be a function of the initial size of the nuclei employed. Although a few such flakes exceed 100 mm in length, a large proportion are between 40 and 60 mm long, while a few diminutive specimens are less than 20 mm in length. Nearly all flakes produced by this technique are larger than their bipolar counterpart, and, while most of these specimens are longer than they are wide, their length rarely exceeds twice their width. Their length–breadth index (breadth/length × 100) is about 90, and, although common plan forms are irregular, other flake types include trapezoidal, triangular (Figure 9.8A), and rectangular specimens, the last of which include rather small artifacts generally fashioned of rock crystal or flint.

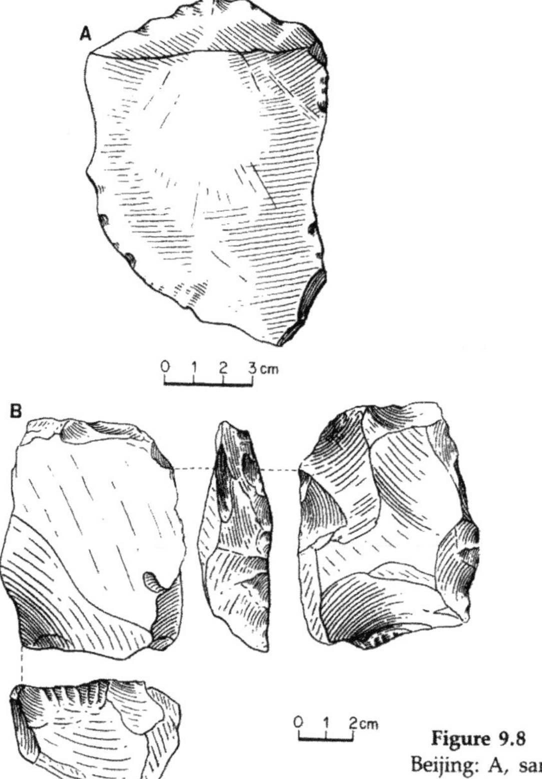

Figure 9.8 Artifacts from Zhoukoudian Locality 1, Beijing: A, sandstone triangular flake; B, flint tabular core with prepared striking platform.

Within the assemblage of flakes produced by simple direct percussion, those with cortex striking platforms constitute about one-third of the total collection. The remaining flakes were struck from simple platforms fashioned on the scar left by the removal of a single initial flake. A few pieces seem to exhibit minimally prepared platforms, the points of percussion are not very concentrated, and their bulbs are similarly not very pronounced. Many simple direct percussion flakes exhibit irregular scars on their dorsal surfaces attesting to the removal of earlier flakes; however, only a few specimens have been found to retain the scars of previously struck regular flakes, these latter specimens being generally thin and relatively regular themselves. Most cores produced through simple direct percussion are larger, exceeding 60 mm in length. These nuclei may be subdivided into single and multiple platform, or polyhedral, varieties, of which the single platform type are generally smaller.

The single platform cores are distinguished by a few short, broad flake scars. The points of percussion tend to be quite concentrated rather than diffuse and the striking platform is generally characterized by many such points. The angle between the striking platform and the worked surface nearly always exceeds 80°, and, from the amount of cortex still present, it is clear most of these nuclei have not been exhausted prior to disposal.

The multiple platform or polyhedral cores, of which more than 100 examples are known from Zhoukoudian, are characterized by the scars of irregular flakes that have been removed from many directions. The productivity of these polyhedral cores exceeds that of the single platform nuclei and some of them are not only symmetrical but are also relatively thin, measuring about 20 to 30 mm thick. Polyhedral cores are mainly irregular, but some are funnel-shaped, cubic, semi-conical, and tabular. One such tabular core (Figure 9.8B) was discovered near the top of the Locality 1 deposits of Locus H in Layers 1–3, and displays a relatively progressive flaking technique.

Large flakes made by the anvil, or block-on-block, technique are less common than those produced by simple direct percussion, and are fashioned almost exclusively on sandstone. A total of 39 flakes and eight cores known to have been produced by the anvil technique are currently known from Locality 1. All the flakes are rather large, exceeding 100 mm in length, although a few measuring less than 40 mm long are also known. With the exception of a few isolated specimens, the widths of these flakes all exceed their lengths.

The nuclei utilized in the anvil technique at Zhoukoudian are correspondingly large, the biggest measuring 245 mm in length, 217 mm in width, 83 mm in thickness, and 5040 g in weight. This specimen is at present the largest known Palaeolithic core in China.

The blanks upon which finished tools were fabricated are of several varieties including flakes produced by the three principal methods outlined above, broken flakes, small chunks of stone, pebbles, and exhausted cores. Tools retouched on flakes comprise 71.3% of the total at Zhoukoudian, while implements chipped from small chunks of raw material account for only 28.7% of the assemblage.

Typological classification of the Zhoukoudian finished tools has resulted in the establishment of six categories: scrapers, points, choppers, gravers, awls, and spheroids.

Scrapers are the most abundant tool type, comprising some 75.2% of the total, laying to rest the notion that the Zhoukoudian Early Palaeolithic industry consists principally of large core tools such as choppers and chopping tools. These small tools, mostly made on flakes, are less than 40 mm in length and weigh less than 20 g. Several types of scrapers are recognized, including straight, convex, and concave side scrapers, double-edge, end and multiple-edge scrapers. Although detailed microwear analyses have not yet been performed on this assemblage, our hypothesis is that theses small tools were employed in a variety of daily tasks, particularly the processing of animal and vegetal products such as skins, tendons, roots, tubers, and bark.

Single-edge side scrapers are the most common variety at Zhoukoudian, the

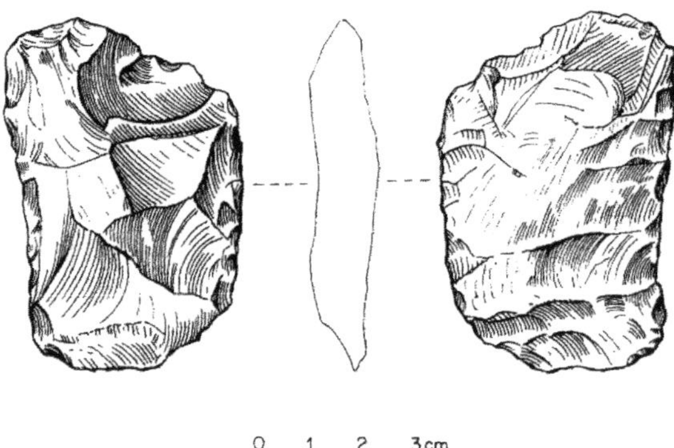

Figure 9.9 Flint scraper retouched by anvil-supported direct percussion, Zhoukoudian Locality 1, Beijing.

majority being rather crudely retouched with sinuous margins. A few exhibit careful trimming and well-proportioned, symmetrical edges, which in most cases are still sharp with edge angles ranging from 60 to 70°.

Double-edge scrapers exhibiting careful retouch outnumber the remaining categories of scraping tools. Most were fashioned by simple direct percussion and then were retouched by bipolar percussion, which in many instances produced microflake scars similar to those resulting from pressure flaking (Figure 9.9).

Points comprise about 13.7% of the Zhoukoudian Locality 1 assemblage and, like scrapers, are principally made on flakes. Almost all points measure less than 40 mm long and weigh less than 10 g; therefore, if average measurements are taken into consideration, the Zhoukoudian points are slightly smaller than the scrapers in the same assemblage. Three types of points are recognized—straight, angled, and double—of which the simple straight points are the most common, accounting for 71.9% of the total points. This artifact class also tends to exhibit finer retouching and more symmetrical plan forms. Crudely retouched irregular points are relatively scarce, even in this Early Palaeolithic context. Almost all the Zhoukoudian point were retouched by simple direct percussion, although three specimens apparently subjected to bipolar retouch have been found. Several modes of retouching are also apparent, of which unidirectional toward the dorsal surface (Figure 9.10) and inverse are the most common at Zhoukoudian.

Choppers (large unifacial artifacts fashioned on flakes, pebbles, exhausted nuclei, and miscellaneous chunks of raw material) are an important element in the Zhoukoudian Locality 1 lithic assemblage. Choppers by definition exceed 100 mm in length and most weigh more than 250 g. Irregular, roughly chipped specimens are far more common than are symmetrical pieces exhibiting refined retouch; thus the cutting edge of most choppers is sinuous and ragged. With the exception of a few specimens apparently chipped by the anvil process, most choppers were fashioned by simple direct percussion with a hard hammer. In most cases these tools were retouched on the dorsal surface by a series of unidirectional blows. A few choppers exhibit what appears to be intentional

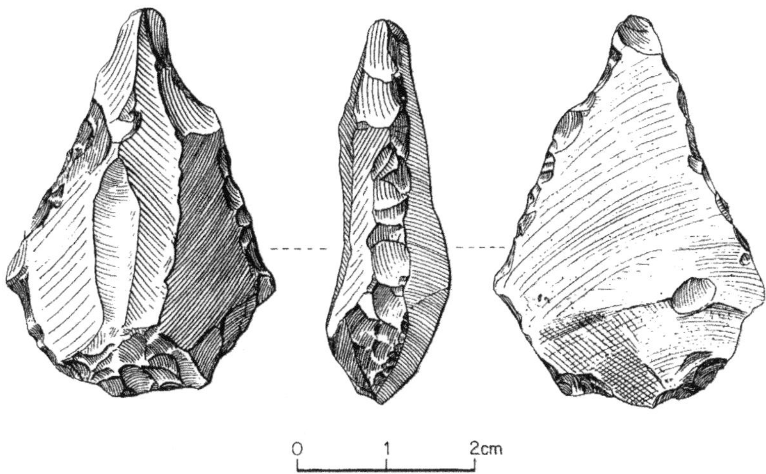

Figure 9.10 Flint point from Zhoukoudian Locality 1, Beijing.

preparation of the tool's surface to facilitate handling (i.e.. blunting of the margin opposite the working edge). The multifunctional character of these implements is attested to by the presence on some specimens of battered areas, suggesting use as a hammerstone.

Choppers are not easily divisible into standardized types, and are only roughly subdivided into single-edge, double-edge, multiple-edge (Figure 9.11), end, and pointed varieties. The function of these implements is at present a topic of intense speculation, although consensus holds that they were employed in a

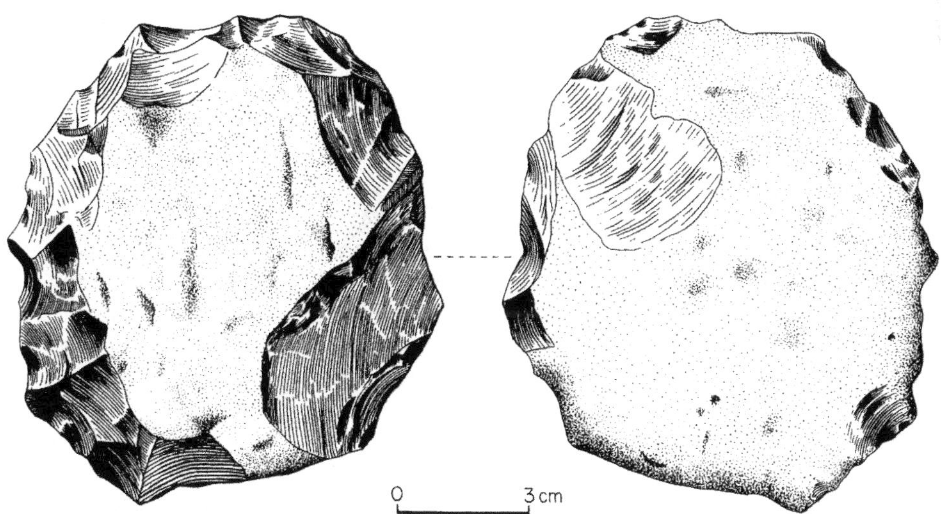

Figure 9.11 Sandstone multiple-edge or discoidal chopper from Zhoukoudian Locality 1, Beijing.

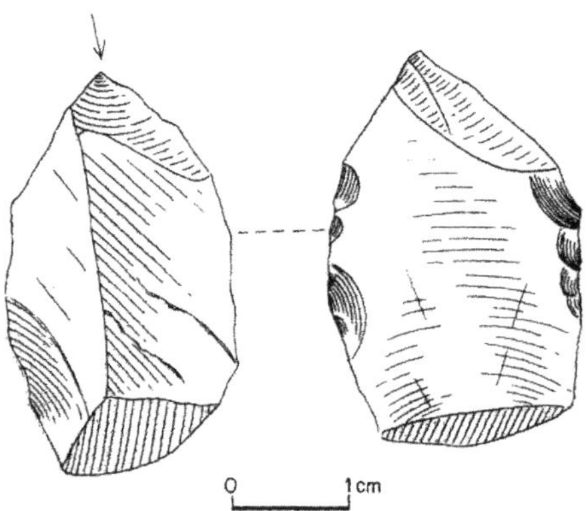

Figure 9.12 Quartz fluted graver from Zhoukoudian Locality 1, Beijing.

variety of cutting and crushing tasks and, in the case of pointed choppers, for light-duty digging.

Gravers, whose function is at present unclear, constitute 4.2% of the total tools from Zhoukoudian. These tools, which are universally fashioned on small flakes, have been recovered in most of the artifact-bearing strata in Locality 1. Three principal types of gravers are currently recognized: fluted (Figure 9.12), angle, and dihedral. The margins of most gravers are not retouched, although a few specimens exhibit minimal chipping on one or two sides. Of these latter tools those with retouching along a single margin far outnumber those with two edges retouched. These edges may be either sharp or blunt, suggesting gravers may also have been employed as scrapers and general-purpose cutting tools in addition to their principal function.

Awls, nearly always fashioned on flakes, have been found from Layer 5 to the top of the Locality 1 deposits. Awls are among the smallest recognized tool types in the Zhoukoudian assemblage. Slender shouldered-awls and short shouldered-awls are the two typological categories into which this range of artifacts may be subdivided. Awls with a slender shouldered point are carefully trimmed by heavy vertical blows producing a relatively long, sturdy point (Figure 9.13). Short shouldered-awls are roughly trimmed in comparison to those with slender points, and the flake blanks upon which these awls are made tend to be rather short and broad, as if the tools' resulting morphology is in part a response to the nature of the raw material available. These awls exhibit retouching on one end, producing a shouldered termination that is short and stout.

The last category of finished tools to be discussed is spheroids. Quartz Horizon 2 in the Gezitang and Layers 1–5 and 8–9 at Locality 1 have yielded a total of eight of these artifacts. They are characterized by a battered appearance with large and small flake scars occurring all over the artifact's surface. An angle constructed across the main flake surfaces of adjacent scars always exceeds 120°. Because this artifact class is characterized by great diversity in size, it is difficult to hypothesize a single function that could account for all the specimens known.

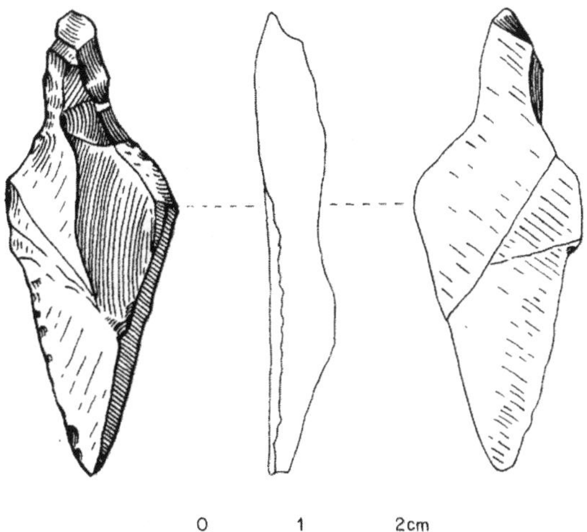

Figure 9.13 Flint slender awl from Zhoukoudian Locality 1, Beijing.

These stone spheroids undoubtedly performed a variety of pounding, hammering, and related tasks, perhaps including use as missile stones.

Large collections of basically unmodified but utilized materials have been amassed from the archaeological deposits at Zhoukoudian. Included in this category of artifacts are flakes, pebbles employed as hammerstones, and anvils. Utilized flakes constitute about 10% of the total flakes recovered at the site, and preliminary analysis suggests most of them may have functioned in a manner similar to scrapers—that is, in a variety of cutting and scraping tasks.

Nineteen stone anvils have been recovered at Zhoukoudian, each exhibiting one or more deep depressions created through use (Figure 9.14). In addition, 17

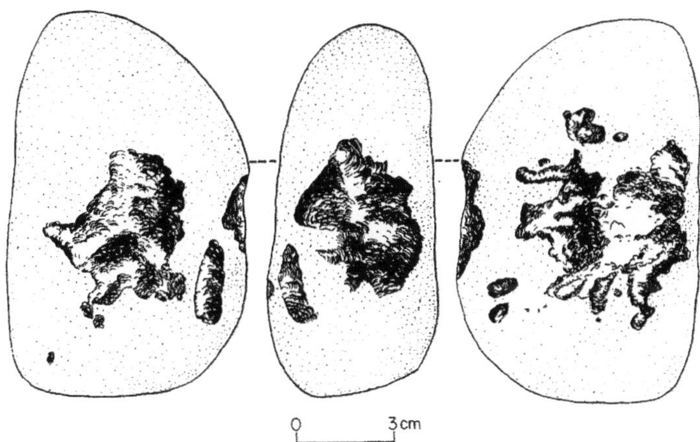

Figure 9.14 Sandstone anvil from Zhoukoudian Locality 1, Beijing.

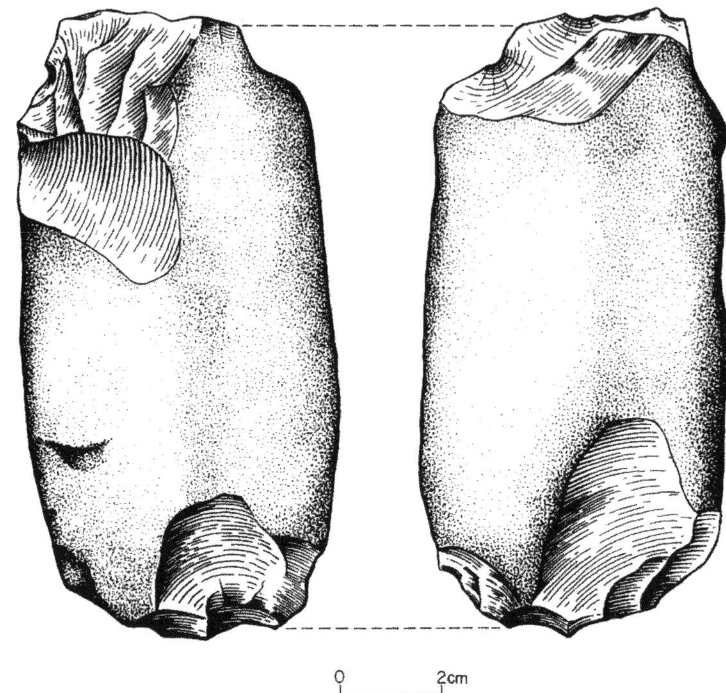

Figure 9.15 Sandstone hammerstone from Zhoukoudian Locality 1, Beijing.

hammerstones with shallow depressions employed in the bipolar process and 44 direct percussion strikers with battered areas on one or both ends have been documented at the site. Hammerstones exhibiting use damage on only one end are more numerous than those having both ends battered (Figure 9.15).

From the descriptions above, and from compiled data relating to the stratigraphic occurrence of these artifacts at Zhoukoudian, we recognize the Locality 1 *Sinanthropus* Industry as characterized by the following points:

1. The principal raw material is quartz, followed in importance by rock crystal, sandstone, and flint. Although 40 additional types of lithic raw material are recognized at Zhoukoudian, these four account for 98.1% of the total stone utilized.
2. Flakes were produced by three techniques: anvil-supported direct percussion or crushing (i.e., bipolar technique), simple direct percussion, and anvil or block-on-block. Bipolar percussion was the technique most frequently employed at Zhoukoudian, with more than 4000 flakes and cores produced by this method having been recovered. Simple direct percussion seems to have been a more important process in obtaining flakes than the anvil technique.
3. Unmodified utilized flakes constitute about 10% of the total flakes re-

covered. The abundance of these and other unmodified tools, including hammerstones of several varieties and anvils, is unique among known Early Palaeolithic sites in China.

4. Tools made on flakes exceed 71% of the total; thus we may properly classify the lithic assemblage at Locality 1 as a flake industry.
5. The assemblage of finished tools includes scrapers, points, choppers, gravers, awls, and spheroids. Scrapers are the most common tool type.
6. No true bifaces have been observed in the Zhoukoudian Early Palaeolithic collections.
7. Small tools that do not exceed 40 mm in length and 20 g in weight comprise over 70% of the total tools recovered, while large tools exceeding 60 mm in length and 50 g in weight occupy only 9 and 10.5% of the assemblage by length and weight, respectively.
8. Tools exhibiting retouch along the left edge only (when viewed dorsally) are more common than those with retouch along the right margin.
9. Retouching was accomplished by three principal methods: simple direct percussion (the most common), bipolar percussion, and anvil or block-on-block. The employment of the bipolar and anvil techniques for retouching at Zhoukoudian is unique among Chinese Early Palaeolithic sites.
10. Application of retouching techniques followed several alternate modes. Tools were most often retouched by oblique blows from a single direction, resulting in edge angles that commonly fall between 60 and 70°. Inverse retouch was also occasionally applied.
11. The *H. erectus* lithic assemblage from Zhoukoudian is diverse and difficult to classify into regular typological categories. Although most pieces recovered from Locality 1 are clearly Early Palaeolithic in character, a few resemble relatively progressive artifacts including blades, microblades, end scrapers, gravers, awls, and a single specimen that compares well with typical Late Palaeolithic Northeast Asian small wedge-shaped blade cores.
12. Most of the Locality 1 assemblage is classifiable into discrete typological categories. In a functional typological sense, the Zhoukoudian assemblage contains some interim forms that do not readily conform to either one or the other of related typological categories. Examples include distinctions between polyhedral cores and some multifaceted choppers, or between some small choppers and large scrapers. In a few cases, assigning scrapers themselves to particular taxonomic units has proven problematic.

On the basis of these specific characteristics it is possible to recognize the differences between the Early Palaeolithic Zhoukoudian assemblage and contemporary industries in Europe, Africa, and West Asia. However, some parallels in tool types and methods of fabrication may be drawn between the Zhoukoudian *Sinanthropus* Industry and Middle Pleistocene archaeological occurrences in Southeast Asia. In spite of these rather superficial similarities, enough points of divergence exist to allow us to apply the term *Sinanthropus Culture* to the archaeological assemblage from Zhoukoudian Locality 1.

On Subdivisions within *Sinanthropus* Culture

The long cycle of deposition reflected in the more-than-30-m deposits of Zhoukoudian Locality 1 has preserved a correspondingly long period of hominid occupation. Archaeological materials gathered over the course of the past 50 years of excavation at Zhoukoudian have allowed us to perceive diachronic change within the lithic assemblage at Locality 1. Our analysis suggests that the Locality 1 Early Palaeolithic industry may be divided into three temporal phases that correspond well with stratigraphic horizons in the site.

The lithic assemblage of the Early Stage occupation at Locality 1, comprising Layers 11–8, is characterized by almost exclusive dependence on quartz and sandstone as raw materials. Tools fashioned from cores, pebbles, and small chunks of stone outnumber those made on flake blanks. This assemblage is typologically simple, consisting primarily of choppers and scrapers. Points and gravers occur only rarely and are very crudely retouched. Large tools predominate, forming roughly 70% of the lithic assemblage. Choppers are common and divisible into several types, many of which appear to be rather carefully crafted. All three techniques of retouching are represented in these strata but the bipolar method occurs only infrequently. The block-on-block technique is rarely present at Zhoukoudian outside these earlier cultural layers. Typological classification is more difficult and tools that are apparently multifunctional are more common than those that seem to be task specific.

The Middle Stage of the Early Palaeolithic sequence at Zhoukoudian is best represented by Quartz Horizon 2 in the Gezitang cave (Layer 7) and by Layer 6 elsewhere in Locality 1. Quartz and rock crystal increase in frequency as raw materials, while sandstone is characterized by a dramatic decrease in utilization. The bipolar method of detaching flakes becomes more developed in these Middle Stage strata, and bipolar nuclei outnumber those fashioned through simple direct percussion for the first time in the Zhoukoudian deposits.

Regular bipolar flakes are also more numerous than those produced by simple direct percussion. The anvil technique is only rarely in evidence. In these Middle Stage deposits, flake tools predominate over core tools for the first time at Zhoukoudian, thus the Locality 1 flake industry may properly be said to begin in these Middle Pleistocene strata. Tool types appear advanced in comparison to those derived from lower strata. End scrapers are found first in these layers, and points exhibiting careful retouch increase in number and diversity while decreasing in overall size. All categories of choppers decrease in these Middle Stage deposits, including the relatively finely chipped specimens characteristic of Layers 11–8.

In all tool types there is a trend toward reduction in size, and implements that measure less than 40 mm long and weigh less than 20 g constitute over 68% of the total assemblage. Methods of retouch undergo some progress, at least in terms of efficiency, for the Middle Stage at Zhoukoudian is characterized by more tools of regularized form. Interim or multipurpose implements are not as common as in the earlier deposits, indicating the production of task-specific implements was an important aspect of tool manufacture at Zhoukoudian by this time.

The Late Stage of the Early Palaeolithic in Locality 1 is reflected in the archaeological assemblage from Layers 5 through 1. Significant technological progress, bearing witness to the evolution of *H. erectus* culture, is the most striking feature of the cultural remains associated with these strata. The morphological changes apparent in the fossils of *H. erectus* throughout the Locality 1 deposits (see Wu and Dong, Chapter 5, this volume) provide important corroborative evidence for such developments.

Vein quartz still constitutes the dominant raw material utilized in these strata, but relatively high-quality milky quartz nodules were also often used in the production of implements. Artifacts made of flint are more numerous here than in earlier deposits and are particularly abundant in contexts near the top of the Locality 1 sequence, such as at Locus H. Based on the sample of artifacts excavated at Locus H in 1966, implements of flint comprise roughly one-third of the entire assemblage.

Flake tools continue their increase in frequency, now constituting nearly three-quarters of the total, while tools made on nuclei amount to only 26.1% of the assemblage.

The bipolar technique remains the dominant method of flake production and both the quantity and quality of the derived flakes indicate this method had become a highly developed skill. Narrow bipolar flakes, some whose length is more than twice their width, are not uncommon. There is also evidence indicating large bipolar flakes were returned to the anvil where they were subsequently reduced to smaller, more regular blanks for the production of finished tools.

Stone awls appear for the first time at Zhoukoudian in these Late Stage layers, and preexisting implement types undergo diversification and increase in quantity. Points in particular become elaborately retouched, and specimens exhibiting careful trimming now constitute about 90% of the total points recovered.

One witnesses a corresponding decrease in the frequency of heavy core tools such as choppers, which, by this stage, amount to only 2.1% of the total finished implements. The trend toward reduction in size begun in the Middle Stage deposits continues in the upper strata and this assemblage is characterized by a much higher percentage of typologically classifiable, regularized tool forms. The number of multifunction tools and implements of uncertain use reaches its lowest point in the Zhoukoudian deposits here.

Simple direct percussion continues to be employed as a means of retouching implements, but the morphology of individual flake scars as well as the complete tools themselves, reflect considerable progress in the application of this technique to the raw material at hand. It is also possible that simple direct percussion had been refined through the use of a soft hammer of wood or bone by this time. By mastering such techniques of production, including the soft hammer and the use of bipolar flaking, the Late Stage inhabitants of Zhoukoudian Locality 1 succeeded in fabricating a number of regular, thin flakes, flake-blades and bipolar flakes resembling blades and even microblades.

According to biostratigraphic and magnetostratigraphic evidence, the age of Locality 1 is later than that of Lantian, Shaanxi. It is clear that the hominid occupation of Zhoukoudian began later than 700,000 years ago and the Early Stage may be tentatively said to range from 660,000 to 400,000 BP. The Middle Stage deposits are thought to be between 400,000 and 300,000 years old, while remains of the Late Stage are thought to have been deposited 300,000 to 200,000 years BP.

Jinniushan, Liaoning

The limestone–dolomite hill called Jinniushan is about 8 km south of Yingkou in southern Liaoning Provice. In the spring of 1974 three of the numerous caves and fissures that penetrate the hill were found to contain fossiliferous deposits. In the fall of the following year excavations were initiated in one such deposit on the western side of the hill (Site C, Field No. 7401C), yielding a rich assemblage of vertebrate fossils and cultural remains.

The excavated deposits were divided into six layers, of which Layers 1–3 are referred to as the *Upper Cultural Zone* and are thought to be of Late Palaeolithic antiquity. Layers 4–6, the *Lower Cultural Zone,* have produced an assemblage of Early Palaeolithic artifacts, evidence of fire utilization, and abundant mammalian fossils. Remains of Early Palaeolithic fire use consists of burned bones, stones, clay, and ash. Samples of the burned bone that have been subjected to chemical analysis have been determined to contain at least 3.1% carbon.

Cultural remains recovered from Site C at Jinniushan include a few bone flakes that may have been intentionally struck and a perforated bone, although the bulk of the assemblage consists of lithic artifacts. In addition to two problematic limestone fragments, 15 stone artifacts were recovered from the Lower Cultural Zone in Site C (Jinniushan Combined Excavation Team 1976, 1978).

Flakes were produced mainly through bipolar percussion. Elongated bipolar cores, bearing evidence of crushing on both ends, have been discovered at Jinniushan and are very similar to those from Locality 1 at Zhoukoudian. Only one triangular quartz flake, clearly produced by simple direct percussion, was found at the site. This specimen is characterized by a very clear point of percussion and a relatively small but convex bulb. Two long, shallow scars formed by the removal of previous flakes appear on its dorsal surface.

Eight finished tools have been recovered from Site C at Jinniushan, including six scrapers, one point, and one graver. All the scrapers discovered thus far are flake tools and may be subdivided into three categories: single-edge side

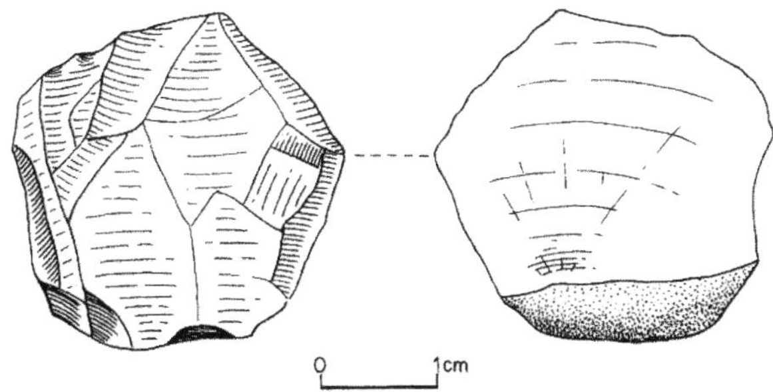

Figure 9.16 Quartz semicircular end scraper from Jinniushan, Liaoning.

scrapers, double-edge side scrapers, and semicircular end scrapers. Although the available sample is very small, it also appears that the single-edge specimens are characterized by straight, convex, and concave subtypes. All single-edge scrapers were roughly retouched on their dorsal surfaces, producing a very sinuous cutting margin with edge angles ranging from 60 to 84°.

Only one double-edge side scraper has been discovered thus far at Jinniushan and, although it has been retouched from many directions, most flake scars appear on the dorsal surface. The edge angles of the two retouched margins are 52 and 72°.

The semicircular end scrapers exhibit relatively careful retouch on their dorsal surfaces (Figure 9.16). The working edge of the tool is much more carefully chipped than are the other margins, and the edge angles of these specimens range from 59 to 75°.

The Jinniushan point, made on a small block of quartz, has a rather blunt working end, while the fluted graver from the site is typical of many recovered in Early Palaeolithic contexts elsewhere in China.

Based on the limited sample of artifacts presently available, we have reached the following conclusions in regard to the Jinniushan Site C Early Palaeolithic assemblage:

1. Flakes were produced mainly by bipolar percussion.
2. The Jinniushan Industry is fashioned principally on small flakes measuring less than 40 mm in length.
3. The assemblage of finished tools is dominated by scrapers.
4. Most tools were retouched by simple direct percussion onto the dorsal surfaces of the implements.

These features are similar in many respects to the Early Palaeolithic assemblage from Zhoukoudian Locality 1 and demonstrate a close relationship between the two sites.

Biostratigraphic evidence indicates the Lower Cultural Zone of Site C at Jinniushan is comparable to the Late Stage cycle of sedimentation at Locality 1 (Jinniushan Combined Excavation Team 1976). The Middle Pleistocene fauna of Liaoning was virtually identical to contemporaneous fossil vertebrate assemblages known elsewhere in North China.

Generally speaking, it appears that the Middle Pleistocene climate of southern Liaoning was warmer and moister than at present and supported a vegetational mosaic including forest and steppe components, a situation not encountered in the Jinniushan vicinity today.

Guanyindong, Guizhou

The Guanyindong (Guanyin Cave) is in Qianxi County, Guizhou Province, and was initially explored during the winter of 1964. The following year, excavations under the leadership of Pei Wenzhong uncovered a stratified sequence of Palaeolithic materials in the site's red clay beds. Subsequent excavations conducted in 1972 and 1973 added to the previously collected lithic remains, producing a total of 3000 artifacts, of which 2323 have been studied in detail by Li and Wen (1978).

Layers 2–8 are the artifact-bearing strata in the Guanyindong. Layer 2 is a red clay bed. Layers 3–7 consist of fossiliferous breccia deposits that are distinguished on the basis of variation in color, consolidation, and size of enclosed limestone blocks. A few artifacts were found on the surface of Layer 8.

Following the terminology proposed by Li and Wen (1978), the artifacts from the red clay beds (Layer 2) are referred to as *Late Stage Guanyindong Culture*, while artifacts derived from the remaining strata are ascribed to the Early Stage.

Given the preliminary nature of the investigations in the Guanyindong, much more research must be conducted before the exact chronological relationships among these strata are properly understood. Only those materials from Layers 3–8 are addressed here. On the basis of macroscopic study, the Guanyindong Early Stage industry is based on black and gray flint and related cryptocrystalline siliceous stones as raw materials. Sandstone, quartz, and a variety of local igneous rocks were also occasionally used in the production of artifacts. In all cases, lithic raw materials seem to have come from deposits, including weathered limestone surfaces, within 2 km of the site.

Hundreds of polyhedral and single-platform cores are known from the site, most of which exceed 100 mm in length and are irregularly shaped. The single platform cores are frequently very simple in execution with striking platforms initiated directly on the cortex surfaces of flint nodules. The polyhedral cores are characterized by a multitude of striking platforms, only a few of which bear any indication of intentional preparation. The morphology of the cores and resulting flakes suggest that simple direct percussion with a hard hammer was the principal means of reducing nuclei.

Although our collection of flakes from the Early stage deposits in the Guanyindong is not large, a few preliminary generalizations can be put forth. Most flakes are small, ranging from 30 to 50 mm in length, although a few exceeding 100 mm are known. Most flakes are irregular; however, triangular, trapezoidal, and bladelike forms are reported. A few flakes exhibiting large, oblique striking platforms and an angle between the ventral surface and the striking platform

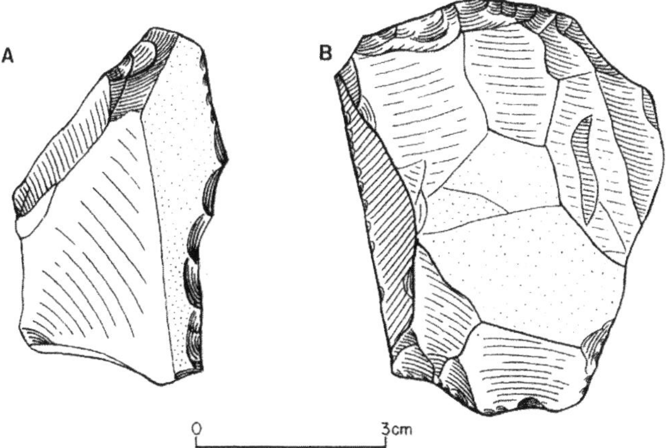

Figure 9.17 Flint implements from Guanyindong, Guizhou: A, concave side scraper; B, end scraper.

exceeding 120° have been found and are thought to have been struck by the anvil or block-on-block technique.

Tools were fabricated principally on simple direct percussion flakes, although a few implements were made on exhausted cores or small chunks of flint. Pebble tools are very rare in the Guanyindong assemblage.

Four types of implements are recognized from the Early Stage strata: scrapers, points, choppers, and gravers. Scrapers comprise roughly 80% of the assemblage and may be subdivided into single- and double-edge side scrapers, end scrapers, and multiple-edge scrapers, the last of which being most numerous. All are small flake tools measuring less than 50 mm long in most cases. All specimens appear to have been retouched by simple direct percussion from many directions resulting in mostly irregular plan forms (Figure 9.17).

Points, including both straight (Figure 9.18) and angled varieties, constitute about 5% of the lithic assemblage; straight points are by far the most common. All examples exhibit rather careful retouch, some having been trimmed on both sides producing biconvex or oblique edges. A few points bear fine retouching on one side and coarse on the other, producing two distinctive working margins. Some points have been retouched by repeated blows to form a relatively long working edge. These specimens are quite similar to many Early Palaeolithic awls (Figure 9.19A), including some with relatively short, stout points (Figure 9.19B). In most cases, the edge angle of the points from these layers exceeds 80°.

Choppers fashioned on nuclei or large flakes comprise about 6% of the total tools. Choppers with multiple edges outnumber those with a single cutting margin. Most multiple-edge choppers still retain at least one unmodified margin, presumably for use as a handle (Figure 9.20). Some implements fashioned on large flakes have had their striking platforms removed by retouching (Figure 9.21), and in all cases choppers are characterized by sinuous cutting margins

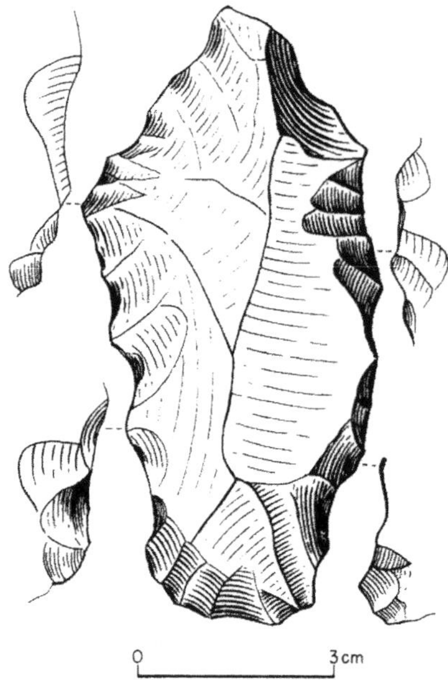

Figure 9.18 Flint straight point trimmed from multiple directions, Guanyindong, Guizhou.

with edge angles often exceeding 80° as a result of their production by simple direct percussion with a hard hammer.

The Guanyindong assemblage includes both angle and fluted gravers that, in addition to their principal working margins, exhibit retouched sides, suggesting these tools may have been employed both as scrapers and as gravers. Unfortunately, the sample of gravers thus far discovered in the Guanyindong is too small to permit detailed interpretation.

General characteristics of the Guanyindong assemblage may be summarized as follows:

1. Flakes seem to have been produced only through simple direct percussion with a hard hammer. Occasional flakes apparently struck by the anvil technique are thought to be accidental.
2. Most of the flakes and cores are irregular. A few flakes bear minimally prepared striking platforms and most cores do not appear to have been prepared prior to reduction. Polyhedral cores outnumber those with a single striking platform.
3. Unretouched utilized flakes are very rare.
4. Most tools are made on small flakes.
5. The proportion of finished tools is relatively high—about 60% of the entire assemblage. Such a high percentage of tools is unique among known Early Palaeolithic cultures in China.
6. The assemblage is typologically simple, with scrapers the most commonly occurring tool type. Points, choppers, and gravers are also reported, but in much smaller quantities.

7. The morphology of the tools varies considerably within each type, and irregular implements are common.
8. Implements with multiple working edges are more common than those with single edges.
9. All specimens were retouched by simple direct percussion with a hard hammer. Application of blows to the tool's surface were directed from a single direction, multiple directions, inversely, or alternately. The predominance of blows directed from multiple directions accounts for the irregular character of most implements.
10. The margins of most tools are relatively blunt with edge angles generally exceeding 80°. Simple direct percussion retouch, utilizing perpendicular or near-perpendicular blows has produced ragged, sinuous cutting edges

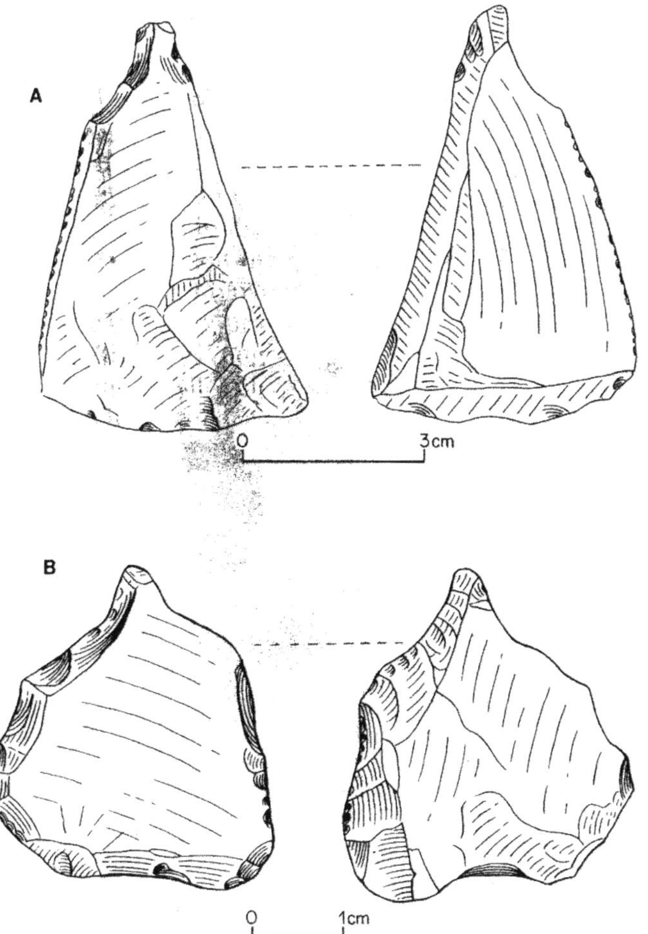

Figure 9.19 Flint points from Guanyindong, Guizhou: A, awl-like point with elongated tip; B, awl-like point with short tip.

in most cases. Very few implements exhibit the small, shallow, parallel flake scars indicative of careful trimming.

11. All categories of tools are characterized by repeated superimposed retouch.

The assemblage of cultural remains from the Guanyindong, Guizhou, has provided prehistorians with a unique glimpse into the Early Palaeolithic of an area previously considered of only marginal significance during the Middle Pleistocene.

As Pei Wenzhong and his colleagues have pointed out (1965), Chinese scholars are faced with a new problem in the study of Palaeolithic archaeology. Taking the Guanyindong as an example, it is likely the abundant caverns of South China will produce evidence of a new cultural tradition, similar in some respects to contemporary traditions in North China but differing significantly from those now thought characteristic of the European Palaeolithic.

New evidence of Early Palaeolithic human activity, seemingly related to the remains in Guanyindong, have already begun to come to light. For example, near the southern shore of the Caohai in Weining County, Guizhou, the Wangjiayuanzi site has recently been found to contain an artifact assemblage similar in many respects to that from Guanyindong (Wu Maolin *et al.* 1983). This is also true of small collections of artifacts from localities scattered across South China, but overall these assemblages contain many elements that do not appear related to the Early Stage artifacts from the Guanyindong, suggesting South China may have been characterized in the Pleistocene by a florescence of Palaeolithic cultures whose general features and local characteristics we are only just beginning to understand (Wu Maolin *et al.* 1983; Zhang 1983).

In spite of regional diversification these southern Chinese sites nonetheless conform in many respects to a generalized Chinese Palaeolithic tradition, as is suggested by parallels that may be drawn between sites such as Guanyindong

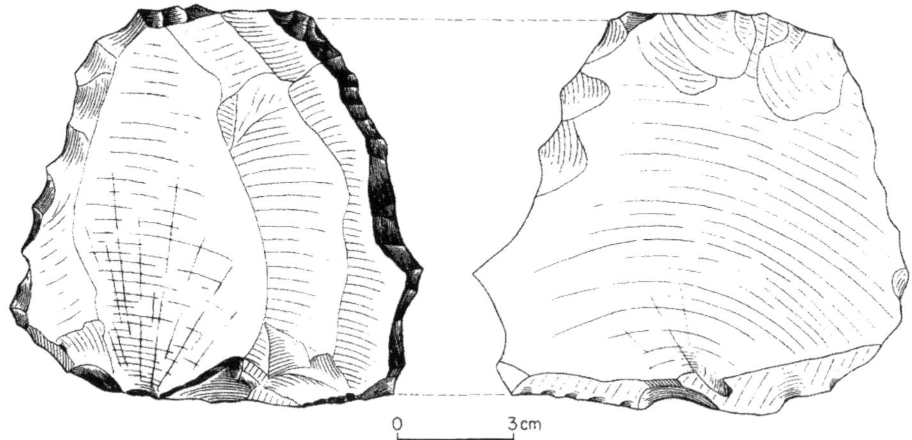

Figure 9.20 Flint multiple-edge chopper from Guanyindong, Guizhou.

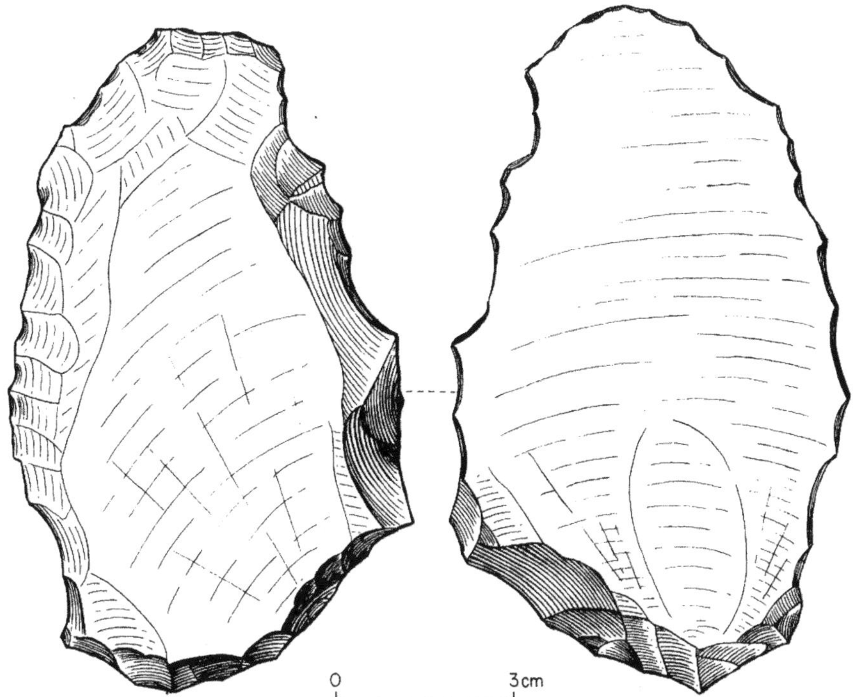

Figure 9.21 Flint multiple-edge chopper from Guanyindong, Guizhou.

and Zhoukoudian Locality 1. For example, both sites are characterized by flakes and cores that are mostly irregular, and specimens with prepared striking platforms are very rare. Polyhedral cores outnumber those with single platforms. Both sites have produced flake industries with scrapers as the dominant tool type. Both industries also contain choppers, points, and gravers, although specific percentages of each implement type vary between the sites. In spite of these broad similarities, it is possible to observe significant points of divergence between these two major Palaeolithic industries, as is summarized in Table 9.1. On the basis of these similarities and contrasts we believe the Early Stage Guanyindong Culture reflects cultural developments that parallel those in North China during the Middle Pleistocene.

The assemblage of mammalian fossils excavated from Layers 3–7 in the Guanyindong belong to a typical Middle–Upper Pleistocene *Ailuropoda–Stegodon* fauna. Lithostratigraphic data are also ambiguous as to the specific period of deposition of these sediments. We are now suggesting a late Middle Pleistocene antiquity for the Early Stage Guanyindong materials principally on typological grounds and also due to the relative stratigraphic position of the finds.

Faunal remains indicate the palaeoenvironment of the Guanyindong area during the period of its occupation was somewhat warmer than at present, and the

Table 9.1
CONTRASTS BETWEEN GUANYINDONG AND ZHOUKOUDIAN LOCALITY 1

Guanyindong Culture: Early Stage	*Sinanthropus* Culture: Zhoukoudian Locality 1
1. Flakes produced mainly by simple direct percussion.	Flakes produced by several methods, with the bipolar technique being most common.
2. Tools with multiple working edges outnumber those with a single edge.	Single-edge tools outnumber those with multiple working edges.
3. Tools were retouched only by simple direct percussion.	Tools were retouched by simple direct percussion, the bipolar technique, and the anvil or block-on-block technique.
4. The working edges of tools are rather blunt due to trimming by near vertical blows. Edge angles usually exceed 80°.	Tools generally trimmed by oblique blows producing relatively sharp edges. Edge angles range between 60 and 70°.
5. Fabricating tools such as hammerstones and anvils have not yet been discovered.	Fabricating tools are well represented.

recovery of such forms as *Elephas*, *Rhinoceros*, and *Tapirus* suggest we may properly consider this environment subtropical or even tropical.

Today, the eroded karst landscape near Guanyindong is nearly devoid of larger shrubs and trees, although the source of a river is nearby. The Middle Pleistocene vegetational community seems to have included grassland, deciduous forest, and bamboo components, all of which are attested to by the recovery of abundant faunal remains valuable as environmental indicators.

Shilongtou, Hubei

The cave site of Shilongtou is on a hill about 30 km west of Daye, between the Yangzi River and Dayi Lake, at an elevation of about 50 m above sea level.

The site was discovered in the winter of 1971 during levee construction that, unfortunately, seriously damaged the artifact-bearing strata in the site before their significance was recognized.

The surviving deposits are divided into three layers: an Upper Layer consisting of 0.5 to 1.5 m of light-brown clay, sands, and weathered limestone containing no fossils or artifacts; a Middle Layer comprising 0.3–1 m of yellow and brown sand and clay, containing blocks of limestone, flint, and quartzite, which has yielded most of the Shilongtou artifacts and fossils; and a Lower Layer 0.3–1 m thick containing reddish-brown clay and several stalactitic lenses with few fossils and artifacts.

The Lower and Middle Layers appear virtually identical in enclosed vertebrate fossils and Palaeolithic artifacts; thus the original investigators consider the two units to be roughly contemporaneous (Li *et al.* 1974).

A total of 88 artifacts were mostly collected *in situ* from the middle layer, fashioned principally from quartzite although quartz and sandstone implements are also known. The 38 cores discovered in the site account for 38.6% of the total artifacts recovered. Most of them bear only a single striking platform with flakes removed from one side or one end. A few irregular polyhedral cores have also been found. In most cases these cores still retain considerable pebble cortex (Figure 9.22A). All the nuclei thus far discovered have been produced by simple direct percussion, and angles between striking platforms and worked surfaces usually approximate 90°. A close examination of these cores and their derived flakes leaves the impression that raw material was not efficiently utilized in this Early Palaeolithic context.

The 27 flakes thus far discovered at Shilongtou constitute 30.7% of the total artifacts, and all seem to have been removed from their nuclei by simple direct

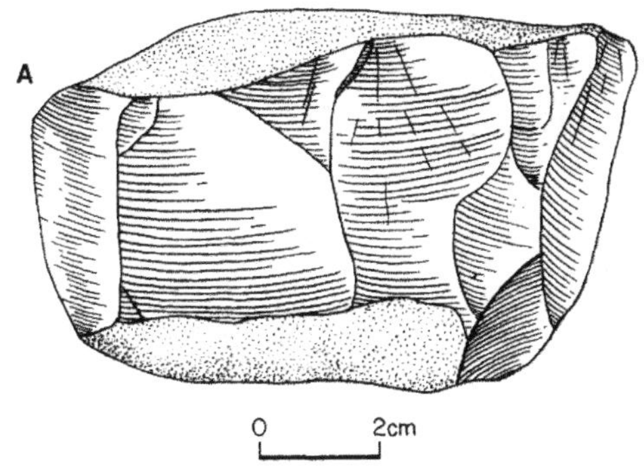

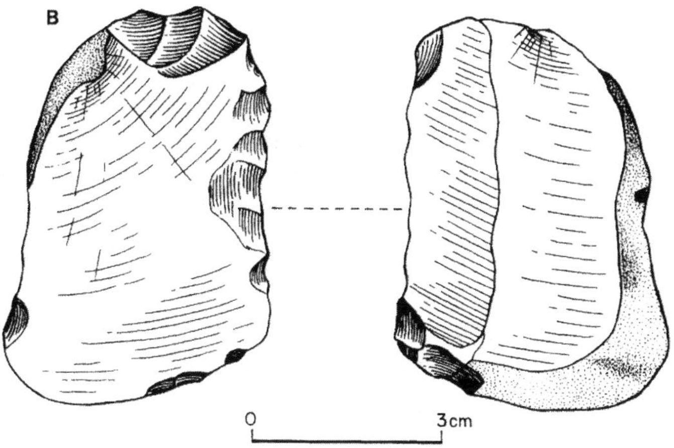

Figure 9.22 Quartzite artifacts from Shilongtou, Hubei: A, core with single striking platform on cortex; B, flake retaining cortex.

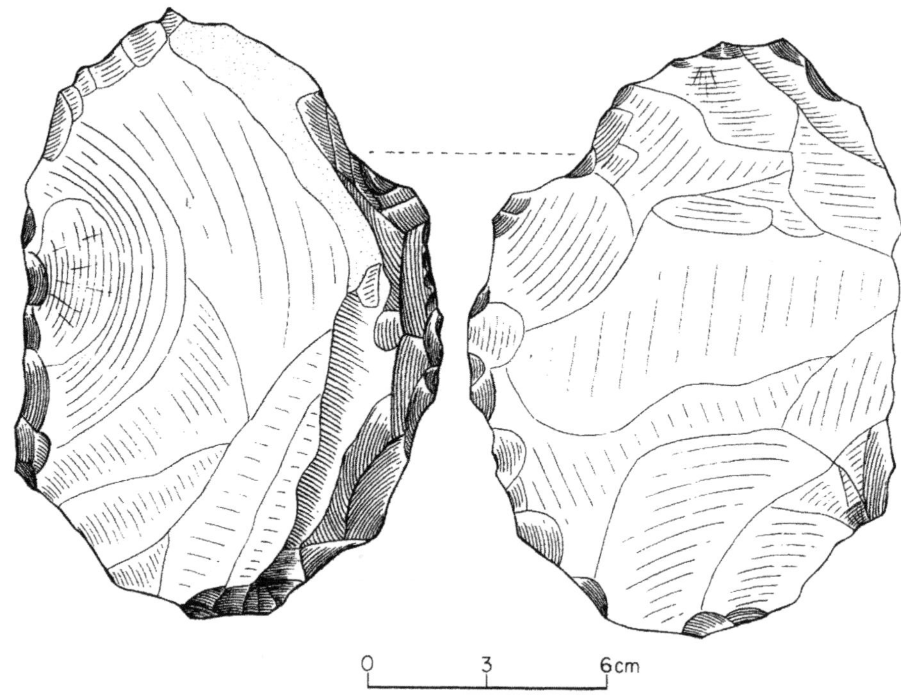

Figure 9.23 Quartzite multiple-edge chopper from Shilongtou, Hubei.

percussion. In most cases these are flakes whose lengths exceed their widths and that are commonly 40–70 mm long. Most specimens exhibit a striking platform on cortex and an angle between the striking platform and the ventral surface of 90 to 125°. Varying amounts of cortex remain on th dorsal surfaces of these flakes and several irregular flake scars are often present (Figure 9.22B).

Twenty-seven finished tools, consisting of choppers and scrapers, were collected in the lower and middle strata at Shilongtou. Core tools account for a little more than half of the assemblage (14 pieces), although this is not statistically significant. Seventeen choppers have been identified, of which only four are flake tools, the remaining 13 having been fashioned on nuclei. Most of these choppers measure between 140 and 150 mm in length and none are less than 80 mm long. Their thickness ranges from 60 to 70 mm. These choppers are principally unifacial, although a few bifacial examples ("chopping tools") do occur. All are characterized by relatively rough retouch producing blunt, sinuous margins. Single-edge implements include both convex and concave varieties. The multiple-edge choppers (Figure 9.23) vary considerably in morphology and include discoidal, end, and complex varieties.

Ten scrapers, of which nine are flake tools and one is fashioned on a small chunk of raw material, have thus far been identified at Shilongtou. These implements are relatively large, ranging from 50 to 90 mm in length, 50 to 70 mm in width, and 15 to 30 mm in thickness. Scrapers with a short, wide body are one of the most characteristic tool types of the Shilongtou Industry. Generally, these scrapers were crudely retouched from many directions, producing blunt, sinuous cutting edges. One specimen, a straight side scraper, was initially shaped by heavy multidirectional blows and subsequently was trimmed by the application of careful blows onto the ventral surface. In addition to this specimen, five convex side scrapers and four multiple-edge scrapers, of which one may be classified as semicircular (Figure 9.24), have also been recovered.

General features of the Shilongtou assemblage may be summarized as follows:

1. Most nuclei and flakes are irregular and were produced by simple direct percussion. Most flakes exhibit striking platforms on cortex, and no specimens with prepared platforms have been observed.
2. Core tools and flake tools occur in roughly equal proportions, although this generalization is based on a very limited sample.
3. Recognized formal tool types include only choppers and scrapers and it is occasionally difficult to distinguish between these categories. The high proportion of choppers in the Shilongtou Industry (about 63% of the total tools) places it second only to Dingcun, Shanxi, in North China in this regard. Surface collections from the Baise Basin in Guangxi also contain a high percentage of choppers but the Shilongtou collection is unique in South China in having been found in a stratified context.
4. Tools with multiple working edges are more common than those with a single edge.
5. As a result of rough trimming, the working margins of these tools are relatively sinuous and blunt.

The overall impression one receives is that the Shilongtou assemblage reflects a stage of technological evolution somewhat less advanced than that in evidence

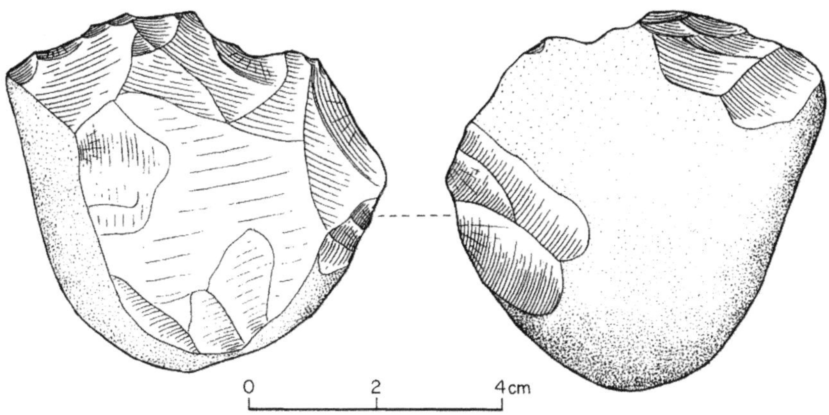

Figure 9.24 Quartzite semicircular end scraper from Shilongtou, Hubei.

at Guanyindong. This situation may reflect the original nature of the assemblage, although it must be remembered that taphonomic factors resulting from the partial destruction of the site may have removed smaller, more carefully prepared implements from the deposits.

Both the Guanyindong and Shilongtou assemblages contain flakes produced and retouched by simple direct percussion blows from many directions. In addition, both feature a predominance of tools with multiple edges.

Points of divergence between these two collections include the fact that the Shilongtou artifacts are generally larger than those found in the Guanyindong. The Guanyindong assemblage is characterized by greater typological diversity than that from Shilongtou, the former being dominated by various types of scrapers and the latter by choppers.

Chronometric dates have not thus far been forthcoming from Shilongtou, but the original investigators concluded that the site is contemporaneous with or slightly later than the deposits in Locality 1 at Zhoukoudian (Li *et al.* 1974). Based on typology alone it is not possible to determine unequivocally the age of this site because of the limited number of specimens collected thus far. Palaeontological evidence indicates a Middle–Upper Pleistocene antiquity for the site, which has yielded an *Ailuropoda–Stegodon* fauna (see Chapter 15, this volume).

Recent investigations suggest that the consolidated condition of the deposits and the composition of the faunal assemblage at Shilongtou strongly resemble those from the site of Changyang, also in Hubei. Because the Changyang locality has produced remains of early *H. sapiens,* it is possible that both of these sites are younger than the *Sinanthropus* deposits at Zhoukoudian and that Shilongtou is not as early as the original estimates indicated.

Discussion and Conclusions

On the basis of data collected thus far, a tentative chronological sequence of China's Early Palaeolithic localities can now be proposed.

The Gongwangling locality, near Lantian, Shaanxi, is the earliest unequivocal archaeological site in China. A series of 27 localities in the Lantian vicinity, including the Pingliang site, have produced artifacts that are typologically equivalent to those at Gongwangling, although the age of these occurrences is not yet known.

Locality 1 at Zhoukoudian, Beijing, preserves a long sequence of strata bearing archaeological remains younger than those at Gongwangling. Artifacts recovered from Zhoukoudian Locality 13 and Chenjiawo, Lantian, Shaanxi, may be correlated with the earlier deposits at Locality 1. The Early Palaeolithic remains from Jinniushan, Liaoning, and Nanhaiyu, Shanxi, are probably equivalent in age to the upper deposits in Locality 1. Kehe, Shanxi Locality 6054 is probably of the same antiquity as Zhoukoudian Locality 1. The Guanyindong, Guizhou, assemblage is thought to be younger than the Locality 1 sequence.

Approximately 30 additional sites scattered across Henan, Shanxi, and Shaanxi have yielded archaeological remains of Early Palaeolithic character (Jia *et al.*

1961), although this interpretation is by no means definite. For example. sites such as Zhangjiawan in Tongguan County, Shaanxi, and Shuigou and Huixinggou in Sanmenxia County, Henan, are classified as Early Palaeolithic due to their geological context and to cultural materials recovered from the sites.

Other localities, including Shilongtou, Hubei, are not definitely associated with Middle Pleistocene deposits nor are their cultural assemblages clearly of Early Palaeolithic antiquity. Such sites may ultimately prove to be Middle Palaeolithic.

The specific character of these Chinese Early Palaeolithic industries, such as the frequent occurrence of very small tools, distinguishes them from contemporary traditions elsewhere in the Old World, although broad similarities may nonetheless be detected. These industries are based principally on flakes, with a variety of scrapers being the most common tool type. Although choppers and some large bifacially flaked implements are known to occur, the Chinese Early Palaeolithic is not typified by the handaxes and cleavers so common in Acheulean industries of the western Old World.

At present we see the sites of Guanyindong and Zhoukoudian Locality 1 as southern and northern variants, respectively, of a common Chinese Early Palaeolithic tradition based on the use of small flakes. The degree to which these industries influenced cultural developments later in the Pleistocene is a matter of current debate in China, but it seems clear that in North China the cultural patterns established at Zhoukoudian in the Middle Pleistocene continued to have an effect on the subsequent florescence of later Quaternary human activities in the region.

Many tool types and methods of fabrication first detected in the *H. erectus*—bearing strata at Zhoukoudian persist into Middle and Late Palaeolithic contexts in China. The bipolar technique in particular, although most common during the Early Palaeolithic, may be viewed as a traditional aspect of Chinese Palaeolithic culture, occurring in the archaeological record up through the close of the Pleistocene. The technological competence with which this approach to stoneworking was executed underwent considerable progress as well.

Although cultural development was very slow during the Early Palaeolithic, Chinese prehistorians now have at their disposal sufficient quantities of data to begin to detect change within this immense temporal frame of reference. In specific terms we can witness the origin, florescence, and eventual abandonment of the anvil or block-on-block method of flake production while simple direct percussion continued to develop. Flakes and nuclei gradually became more regularized through time, as did the hammers used to produce them. Beginning with simple natural elongated pebbles, the Palaeolithic inhabitants of China eventually began to use more specialized strikers and finally batons of bone and wood for the production of more regularized flakes. Flake tools increase dramatically in relation to core tools during the Chinese Early Palaeolithic, while tool types similarly increase in variety and regularity.

Specific implement types may be seen to have undergone diachronic change as well. Scrapers, for example, tend to become smaller through time and to exhibit increasingly regular, finely retouched margins. The absolute number of points associated with any particular Early Palaeolithic assemblage in China also increased and they gradually became more refined. Choppers seem to have followed an opposite course of development in that they became demonstrably less sophisticated throughout the Early Palaeolithic and their absolute number also decreased. Presumably this is a result of their eclipse by smaller, more efficient task-specific implements.

Simple direct percussion persists throughout the Palaeolithic as the principal means of retouching artifacts, although some of the specific techniques employed, such as alternating retouch, disappear from most later Palaeolithic contexts. The modification of flakes in general became more efficient through time, and tools exhibiting a symmetrical plan form, shallow flake scars, and regular edges eventually dominate the collections.

The ability to use and control fire, one of the most important developments of the Early Palaeolithic, is attested to by the discovery of massive quantities of burned stone, bones, clay, and ash in the *H. erectus* occupation levels at Zhoukoudian, especially in the upper strata such as Layers 3 and 4.

These combined data clearly refute the idea that the Early Palaeolithic of China is monotonous and nonprogressive (Teilhard 1941). Movius (1949) proposed the idea that southern and eastern Asian Palaeolithic industries were best ascribed to a Chopper–Chopping Tool Tradition that was characterized by a lack of large bifacial implements (i.e., handaxes). Movius's notion placed too much emphasis on the importance of choppers in Chinese Palaeolithic assemblages and virtually ignored the overwhelming abundance of small flake tools, especially scrapers. At Zhoukoudian, choppers only amount to 1.85% of the total artifacts recovered, or 5.4% of the retouched tools. At Guanyindong, choppers comprise only 6% of the total implements unearthed. Finally, large bifacial implements, albeit relatively few, are known from a number of localities in East Asia, including China, thus bringing Movius's interpretation seriously into question.

Concomitant with the development of all the palaeoanthropological sciences in China, we hope to continue to make contributions to the understanding of past human behavior by continued field and laboratory analyses of China's Early Palaeolithic archaeological record.

References

Black, Davidson

1931 Evidences of the use of fire by *Sinanthropus*. *Bulletin of the Geological Society of China* 11(2):107–108.

Black, Davidson, P. Teilhard de Chardin, Yang Zhongjian (C. C. Young), and Pei Wenzhong (Pei Wen-chung)

1933 Fossil man in China. *Memoirs of the Geological Survey of China*, Series A 11:1–166.

Chaney, Ralph and Lyman Daugherty

1933 The occurrence of *Cercis* associated with remains of *Sinanthropus*. *Bulletin of the Geological Society of China* 12(3):323–328.

Dai Erjian
1966 The paleoliths found at Lantian Man locality of Gongwangling and its vicinity. *Vertebrata PalAsiatica* 10(1):30–34.
Dai Erjian and Xu Chunhua
1973 New finds of palaeoliths from Lantien. *Acta Archaeologica Sinica* 2:1–12.
Gai Pei and You Yuzhu
1976 Some characters of palaeolithic artifacts in Lantian, Shaanxi. *Vertebrata PalAsiatica* 14(3):198–203.
Huang Weiwen
1964 On a collection of palaeoliths from Sanmen area in western Honan. *Vertebrata PalAsiatica* 8(2):162–181.
Jia Lanpo (Chia Lan-po)
1959 Report on the excavation of *Sinanthropus* site in 1958. *Gu Jizhuidongwu yu Gu Renlei (Palaeovertebrata et Palaeoanthropologia)* 1(1):21–26.
Jia Lanpo (Chia Lan-po), Gai Pei, and Huang Weiwen
1966 The palaeoliths of the Lantian, Shaanxi region. In *Shaanxi Lantian Xinshengjie Xianchang Huiyi Lunwenji (Symposium on the Lantian Cenozoic of Shaanxi Province)*. Beijing: Science Press. Pp. 151–156.
Jia Lanpo (Chia Lan-po), Wang Zeyi, and Qiu Zhonglang
1961 Palaeoliths of Shansi. *Memoirs of the Institute of Vertebrate Palaeontology and Palaeoanthropology*, Series A 4:1–48.
Jia Lanpo (Chia Lan-po), Wang Zeyi, and Wang Jian (Wang Chien)
1962 Kóho: An Early Palaeolithic site in south-western Shansi. *Memoirs of the Institute of Vertebrate Palaeontology and Palaeoanthropology*, Series A 5:1–40.
Jinniushan Combined Excavation Team
1976 New material of Pleistocene mammalian fossils in Jinniushan from Yingkou, Liaoning province and their significance. *Vertebrata PalAsiatica* 14(2):120–127.
1978 A preliminary study of Palaeolithic artifacts of Jinniushan, Yingkou, Liaoning. *Vertebrata PalAsiatica* 16(2):129–136.
Li Yanxian and Wen Benheng
1978 The discovery and significance of the Guanyindong Palaeolithic culture, Qianxi, Guizhou. In *Gurenlei Lunwenji (Collected Papers of Palaeoanthropology)*, edited by the Institute of Vertebrate Palaeontology and Palaeoanthropology, Chinese Academy of Sciences. Beijing: Science Press. Pp. 77–93.
Li Yanxian, Yuan Zhenxin, Dong Xingren, and Li Tianyuan
1974 Report on the excavation of a Palaeolithic station known as Shilongtou at Daye, Hubei. *Vertebrata PalAsiatica* 12(2):139–157.
Movius, Hallam L., Jr.
1949 The Lower Palaeolithic cultures of southern and eastern Asia. *Transactions of the American Philosophical Society* 38(4):329–420.
Pei Wenzhong (Pei Wen-chung)
1931 Notice of the discovery of quartz and other stone artifacts in the Lower Pleistocene hominid-bearing sediments of the Choukoutien cave deposit. *Bulletin of the Geological Society of China* 11(2):109–146.
Pei Wenzhong (Pei Wenzhong), Yuan Zhenxin, Lin Yipu, Zhang Yinyun, Cao Zetian
1965 Discovery of Palaeolithic chert artifacts in Kuan-yin-tung Cave in Ch'ien-Hsi-hsien of Kweichow province. *Vertebrata PalAsiatica* 9(3):270–279.
Pei Wenzhong (Pei Wen-chung) and Zhang Senshui
n.d. Investigation of *Sinanthropus* artifacts. Beijing: Science Press. In press.
Teilhard de Chardin, Pierre
1941 Early man in China. *Institut de Géo-Biologie, Publication* 7:1–99.
Teilhard de Chardin, P. and Pei Wenzhong (Pei Wen-chung)
1932 The lithic industry of the *Sinanthropus* deposits in Choukoutien. *Bulletin of the Geological Society of China* 11(4):315–364.

1941 The fossil mammals from Locality 13 of Choukoutien. *Palaeontologia Sinica,* New Series C 11:1–118.

Wang Zeyi, Qiu Zhonglang, and Bi Chuzhen

1959 Report on the excavation of a Palaeolithic site from Nanhai-yu, Yuan-chu, Shansi. *Gu Jizhuidongwu yu Gu Renlei (Palaeovertebrata et Palaeoanthropologia)* 1(2):88–91.

Wu Maolin, Zhang Senshui, and Lin Shuji

1983 New discovery of the Palaeoliths in Guizhou province. *Acta Anthropologica Sinica* 2(4):320–330.

Zhang Senshui

1962 Some problems concerning the *Sinanthropus* Industry of Choukoutien. *Vertebrata Pal-Asiatica* 6(3):270–279.

1983 New discoveries in Guizhou and their significance to Chinese Palaeolithic archaeology. *Guiyang Shiyuan (Shehui Kexue Ban) Xuebao* 3:15–24.

10

The Middle Palaeolithic of China

QIU ZHONGLANG

Introduction

In the past the so-called Ordos Culture of Inner Mongolia was considered to be the type Middle Palaeolithic assemblage for North China, but the discovery of a perforated ornament at Shuidonggou in the Ningxia Hui Autonomous Region, within the Ordos sphere of distribution, resulted in the reinterpretation of the Ordos Culture as Late Palaeolithic (Qiu and Li 1978).

During the 1950s a series of discoveries in the vicinity of Dingcun in the Fen River valley of Shanxi supplanted the Ordos assemblages as North China's characteristic Middle Palaeolithic industry. However, in the past 25 years the discovery of a number of additional Middle Palaeolithic localities has refined and amplified our view of this stage of technological development.

The most significant of China's currently recognized Middle Palaeolithic sites also include Jiangjiawan and Sigoukou, Gansu; Xujiayao, Shanxi; Dali and Yaotougou, Shaanxi; Gezidong, Liaoning; and Tongzi, Guizhou. In addition, the assemblage of cultural remains excavated in Locality 15 at Zhoukoudian near Beijing, originally thought to be of Early Palaeolithic antiquity (Pei 1938), has, on the basis of archaeological and biostratigraphic evidence, been reclassified as Middle Palaeolithic. Table 10.1 summarizes the current state of our understanding of associated human fossils and artifactual assemblages that are considered Middle Palaeolithic.

In North China the Middle Palaeolithic is largely synchronous with the early Upper Pleistocene, a fact corroborated principally on biostratigraphic grounds. Characteristic Tertiary and Lower Pleistocene forms are essentially absent in

Palaeoanthropology and
Palaeolithic Archaeology in the
People's Republic of China

ISBN 0-12-601720-4

Table 10.1

PRINCIPAL MIDDLE PALAEOLITHIC SITES AND EARLY *HOMO SAPIENS* FOSSIL LOCALITIES IN CHINA

Site	Hominid fossils	Principal artifacts	Depositional context	Age (Pleistocene)	References
Zhoukoudian, Locality 15	None	Nuclei and flakes, hammerstones, choppers, scrapers, points, gravers	Cave	Middle–Upper	Pei 1938
Zhoukoudian, Locality 4	Tooth	Utilized bones, flakes	Cave	Middle–Upper	Gu 1978; Pei 1939
Zhoukoudian, Locality 22	None	Nuclei, flakes, scrapers	Cave	Upper	Zhang 1963
Xujiayao, Shanxi	Parietal, occipitals, maxillae, mandible, teeth	Nuclei, flakes, scrapers, points, spheroids, gravers, anvils, choppers, bone artifacts	Lacustrine	Upper	Jia and Wei 1976; Jia *et al.* 1979; Wu Maolin 1980
Dingcun, Shanxi	Teeth, parietal	Nuclei, flakes, choppers, scrapers, heavy trihedral points, spheroids, protobifaces	Fluviolacustrine	Upper	Movius 1956; Pei *et al.* 1958; Wu 1976
Nanliang, Shanxi	None	Nuclei, flakes	Fluviolacustrine	Upper	Wang *et al.* 1959
Licunxigou, Shanxi	None	Nuclei, flakes, scrapers, choppers, points, spheroids	Fluviolacustrine	Upper	Jia 1959
Huoxian, Shanxi	None	Nuclei, flakes, scrapers, heavy trihedral points, spheroids	Fluvial	Upper	Wang 1965

Fanjiazhuang, Shanxi	None	Nuclei, flakes, scrapers, points, choppers	Mostly surface finds	Upper	Jia and Wang 1957
Hougedafeng, Shanxi	None	Nuclei, flakes, scrapers, points, choppers	Fluviolacustrine	Upper	Jia *et al*. 1961
Pingding and Shouyang, Shanxi	None	Scrapers, points, choppers	Open air (loess)	Upper	Jia *et al*. 1961
Gezidong, Liaoning	None	Nuclei, flakes, scrapers, choppers, points	Cave	Upper	Gezidong Excavation Team 1975
Laochihegou, Lantian, Shaanxi	Humerus	Nuclei, flakes, scrapers, points, choppers	Fluviolacustrine	Upper	Dai 1966
Yaotougou, Shaanxi	Teeth	Nuclei, flakes, choppers, scrapers, points	Fluviolacustrine	Upper	Gai and Huang 1982
Dali, Shaanxi	Cranium	Nuclei, flakes, scrapers, points, gravers, awls.	Fluvial	Middle–Upper	Wu and You 1979, 1980
Jiangjiawan, Gansu	None	Nuclei, flakes, scrapers, choppers, spheroids	Fluciolacustrine	Upper	Xie and Zhang 1977
Sigoukou, Gansu	None	Nuclei, flakes, scrapers, points, spheroids	Fluviolacustrine	Upper	Xie and Zhang 1977
Guojiuyan, Changyang, Hubei	Calvarium	None	Fluviolacustrine	Upper	Li 1981
Longdong, Changyang, Hubei	Maxilla, teeth	None	Cave	Upper	Jia 1957
Maba, Guangdong	Cranium	None	Cave	Upper	Wu and Peng 1959
Tongzi, Guizhou	Teeth	Nuclei, flakes, scrapers	Cave	Upper	Wu *et al*. 1975

these contexts, and typical Middle Pleistocene species such as *Sinomegaceros pachyosteus* and *Equus sanmeniensis* are greatly diminished, while new species including *Equus przewalskyi*, *E. hemionus*, *Bos primigenius*, *Cervus* (*Elaphus*) *canadensis*, and *Megaloceros ordosianus* appear for the first time. In South China a generalized *Ailuropoda–Stegodon* fauna persisted into the early Upper Pleistocene and only minor fluctuations in species content have been detected at sites dating to this period.

Chronometric dates for the Chinese Middle Palaeolithic are scarce, as they are everywhere for this difficult period of time. In comparison with the Early and Late Palaeolithic sequences of China, Middle Palaeolithic remains are still under-represented, but sufficient localities are now known to indicate that no single Middle Palaeolithic site may be viewed as typical of even such a relatively homogeneous zone as early Upper Pleistocene North China.

Following are detailed descriptions of China's most thoroughly investigated Middle Palaeolithic localities, which should serve to emphasize the diversity of these archaeological assemblages.

Principal Middle Palaeolithic Sites

Dingcun, Shanxi

In the spring of 1953 stone artifacts were uncovered during excavation of sand for construction near Dingcun, Xiangfen County, Shanxi. Scientific investigations conducted the following year resulted in the identification of 10 localities scattered along a 15-km stretch of the east bank of the Fen River (Localities 54.90, 54.93–100, and 54.102). Three fossil human teeth were initially unearthed at Locality 54.100 (Pei *et al.* 1958) and in 1976 a human parietal was also recovered (Wu 1976).

Geological conditions at all 10 of the principal Dingcun localities are similar, and for the purpose of discussion we may take the section exposed at Locality 54.98 as typical. The upper member is a 4.5-m thick deposit of sandy loess. This unit is underlain by a 0.6-m thick gravel lense that caps a series of cross-bedded sands and gravels of undetermined depth. The 1954 excavations penetrated to a

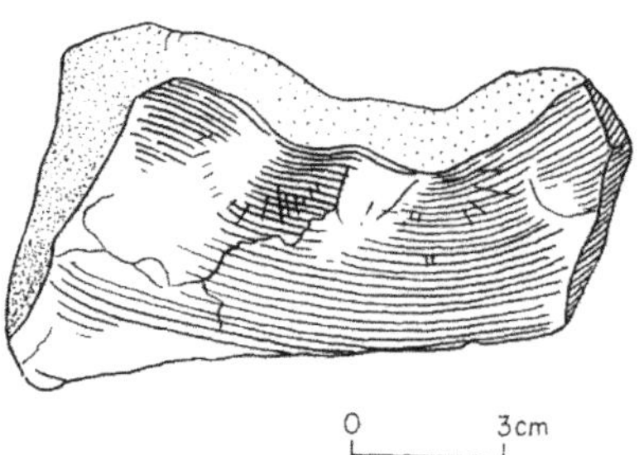

Figure 10.1 Hornfels flake made by the block-on-block technique, exhibiting twin bulbs of percussion, from Dingcun, Shanxi.

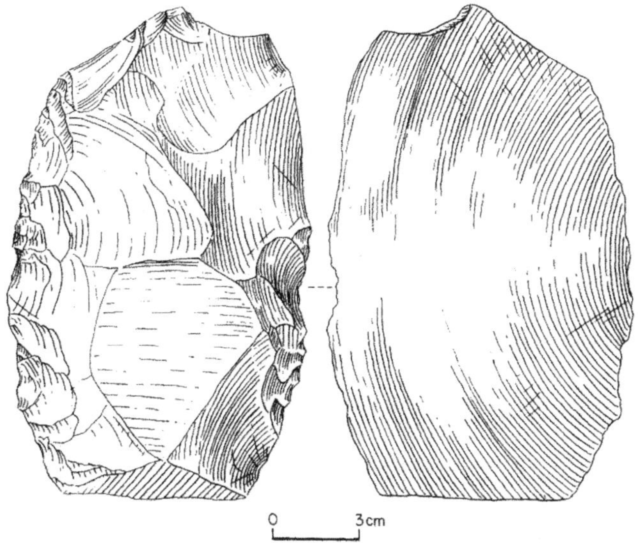

Figure 10.2 Hornfels chopper from Dingcun, Shanxi.

depth of 4 m, yielding fossils and cultural remains in both the middle and lower layers. A total of 2005 artifacts were collected in 1954, including surface finds. Over 94% of the tools are fashioned from dark hornfels while the remaining minority were made of chert, limestone, basalt, and quartzite.

Observation and experimental replication indicate the early Upper Pleistocene inhabitants of Dingcun used the simple direct percussion, anvil-supported direct percussion, and throwing techniques in the production of flakes. Flakes fashioned through anvil-supported direct percussion are the most common at Dingcun, being characteristically very broad with oblique striking platforms and a platform angle generally in excess of 110°. These specimens possess obvious bulbs and many flakes exhibit double points of percussion (Figure 10.1). Both large and small nuclei produced by these three techniques have been recovered, the small cores being particularly varied with cubic, polyhedral, and conical forms present. The polyhedral nuclei exhibit signs of flake removal using both simple and anvil-supported direct percussion.

Most of the Dingcun assemblage consists of flake tools; less than one-third of the finished implements were fashioned on nuclei. The most common tool types include choppers, heavy and light points, and scrapers. A total of 32 unifacial choppers made on large flakes were recovered that are characterized by either single or multiple working edges (Figure 10.2). Eleven heavy points from Dingcun were fashioned on thick flakes and exhibit retouch from the ventral to the dorsal side along two edges. No alternating retouch has been observed on these specimens. These heavy points, which may be typologically classified into trihedral and picklike forms, are considered index fossils of the Dingcun Middle Palaeolithic (Figures 10.3 and 10.4). Five smaller points were chipped from thin

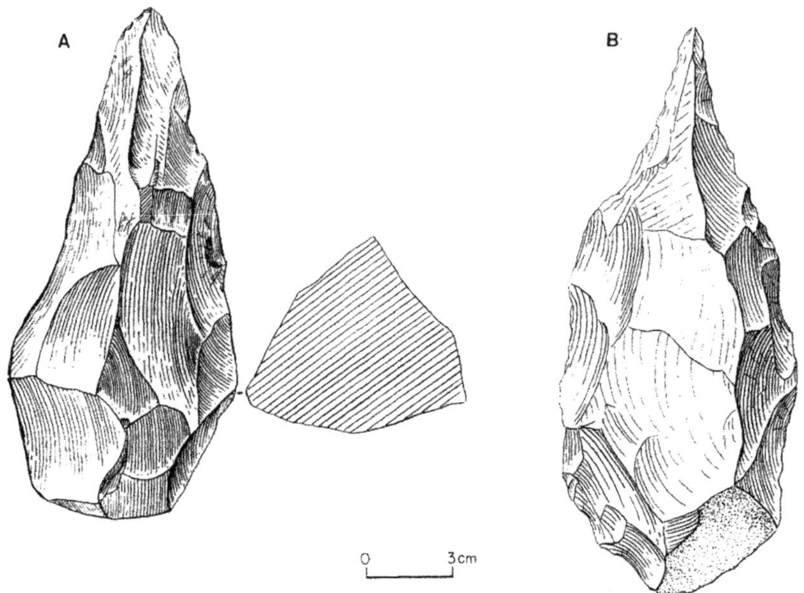

Figure 10.3 Two heavy trihedral points in hornfels, from Dingcun, Shanxi.

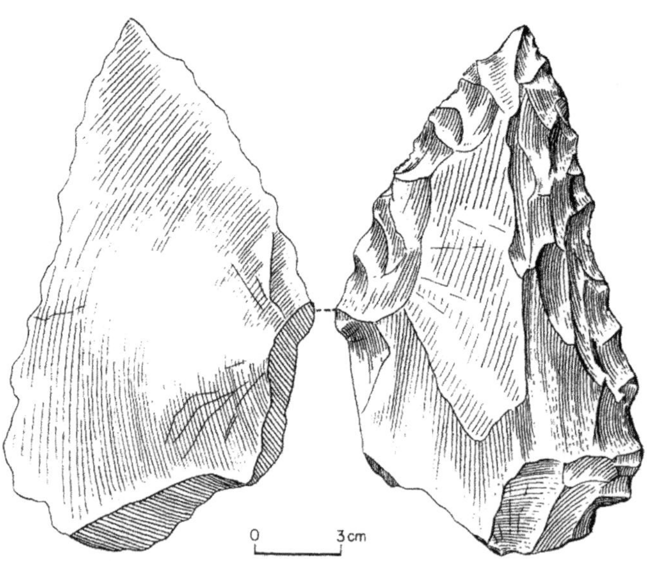

Figure 10.4 Unifacially flaked heavy trihedral point made on a large hornfels flake, from Dingcun, Shanxi.

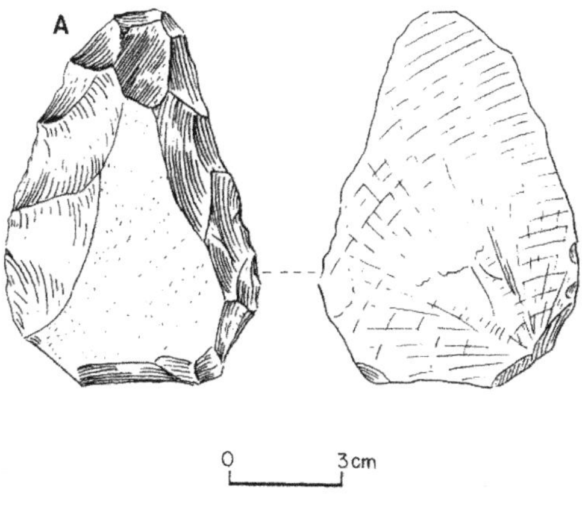

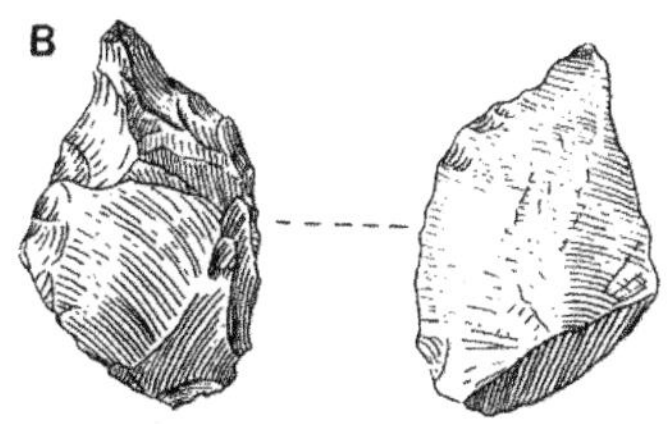

Figure 10.5 Two small points made on hornfels flakes, from Dingcun, Shanxi.

flakes (Figure 10.5) and are also characterized by retouching from their ventral to dorsal surfaces. A large number of end scrapers were also found at Dingcun, although only 10 specimens possess secondary retouch.

Core tools include bifacial chopping tools, handaxe-like implements, and missile stones or spheroids. The 18 bifacially flaked chopping tools from Dingcun are subdivided according to whether they possess single or multiple working edges (Figure 10.6). The handaxe-like implement is unfortunately a surface find (Figure 10.7) and, although it does not typologically resemble anything found in later lithic assemblages in the region, this enigmatic piece cannot with complete confidence be associated with the Middle Palaeolithic Dingcun Industry. A number of stone spheroids were discovered at Dingcun, ranging from 1500 to 200 g in weight. Although the function of these artifacts is unclear, they are presumed to be missiles and are found at many Palaeolithic localities in North China.

In comparison with earlier Palaeolithic assemblages, the Dingcun Industry exhibits a number of relatively progressive features. For example, some of the points display careful, even trimming and many of the unmodified flakes recovered at the site are highly regularized in form. The assemblage as a whole permits distinct typological classification in contradistinction to earlier Chinese Palaeolithic industries, although the Dingcun stone tools also seem to retain some of the technological traditions of their predecessors. These surving traits include the dominance of flake tools in the industry, the prevalence of unifacial retouching, and the common occurrence of points within the assemblage of finished tools.

Most of the fundamental tool types of the Chinese Palaeolithic were in evidence by the Early Palaeolithic, although they of course became more refined through time. By examining these shared characteristics it is possible to trace the developmental relationships among such early Palaeolithic assemblages as Lantian and Kehe and the Middle Palaeolithic Dingcun Industry (Qiu and Li 1978).

Biostratigraphic evidence suggested to the sites' original investigators that the majority of the Dingcun localities were of Middle Pleistocene antiquity, but Movius (1956) and Pei and his colleagues (1958) later revised this estimate to the Upper Pleistocene. It should be noted that there is still no universal agreement on the absolute antiquity of the Dingcun localities. Many of the fossil vertebrates recovered suggest an earlier period of deposition for many of the Dingcun localities. In addition, investigations in recent years have indicated that the artifacts unearthed in the Dingcun vicinity are not all of Middle Palaeolithic antiquity. Rather, Early, Middle, and Late Palaeolithic cultural remains all seem to be present.

Archaeological assemblages that conform to a series of technological and typological traits that we may label Dingcun Culture are widely distributed in the Fen River area. On the lower reaches of the river, the sites of Licunxigou in Quwo County (Jia *et al.* 1961) and Nanliang in Houma (Wang *et al.* 1959) have produced Dingcun Culture assemblages. The middle course of the Fen River has yielded similar materials at Fanjiazhuang in Jiaocheng County (Jia and Wang 1957) and Gujiao in Taiyuan (Jia *et al.* 1961). The Chengfeng Mountain site, on the upper reaches of the Fen River (Jia *et al.* 1961), has also produced archaeological remains very similar to those discovered at Dingcun.

On the basis of our investigations, it seems clear that Middle Palaeolithic assemblages related to those originally described from Dingcun are distributed

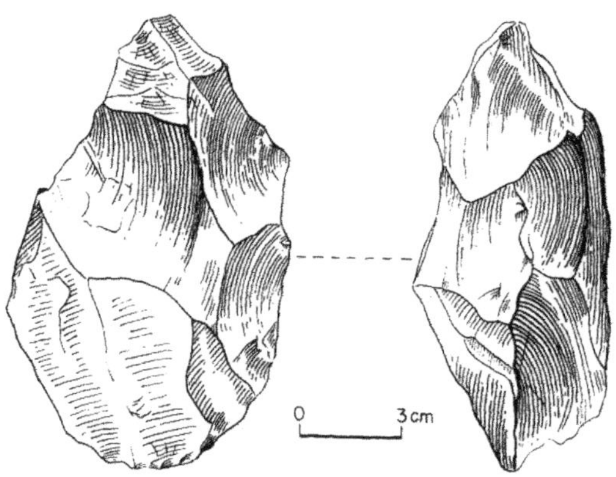

Figure 10.6 Chopping tool or protobiface of hornfels, from Dingcun, Shanxi.

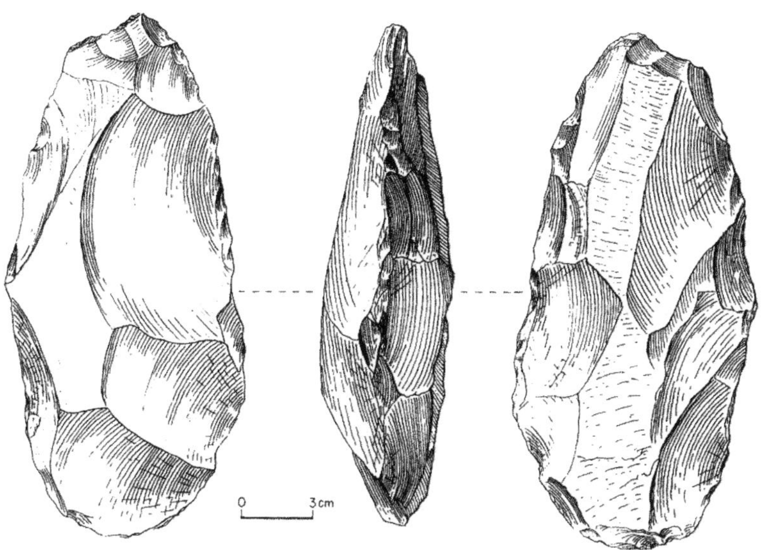

Figure 10.7 Large hornfels biface collected on the surface, Dingcun, Shanxi.

throughout the Fen River valley in Shanxi. Continued field studies will, it is hoped, allow us to refine our understanding of the dynamics and development of the Dingcun Culture.

Yaotougou, Shaanxi

Discovered in 1972, the Yaotougou site is located near the town of Changwu on the middle course of the Wei River in Shaanxi Province. The lithic assemblage was found enclosed in gray sandy clay and gravels beneath a thick loess deposit in association with fossil remains of *Myospalax* sp. indet., *Equus* cf. *przewalskyi*, *E. hemionus*, *Coelodonta* sp. indet., *Sinomegaceros* sp. indet., *Cervus* (*Pseudaxis*) sp. indet., and Bovidae gen. et sp. indet. The biostratigraphic data indicate an early Upper Pleistocene age for the Yaotougou assemblage (Gai and Huang 1982).

The artifacts discovered at the site thus far include 40 nuclei, 120 unmodified flakes, 2 points, 11 scrapers, and 3 choppers of quartz or quartzite, in addition to 10 nuclei and 35 flakes of flint. The nuclei include polyhedral, pebble, and tabular varieties and the resulting flakes are also varied with rectangular, triangular, and broad irregular specimens present, some of which retain pebble cortex. One triangular flake exhibits a retouched platform and a dorsal surface bearing the scars of two previously removed flakes, one triangular (Figure 10.8) and one rectangular.

Scrapers, which constitute the majority of the Yaotougou assemblage, are coarsely retouched, their plan form having been largely predetermined by the shape of the flakes on which they were fabricated. Although small in number, the Yaotougou points are finely crafted. These points are triangular in cross-

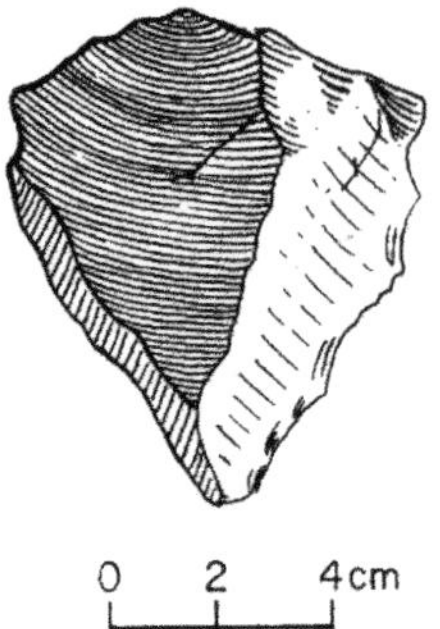

Figure 10.8 Triangular quartzite flake from Yaotougou, Shaanxi.

section and exhibit abrupt retouch near their points. This retouch is generally quite invasive, while trimming scars are quite small, yielding an edge angle of about 69°. The bases of these points are retouched to produce an intentionally round, blunt margin (Figures 10.9 and 10.10).

Gai and Huang (1982) have included the Yaotougou assemblage with those from Hougedafeng, Shanxi; Jujiayuan and Luofangzi, Gansu; Laochihegou, Shaanxi; and Mengcun, Henan, in a larger tradition, the Jing–Wei Culture. The purpose here is to contrast the Middle Palaeolithic industries of the Fen River

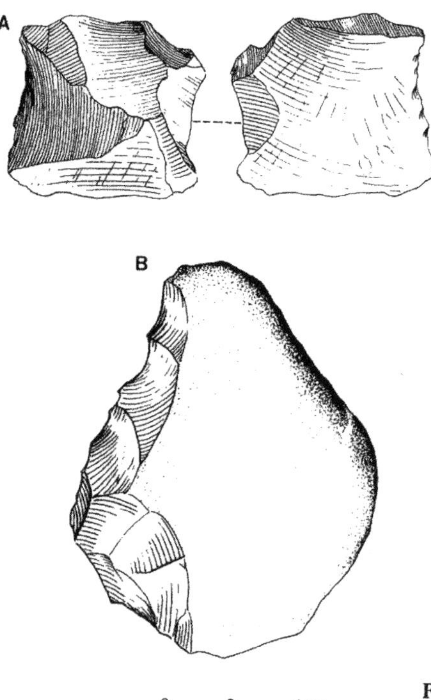

Figure 10.9 Quartzite artifacts from Yaotougou, Shaanxi: A, hard hammer flake; B, pebble chopper.

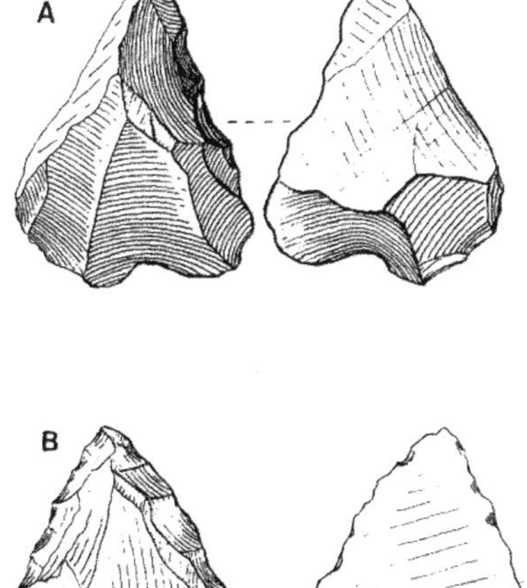

Figure 10.10 Quartzite implements from Yaotougou, Shaanxi: A, small side scraper; B, unifacial point.

valley with those of the Jing and Wei river valleys. In the opinion of Gai and Huang (1982) the Late Palaeolithic materials from Shuidonggou, Ningxia, show closer affinities to the Jing–Wei Culture than they do to the Dingcun assemblage. The implication here is that China may have been characterized by a number of Middle Palaeolithic traditions, each of which contributed to the formation and development of Late Palaeolithic culture in various areas.

Jiangjiawan and Sigoukou, Gansu

The Jiangjiawan site is on the west bank of the Bajiazhui Reservoir, 18 km west of Xifengzhen in Zhenyuan County, Gansu. Stone artifacts were originally reported from this locality in 1965 and additional investigations in 1974 produced tools in association with vertebrate fossils.

The uppermost stratigraphic unit at the site consists of a 5-m-thick deposit of brownish-red fine sand and clay. The artifacts were recovered from a greenish-gray sand and clay bed immediately underlying this deposit.

The related site of Sigoukou is located at Longyagua near Gougoucun at the confluence of the Pu and Ru rivers about 20 km from the Jiangjiawan locality. The Sigoukou stratigraphic section is identical to that at Jiangjiawan and artifacts were also found here in a greenish-gray sand and clay bed.

The vertebrate fossils recovered in association with artifacts at both sites in-

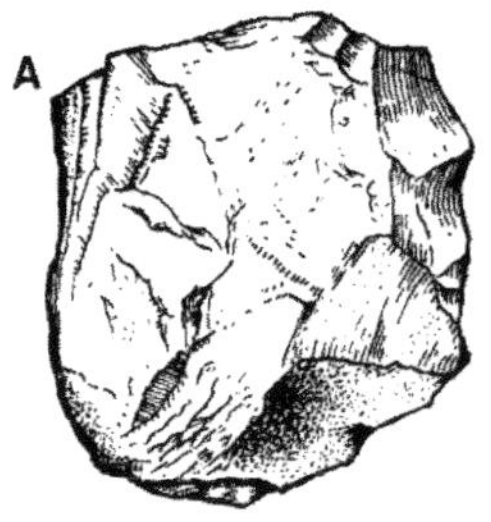

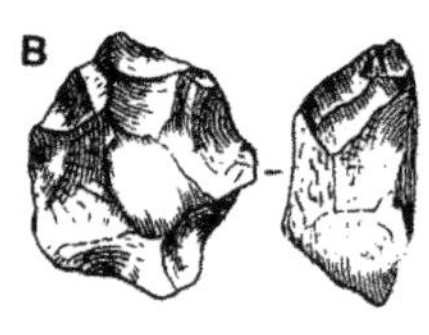

Figure 10.11 Artifacts from Zhenyuan County, Gansu: A, chopper of igneous rock; B, chert discoidal tool; C, quartzite point-scraper.

clude *Coelodonta antiquitatis, Equus* cf. *przewalskyi,* and *Sinomegaceros* sp. indet. Biostratigraphic and typological evidence both suggest the Jiangjiawan and Sigoukou assemblages are younger than the Middle Pleistocene deposits at Zhoukoudian Locality 1 and yet antedate the Late Palaeolithic materials from the Sjara-osso-gol (Salawusu) Valley in Inner Mongolia (Xie and Zhang 1977).

Thirty-nine stone artifacts were recovered at Jiangjiawan: 10 nuclei, 4 flakes, 3 choppers, 17 scrapers, 1 spheroid, and 4 pitted stones. All the flakes seem to have been produced by simple direct percussion without the benefit of platform preparation. The choppers were uniformly flaked onto their dorsal surfaces and some still retain substantial pebble cortex. The coarsely retouched scrapers are varied in form including discoidal, multiple-edge, convex, straight, and concave varieties (Figure 10.11).

The nine stone artifacts recovered from Sigoukou include nuclei, flakes, discoidal and convex scrapers, points, spheroids, and several unclassifiable pieces. Being largely similar to those recovered from Jiangjiawan, the Sigoukou artifacts exhibit rather crude trimming.

Xujiayao, Shanxi

The Xujiayao site is on Gucheng People's Commune in Yanggao County, Shanxi. Excavations have been concentrated along the bluffs bordering Liyi Gully about 1 km southeast of Xujiayao Village, which falls under the administrative jurisdiction of Yangyuan County, Hebei. Excavations conducted in 1974, 1976, and 1977 yielded over 14,000 stone and bone artifacts, vertebrate fossils, and the remains of more than 10 individual humans in a yellowish-green clay lacustrine deposit more than 8 m below present ground surface (Jia *et al.*

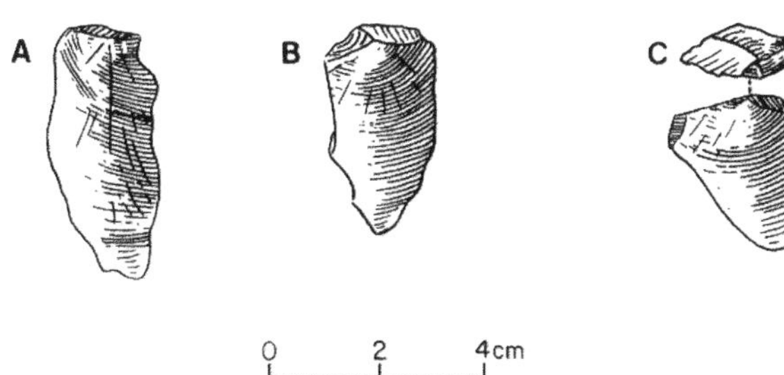

Figure 10.12 Artifacts from Xujiayao, Shanxi: A, simple platform flake of igneous rock; B, faceted platform flake of igneous rock; C, chert prepared platform flake.

1979). The human fossils are thought to be those of early *Homo sapiens* (Wu 1980) and several age classes are represented.

The stone artifacts unearthed at Xujiayao in 1974 and 1976 are generally quite small, having been fashioned on a variety of raw materials including vein quartz, chert, agate, quartzite, metamorphic limestone, and other siliceous and igneous rocks. Both simple direct percussion and anvil-supported direct percussion, including the bipolar technique, were used to produce flakes. Most of the Xujiayao flakes are irregular, some exhibiting trimmed and prepared platforms while others retain cortex platforms (Figure 10.12). Unfortunately, none of the Xujiayao nuclei discovered thus far bear clearly prepared striking platforms. Discoidal, protoprismatic, and funnel-shaped cores are present (Figure 10.13), and it is thought that the discoidal and protoprismatic forms may be the antecedents of China's Late Palaeolithic cylindrical and conical nuclei (Jia *et al.* 1979). Only a few bipolar flakes were recovered, but they are very similar to those found in Early Palaeolithic contexts in Zhoukoudian Locality 1, attesting to the

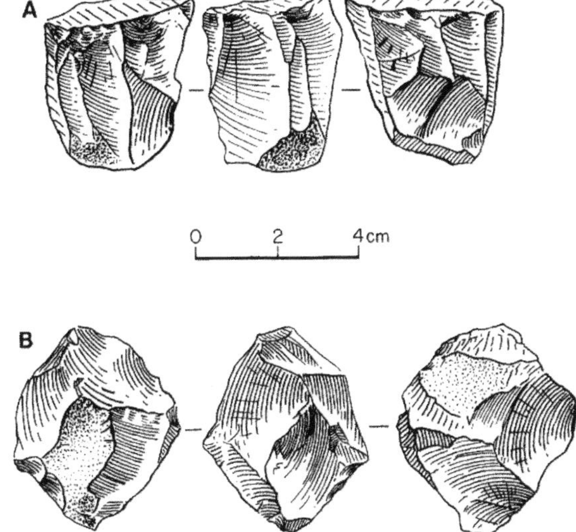

Figure 10.13 Chert nuclei from Xujiayao, Shanxi: A, protoprismatic nucleus; B, discoidal nucleus.

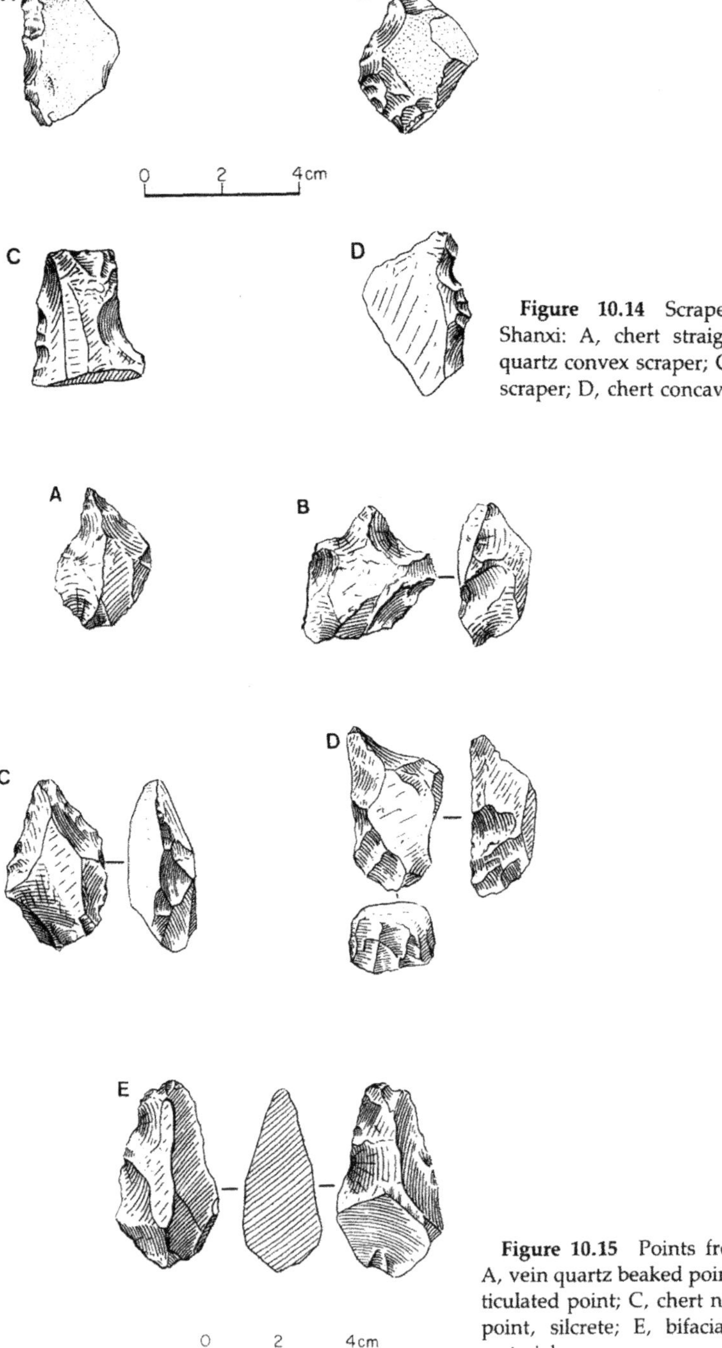

Figure 10.14 Scrapers from Xujiayao, Shanxi: A, chert straight scraper; B, vein quartz convex scraper; C, chert double-edge scraper; D, chert concave scraper.

Figure 10.15 Points from Xujiayao, Shanxi: A, vein quartz beaked point; B, vein quartz denticulated point; C, chert nosed point; D, keeled point, silcrete; E, bifacial point of uncertain material.

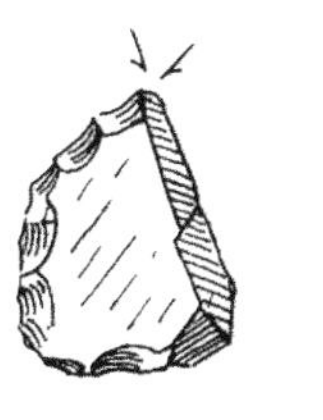

Figure 10.16 Vein quartz dihedral graver from Xujiayao, Shanxi.

persistence of this fabrication technique and the developmental relationship among Palaeolithic cultures in North China.

Stone tools exhibiting secondary retouch account for just over 50% of the Xujiayao assemblage, and finished tools include scrapers, points, anvils, gravers, choppers, spheroids, and multiple-function implements. Scrapers were the most commonly encountered artifact type, accounting for over 38% of the assemblage. Scraper types from Xujiayao include straight, concave, convex, and end varieties with single, double, or multiple working edges (Figure 10.14). The short end scrapers are similar to the thumbnail scrapers seen in later Palaeolithic microlithic assemblages, and are consequently thought to be ancestral to this tool type. Points constitute 4.1% of the total, of which denticulated, beaked, and bifacial varieties are known (Figure 10.15). Gravers account for only a little more than 3% of the assemblage (Figure 10.16).

The Xujiayao stone spheroids are of particular interest since well over 1000 have been discovered at the site, a quantity unequaled at any other Chinese Palaeolithic locality. The spheroids may be divided into three categories according to their size, the largest weighing over 1500 g and measuring over 100 mm in diameter, while the smallest weigh less than 100 g and are less than 50 mm in diameter. Although the function of these finely made, symmetrical spheroids is not yet known, it is thought that they may have been employed as missile stones or bolas.

Because the Xujiayao stone industry is based on small tools, it is thought that it may constitute one of the principal forerunners of the North Chinese microlithic tradition.

The Xujiayao faunal assemblage (see Chapter 15, this volume) indicates an early Upper Pleistocene antiquity, but in recent years some scholars have suggested on palaeoclimatic grounds an even earlier date for this assemblage, perhaps as early as the late Riss or Lushan glacial period (Jia *et al.* 1979).

Locality 15, Zhoukoudian, Beijing

Situated some 70 m south of Locality 1 and 10 m east of Locality 4, the fossiliferous fissure of Zhoukoudian Locality 15 was discovered in 1932 and excavated between 1934 and 1937. The excavated portion of the fissure extended

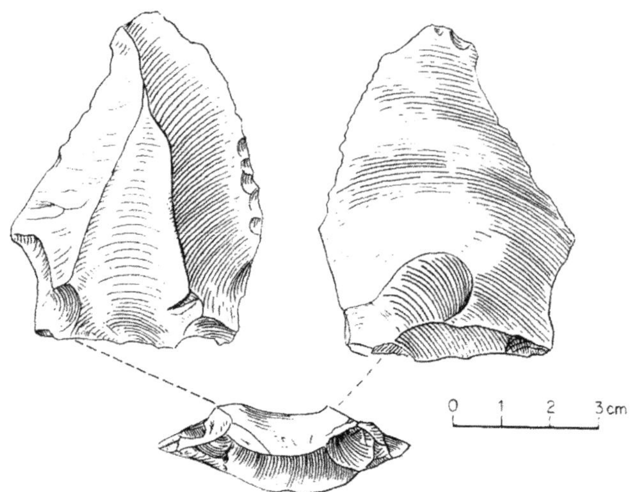

Figure 10.17 Large triangular chert flake from Zhoukoudian Locality 15, Beijing.

13 m east–west, 16 m north–south, and reached a maximum depth of 6 m. The deposit consisted of relatively homogeneous layers of yellow loam and red loam with weathered limestone inclusions. Stone artifacts and mammalian fossils were found distributed throughout the deposit, while ash, *Celtis* seeds, and burned bones were unearthed near the middle of the stratigraphic sequence (Pei 1938).

More than 10,000 stone artifacts were collected including pieces flaked on quartz, chert, sandstone, and various volcanics. Simple direct percussion was the principal means employed in the reduction of cores, the bipolar technique apparently having been rarely used. Most of the Locality 15 flakes are small and pieces with clear striking platforms outnumber those exhibiting platforms on cortex. Some of the flakes appear to have retouched and trimmed platforms, although on most nuclei it is difficult to clearly discern these processes. The Locality 15 assemblage is characterized by a high percentage of regularized tool types including substantial improvement in stoneworking capabilities over earlier Zhoukoudian industries (Figure 10.17). Shallow bulbs of percussion suggest the adoption of simple direct percussion with a soft hammer of wood or bone.

Both the tool types and mode of retouch are similar to those of the Zhoukoudian Locality 1 industry; however, at Locality 15 substantially improved regularity in tool types is an important feature of the stone assemblage. The Locality 15 tool types consist principally of scrapers and points, with a small number of choppers and gravers also present. Among the scrapers, straight-edge specimens fashioned on small flakes or pebbles are the most common. Other scraper types include double-edge, discoidal, and complex forms (Figure 10.18) also made on small flakes. The Locality 15 points, mainly made on small flakes or tabular pebbles, include varieties with either sharp or rounded points (Figure 10.19).

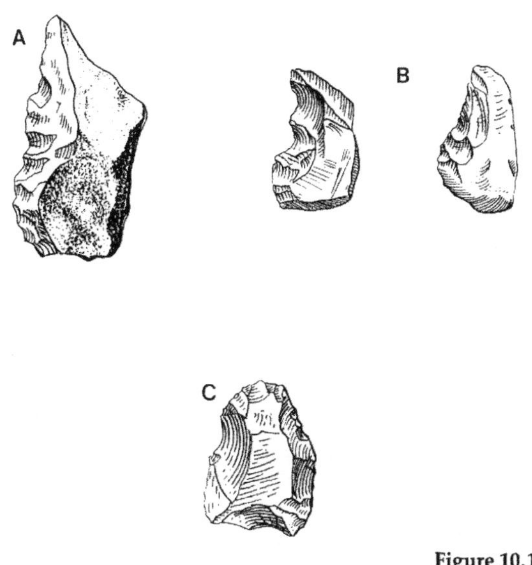

Figure 10.18 Scrapers from Zhoukoudian Locality 15, Beijing: A, quartz straight scraper; B, quartz crystal concave scrapers; C, chert convex scraper.

The choppers exhibit relatively coarse retouch. Some were fashioned on round, oval, or rectangular pebbles unifacially retouched, while others were bifacially chipped. Another category of choppers from Locality 15 was made on chert flakes, the thick bulbar end having been trimmed apparently to facilitate handling (Figure 10.20).

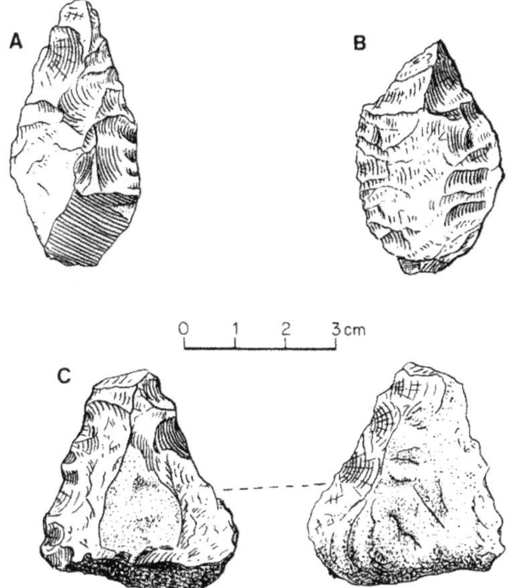

Figure 10.19 Points from Zhoukoudian Locality 15, Beijing: A,B, quartz bifacial points; C, quartz alternately flaked point.

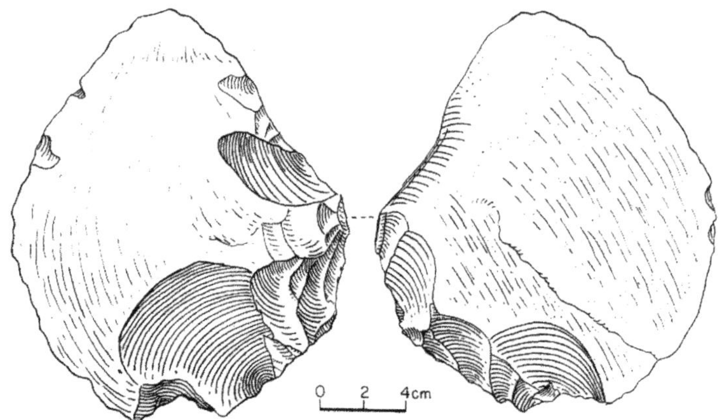

Figure 10.20 Heavy flake of igneous rock with trimmed butt, from Zhoukoudian Locality 15, Beijing.

Typical gravers, similar to the burins so characteristic of the later Palaeolithic industries of Europe, are not known from any locality at Zhoukoudian (Movius 1956), but 20 specimens discovered in the site have been classified as gravers due to the morphology of their working edges (Figure 10.21).

Thirty-three fossil mammalian species were found in association with the lithic industry at Locality 15 including *Coelodonta antiquitatis, Sinomegaceros pachyosteus, Pseudaxis* sp. indet., *Cervus* (*Elaphus*) *canadensis, Gazella przewalskyi,* and *Palaeoloxodon* cf. *namadicus.* These biostratigraphic data and the relatively advanced character of the artifacts indicate that the age of the Locality 15 deposit is later than that of Locality 1, placing it in the early Upper Pleistocene.

Gezidong, Liaoning

Located near Wafang, on the Shuiquan People's Commune in Kazuo County, Liaoning, the Gezidong site was the first Palaeolithic cave locality to be discovered in China's Northeast.

In the 1973 and 1975 excavations, 68 stone artifacts and traces of fire were unearthed in Cave A, while a large assemblage of mammalian fossils was derived from both Caves A and B (Gezidong Excavation Team 1975).

The site's strata consist mainly of breccia, ash, and gray soil, the artifacts and fossils having been recovered principally in the breccia and ash lenses.

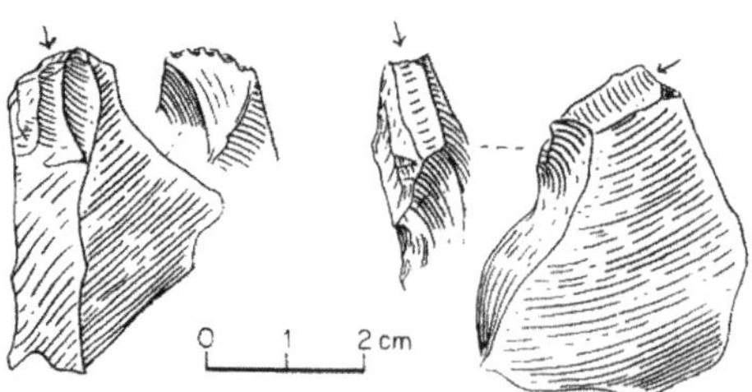

Figure 10.21 Quartz or chert gravers from Zhoukoudian Locality 15, Beijing.

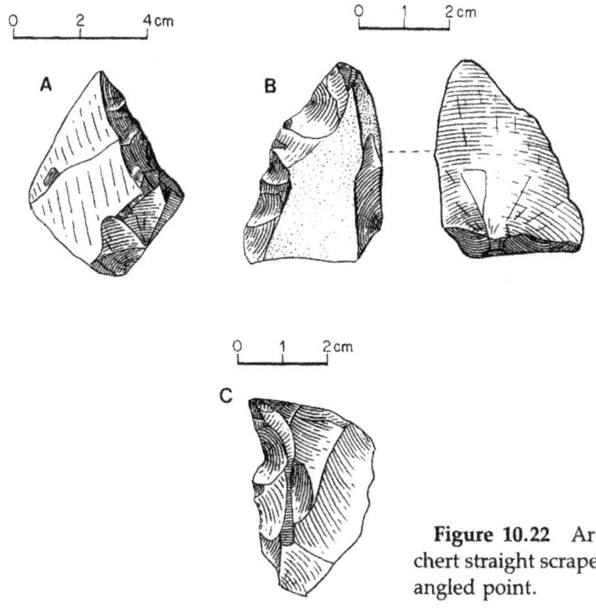

Figure 10.22 Artifacts from Gezidong, Liaoning: A, chert straight scraper; B, chert(?) convex scraper; C, chert angled point.

The 68 lithic artifacts include polyhedral and discoidal nuclei, flakes, and finished tools. Most of the flakes have been retouched by simple direct percussion, while some of them bear signs of bipolar retouch. Finished tools from the Gezidong include scrapers, points, choppers, and chopping tools.

The scrapers, of which straight, convex, and double-edge varieties have been identified, were generally retouched onto their dorsal surfaces. All the points, choppers, and chopping tools exhibit relatively coarse retouch (Figure 10.22).

The original researchers believe the Gezidong stone assemblage bears conspicuous similarities to those in the upper levels of Zhoukoudian Locality 1 and Locality 15 in terms of type, size, and retouch techniques (Gezidong Excavation Team 1975). At the same time, the Gezidong Industry appears quite different from those of the Sanmen Gorge region of western Henan and from the Dingcun Culture of Shanxi. Therefore, the Gezidong assemblage seems to be an extension of the lithic tradition established at Zhoukoudian.

The mammalian fossils recovered from Caves A and B consist principally of *Canis* cf. *chihliensis*, *Felis* cf. *microta*, *Crocuta c. ultima*, *Coelodonta antiquitatis*, *Equus przewalskyi*, and *E. hemionus*, suggesting an Upper Pleistocene antiquity for Gezidong Caves A and B, perhaps somewhat later than Zhoukoudian Locality 15.

Tongzi, Guizhou

Located on the southern slope of Chaishangang Mountain in Yufeng Brigade, Jiuba People's Commune, Tongzi County, Guizhou, the Yanhui Cave was the first site containing fossils of *Homo sapiens* discovered anywhere in the province.

Excavations in 1971 and 1972 have shown that the deposits in the cave contain seven layers. The human fossils, stone artifacts, burned bones, and mammalian fossils were all unearthed in the fourth layer, a stratum of greyish-yellow sand and gravel (Wu *et al.* 1975). The human fossils from the initial excavations consist of an incisor and premolar very similar to those of *H. erectus* from Zhoukoudian Locality 1. Only 12 stone artifacts have been discovered, most of which are fashioned on chert, although a few chipped from various volcanics, siliceous limestone, and quartzite were also found. An examination of the Tongzi nuclei indicate simple direct percussion was the primary means of core reduction. Unidirectional retouch was more common than alternating retouch and the majority of the Tongzi assemblage consists of coarsely retouched scrapers (Figure 10.23).

A large assemblage of mammalian fossils, mostly isolated teeth, were found in association with the stone artifacts. More than 25 species are represented, including *Hylobates* sp. indet., *Ailuropoda* sp. indet., *Ursus thibetanus kokeni*, *Crocuta c. ultima*, *Stegodon orientalis*, *Megatapirus* sp. indet., and *Rhinoceros sinensis*. The fauna suggests a Middle–Upper Pleistocene range, but the archaeological evidence is consistent with an Upper Pleistocene age.

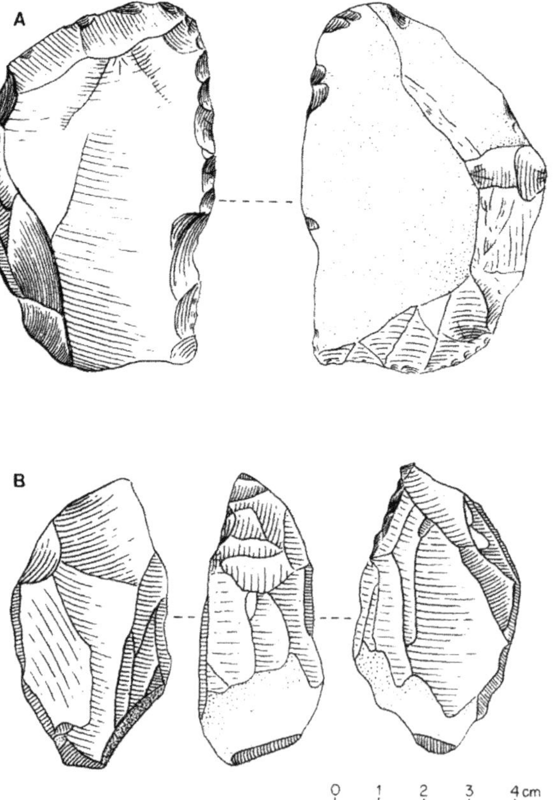

Figure 10.23 Scrapers from Tongzi, Guizhou: A, quartzite straight scraper; B, chert complex scraper.

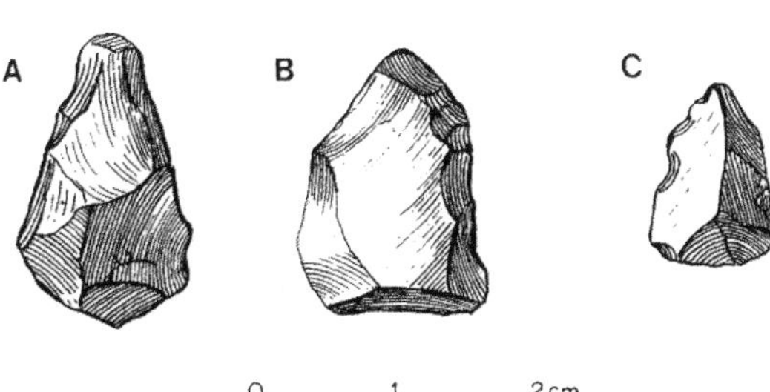

Figure 10.24 Three scrapers of uncertain material, from Dali, Shaanxi.

Dali, Shaanxi

The Dali site is near Jiefangcun on the Duanjia People's Commune in Dali County, Shaanxi. Excavations in 1978 and 1979 yielded a fossilized hominid cranium, 481 stone artifacts, and an abundant fossil mammalian fauna.

The hominid cranium and stone implements were found buried in a gravel layer at the base of a 50-m terrace in the Wei River valley. The stratigraphic section at Dali contains a total of 13 layers, starting from the bottom of the sequence. Animal fossils and stone tools were recovered from Levels 5–3, while the human remains were found only in Level 3 (Wu and You 1979, 1980; Zhang and Zhou 1984).

The Dali cranium, derived from a young male individual, is thought to be that of an archaic *H. sapiens* (Wu 1981). The stone artifacts show little change from Levels 5–3, all being chiefly made of quartzite, vein quartz, and flint. Most flakes were produced by simple direct percussion, although a few bipolar specimens were also uncovered. The nuclei are small and irregular with no evidence of platform preparation. Most of the finished tools were fabricated on small flakes and include scrapers, points, gravers, and awls. Scrapers alone account for 68.9% of the assemblage (Figure 10.24) and no choppers or spheroids were collected during the two seasons of excavation. Retouching on both dorsal and ventral surfaces of flakes has been observed, as has alternate flaking.

The mammalian fossils found in association with the Dali lithic industry include *Equus hemionus* and *Sinomegaceros pachyosteus* in Level 5, and *Cervus elaphus* in Level 4. Level 3, which yielded the Dali hominid cranium, produced remains of *Castor* sp. indet., *Palaeoloxodon* cf. *namadicus*, *Equus* sp. indet., *Rhinoceros* sp. indet., *Bubalus* sp. indet., *Gazella przewalskyi*, and *Sinomegaceros pachyosteus*. The recovery of these species indicates that Levels 5–3 at Dali are probably of Upper Pleistocene antiquity.

Conclusions

On the basis of this brief overview we may draw the following conclusions:

1. Chinese Middle Palaeolithic culture was extensively distributed in both North and South China, although central Shanxi seems to have been an area of particularly intensive occupation. Thus far, 21 Middle Palaeolithic localities have

been identified in China, of which 8 sites have produced the bulk of our presently available data. These sites, arranged in chronological order beginning with the oldest are: Dali, Zhoukoudian Locality 15, Dingcun, the allied sites of Jiangjiawan and Sigoukou, Yaotougou, Xujiayao, Gezidong, and Tongzi.

2. Chinese Middle Palaeolithic cultures seem to have developed directly out of an indigenous Early Palaeolithic base. Persistent Early Palaeolithic cultural features—such as the reliance on flakes as blanks for tools, and the presence of pebble choppers—link the Chinese Middle Palaeolithic with its local forerunners.

3. Principal artifact types include scrapers, points, choppers, and chopping tools, most of which exhibit only unifacial retouch. Regional and temporal variation are features of Chinese Middle Palaeolithic industries. At Dingcun for example, the tradition of heavy chopper–chopping tools is maintained, while at Zhoukoudian Locality 15 the Locality 1 techniques of artifact production are perpetuated with refinements. Although the Xujiayao assemblage is likewise dominated by small flake tools, stone spheroids are also an important component, indicating yet another variant on a generalized Middle Palaeolithic theme.

These examples illustrate that the Chinese Middle Palaeolithic should not continue to be considered the homogeneous entity that earlier publications have tended to suggest. On the contrary, these early Upper Pleistocene industries are an important link between the relatively uniform Early Palaeolithic cultures of China and their highly diversifed Late Palaeolithic descendants.

References

Dai Erjian

1966 The palaeoliths found at Lantian Man locality of Gongwangling, and its vicinity. *Vertebrata PalAsiatica* 10(1):30–34.

Gai Pei and Huang Wanbo

1982 Middle Palaeolithic remains found in Zhangwu county, Shaanxi. *Acta Anthropologica Sinica* 1(1):30–34.

Gezidong Excavation Team

1975 Discovery of Palaeolithic artifacts in Gezidong Cave in Liaoning province. *Vertebrata PalAsiatica* 13(2):122–136.

Gu Yumin

1982 New Cave Man of Zhoukoudian and his living environments. In *Gurenlei Lunwenji (Collected Papers of Palaeoanthropology)*, edited by the Institute of Vertebrate Palaeontology and Palaeoanthropology, Chinese Academy of Sciences. Beijing: Science Press. Pp. 158–174.

Jia Lanpo (Chia Lan-po)

1957 Notes on the human and some other mammalian remains from Changyang, Hupei. *Gu Jizhuidongwu Xuebao (Vertebrata PalAsiatica)* 1(3):247–258.

1959 The Palaeolithic site of Li-ts'un Hsi-kou, Ch'u-wo, Shansi. *Kaogu* 1:18–20.

Jia Lanpo (Chia Lan-po) and Wang Zeyi

1957 The discovery of the Jiaocheng, Shansi Palaeolithic culture. *Kaogu Tongxun* 5:12–18.

Jia Lanpo (Chia Lan-po), Wang Zeyi, and Qiu Zhonglang
1961 Palaeoliths of Shansi. *Memoirs of the Institute of Vertebrate Palaeontology and Palaeoanthropology*, Series A 4:1–48.
Jia Lanpo (Chia Lan-po) and Wei Qi
1976 A Palaeolithic site at Hsu-chia-yao in Yangkao county, Shansi province. *Acta Archaeologica Sinica* 2:97–114.
Jia Lanpo (Chia Lan-po), Wei Qi, and Li Chaorong
1979 Report on the excavation of Hsuchiayao Man site in 1976. *Vertebrata PalAsiatica* 17(4):277–293.
Li Tianyuan
1981 The discovery of human fossils at Guojiuyan, Changyang county, Hubei. *Vertebrata PalAsiatica* 19(2):194.
Movius, Hallam L., Jr.
1956 New Palaeolithic sites near Tingtsun on the Fen River, Shansi province, North China. *Quaternaria* 3:13–26.
Pei Wenzhong (Pei Wen-chung)
1938 A preliminary study of a new Palaeolithic station known as Locality 15 within the Choukoutien region. *Bulletin of the Geological Society of China* 19(2):147–187.
1939 New fossil materials and artifacts collected from the Choukoutien region during the years 1937 to 1939. *Bulletin of the Geological Society of China* 19(3):207–232.
Pei Wenzhong (Pei Wen-chung), Wu Rukang (Woo Ju-kang), Jia Lanpo (Chia Lan-po), Zhou Mingzhen (Chow Min-chen), Liu Xianting, and Wang Zeyi
1958 Report on the excavation of Palaeolithic sites at Tingtsun, Hsiangfenhsien, Shansi province, China. *Memoirs of the Institute of Vertebrate Palaeontology and Palaeoanthropology*, Series A 2:1–111.
Qiu Zhonglang and Li Yanxian
1978 Chinese Palaeolithic archaeology in the past 26 years. In *Gurenlei Lunwenji (Collected Papers of Palaeoanthropology)*, edited by the Institute of Vertebrate Palaeontology and Palaeoanthropology, Chinese Academy of Sciences. Beijing: Science Press. Pp. 43–66.
Wang Zeyi
1965 Palaeoliths from Huoxian, Shanxi. *Vertebrata PalAsiatica* 9(4):399–402.
Wang Zeyi, Hu Jiarui, and Li Yujie
1959 Some palaeoliths found in Nan-liang, Hou-ma, Shansi province. *Gu Jizhuidongwu yu Gu Renlei (Palaeovertebrata et Palaeoanthropologia)* 1(4):187–188.
Wu Maolin
1980 Human fossils discovered at Xujiayao site in 1977. *Vertebrata PalAsiatica* 18(3):229–238.
Wu Maolin, Wang Linghong, Zhang Yinyun, and Zhang Senshui
1975 Fossil human teeth and associated fauna from northern Guizhou. *Vertebrata PalAsiatica* 13(1):14–23.
Wu Rukang (Woo Ju-kang) and Peng Ruce
1959 Fossil human skull of early Palaeoanthropic stage found at Mapa, Shaokuan, Kwangtung province. *Gu Jizhuidongwu yu Gu Renlei (Palaeovertebrata et Palaeoanthropologia)* 1(4):159–164.
Wu Xinzhi
1976 Turning grief into strength: excavating Neoanthropus fossils at Dingcun. *Vertebrata PalAsiatica* 14(4):270.
1981 The well preserved cranium of an early *Homo sapiens* from Dali, Shaanxi. *Scientia Sinica* 2:200–206.
Wu Xinzhi and You Yuzhu
1979 A preliminary observation of Dali Man site. *Vertebrata PalAsiatica* 17(4):294–303.
1980 Dali Man and his culture. *Kaogu yu Wenwu* 1:2–6.
Xie Junyi and Zhang Luzhang
1977 Palaeolithic artifacts in Qingyang district, Gansu. *Vertebrata PalAsiatica* 15(3):211–222.

Zhang Senshui
1963 Some palaeoliths from Loc. 22 of Choukoutien. *Vertebrata PalAsiatica* 7(1):84–86.
Zhang Senshui and Zhou Chunmao
1984 A preliminary study of the second excavations in the Dali Man locality. *Acta Anthropologica Sinica* 3(1):19–29.

11

The Late Palaeolithic of China

JIA LANPO AND HUANG WEIWEN

Introduction

On June 4, 1920 the French collector Emile Licent discovered a quartzite core in the loess at Xingjiagou, 55 km north of Qingyang in Gansu Province. The discovery of this nucleus, the first Palaeolithic artifact recorded from Chinese territory, spurred further investigation and in 1923 Licent and the French palaeontologist Pierre Teilhard de Chardin discovered Pleistocene archaeological sites at Shuidonggou in the Ningxia Hui Autonomous Region and at Salawusu (Sjara-osso-gol) in the Inner Mongolia Autonomous Region (Licent and Teilhard 1925). All these assemblages were determined to be of Upper Pleistocene, Late Palaeolithic antiquity.

The field reconnaissances of Teilhard and the Chinese palaeontologist Yang Zhongjian (C. C. Young) in the loesslands of western Shanxi and northern Shaanxi provinces during the summer of 1929 yielded additional Late Palaeolithic remains (Teilhard and Yang 1930), as did excavations conducted in 1933–1934 in the Upper Cave at Zhoukoudian, near Beijing (Pei 1939).

Since the founding of the People's Republic of China in 1949 there has been a staggering increase in the number of known Late Palaeolithic remains. For example, in North China, which is characterized by a history of sound archaeological field investigations, important Late Palaeolithic sites have been discovered at Shiyu, Shanxi (Jia *et al.* 1972); Xiaonanhai, Henan (An 1965); Xiachuan, Shanxi (Wang *et al.* 1978); Xueguan, Shanxi (Wang *et al.* 1983); Liujiacha, Gansu (Gansu Provincial Museum 1982); and Hutouliang, Hebei (Gai and Wei 1977). South China and the Northeast (formerly known as Manchuria), which

ISBN 0-12-601720-4

had yielded no Pleistocene archaeological remains prior to Chinese Liberation in 1949, have subsequently produced a number of important Palaeolithic localities including Fulin, Sichuan (Yang 1961; Zhang 1977); Lunan, Yunnan (Li and Huang 1962; Pei and Zhou 1961); Tongliang, Sichuan (Li and Zhang 1981; Zhang *et al.* 1982); Maomaodong, Guizhou (Cao 1982a,b); Baise, Guangxi (Li and You 1975); and Xibajianfang, Liaoning (Liaoning Provincial Museum 1973). Even on the high Qinghai—Tibet Plateau in southwest China, where relatively little archaeological fieldwork has yet been conducted, evidence of Pleistocene occupation has been discovered (Qiu 1958; Zhang 1976).

In recent years the related questions of chronology and cultural diversification have drawn the attention of prehistorians. The increasingly frequent application of chronometric dating techniques and palynological studies in China in recent years has greatly expanded our knowledge of the interface between environment and culture during the Pleistocene.

Stratigraphic Units and Environment

In China the Late Palaeolithic is correlated with the middle and late Upper Pleistocene of roughly 40,000 to 10,000 years ago. The massive global temperature fluctuations that took place during this period are conspicuously reflected in China by varying rates of sedimentary deposition and erosion as well as by the changing distribution of plant and animal communities. The meters-thick loess deposits, so characteristic a feature of the North Chinese landscape, were formed during this period. Generally speaking, the eolian processes responsible for these substantial deposits of silty loess were correlated with relatively cold and dry climatic conditions. The loessic sequences are frequently interbedded with fluviolacustrine facies such as sand, gravel, and clay, which reflect the cyclical replacement of the loess depositional regime with relatively mesic conditions accompanied by warmer or colder average temperatures (You 1984).

In northeastern China, such fluviolacustrine facies and bog deposits, including a black, organic palaeosol, are thought to be associated with a predominantly cold and wet climate. North China during the Upper Pleistocene was inhabited by the Salawusu Fauna (see Chapter 15, this volume). Important members included *Palaeoloxodon namadicus*, *Equus hemionus*, *E. przewalskyi*, *Coelodonta antiquitatis*, *Camelus knoblocki*, *Cervus elaphus*, *Megaloceros ordosianus*, *Bubalus wansjocki*, *Bos primigenius*, and *Crocuta c. ultima*.

Most of these forms are associated with steppe–desert niches, although a few probably preferred riparian habitats or thinly wooded forests. During the same period, the Northeast was inhabited by a *Mammuthus–Coelodonta* fauna fundamentally the same as Siberia's Upper Pleistocene vertebrate community and including such forms as *Canis lupus*, *Ursus spelaeus*, *Mammuthus primigenius*, *Equus caballus*, *Coelodonta antiquitatis*, *Elaphus* sp. indet., *Bison exiguus*, and *Bos primigenius.* This northern fauna was very similar to its contemporary in North China proper in percentages of forms now extinct; however, the latter did not feature such species as *Mammuthus primigenius* and *Bison exiguus.* From an ecological standpoint most of the fauna of the Upper Pleistocene of China's Northeast were adapted to that region's boreal forests and steppes, while a few seem to have preferred more mesic niches along the courses of rivers and in swampy areas.

Palynological analyses indicate that 40,000 years ago North China's climate was mild, with the lakes and rivers of the Ordos Plateau supporting associated mixed deciduous forests (Yuan 1978).

About 30,000 years ago mean annual temperatures seem to have dropped drastically. As a result, the subalpine coniferous forests that had previously been restricted to montane regions and the higher latitudes began to dominate the hills and valleys of North China. The boreal forests of Northeast China's Pacific coast, dominated by *Picae, Abies,* and *Betula,* were particularly affected by this change.

Between 22,000 and 13,000 years ago, during the last glacial maximum, the climate became extremely dry and cold and China's northeastern provinces were once again transformed into steppe or steppe–desert zones dominated by a vegetational community including *Artemesia* spp., *Populus, Tamarix, Stipa* spp., *Festuca,* and *Koeleria.*

By 12,000 years ago temperatures had begun to rise, resulting in the retreat of glacial masses and the expansion of *Tilia*-dominated broad-leaved deciduous forests in North China (Kong and Du 1980). At that time South China was characterized by extensively distributed yellow cave sediments and fluviolacustrine deposits in river valleys and basins.

During the Pleistocene South China was inhabited by the *Ailuropoda–Stegodon* Fauna (see Chapter 15, this volume) reflecting a relatively warm, wet climate with associated woodlands. By Middle and Upper Pleistocene times, the fauna of South China had come to closely resemble that of modern Southeast Asia. The relative stability of the South Chinese Pleistocene climate is attested to by the lack of substantial change in the region's fauna throughout this period. This stability is in marked contrast to contemporary faunas from higher latitudes where drastic changes are apparent as a function of fluctuating climatic conditions.

Cultural Remains

In comparison with earlier Pleistocene archaeological assemblages, those of the Late Palaeolithic are characterized by greater diversity and refinement both in techniques of artifact manufacture and in the finished products themselves. The tradition based on small flake tools—represented by such Early Palaeolithic sites as Zhoukoudian Localities 1 and 15 and the Middle Palaeolithic Xujiayao site—maintained their dominance in the North Chinese Late Palaeolithic. Sites such as Salawusu, Inner Mongolia; Shiyu, Shanxi; Liujiacha, Gansu; and Xiaonanhai, Henan, are all characteristic of this period. They inherited from preceding small tool industries such basic characteristics as the use of small, irregular flakes and the employment of simple direct percussion in the fabrication and retouching of tools. However, these Late Palaeolithic assemblages are characterized by more sophisticated and refined applications of these time-tested principles, and a variety of new tool types made their appearance in these sites.

The Salawusu Valley in the southeastern extremity of the Ordos Plateau in Inner Mongolia (37°10–59′N, 108°10–58′E) has yielded stone and bone artifacts as well as traces of fire utilization that are of Late Palaeolithic origin. Most of the artifacts were made on a variety of black or gray siliceous pebbles, brown quartzite, and gray or white quartz. Most utilized pebbles originally ranged from 20 to 40 mm in diameter; consequently the artifacts made from these raw materials are particularly minute. Most implements are flake tools, although some fashioned on nuclei or pebbles have also been recovered. Simple direct percussion seems to have been the most commonly applied means of both core reduction and retouching. In most cases, retouching on the Salawusu specimens is meticulous and fine, although the cutting margins on most implements are rather sinuous. Typical implements include points, borers, side scrapers, nosed end scrapers, thumbnail scrapers, and burins, of which the side scrapers are the most diverse, with simple, straight, double-edge, convergent, and transverse varieties represented (Figure 11.1).

According to stratigraphic and faunal comparisons, Pierre Teilhard de Chardin and Emile Licent maintained that the Salawusu culture approximated that of the Mousterian or Chatelperronian of Western Europe (Boule *et al.* 1928:26). Recent uranium series dates place the Salawusu materials in the 50,000–37,000 BP range (Yuan *et al.* 1983).

The Shiyu site is in the southwestern part of the Datong Basin in northern Shanxi Province (39°25′N, 112°17′E), where more than 15,000 stone artifacts and other cultural remains were discovered in Pleistocene fluvial sands and gravels (Jia *et al.* 1972). A typical Salawusu Fauna is present in the localities at Shiyu and a radiocarbon date of 28,945 ± 1370 BP (ZK-190-0) has been determined. The

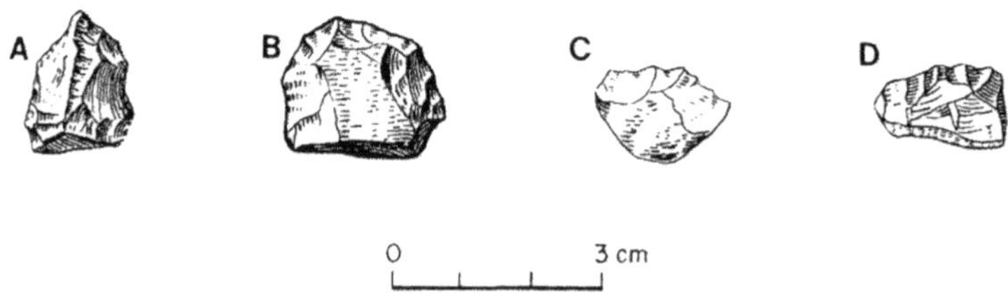

Figure 11.1 Chert implements from the Salawusu (Sjara-osso-gol) Valley, Inner Mongolia: A, point; B–D, scrapers. (After Boule *et al.* 1928.)

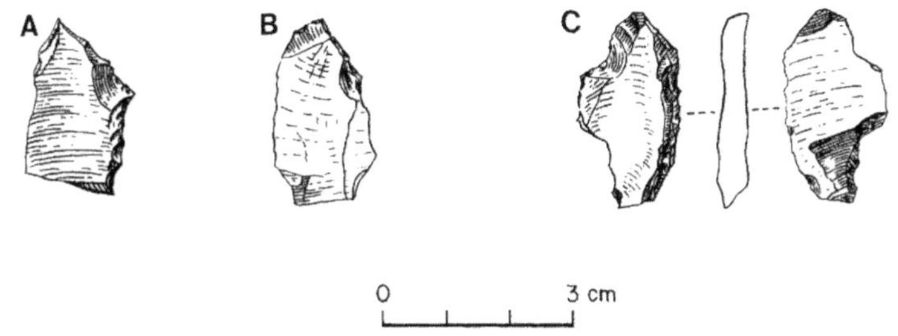

Figure 11.2 Small implements from Shiyu, Shanxi: A, chert graver; B, chert(?) projectile point; C, quartz crystal crescentic knife. (After Jia *et al.* 1972.)

Shiyu artifacts are predominantly made on pebbles of vein quartz, quartzite, siliceous limestone, and a small number of igneous rocks. Although the techniques of fabrication are nearly identical to those employed at Salawusu, the Shiyu site has yielded a number of previously undocumented tool types such as projectile points, an axelike knife, and small blades (Figure 11.2). Standardization of tool types seems to have been an important factor in the production of stone implements at Shiyu and bipolar cores and, in contrast to Salawusu, flakes are present in the site's cultural inventory.

Late Palaeolithic sites of the small tool tradition also include Liujiacha (39°29′N, 107°06′E) in Huanxian County on the eastern Gansu loessic plateau (Gansu Provincial Museum 1982), and the cave deposits of Xiaonanhai (36°5′N, 114°15′E) near Anyang in northern Henan on the western edge of the North China Plain (Aigner 1981:88–96; An 1965). A radiocarbon date of 13,075 ± 220 BP (ZK-170-0) has been generated for the Xiaonanhai deposits.

Both the Xiaonanhai and Liujiacha sites contain a typical Salawusu Fauna, although the latter site is thought to be somewhat older, approximating Salawusu itself in antiquity.

Another variant of Late Palaeolithic culture in North China is represented by the Shuidonggou site in Lingwu County, some 30 km southeast of Yinchuan, the capital of the Ningxia Hui Autonomous Region. In 1923 Pierre Teilhard de Chardin and Emile Licent discovered a very rich assemblage of stone artifacts and vertebrate fossils in Pleistocene fluvial sands and gravels at Shuidonggou. Since the 1960s Chinese scholars have conducted several excavations at the site, greatly supplementing the data originally gathered in the 1920s (Jia *et al.* 1964).

The artifacts from Shuidonggou were fashioned mainly on siliceous limestone and large quartz pebbles. A number of the tool types from Shuidonggou, including small points, scrapers of several varieties, and many irregularly flaked pieces, strongly resemble implements from the Salawusu assemblage. Parallels have also been drawn between some of the larger Shuidonggou stone artifacts, such as transverse retouched points, and tools from the Middle Pleistocene deposits at Zhoukoudian Locality 1.

Large implements dominate the Shuidonggou Industry and in this respect it bears resemblances to Mousterian and Aurignacian industries in Western Eu-

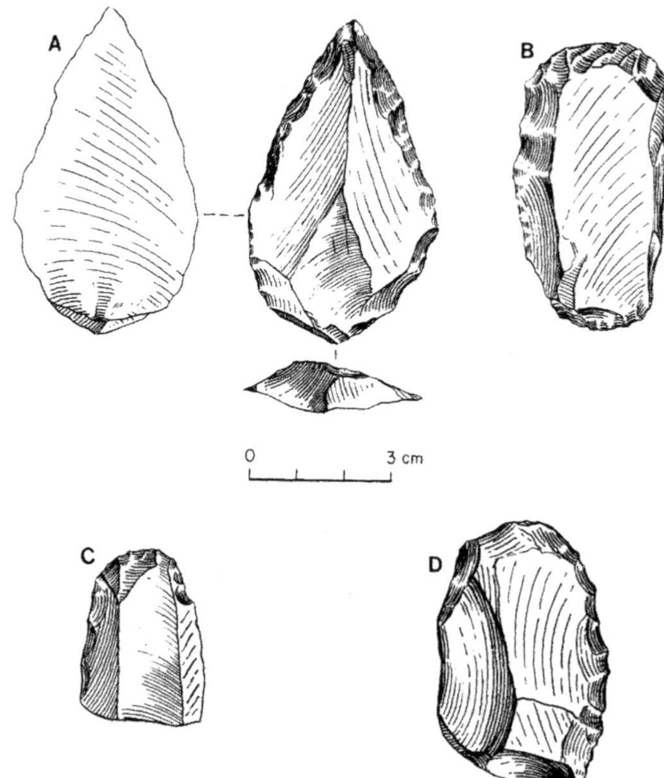

Figure 11.3 Quartzite implements from Shuidonggou, Ningxia Hui Autonomous Region: A, point similar to a Western European Mousterian point; B,C, end scrapers; D, side scraper. (After Jia *et al.* 1964).

rope. For example, artifacts such as discoidal cores, semicircular scrapers, and triangular and foliate points chipped on flakes removed from prepared cores (Figure 11.3) are all characteristic elements in the stone industries of both of these regions. In particular, triangular points have been discovered at Shuidonggou that are essentially identical to Mousterian points found in Europe. The Shuidonggou elongated nuclei and end scrapers made on blades with trimmed platforms closely resemble such implements recovered in Aurignacian contexts to the west.

Basing his conclusions on the material collected in 1923, Henri Breuil remarked that the Shuidonggou culture resembled a highly evolved Mousterian and an incipient Aurignacian culture, or perhaps a combination of the two (Boule *et al.* 1928:121). Subsequently, Jia Lanpo and his colleagues, after examining a new series of artifacts collected at the site, also concluded that the Shuidonggou assemblage

> exhibits characteristics of both Middle and Late Palaeolithic cultures. On the basis of the material collected thus far, there is difficulty in positively asserting that any of the cultural inventory is of Middle Palaeolithic origin. A more reliable estimate of the site's age is Late Palaeolithic as these cultural features are exhibited more distinctly than the others. (Jia *et al.* 1964:80)

Stone industries similar to that of Shuidonggou but probably earlier are those excavated at Changwu, Shaanxi (Gai and Huang 1982), and the slightly later series of localities discovered along the course of the Qingshui River in south-central Inner Mongolia (Zhang 1959). Although the last are all surface finds without clear stratigraphic provenance, on typological grounds they are believed to be Late Palaeolithic.

In recent years several important Late Palaeolithic sites have been discovered in North China. The abundance of microlithic tools including blades and nuclei produced by indirect percussion and pressure-flaked tools have aroused immense interest among Chinese prehistorians (Chen 1983). The most important of these new localities include Xiachuan and Xueguan in Shanxi and Hutouliang in Hebei.

The Xiachuan site, earliest and richest of the three, is located near Lishan Peak in the Zhongtiao Range east of the Fen River valley in Qinshui County, southern Shanxi Province (35°25′N, 111°59′E). The Palaeolithic remains, widely distributed in river sediments and as a relic deposit formed by weathering, occur commonly as surface exposures in the area (Wang *et al.* 1978). In the strata containing both stone artifacts and broken animal bones, charcoal and ash yielded ^{14}C dates ranging from 21,700 ± 1000 BP (ZK-384) to 19,600 ± 600 BP (ZK-634).

Late Palaeolithic remains are abundant at Xiachuan. The 1978 report alone includes the analysis of over 1800 artifacts, the overwhelming majority of which (95.3%) are microlithic. These minute tools were made on flakes and blades struck from a variety of flint nuclei including conical and boat-shaped cores worked by indirect percussion (Chen 1983). The assemblage of finished tools from Xiachuan is dominated by backed knives, angle and parrotbeak burins, small triangular points, bifacial foliate points, awls, borers, and end scrapers, all produced by pressure flaking (Figure 11.4). The craftsmanship apparent in these small implements is very refined. The large tools from Xiachuan, comprising only 4.7% of the total assemblage, include axelike pieces, scrapers, millingstones, and hammers fashioned most commonly from vein quartz and quartzite.

The Xueguan site (36°27′N, 111°E) is situated in the Luliang Mountains in the western Fen River valley of southern Shanxi (Wang *et al.* 1983). The stone artifacts from this site were buried in the diluvial sands and loess above the river terraces. Associated faunal remains include *Equus* cf. *przewalskyi*, *E. hemionus*, *Gazella* sp. indet., *Bos* sp. indet., *Cervus* sp. indet., and *Struthio* sp. indet., among others, all ^{14}C dated to approximately 13,550 ± 150 BP. The microlithic tools that predominate at this site are typified by wedge-shaped, boat-shaped, and conical

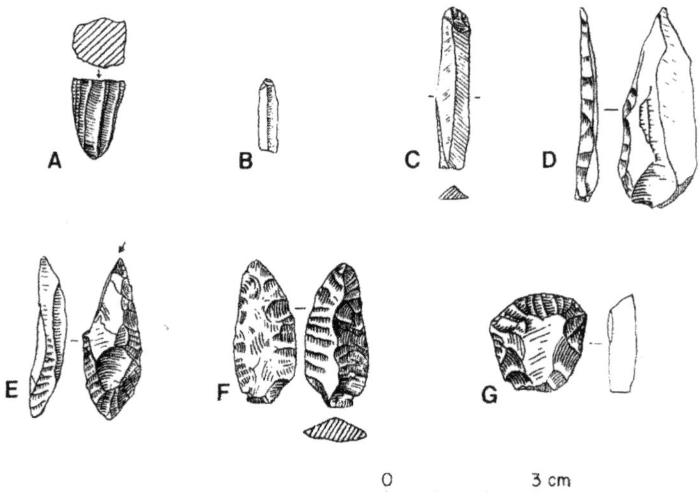

Figure 11.4 Microlithic chert tools from Xiachuan, Shanxi: A, conical core; B,C, microblades; D, backed blade; E, graver; F, projectile point; G, thumbnail scraper. (After Wang *et al.* 1978.)

flint cores, as well as by blades, backed knives, and burins or gravers. Techniques of production seem to parallel those observed at Xiachuan. The larger tools from Xueguan, made of flint and quartzite, include semilunar scrapers, double-end points, and axelike implements.

The Hutouliang site (40°N, 114°11′E) is near Nihewan Village northwest of Beijing in Yangyuan County, Hebei (Gai and Wei 1977). Stone artifacts were found in a sandy loess deposit above a river terrace in association with fossils of *Microtus brandtiodes, Myospalax fontanieri, Struthiolithus* sp. indet., *Canis lupus, Equus przewalskyi, E. hemionus, Gazella subgutturosa, Cervus* sp. indet., *Sus scrofa,* and *Bos* sp. indet. A single radiocarbon date of 11,000 ± 210 BP (PV-4) has been generated, correlating well with the faunal remains to suggest a terminal Pleistocene age for the site.

Both microlithic and larger stone tools of quartzite, flint, and a number of other raw materials have been discovered. The microlithic assemblage includes wedge-shaped cores, fine blades, and a wide variety of small, carefully flaked implements. The larger lithic tools from Hutouliang are typified by quartzite points; unifacial and bifacial pieces such as choppers, end scrapers, discoidal scrapers, and semilunar scrapers; as well as hammerstones, anvils, and perforated stone ornaments.

Nonlithic artifacts recovered from Hutouliang include bird-bone beads, ostrich-eggshell pendants, and perforated shells.

Northeast China has also produced a series of important Upper Pleistocene archaeological sites in the past decade. The Xibajianfang site (41°15′N, 119°15′E) in Lingyuan County, southwest Liaoning (Liaoning Provincial Museum 1973) has yielded artifacts in a fluvial sand and gravel terrace accompanied by remains of *Myospalax fontanieri, M.* cf. *psilurus, Spermophilus* (*Citellus*) *undulatus, Gazella przewalskyi, Cervus* sp. indet., and *Bos primigenius*, an assemblage that suggests a late Upper Pleistocene age. The stone implements themselves consist of nuclei, flakes, points, nosed end scrapers, thumbnail scrapers, concave side scrapers, straight side scrapers, and backed knives. Techniques of fabrication are identical to those in evidence at other North Chinese Late Palaeolithic localities.

In South China, Late Palaeolithic sites also show a tendency toward great variety and technological progress in their lithic inventories. At the same time, however, these sites exhibit closer correlations to the earlier Palaeolithic traditions of North China than they do to Upper Pleistocene cultural stations in the same area.

The first of these important southern Chinese localities to be considered is Tongliang, about 110 km northwest of Chongqing, Sichuan (29°56′N, 106°02′E). Stone artifacts were found buried in Pleistocene bog facies within a lake basin in association with an *Ailuropoda–Stegodon* Fauna radiocarbon dated to 21,550 ± 310 BP (BKY-76050) (Li and Zhang 1981; Zhang *et al.* 1982).

The Tongliang artifacts were made principally on quartzite and flint nuclei, flakes having been produced by simple direct percussion or the anvil (block-on-block) technique. Scrapers, points, and chopper–chopping tools are known (Figure 11.5), most of which exceed 60 mm in length. Fabrication techniques included rather crude abrupt retouch, resulting in tools with blunt edges, most of which exceed 80°. The working edge often occupies the majority of the tool's margin and retouch can be identified on many edges of most artifacts. These same characteristics are also seen in the Early Palaeolithic tradition of South China, exemplified by the Guanyindong site in western Guizhou. This unique combination of technological features is not currently recognized elsewhere in China.

Another variant of Late Palaeolithic culture in South China is represented by the Fulin site (Yang 1961). It is in a mountainous basin at an elevation of 790 m above sea level in Hanyuan County, Sichuan, over 300 km southwest of Chengdu. (29°29′N, 102°42′E). The Fulin cultural remains were excavated from an ancient terrace 20–25 m above the present bed of a nearby river. Accompanying faunal remains were scarce: only *Ursus thibetanus, Sus* sp. indet., *Rusa* sp. indet., *Mun-*

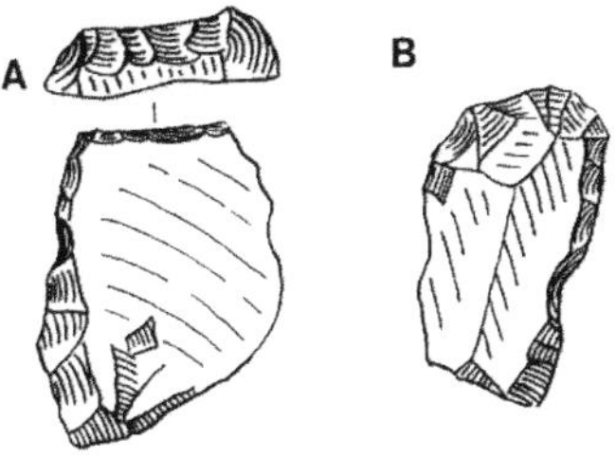

Figure 11.5 End scrapers from Tongliang, Sichuan. (After Li and Zhang 1981.)

tiacus sp. indet., and an as-yet-unidentified mollusk have been found. Based on these biostratigraphic data, the Fulin assemblage is thought to date to the last phase of the Late Palaeolithic. The stone artifacts were mostly made on tabular flint concretions and nearly all flakes exhibit trimmed platforms. Simple direct percussion was used to produce side scrapers, end scrapers, points, gravers, and chopping tools. One salient characteristic of the Fulin tools is their small size, averaging 26.1 mm in length by 19.2 mm in width. Such small tools are rarely seen in South Chinese Palaeolithic assemblages, but closely resemble their contemporaries to the north.

Additional divergent lithic traditions include that identified at Lunan in the Nanpan River area on the upper reaches of the Pearl River in Yunnan Province (24°6′N, 103°15′E). Stone artifacts from the Lunan site include pieces that resemble some of the end scrapers of Late Palaeolithic Europe (Li and Huang 1962).

Another example is the Maomaodong site in Guizhou Province (25°6′N, 104°57′E), which has yielded an assemblage of meticulously produced points similar to those found in the North Chinese sites of Shuidonggou, Qingshui River, Xueguan, and Hutouliang. The Maomaodong points were flaked from their dorsal face to the ventral surface, in contrast to those from the northern localities (Cao 1982a). Also excavated at Maomaodong were 14 bone awls, knives, and antler spades (Cao 1982b), which were fashioned by a combination of percussion, cutting, scraping, and grinding.

Reconstruction of Late Palaeolithic Lifestyles

In recent years there has been developing among Chinese prehistorians an increasing interest in understanding the behavioral and economic aspects of Palaeolithic archaeology. Toward this end, numerous Pleistocene localities in North China have been closely examined for evidence of past subsistence strategies and economic lifestyles.

At Salawusu in Inner Mongolia, large quantities of faunal remains, including fossils of *Gazella, Equus przewalskyi, E. hemionus,* and *Coelodonta antiquitatis* have been found in association with a rich assemblage of stone artifacts. Remains of *Gazella* predominate; the 1923 materials alone produced more than 300 antelope horn cores representing over 150 individuals (Licent and Teilhard 1925). Most of these *Gazella* elements had been subjected to intentional breakage and some bore traces of burning, suggesting this faunal collection is the product of human activity and that *Gazella* constituted the chief game of the Upper Pleistocene inhabitants of the Ordos Plateau.

The 1963 excavation at Shiyu, Shanxi, also yielded a large collection of animal remains, including more than 5000 mammalian teeth representing many species (Jia *et al.* 1972). Like the Salawusu materials, the bones from Shiyu are highly fragmented and burned. At Shiyu however, the identifiable elements consisted chiefly of *Equus przewalskyi* and *E. hemionus*. Based on an incomplete analysis of

E. przewalskyi right upper third molars and the right upper first molars of *E. hemionus*, at least 130 wild horses and 88 wild asses are represented at Shiyu.

These examples illustrate not only that large-game hunting was a crucial aspect of subsistence in Upper Pleistocene North China, but that the specific strategies and tactics involved were not uniform throughout this large and environmentally diverse region. The concentration of hunting activities on one or two large herbivores provides evidence of specialization and the appearance of "professional" hunters.

Throughout China, Late Palaeolithic sites tend to be located near permanent bodies of water, in river valleys, and along the margins of Pleistocene lakes. Other than the cultural remains found in cave sites such as Maomaodong, Guizhou, there is no evidence as yet in China for substantial Palaeolithic dwellings.

The discovery of bone needles in sites such as the Upper Cave at Zhoukoudian and the almost universal evidence of fire utilization in these Upper Pleistocene localities suggests China's Late Palaeolithic inhabitants were well equipped to deal with the realities of a harsh boreal climate through the use of clothing and controlled fire. Cave and rockshelter sites preserving a record of human habitation—such as at Xiaonanhai, Henan—are comparatively scarce, and yet people survived the severe climatic conditions of Pleistocene North China.

As yet no parietal arts such as those typical of the Late Palaeolithic of Western Europe have been discovered in Pleistocene contexts in China. A number of localities, however, have yielded small ornaments of several varieties. In addition to the perforated shells, bones, and ostrich eggshells from the Hutouliang site mentioned earlier, the Upper Cave at Zhoukoudian has also produced an interesting assemblage of decorative artifacts. Perforated marine shells (*Arca* sp. indet.), perforated pebbles, and beads made of stone, fish bone (the supraorbital of *Ctenopharyngodon idellus*), bird bone, and the drilled canine teeth of *Meles* and *Vulpes* were all discovered in the cave. In the Upper Cave three complete human skulls and postcranial elements of several more individuals were discovered resting on a layer of hematite powder, attesting to the ritual significance of these intentional burials. Interestingly, many of the ornaments recovered in association with these interments were also stained red with hematite, indicating that by the Late Palaeolithic a complex suite of spiritual beliefs and rituals had begun to develop in North China.

Research into the Late Palaeolithic prehistory of China continues at an ever-increasing pace. As more data are accumulated our picture of late Upper Pleistocene China more and more becomes one of diverse ecological zones, each characterized by specialized human adaptations that share, in broad terms, features in common with their contemporaries in adjacent environmental niches. Moreover, a clear pattern of continuity can be established between these Late Palaeolithic cultures and their earlier Pleistocene forebears. The illumination of these synchronic and diachronic relationships constitutes a major goal for future Palaeolithic studies in China.

References

Aigner, Jean S.

1981 *Archaeological remains in Pleistocene China*. Forschungen zur Allgemeinen und Vergleichenden Archäologie, Band 1. Munich: Verlag C. H. Beck.

An Zhimin

1965 Trial excavations of the Palaeolithic cave of Hsiao-nan-hai in Anyang, Honan. *Acta Archaeologica Sinica* 1:1–28.

Boule, M., H. Breuil, E. Licent, and P. Teilhard de Chardin

1928 *Le Paléolithique de la Chine*. Archives de l'Institut de Paléontologie Humaine 4:1–138.

Cao Zetian

1982a On the Palaeolithic artifacts from Maomaodong (the rock-shelter site), Guizhou province. *Vertebrata PalAsiatica* 20(2):36–41.

1982b The preliminary study of bone tools and antler spades from the rock-shelter site of Maomaodong. *Acta Anthropologica Sinica* 1(1):18–29.

Chen Chun

1983 Preliminary exploration of the typology and technology of microcores in China—also of the culture relationship between Northeast Asia and Northwestern North America. *Acta Anthropologica Sinica* 2(4):331–341.

Gai Pei and Huang Wanbo

1982 Middle Palaeolithic remains found in Zhangwu county, Shaanxi. *Acta Anthropologica Sinica* 1(1):30–34.

Gai Pei and Wei Qi

1977 Discovery of the Late Palaeolithic site at Hutouliang, Hebei. *Vertebrata PalAsiatica* 15(4):287–300.

Gansu Provincial Museum

1982 The Palaeolithic site at Liujiacha, Huanxian county, Gansu province. *Acta Archaeologica Sinica* 1:35–48.

Jia Lanpo (Chia Lan-po), Gai Pei, and Li Yanxian

1964 New materials from the Shuidonggou Palaeolithic site. *Vertebrata PalAsiatica* 8(1):75–83.

Jia Lanpo (Chia Lan-po), Gai Pei, and You Yuzhu

1972 Report of excavation in Shi Yu, Shanxi—a Palaeolithic site. *Acta Archaeologica Sinica* 1:39–60.

Kong Zhaochen and Du Naiqiu

1980 Vegetational and climatic changes from 30,000 to 10,000 BP in Beijing. *Acta Botanica Sinica* 22(4):330–338.

Li Xuanmin and Zhang Senshui

1981 On Palaeolithic culture of Tongliang county. *Vertebrata PalAsiatica* 19(4):359–371.

Li Yanxian and Huang Weiwen

1962 Preliminary report on the investigation of Palaeolithic artifacts from Yiliang district, Yunnan province. *Vertebrata PalAsiatica* 6(2):182–189.

Li Yanxian and You Yuzhu

1975 On the discovery of palaeoliths in Baise, Guangxi. *Vertebrata PalAsiatica* 13(4):225–228.

Liaoning Provincial Museum

1973 The Xibajianfang Palaeolithic site in Lingyuan county. *Vertebrata PalAsiatica* 11(2):223–226.

Licent, Emile and Pierre Teilhard de Chardin

1925 Le Paléolithique de la Chine. *L'Anthropologie* 35(4):201–234.

Pei Wenzhong (Pei Wen-chung)

1939 The Upper Cave Industry of Choukoutien. *Palaeontologia Sinica* New Series D 9:1–41.

Pei Wenzhong (Pei Wen-chung) and Zhou Mingzhen (Chow Min-chen)

1961 Discovery of palaeoliths in Yunnan. *Vertebrata PalAsiatica* 2:182–189.

Qiu Zhonglang
1958 Discovery of palaeoliths on the Tsinghai—Tibet Plateau. *Gu Jizhuidongwu Xuebao* (*Vertebrata PalAsiatica*) 2(2–3):157–163.

Teilhard de Chardin, P. and Yang Zhongjian (C. C. Young)
1930 Preliminary observations on the pre-Loessic and post-Pontian Formation in western Shanxi and northern Shaanxi. *Memoirs of the Geological Society of China* Series A 8:1–37.

Wang Jian (Wang Chien), Wang Xiangqian, and Chen Zheying
1978 Archaeological reconnaissances at Hsia Chuan in Chin Shui county, Shansi province. *Acta Archaeologica Sinica* 3:259–288.

Wang Xiangqian, Ding Jianping, and Tao Fuhai
1983 Microliths from Xueguan, Puxian county, Shanxi. *Acta Anthropologica Sinica* 2(2):162–171.

Yang Ling
1961 Discovery of the palaeoliths from Fulinchen, Hanyuan, Szechuan. *Vertebrata PalAsiatica* 2:139–142.

You Yuzhu
1984 Distribution and burying of Late Palaeolithic culture in North China. *Acta Anthropologica Sinica* 3(1):68–75.

Yuan Baoyin
1978 Sedimentary environment and stratigraphic subdivisions of the Sjara-osso-gol Formation. *Acta Geologica Sinica* 3:220–234.

Yuan Sixun, Chen Tiemei, and Gao Shijun
1983 Uranium series dating of "Ordos Man" and "Sjara-osso-gol Culture." *Acta Anthropologica Sinica* 2(1):90–94.

Zhang Senshui
1959 Discovery of Late Palaeolithic artifacts in Inner Mongolia and north-west Shansi. *Gu Jizhuidongwu yu Gu Renlei (Palaeovertebrata et Palaeoanthropologia)* 1(1):30–40.
1976 Newly discovered Palaeolithic artifacts from Dingri, Tibet. In *Report on a Scientific Survey in the Mount Qomolangma Area (1966–1968), Quaternary Geology*. Beijing: Science Press, pp. 105–109.
1977 On Fulin Culture. *Vertebrata PalAsiatica* 5(1):14–27.

Zhang Senshui, Wu Yushu, Yu Qianli, Li Xuanmin, and Yang Xinglong
1982 Discussion of natural environment of Palaeolithic site of Tong-liang. *Vertebrata PalAsiatica* 20(2):165–179.

12

Microlithic Industries in China

GAI PEI

Introduction

Only a decade has passed since the analysis of microlithic remains was incorporated within Palaeolithic studies in China. Previously, this research fell entirely within the purview of Neolithic archaeology (An 1958; Pei 1963; Teilhard and Pei 1944), but, as a result of the discovery during the past 10 years of large quantities of microlithic artifacts in a number of Chinese Palaeolithic sites, great changes have taken place in the research techniques employed and resulting conclusions concerning China's microlithic cultures. One of the most important of these fundamental changes has been the recognition that these microlithic industries represent an important link between China's Late Palaeolithic cultures and those of the Early Neolithic.

Beginning at the turn of the present century, several dozen Chinese and foreign scholars began to accumulate microlithic material across a broad section of North China (Andersson 1923, 1945; Boule *et al.* 1928; Teilhard and Pei 1944; Teilhard and Yang 1932). Large-scale expeditions that were focused on a variety of scientific subjects collected quantities of microlithic remains, the analysis of which has contributed greatly to current research on the origin, spatial distribution, and regional differences among these cultures.

In recent years Chinese archaeologists have published many articles devoted to the study of microlithic remains (see especially An 1957, 1978; Gai and Wang 1983; Gai and Wei 1977; Jia 1978; Pei 1963; Tong 1979). Particular attention has

ISBN 0-12-601720-4

been focused on the problem of the origin of Chinese microlithic industries and their relationship to similar assemblages in neighboring regions. In fact, it is the integration of data from many geographic areas that provides the best information on such crucial questions as modes of ecological adaptation, technological developments, and patterns of cultural interaction. In particular, the nearly simultaneous appearance of microlithic traditions in Northeast Asia and North America is a subject worthy of intense investigation along these lines (Gai 1977b, 1978, 1983; Chen 1983). Clearly we cannot hope to illuminate such complex questions through the analysis of archaeological materials from a single region.

Because contemporary research on microlithic industries in China is a massive and complicated subject, it is impossible to present all the relevant data and various scholarly viewpoints within a single article. Consequently, this summary endeavors to provide an overview of this complex and multifaceted topic.

Throughout the history of Chinese research into the subject, the meaning of the term *microlithic* has undergone many fundamental changes. In the 1930s and 1940s the word had a very broad meaning and was applied generally to small tools from both Palaeolithic and Neolithic contexts. For example, Teilhard and Pei (1932) referred to the collection of small flake tools excavated from Locality 1 at Zhoukoudian near Beijing as an "almost microlithic industry." Pei Wenzhong (1939) maintained that the small tools from Zhoukoudian Locality 15 were also microlithic and included concave side scrapers and microblades.

To the west, in southern Inner Mongolia and northern Shaanxi, Upper Pleistocene stone artifacts from the Salawusu (Sjara-osso-gol) region were classified as "Microlithic Palaeolithic" by Teilhard and Pei (1944). In the same publication, they referred to Neolithic remains from Mongolia as the "Mongolian Microlithic" or the "Desert Microlithic." Here the term *microlithic* was used in reference to an artifact assemblage containing not only small stone tools such as microcores, blades, and projectile points, but also various other artifacts including large knives, mortars and pestles, pottery, and large pieces of agricultural equipment (Teilhard and Pei 1944:25–27). Following such precedent, the term *microlithic* appeared in many Chinese publications in reference to a bewildering variety of cultural contexts and stages of technological development.

Many Chinese prehistorians rejected the phrase *microlithic culture* (An 1957; Tong 1979; Xia 1959), arguing that microliths represent only one element in a large complex of artifacts, most of which are characterized by much more rapid and dramatic change through time and space than are microliths. In fact, the modern concept of a microlithic culture in China is very similar to what is meant by the term *microblade industry* in the writings of many North American archaeologists. However, the names *microblade industry* and *microlithic industry* are still seldom used in China.

In the minds of contemporary Chinese archaeologists, the concept of a microlithic industry has become more clearly defined and limited in scope and is no longer used in reference to small tools in general. Today, the term *microlithic*

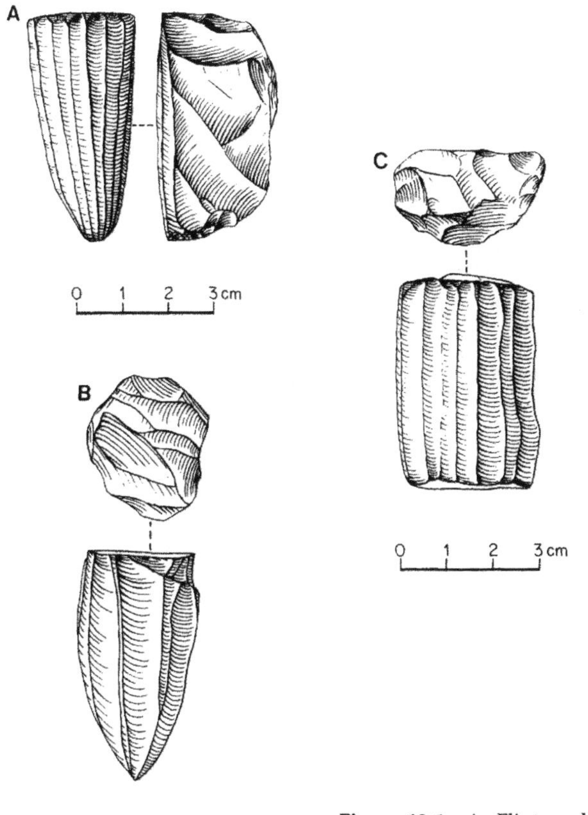

Figure 12.1 A, Flint wedge-shaped microblade core; B, jasper conical microblade core; C, flint cylindrical microblade core.

industry usually indicates an assemblage of artifacts that includes microblades, scrapers, points, small projectile points with flat or concave bases, and a variety of microcores used to produce the blades themselves. *Microblades* are defined as thin strips of stone about 2 mm in thickness with a triangular or trapezoidal cross section. Typical microblades are characterized by roughly parallel sides with a maximum width of less than 10 mm. Microlithic blades are further defined as being between 20 and 60 mm in length (Figures 12.1 and 12.2).

Because the most common elements in any such assemblage are microblades and cores, An Zhimin (1978) has limited the definition of *microlith* to include only very small cores, microblades, and tools made on microblades. In fact, microcores have received the most attention from Chinese prehistorians interested in the origin and subsequent development of northeast Asia's microlithic tradition (An 1978; Gai 1977a, Jia 1978).

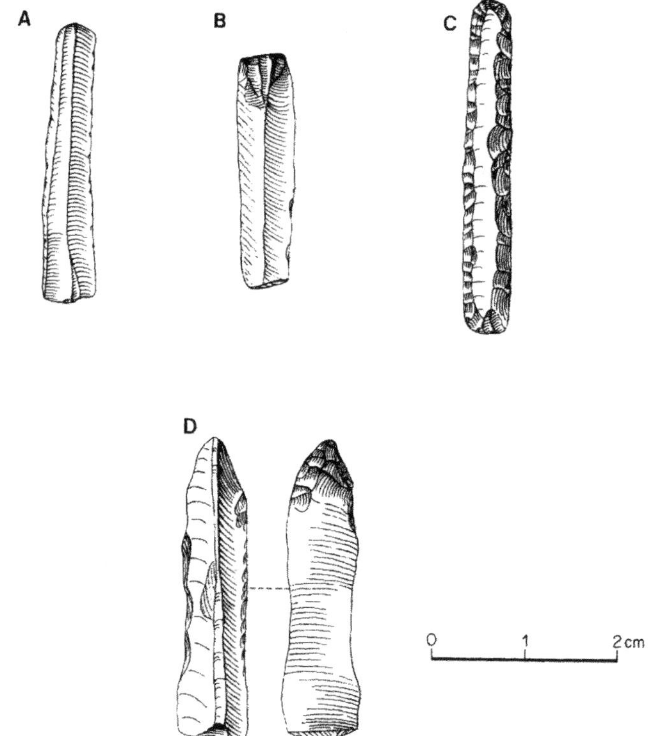

Figure 12.2 A, Jasper prismatic microblade, exhibiting use damage; B, flint prismatic microblade; C, flint unifacially retouched microblade; D, quartz crystal point made by retouching microblade on ventral surface.

Spatial Distribution of Microliths in China

Microlithic artifacts are widely distributed in China. The northernmost of these sites occur in the Heilongjiang (Amur River) area on the Sino–Soviet frontier (Anonymous 1978), while the southernmost sites are located in the vicinity of Guangzhou in Guangdong Province (Guangdong Provincial Museum 1959; Huang *et al.* 1982) (Figure 12.3). Microlithic artifacts have been found in western Xinjiang (Teilhard and Yang 1932) and as far east as the Yellow Sea coast (Li *et al.* 1980). In all, this area of distribution extends some 3500 km north–south by 4600 km east–west. Figure 12.3 illustrates clearly that in spite of this broad areal distribution, microlithic artifacts are found concentrated in the Northeast (the area formerly referred to as Manchuria), Inner Mongolia, and Xinjiang (Inner Mongolia Autonomous Region Bureau of Culture, Cultural Relics Work Group 1957). Particularly dense occurrences of microliths are found on the Songhua (Sungari) River–Nen River Plain in northeast China.

Between 1927 and 1935, the Sino–Swedish Expeditions under the general direction of Sven Hedin recovered more than 50,000 mostly microlithic imple-

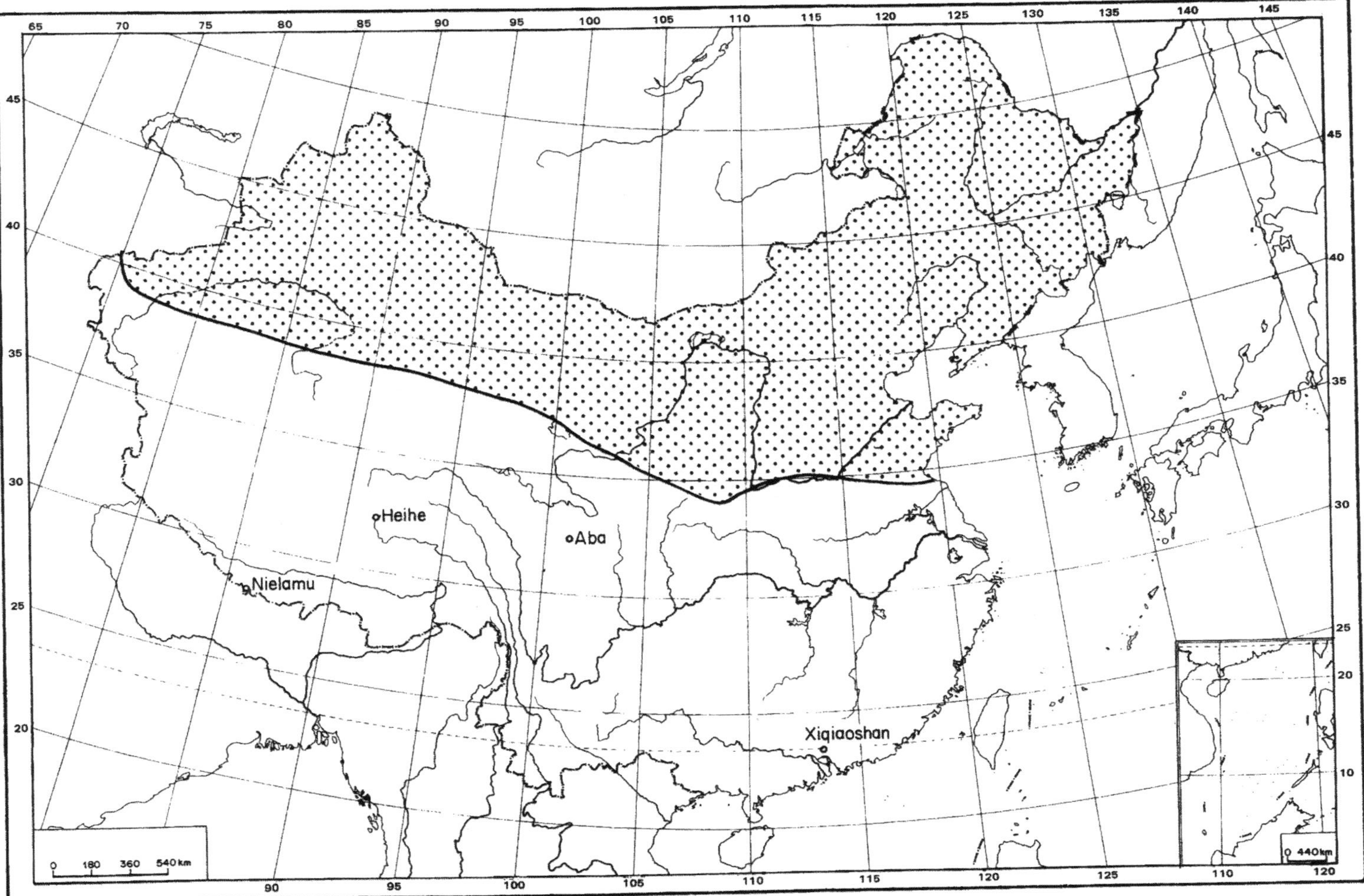

Figure 12.3 Known geographic distribution of Chinese microlithic industries. Shaded area indicates region of densest concentration. Recently discovered sites outside this core area include Nielamu, Xizang (Tibet); Heihe and Aba, Qinghai; and Xiqiaoshan, Guangdong.

ments at 327 localities from Zhangjiakou, Hebei, in the east, to Hami, Xinjiang, in the west (Maringer 1950; Sommarström 1956, 1958), demonstrating the relative abundance of such remains in this area.

In China microlithic remains are associated with a broad spectrum of ecological niches including desert, steppe, and lakeside environments. Microlithic remains are also known to occur above the 4000-m level on the Tibetan Plateau. In 1966 a surveying team sent by the Chinese Academy of Sciences to Tibet excavated 6 microcores and 11 blades near Yali Village in Nielamu County at the foot of the southern face of the Himalayan massif. One of the specimens was found in a travertine deposit on the first terrace of the Qubo River at an elevation of 4300 m above sea level (An and others 1982; Dai 1972, 1976).

At the opposite extreme of the altitudinal scale, microlithic assemblages have been found along the coast of the Yellow Sea less than 100 m above sea level. For example, in 1980 Gai Pei and other archaeologists discovered typical microcores, end scrapers, and small projectile points near Lianyungang in Jiangsu Province.

In the 1940s it was generally believed that microlithic assemblages did not occur south of the Great Wall, or roughly 40°N (Pei 1963; Teilhard and Pei 1944). However, subsequent investigations have demonstrated that the distribution of microlithic remains is not limited to China's northernmost provinces. In 1957, An Zhimin and other archaeologists unearthed typical microcores, microblades, small projectile points, and scrapers in the Shayuan region northeast of Xi'an, Shaanxi (An and Wu 1957). Bearing striking similarities to microlithic artifacts discovered previously in Inner Mongolia (Figures 12.4 and 12.5), this Shayuan assemblage is associated with a complex dune field thought to be of Early Neolithic or possibly Mesolithic age.

An important locality producing microliths at Lingjing, near Xuchang, Henan, south of the Yellow River, was investigated in 1965 by Zhou Guoxing (1974). During the construction of a reservoir at this locality, the excavated fine sands began to yield microlithic tools including cores, blades and scrapers.

These sites and many others that continue to be discovered and investigated within this sphere of distribution clearly indicate China's microlithic assemblages are not phenomena restricted to particular geographical or environmental zones.

A

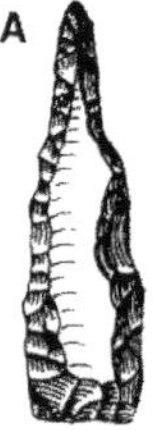

B

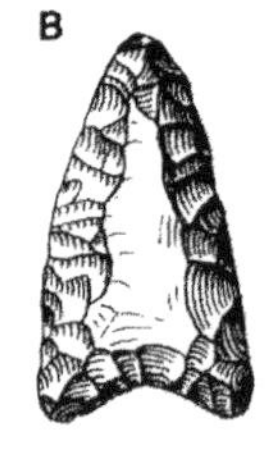

C

0 1 2 cm

Figure 12.4 A, Flint awl made by unifacially retouching microblade on dorsal surface; B, flint projectile point with concave base; C, flint projectile point with straight base.

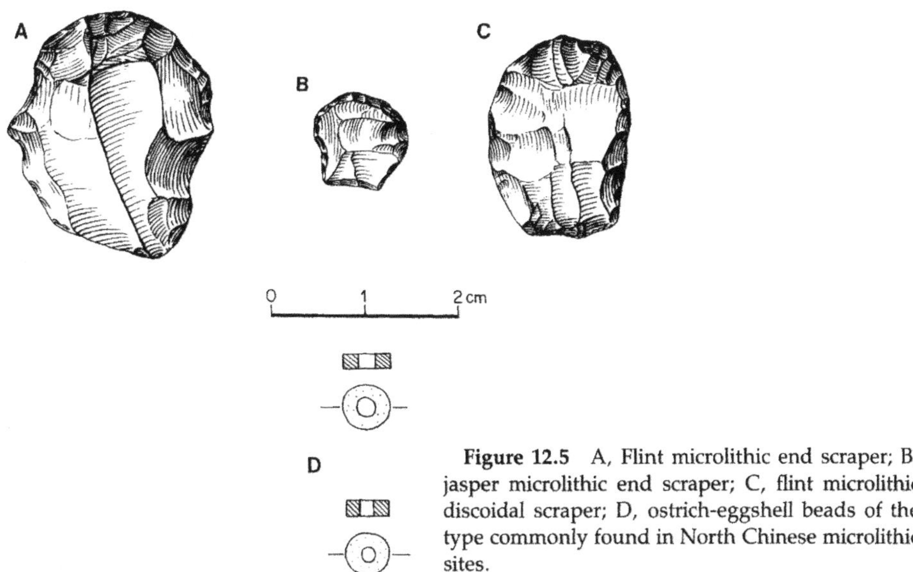

Figure 12.5 A, Flint microlithic end scraper; B, jasper microlithic end scraper; C, flint microlithic discoidal scraper; D, ostrich-eggshell beads of the type commonly found in North Chinese microlithic sites.

Chronology of Chinese Microlithic Assemblages

Precise chronological placement of China's microlithic assemblages has been a subject of constant discussion. These artifacts are characterized by a persistence in the archaeological record virtually unmatched by any other category of cultural remains in the later prehistoric period. With a diachronic range beginning in the Late Palaeolithic, microlithic tools are present in Neolithic contexts and survived well into the historic Bronze Age in the first millennium BC.

Until the early 1970s consensus of opinion held that most Chinese microliths were of Mesolithic or Neolithic age (Teilhard and Pei 1944); however, in 1972 Gai Pei and Wei Qi discovered abundant microlithic remains in a Late Palaeolithic context at Hutouliang, Hebei, about 100 km west of Beijing (Gai and Wei 1977). Hearth features discovered at the site are believed to contain the charred remains of ostrich eggshells and mammal bones. The site's artifact inventory includes a total of 236 microcores, more than 300 blades, and 114 end scrapers. Biostratigraphic and geological data suggest the deposit is Upper Pleistocene, and an associated radiocarbon date of 11,000 ± 210 BP (PV-156) tends to confirm this conclusion.

In 1973 excavations at the Xiachuan site in southern Shanxi Province (35°23′–35°31′N, 111°58′–112°16′E) yielded about 180 microcores, 180 blades, ad more than 300 end scrapers (Wang *et al.* 1978). Six calibrated radiocarbon dates have been obtained thus far ranging from 14,450 ± 900 BC (ZK-385) to 21,950 ± 100 BC (ZK-417).

Microlithic cores have also been recovered in earlier Palaeolithic contexts. Beginning in 1963, Locality 63661 near Shiyu in Suoxian County, Shanxi (39°25′N,

112°E), has produced a wide variety of archaeological and faunal remains (Aigner 1981:226–228; Jia *et al.* 1972) with an associated ^{14}C date on *Bubalus* bone of 28,135 ± 1330 BP (ZK-109). In 1972, the discovery of a microlithic core and blades in association with such animals as *Struthio* sp. indet., *Crocuta* sp. indet., *Cervus elaphus, Megaloceros ordosianus, Coelodonta antiquitatis, Equus przewalskyi,* and *E. hemionus* suggests a rather cool, steppe environment may have prevailed during the period of the site's occupation.

In southern Inner Mongolia, within the great bend of the Yellow River, sites in the Ordos (Hetao) Region such as those in the Salawusu (Sjara-osso-gol) Valley have also yielded microlithic tools. The French archaeologist Henri Breuil first suggested many of these artifacts were burins (in Boule *et al.* 1928), but this determination was later revised by the American archaeologist Jason Smith (1974), who considered the artifacts to be microcores, a position with which Chinese archaeologists agree (An 1978; Gai 1977b, 1978). The Salawusu deposits have yielded a radiocarbon date of 35,340 ± 1900 BP (PV-177) and uranium series determinations suggest a range of 37,000 to 50,000 years BP.

Evidence accumulated from the opposite end of the temporal continuum suggests microlithic equipment continued to be used well into China's historic period. At the Fuhegoumen site in Zhaowuda League, Inner Mongolia, microcores, blades, and small points fashioned on microblades occur in association with ground-stone agricultural implements and simple brown ceramics in an essentially Neolithic archaeological context radiocarbon dated to 2785 ± 110 BC (ZK-188) (An 1981).

Also in China's Northeast, microblades, small projectile points, and end scrapers were found among the funerary goods in the Dongshantou tomb in Da'an County, Jilin (Jilin Provincial Museum 1961a,b). Specific objects found in this Bronze Age tomb included yellow-brown geometric design pottery vessels, bronze buttons, and knives, suggesting the persistence of this microlithic tradition. In Xifeng County, Liaoning Province, another historic Xiongnu culture tomb excavated at Xichagou produced stone microblades and small projectile points in association with a Han dynasty bronze mirror, as well as Han *banliang* and *wushu* coins (Sun 1960). According to An Zhimin (1981), the use of microlithic equipment in the late historic period is attested to by its discovery in archaeological assemblages dating to periods as late as the Liao and Jin dynasties (AD 916–1234).

In spite of the great temporal durability of the microlithic tradition itself, the cultural remains found in association with microliths changed significantly.

Assemblages consisting solely of microlithic artifacts have been reported from Nielamu County, Tibet; Hongfangzi, Xinjiang; and Yi'erdingmanha (Irdin Manha), Inner Mongolia. The fact that large chipped-stone implements, ground-stone tools, and ceramics do not occur at all at localities such as these suggests that at one time parts of China may have been inhabited by cultures utilizing exclusively microlithic technologies. Unfortunately, due to the fact that only relatively small samples were collected, without any stratigraphic control, it is difficult to determine their absolute chronology.

In most Palaeolithic sites, microlithic elements occur in association with various kinds of larger chipped-stone implements. For instance, "ulu" knives, gouges, points, and a small number of chopping tools were found at Hutouliang, Hebei, in addition to a large array of microcores, blades, and scrapers (Gai and Wei 1977). At Xiachuan, in Shanxi Province, microlithic remains occur alongside larger chipped-stone tools as well as with infrequent ground-stone pieces (Wang *et al.* 1978).

In the Badan Jilin (Badain Jaran) Desert of western Inner Mongolia, microlithic implements are found in conjunction with larger tools, but, as these pieces bear a striking morphological resemblance to polished Neolithic stone artifacts, it is possible these sites may be no earlier than the Neolithic period (Maringer 1950).

In Qinghai Province, some 200 km southwest of Xining, the Layihai site has yielded microlithic remains in association with both flaked- and ground-stone tools; however, no polished-stone artifacts or potsherds were recovered. A single radiocarbon determination of 6745 ± 85 BP (PV-199) is similar to dates derived from middle Neolithic contexts in central China (Gai and Wang 1983).

In the Hunshandake Desert of central Inner Mongolia, microlithic implements are occasionally found in context with a few polished-stone artifacts and brown-gray potsherds. On the Songhua (Sungari) River–Nen River Plain in China's Northeast, microlithic assemblages are found in archaeological sites that also contain polished-stone tools, bone harpoons, and brownish pottery. In the Ordos (Hetao) Region of southern Inner Mongolia and northern Shaanxi, microliths occur in association with polished-stone axes and hoes as well as chipped-stone tools and red-brown ceramics. Microliths have also been found with Neolithic painted pottery, polished-stone axes and hoes, and chipped-stone tools in the Xilamulun River region of eastern Inner Mongolia (Tong 1979).

The complex nature of the archaeological occurrence of microlithic tools in China does not diminish the fact that in all the previously cited contexts microliths constitute a major element in the total cultural assemblage. This persistent presence in the archaeological record underscores the difficulties involved in establishing precise chronological control for the temporal distribution of microliths in China.

Changes in the Composition of Microlithic Industries

Another aspect of the complicated research questions surrounding the occurrence of microliths in China concerns changes apparent within the composition of the assemblages themselves. The three principal changes to which I refer are functions of time, spatial distribution, and technique of manufacture.

Microliths in China conform to an interesting pattern of frequency through time, and each period is characterized by particular methods of fabrication. For example, the earliest known true microliths in China occur in only very small quantities at some localities. The cores were either entirely unretouched or exhibit very coarse trimming. Blades are very rare and do not conform to our definition of microlithic, particularly since their dimensions vary considerably throughout each assemblage. Our present impression is that the technologies that eventually led to the manufacture of true microlithic cores may have begun in the Upper Pleistocene or even earlier.

The second stage in the development of microlithic technologies in China includes the Late Palaeolithic and Early Neolithic periods. At this time, microlithic industries seem to have undergone a marked florescence and become widely distributed in North China. The variety of techniques used to produce these artifacts similarly increased, although finely retoched microlithic blades are not yet associated with these assemblages.

The salient feature of the third stage of this developmental continuum, including the Late Neolithic period, is the maturity of the fabrication techniques employed in the production of microlithic blades. Typical occurrences of these mature microlithic industries may be found on the Hulunbei'er Steppes of eastern Inner Mongolia, where characteristic elements include large numbers of long, thin blades as well as retouched tools fashioned on such blades. In most areas of China, the early Bronze Age witnessed the rapid decline of microlithic technologies, although the basic techniques of manufacture persisted in some areas well into the historic period.

It should be noted that these three stages of microlithic development do not coincide with the broad cultural designations Palaeolithic, Neolithic, and historic. For example, microlithic nuclei typical of the second stage are found in association with both Late Palaeolithic stone industries and Early Neolithic assemblages containing ceramics. Remnants of the technologically simple first-stage microcores are also known from Late Palaeolithic sites, and occasionally rather sophisticated microlithic tools are found in essentially Early Neolithic contexts. Microlithic end scrapers appear first in sites of Late Palaeolithic age, but in Early Neolithic contexts end scrapers and circular scrapers characterized by much smaller overall dimensions and finer retouch occur in large quantities.

Certain important microlithic tool types have not been discovered thus far in any Palaeolithic assemblage. These include awls and small projectile points with straight and concave bases that, due to their frequent occurrence in later microlithic collections, may be characterized by a relatively rapid process of development. Unfortunately, we have no data as yet to illuminate this important sequence. Some projectile points, such as the so-called leaf-shaped arrowheads with fine retouch on their ventral surfaces, occur in only a few isolated localities in eastern Inner Mongolia and Heilongjiang such as Angangxi, Fuhegoumen, Ordos (Hetao), and Yi'erdingmanha (Irdin Manha), among others.

Detailed analysis of microlithic occurrences in China reveals substantial synchronic regional variation within the industry as a whole. One of the most striking patterns to be illuminated thus far is the tendency for microlithic assemblages in eastern China to be characterized by much more technological variation than those to the west. For example, in the Badan Jilin Desert of western Inner Mongolia, only a few types of microlithic tools are known. Farther to the east, in the Hunshandake Desert, both the variety and absolute number of microliths are greater. And finally, on the Songhua (Sungari) River–Nen River Plain in Heilongjiang, Jilin, and eastern Inner Mongolia, large numbers of microlithic tools can be found including cores, projectile points, circular scrapers, end scrapers, awls, and blades. At present, problems in the establishment of an absolute chronology for these various assemblages limit our ability to determine to what extent we may be witnessing a west to east flow of technological innovation (Heilongjiang Provincial Museum 1974; Liang 1959). This is a research question we intend to address in the future.

Two Hypotheses Concerning the Origin of Chinese Microlithic Industries

Teilhard and Pei (1944) proposed the idea that Chinese microlithic industries were largely derived from preexisting culture complexes in the area of Lake Baikal in the southern U.S.S.R. Their argument further suggests that Late Palaeolithic microlithic industries in south Siberia gradually extended southward, converging with local Chinese agricultural complexes forming a so-called mixed culture. An important aspect of Teilhard and Pei's hypothesis was their idea that such microlithic remains in China were restricted to the northern quarter of the country, further reinforcing the concept of strong links with Late Palaeolithic Siberia. Even though this hypothesis provided a comprehensive explanation for the archaeological record as it was then known, this idea was challenged on the basis of new evidence and interpretations.

By the late 1950s a number of localities south of the Great Wall and the Yellow River had been discovered, containing large quantities of microlithic remains. Among the most important of these sites are those in the Shayuan region of Shaanxi Province (An and Wu 1957) and Lingjing, Henan (Zhou 1974).

The original thesis of Teilhard and Pei is further weakened by the recognition in recent years that the southern Siberian Palaeolithic microlithic industries probably do not constitute the basal stock from which their Chinese counterparts developed.

Finally, and perhaps most important, microlithic tools have been found in Upper Pleistocene Palaeolithic contexts in China itself. These new data on the spatial distribution and origins of microlithic industries in China have resulted in the abandonment of Teilhard and Pei's 1944 thesis and the formulation of new explanations.

In 1972 Chinese scholars proposed a new hypothesis explaining the origin and florescence of the Chinese microlithic tradition (Jia *et al.* 1972). Their first step was a reclassification of Chinese archaeological sites beginning with the Early Palaeolithic into units that they perceived as having shared traits. They concluded that even the smaller tools derived from the Middle Pleistocene *Homo erectus* occupation site at Zhoukoudian Locality 1 exhibit sufficient characters to allow them to be included in a general continuum of technological features that culminated in the typical microlithic cultures of North China. Their chronological sequence continues with the inclusion of Zhoukoudian Locality 15; Salawusu, Inner Mongolia; Hougedafeng and Shiyu, Shanxi; and Xiaonanhai, Henan. Jia Lanpo and others believe that the highly developed microlithic industries of early Holocene China are an outgrowth of this lineage. When this concept was originally proposed a disconcerting gap existed in the archaeological record between the microlithic industries exemplified by such Palaeolithic occurrences as Shiyu and Salawusu and the abundant microlithic remains of the Neolithic period. Jia and his colleagues predicted that this hiatus would be filled through the discovery of Late Palaeolithic sites whose industrial complexes would be based largely on microlithic tools. The discovery and analysis of microlithic assemblages at the sites of Xiachuan, Shanxi (Wang *et al.* 1978), and Hutouliang, Hebei (Gai and Wei 1977), have proven this prediction entirely correct, and Chinese archaeologists now believe the origin and subsequent development of local microlithic industries to be deeply rooted in North China's Palaeolithic prehistoric record.

The Role of Technological Diffusion

Microlithic industries are not a cultural phenomenon unique to China. In fact, microlithic remains identical or very similar to Chinese assemblages are widely distributed throughout Siberia, the Mongolian People's Republic, the Korean peninsula, the Japanese archipelago, and northwestern North America. In the Soviet Union, wedge-shaped microlithic cores are distributed along the Obi River in the west (Panichkina 1959) and in the Aldan River area of eastern Siberia as far north as 70°N. In his study of the famous Dyuktai culture of Siberia, the Soviet archaeologist Ju. A. Mochanov concluded that the origins of this late Palaeolithic industry lay in the region of North China between the Amur River (Heilongjiang) and the Yellow River (Mochanov 1969). Based on our current analyses of microlithic assemblages from both eastern Siberia and North China, it now seems that Mochanov's conclusion is supportable.

Some Soviet archaeologists, however, suggest the microlithic tradition of Central and East Asia was derived from an eastern Mongolian Levallois prepared-core technology (Okladnikov 1974:337; Vasilevsky 1976:150). For example, Okladnikov and Vasilevsky both propose the following features as traits shared by both Levallois and microlithic traditions: (1) removal of blades from only one side of the core; (2) the blade removal surface is beveled in relation to the striking platform, rather than being perpendicular; and (3) the core's working surface was prepared by special retouching of the edges. Okladnikov's conclusion is that because the microlithic nuclei of East Asia (the so-called Gobi cores) also share these traits, they were therefore derived from a Palaeolithic Levallois-based industry. In our view, this position is unsupportable. First, we do not believe a true Levallois technology was widely distributed in East Asia. In the past, there has been a tendency to label any prepared-platform core technology *Levallois*, and a great deal of confusion has resulted.

As for Okladnikov's and Vasilevsky's three points of congruence between Levallois and microlithic industries, we would comment that none is restricted to the two industries mentioned. The morphology and function of Levallois flakes are quite distinct matters, and the techniques employed to obtain Levallois flakes (direct percussion) and microblades (indirect percussion) are also different. There is no reason to see a developmental, functional relationship between these two traditions, because microliths were presumably used principally as inserts in composite tools while Levallois flakes served as blanks for larger implements.

We believe that the suggestion is in error that Gobi cores are characterized by blade-removal surfaces that are beveled in relation to the striking platform. Nearly all the East Asian microblade nuclei with which we are familiar, including the famous Gobi cores, are typified by blade-removal surfaces that are essentially perpendicular to their striking platforms. Vasilevsky's plate depicting microlithic materials from the Khere-Uul site in eastern Mongolia illustrates this point well (1976:149).

The microlithic artifacts of Japan share many features in common with their North Chinese counterparts. It is likely these similarities result, at least in part, from the physical proximity of the Japanese archipelago to the East Asian mainland in both the north and south during the Pleistocene epoch (Aikens and Higuchi 1982; Gai 1977a,c; Pei 1978).

In regard to the Dyuktai culture itself, we believe the links between North America and Asia in the Upper Pleistocene may best be understood through careful analysis of these archaeological materials. Clearly, an approach to such large questions based on data from a limited geographic area cannot be expected to produce definitive results. The radiocarbon dates from Dyuktai Cave need to be reexamined, as there is confusion in the stratigraphic sequence between the upper and lower deposits. In addition, detailed comparisons must be made between the Dyuktai materials and similar assemblages in both North America and North China. In North America as early as the 1930s, American archaeologist Nels C. Nelson found that the microlithic artifacts of Alaska bore apparent relationships to their counterparts in Central Asia (Nelson 1937). More recently, parallels between microlithic remains obtained in North China and northwestern North America continue to suggest the validity of Nelson's view (Chen 1983; Gai 1977a, 1983; Smith 1974). Microcores recovered from the Campus Site in Fairbanks, Alaska (Nelson 1937), from the Healy Lake Village and

Akmak sites in northwest Alaska (Anderson 1970; McKennan and Cook 1968), and from Ice Mountain in British Columbia (Smith 1974) are all similar to microlithic assemblages excavated recently in North China (Gai 1977b, 1983; Gai and Wei 1977). The apparently widespread geographic distribution of microlithic artifacts throughout northeast Asia and northwest North America may be attributed to one or a combination of two factors. First, the technology itself may have spread through stimulus diffusion to incorporate broad expanses of the Asian and North American continents. Second, it is possible that the physical movement of human populations, carrying with them a developed microlithic technology, may account for the distribution of these assemblages as recognized in the archaeological record. Given what we know about the vast geographic distribution and temporal persistence of the microlithic tradition, it is likely both of these processes had an effect on the florescence of this phenomenon.

That microlithic technologies bridge the gap between hunting–gathering–fishing cultures and those engaged in full-fledged agriculture in East Asia is an important point to consider. Microlithic assemblages are found in association with cultures whose principal subsistence strategies include the procurement of terrestrial and marine mammals, the collection of wild vegetal resources, mature agriculture, and various combinations of these activities. That microlithic industries are found in such a diverse spectrum of environmental and cultural contexts suggests adaptability is an important aspect of this technology.

Our research in China during the past decade has begun to indicate clearly the complex nature of the archaeological occurrence of microlithic assemblages in this region. It is hoped that continued field studies and laboratory analyses will further clarify some of the points made in this essay, particularly the question of northeast Asian–North American connections during the Upper Pleistocene.

References

Aigner, Jean S.

1981 *Archaeological remains in Pleistocene China.* Forschungen zur Allgemeinen und Vergleichrenden Archäologie, Band 1. Munich: Verlag C. H. Beck.

Aikens, C. Melvin and Takayasu Higuchi

1982 *Prehistory of Japan.* New York: Academic Press.

An Zhimin

1957 Microlithic cultures. *Kaogu Tongxun* 2:36–47.

1958 The Neolithic. In *Kaoguxue Jichu,* edited by the Institute of Archaeology, Chinese Academy of Social Sciences. Beijing: Science Press. Pp. 30–59.

1978 Mesolithic remains in Haila'er: On the origin of the microlithic tradition. *Acta Archaeologica Sinica* 3:289–316.

1981 The Neolithic age of China. *Kaogu* 3:252–260.

An Zhimin and others (Yi Zesheng and Li Bingyuan)

1982 Palaeoliths and microliths from Shenja and Shuanghu, Northern Tibet. *Current Anthropology* 23(5):493–499.

An Zhimin and Wu Ruzuo
1957 Stone Age remains in the Sha-wan region, Chao-yi and Ta-li counties, Shensi. *Acta Archaeologica Sinica* 3:1–12.
Anderson, Douglas D.
1970 Akmak: An early archaeological assemblage from Onion Portage, northwest Alaska. *Acta Arctica* XVI. Copenhagen: Munksgaard.
Andersson, J. Gunnar
1923 The cave deposit at Sha Kuo T'un in Fengtien. *Palaeontologia Sinica* Series D 1(1):1–43.
1945 The site of Chu Chia Chai. *Bulletin of the Museum of Far Eastern Antiquities* 17:1–63.
Anonymous
1978 Discovery of a Palaeolithic site on the right bank of the Heilongjiang. *Renmin Ribao* January 24, p. 4. Beijing.
Boule, M., H. Breuil, E. Licent, and P. Teilhard de Chardin
1928 *Le Paléolithique de la Chine*. Archives Institut de Paléontologie Humaine, Memoire 4:1–138. Paris: Masson et Cie.
Chen Chun
1983 Preliminary exploration of the typology and technology of microcores in China—also of the culture relationship between Northeast Asia and Northwestern North America. *Acta Anthropologica Sinica* 2(4):331–341.
Dai Erjian
1972 Stone artifacts unearthed in Nielamu, Tibet. *Kaogu* 1:43–44.
1976 Stone artifacts unearthed in Nielamu, Tibet. In *Report on a Scientific Survey in the Mount Qomolangma Area (1966–1968), Quaternary Geology*. Beijing: Science Press. Pp. 110–112.
Gai Pei
1977a The water of the Yellow River flows to Japan. *People's China* 10–11:36–39.
1977b On the Palaeolithic connections between China and North America. *Huashi* 2:1–4.
1977c The cultural relationship between China and Japan in Late Palaeolithic times. *Huashi* 3:2–10.
1978 Evidence linking Palaeolithic culture in China with North America. *China Reconstructs* 27(5):46–48.
1983 New research on Chinese origins of the first Americans. *China Reconstructs* 32(1):38–40.
Gai Pei and Wei Qi
1977 Discovery of the Late Palaeolithic site at Hutouliang, Hebei. *Vertebrata PalAsiatica* 15(4):287–300.
Gai Pei and Wang Guodao
1983 Excavation report on a Mesolithic site at Layihai on the upper Yellow River. *Acta Anthropologica Sinica* 2(1):49–59.
Guangdong Provincial Museum
1959 Stone tools excavated at Hsi-ch'iao-shan, Nan-hai county, Kwangtung. *Acta Archaeologica Sinica* 4:1–15.
Heilongjiang Provincial Museum
1974 Investigation of the Angangxi Neolithic site. *Kaogu* 2:99–108.
Huang Weiwen, Li Chunchu, Wang Honshou, and Huang Yukun
1982 Reexamination of a microlithic site at Xiqiaoshan, Nanhai county, Guangdong. *Current Anthropology* 23(5):487–492.
Inner Mongolia Autonomous Region Bureau of Culture, Cultural Relics Work Group
1957 Microlithic culture sites discovered in the Inner Mongolia Autonomous Region. *Acta Archaeologica Sinica* 1:9–20.
Jia Lanpo (Chia Lan-po)
1978 On the phase, origin, and tradition of Microtool Industry in China. *Vertebrata PalAsiatica* 16(2):137–143.

Jia Lanpo (Chia Lan-po), Gai Pei, and You Yuzhu
1972 Report of excavation in Shi Yu, Shanxi—a Palaeolithic site. *Acta Archaeologica Sinica* 1:39–60.

Jilin Provincial Museum
1961a The Dongshantou microlithic site in Da'an, Jilin. *Kaogu* 8:404–406.
1961b Microlithic sites in Zhen'gai, Jilin. *Kaogu* 8:398–403.

Li Yanxian, Lin Yipu, Ge Zhigong, and Zhang Zufang
1980 On a collection of chipped stone artifacts from Donghai, Jiangsu. *Vertebrata PalAsiatica* 18(3):239–246.

Liang Siyong
1959 The Angangxi prehistoric site. In *Liang Siyong Kaogu Lunwenji, Kaoguxue Zhuankan*, Series A 5:58–90.

Maringer, Johannes
1950 Contribution to the prehistory of Mongolia. *The Sino-Swedish Expedition Publication 34*. Stockholm: Statens Etnografiska Museum.

McKennan, Robert A. and John P. Cook
1968 Prehistory of Healy Lake, Alaska. *Proceedings of the 8th International Congress of Anthropological and Ethnological Sciences* 3:182–184.

Mochanov, Ju. A.
1969 Earliest stages in the habitation of northeast Asia and Alaska (On the question of man's earliest migrations into America). *Sovetskaia Etnografia* 1:79–86.

Nelson, Nels C.
1937 Notes on cultural relations between Asia and America. *American Anthropologist* 2(4):267–272.

Okladnikov, Aleksei Pavlovich
1974 A Stone Age settlement on the Khere-Uul Mountain (eastern Mongolia) and preceramic cultures of Japan. *Investigations in History and Philology: Articles Collected in Honor of Academician N. I. Conrad*. Moscow: Nauka. Pp. 322–338.

Panichkina, M. Z.
1959 Palaeolithic cores. *Arkheologicheskii Sbornik* 1:7–77.

Pei Wenzhong (Pei Wen-chung)
1939 A preliminary study of a new Palaeolithic station known as Locality 15 within the Choukoutien region. *Bulletin of the Geological Society of China* 19(2):147–187.
1963 *The Stone Age of China*. Beijing: Young People's Press.
1978 Connections between China and Japan in view of ancient cultures and animals. *Kexue Tongbao* 23(12):705–708.

Smith, Jason W.
1974 The northeast Asian—Northwest microblade tradition. *Journal of Field Archaeology* 1(3–4):347–364.

Sommarström, Bo
1956 Archaeological researches in the Edsen-gol region, Inner Mongolia, Part I. *The Sino-Swedish Expedition Publication 39*. Stockholm: Statens Etnografiska Museum.
1958 Archaeological researches in the Edsen-gol region, Inner Mongolia, Part II. *The Sino-Swedish Expedition Publication 41*. Stockholm: Statens Etnografiska Museum.

Sun Shoudao
1960 Discovery of ancient Xiongnu Xichagou culture tombs. *Wenwu* 8–9:25–32.

Teilhard de Chardin, P. and Pei Wenzhong (P'ei Wen-chung)
1932 The lithic industry of the *Sinanthropus* deposits in Chouk'outien. *Bulletin of the Geological Society of China* 11(4):315–364.
1944 Le Neolithique de la Chine. *Institut de Géo-Biologie* 10:1–98.

Teilhard de Chardin, P. and Yang Zhongjian (C. C. Young)
1932 On some Neolithic (and possibly Palaeolithic) finds in Mongolia, Sinkiang, and west China. *Bulletin of the Geological Society of China* 12(1):83–104.

Tong Zhuchen
1979 On the question of microlithic cultures in north and northeast China. *Acta Archaeologica Sinica* 4:403–422.

Vasilevsky, R. S.
1976 The Pacific microlithic traditions and their Central-Asian roots. In *Le Paléolithique Inférieur et Moyen en Inde, en Asie Centrale, en Chine et dans le Sud-est Asiatique,* edited by A. K. Ghosh. UISPP IX Congres, Colloque VII. Nice: CNRS. Pp. 131–153.

Wang Jian (Wang Chien), Wang Xiangqian, and Chen Zheying
1978 Archaeological reconnaissances at Hsia Chuan in Chin Shui county, Shansi province. *Acta Archaeologica Sinica* 3:259–288.

Xia Nai
1959 On the problem of assigning names to archaeological cultures. *Kaogu* 4:171–172.

Zhou Guoxing
1974 Stone Age remains from Lingjing, Xuchang, Henan. *Kaogu* 2:91–98.

13

Aspects of the Inner Mongolian Palaeolithic

WANG YUPING AND JOHN W. OLSEN

Introduction

Although the first unquestionable Palaeolithic artifacts to be brought to light in China were those found by Emile Licent in the Qingyang region of eastern Gansu as early as 1920 (Teilhard and Licent 1924; Xie and Zhang 1977), the Pleistocene prehistory of China's steppe and desert provinces northwest of approximately 35°N and 110°E is still poorly understood.

The Sino–Swedish Expeditions of 1927 to 1935 (Bergman 1945; Maringer 1950a, 1963; Sommarström 1956, 1958) and the reconnaissances of Pierre Teilhard de Chardin and Yang Zhongjian in 1930–1931 (Teilhard and Yang 1932) yielded the majority of the Inner Mongolian data upon which many subsequent interpretations were based. The Andrews Central Asiatic Expeditions provided complementary data from the area of what is now the Mongolian People's Republic during two field campaigns in 1922–1923 and 1928–1929 (Berkey and Nelson 1926; Nelson 1926, 1939). More recently Soviet and Mongolian scholars have augmented these earlier studies with additional information (Dorj 1971; Elisseeff 1950; Okladnikov 1951). Unfortunately, of all the Stone Age material collected in both Inner Mongolia and the Mongolian People's Republic by these earlier expeditions, only that discovered by the Sino–Swedish Expeditions has been fully described and published.

In the past two decades, however, a number of important advances have been made in the Palaeolithic archaeology of the Inner Mongolia Autonomous Region

Palaeoanthropology and
Palaeolithic Archaeology in the
People's Republic of China

ISBN 0-12-601720-4

on the eastern boundary of China's vast arid territories. It is the purpose of this essay to outline some of these discoveries in the context of the Pleistocene prehistory of North China.

Principal Inner Mongolian Palaeolithic Sites

Dayao, Hohhot

Located near Dayao Village on the Baoheshao Commune some 33 km northeast of Hohhot, the Dayao Palaeolithic locality is one of the most important Pleistocene archaeological sites yet discovered in China's steppe zone (Wang 1979, 1980). In 1973 archaeologists began a long-term program of investigation at the site, which is situated in the foothills of the Daqing Mountains immediately south of Dayao Village. During excavations in 1976, 1979, 1981, and 1983 it was determined that the site is a quarry–workshop covering an area of more than 3 km^2 and reflects a long sequence of utilization. The three hills that comprise the locality are characterized by outcroppings of flint and quartz that, in this area of thick loess deposits and generally small, intractable, fluvially derived pebbles, seems to have been an attractive source of raw material.

Quarry–workshops are among the scarcest archaeological site-types in China; only the Neolithic localities of Xiqiaoshan in Nanhai County, Guangdong (Guangdong Provincial Museum 1959; Huang *et al.* 1982; Zhongshan University Investigation Group 1959), and E'maokou in Huairen County, Shanxi (Jia and You 1973), have been investigated to any significant extent. Consequently, Dayao has provided a heretofore unparalleled opportunity to investigate changing patterns of lithic resource utilization in North China during the Upper Pleistocene.

Although many of the Dayao archaeological occurrences consist of surface scatters—clearly the waste products of innumerable generations of stone knappers, including those of the Neolithic—the late Pleistocene loess deposits in some areas of the site preserve artifacts in stratified primary context. Only one of the three low hills comprising the Dayao site is characterized by a succession of loessic deposits including Upper Pliocene (Baode), Middle Pleistocene (Lishi), and Upper Pleistocene (Malan) components. In other areas of the site the bedrock outcrops utilized as a source of raw material are covered directly by the Malan loess, which is at least in part a result of differential erosion (for a thorough discussion of China's loess deposits, see Derbyshire 1983). In all areas of the site the loessic sequence at Dayao is capped by a gray-black loam that is up to 6 m thick in areas protected from eolian deflation.

The natural erosional gullies that have dissected the Dayao site provide several 15-m-deep sections in which Palaeolithic artifacts may be observed in primary context within the site's Upper Pleistocene loess beds and in the reddish palaeosol that invades it.

Excavations at Dayao have yet to reveal any evidence of Upper Pleistocene structures, but in 1981 and 1983 the authors examined concentrated horizons of apparently scorched loess thought to be remnants of hearth features. It is hoped that such loci will provide charred organic remains from which radiocarbon determinations may be derived.

The 1979 and 1981 excavations conducted by the Inner Mongolia Museum also yielded evidence of much earlier utilization of the Dayao flint source. Excavating below the bed of one of the principal erosional gullies (Sidaogou) on the north slope of Tu'er Hill, archaeologists encountered a large number of flint boulders, some measuring as much as 1.7 m in length. The boulders, which occur in a red Middle Pleistocene palaeosol, are characterized by severe battering, for the most part resulting from the intentional reduction of these monoliths for raw material. Discovered strewn about these boulders were large quantities of débitage and a few completed tools; consequently, there can be little doubt of the archaeological nature of this assemblage. In addition, the Sidaogou at Dayao has yielded purposefully arranged patterns of stones, including one thought to be the foundation of a circular structure about 1 m in diameter, and containing a deposit of ash and highly fragmented bone.

The implications of these most recent finds are quite significant. The archaeological materials contained in the upper loess beds at Dayao constitute China's first well-documented Palaeolithic quarrying debris. If the materials from the lower strata of the Sidaogou can be determined to be of Middle Pleistocene antiquity, the documented prehistory of Inner Mongolia can be pushed back by a factor of 10 from the roughly 30,000 to 50,000-year-old Palaeolithic sequences in the Salawusu (Sjara-osso-gol) Valley. If we accept the lower Sidaogou assemblage at Dayao as being of Middle Pleistocene origin, it is of additional interest in that these remains do not closely resemble Early Palaeolithic finds from other areas of North China including those from Lantian, Shaanxi; Kehe, Shanxi; and Zhoukoudian Locality 1, Beijing.

Whereas the Early Palaeolithic industries of these latter localities are based mainly on the use of fluvial pebbles and relatively small nodules of siliceous stone as raw material, at Dayao it is apparent substantial energy was expended in reducing large flint boulders into manageable blanks. This disparity in primary production techniques may simply be a function of the type of raw materials available.

One of our principal goals for the future is to gather sufficient data to allow us to determine unequivocally the age of these assemblages. Thus far, aside from geological context and typological considerations, chronological data are scarce. Faunal remains associated with this earlier component are poorly preserved and include species that are not unique to the Middle Pleistocene.

Cultural remains from the Dayao locality show little variation between the upper and lower deposits in the Sidaogou, which may be partially a result of the fact that as a quarry–workshop site, few finished artifacts are present in either depositional context. In a qualitative sense, the earlier assemblage is charac-

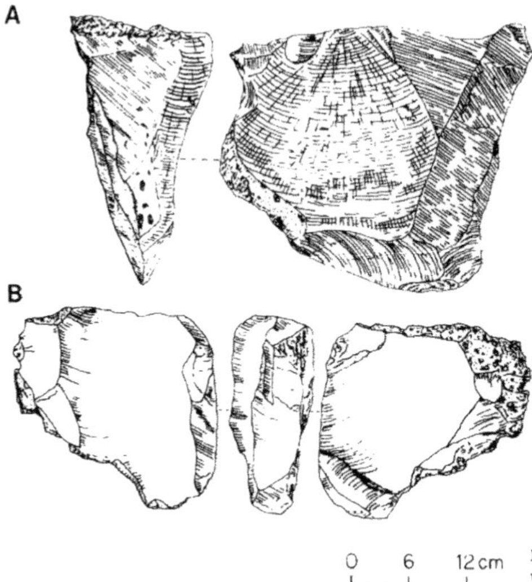

Figure 13.1 Two large co ı Dayao, Inner Mongolia: A, unifacial; ıcial. (After Wang 1980.)

terized by larger, thicker flakes, and retouched pieces constitı ly a very small percentage of the whole.

With the exception of odd Neolithic surface materials the only d of flake production in evidence is direct percussion with a hard hamm ɜither the indirect percussion nor pressure techniques have yet been idє l, further emphasizing the Palaeolithic character of these finds.

The lithic assemblage from the upper loess unit at Dayao con . range of typologically classifiable implements in addition to the waste ļ :ts of the manufacturing process. Six types of nuclei are recognized. Alt ·ly struck large cores are among the most numerous and include several sp ·ns found in close proximity to conjoining flakes (Wang 1980:3). Other cor s include unifacial and bifacial (Figure 13.1), triangular, pillar shaped, ; ɔlyhedral varieties, of which the last may be subdivided into those wi ee or six primary flake-removal surfaces.

Flakes derived from these cores are at present classified i ree morphological types: multiple-edge, bipointed, and "plate shape *nxing*) or discoidal (Figure 13.2). Bladelike flakes, ranging from 1.3 to 12. n length, occur infrequently at the site.

Finished implements from the loessic deposits at Dayao includ ·pers that are all alternately flaked by direct percussion. Choppers from :e are typologically subdivided into those with a single working edge and with two or more cutting margins (Figure 13.3). Dayao is not the only Ir :ongolian locality to produce such implements. In 1976 late Pleistocene l ediments yielded two such tools at Naimoban, about 10 km south of Day

Stone spheroids similar to those often described as "missile stc ecovered from many Palaeolithic localities in North China have also bee ɔvered at

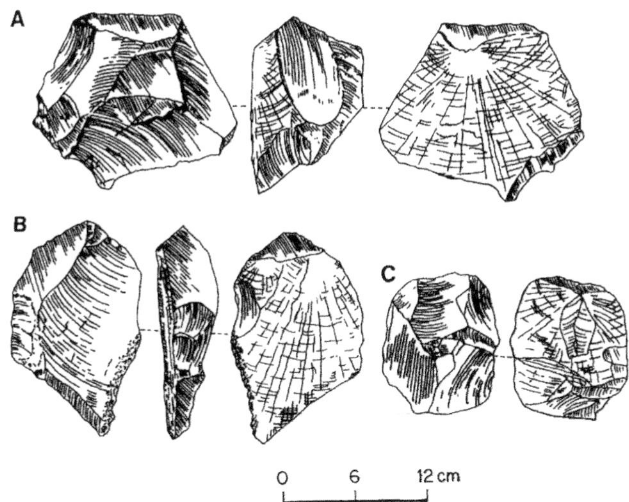

Figure 13.2 Direct percussion hard-hammer flakes from Dayao, Inner Mongolia: A, multiple-edge flake; B, bipointed flake; C, "plate-shaped" (*panxing*) or discoidal flake. (After Wang 1980.)

Dayao (Figure 13.4). Although the function of these tools is not yet known, their presence at Dayao provides an important link between this site and at least one facies of the North Chinese Palaeolithic exemplified by such sites as Dingcun and Xujiayao in Shanxi.

Side scrapers and "tortoise back" (*guibei*) or keeled scrapers comprise a highly diverse and abundant category of finished tools at Dayao (Figure 13.5). Further typological study of this collection will probably allow refinement of the classifi-

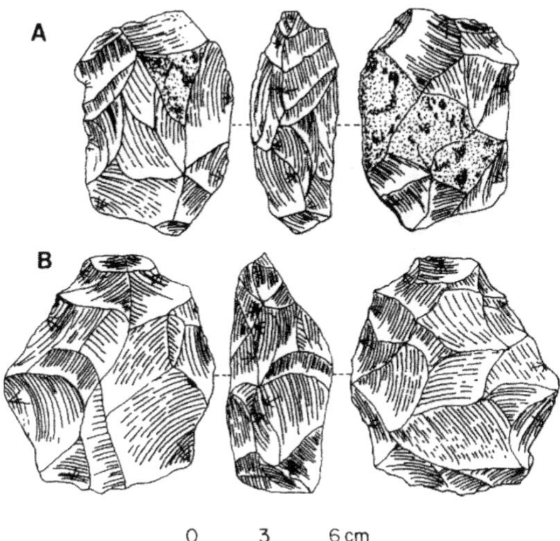

Figure 13.3 Multiple-edge choppers from Dayao, Inner Mongolia. (After Wang 1980.)

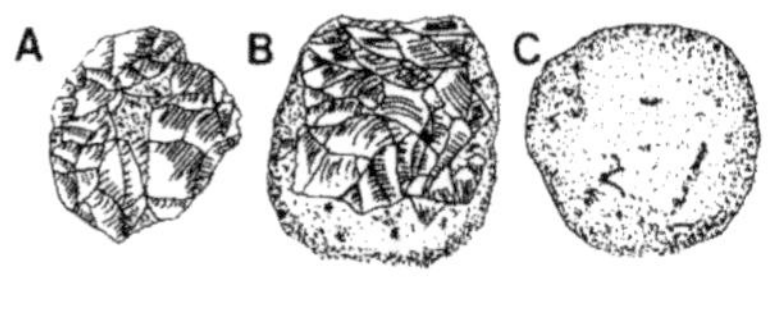

Figure 13.4 Spheroids from ɪo, Inner Mongolia. (After Wang 1980.)

cation now in use, but for the present a broad range of morpł ical implements is subsumed within these two categories.

Pointed tools (*jianzhuangqi*) are represented at Dayao by three ct types—wide bodied (*kuanshen*), tongue shaped (*shexing*), and shuttle sha *uoxing*)—most of which are fashioned on flakes (Figure 13.6). Many of the .o pointed tools exhibit retouch on their dorsal surfaces. The shuttle-shape nted tools are of particular interest since many are chipped on small chunł lint rather than on specially struck flakes. These implements may in so spects be compared with the heavy trihedral points of the Fen River Ding ıdustry in Shanxi, although the Inner Mongolian examples are generally ı smaller. Unfortunately, stratigraphic data do not yet allow us to accura lace these shuttle-shaped pointed tools within the continuum of Palaeoli emains at Dayao, so for the present our comparisons of these specimer st remain speculative.

Circular scrapers, which comprise the final category of finish ıplements excavated at Dayao, are light-duty tools, unifacially flaked with c .y worked

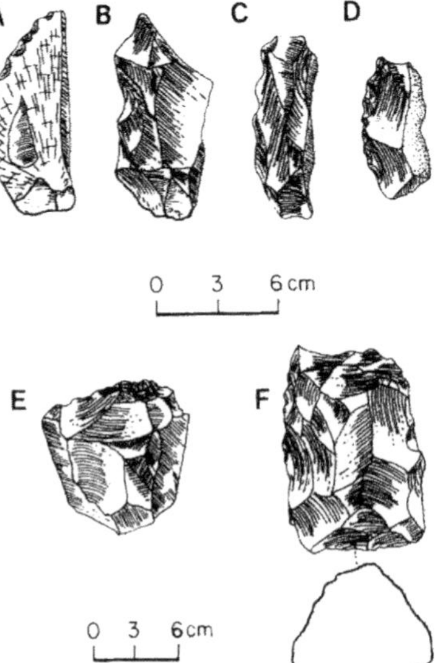

Figure 13.5 Scrapers from Dayao, I ɔngolia: A–D, side scrapers; E,F, tortoise-back (*guil* pers. (After Wang 1980.)

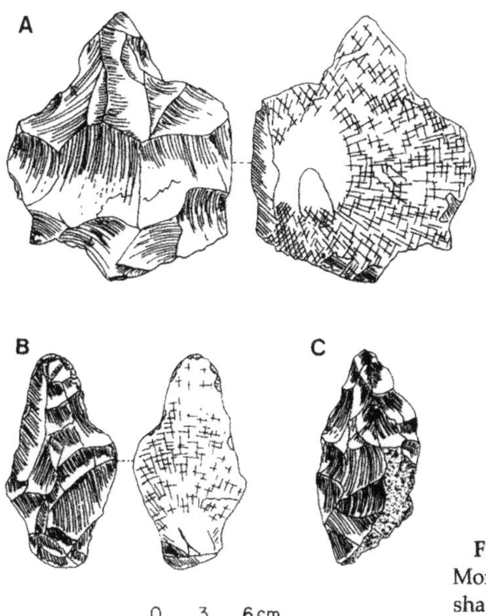

Figure 13.6 Pointed tools from Dayao, Inner Mongolia: A, wide bodied (*kuanshen*); B, tongue shaped (*shexing*); C, shuttle shaped (*suoxing*). (After Wang 1980.)

dorsal surfaces. These circular scrapers constitute a very homogeneous group of implements, exhibiting little change throughout the sequence.

Substantial revisions of the original Dayao typology proposed in 1977 by the Inner Mongolia Museum and Inner Mongolia Cultural Relics Work Team have been published in Wang (1980). For example, the "handaxes" described in the original (1977:11–12) publication are now included in the chopper category, and further refinements are foreseen.

Faunal remains unearthed in this archaeological context include a range of typical Upper Pleistocene forms such as *Coelodonta antiquitatis, Equus* cf. *przewalskyi, Bos primigenius, Procapra picticaudata,* and *Cervus elaphus*. Vertebrate fossils recovered thus far in the Middle Pleistocene red palaeosol containing Dayao's earlier Palaeolithic component are both scarce and highly fragmented. The depth of the loess deposits that cover the site precludes areal excavation on a large scale, so for the present investigations can only be continued at the bottom of the Sidaogou where natural erosion first brought to light these earlier Palaeolithic remains.

Other Quarry–Workshop Localities

In the decade that has elapsed since the discovery of the Dayao site, numerous additional Late Palaeolithic and early Neolithic stone-processing localities have been discovered in Inner Mongolia. Investigations in the vicinity of the Yinshan Range that separates Inner Mongolia's steppe province in the north from the

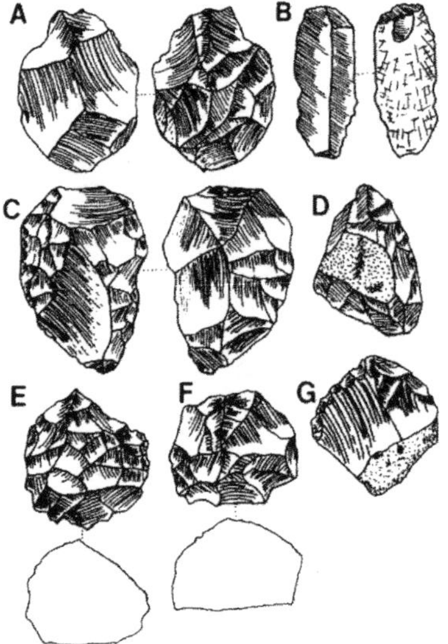

Figure 13.7 Stone tools from Nanshuichuan, Inner Mongolia: A, discoidal core; B, blade; C, large scraper; D, pointed tool; E–G, small scrapers. All approximately × $\frac{1}{4}$. (After Wang 1981.)

fertile alluvial plains of the Huanghe to the south have yielded a number of quarry–workshop sites that are variously considered Late Palaeolithic, Mesolithic, or early Neolithic (Wang 1981:129). It is also apparent that all these sites are not contemporary with one another and may reflect human occupation over a period of several thousand years on both sides of the Pleistocene–Holocene boundary.

Wang (1981) has reported on a series of eight unstratified quarry–workshops in the Yinshan region of central Inner Mongolia within an area of roughly 420 km east–west by 125 km north–south. This geographic sample includes both the altitudinal variation of the Yinshan Range itself in addition to the various ecolog-

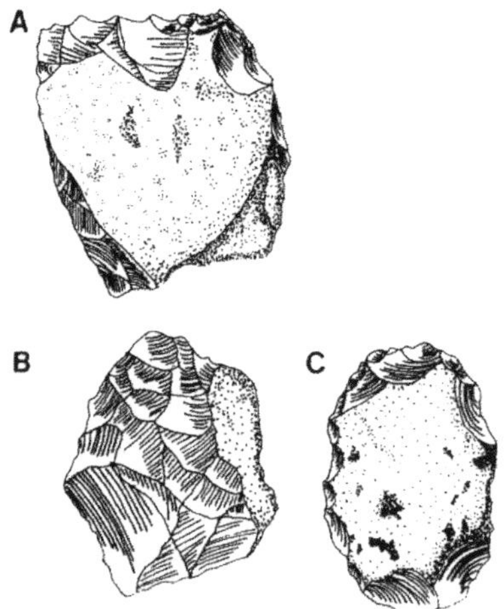

Figure 13.8 Scrapers from Amawusu, Inner Mongolia; all approximately × $\frac{1}{4}$. (After Wang 1981.)

ical zones that border it, ranging from steppe grassland and alluvial plains in the north and south, respectively, to arid steppe and stony desert at the western fringe of the mountain chain.

The following sites are considered typical of these occurrences:

1. Nanshuichuan and Wopuyao, both on the Baoheshao Commune about 30 km northeast of Hohhot (Figure 13.7);
2. Mazongshan, on the east bank of the Dahei River, Yulin Commune, about 35 km east of Hohhot;
3. Houjianzi, about 65 km east of Hohhot on the Sandaojian Commune in Zhuozi County;
4. Huoshiyaogou on the Hadatu Commune, also in Zhuozi County;
5. Erdaowa on the Daqingshan Commune in Wuchuan County, about 25 km north of Hohhot;
6. Amawusu on the Gongjitang Commune in Siziwang Banner, about 65 km northeast of Ulan Hua (Figure 13.8); and
7. Hanggai Gobi in western Wulate Zhonghoulianhe Banner, Bayan Nur League, 100 km north of Linhe (Figure 13.9).

These surface localities are characterized by the presence of nuclei, flakes, débitage, and finished implements including scrapers, choppers, and pointed tools usually fashioned from white or yellowish flint. All these sites differ in fundamental ways from their closest functional parallel at E'maokou, Shanxi (Jia and You 1973), and from the abundant late Pleistocene and early Holocene microlithic cultures of North China (An 1978; Inner Mongolia Autonomous Region Bureau of Culture, Cultural Relics Work Group 1957).

None of the quarry–workshop sites mentioned above has produced ceramics, projectile points, ground-stone agricultural equipment, ornamental stone rings,

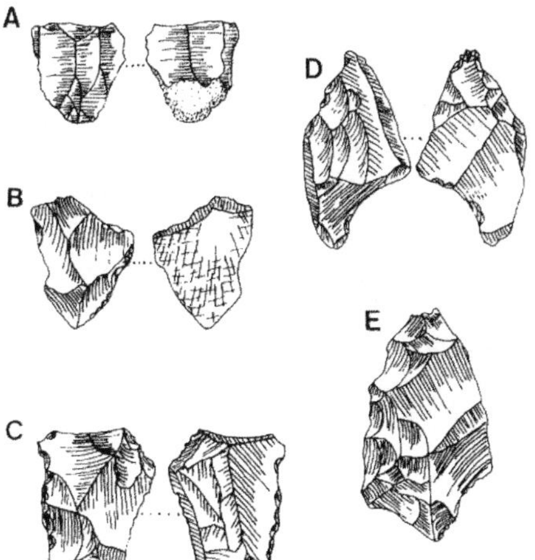

Figure 13.9 Stone tools from Hanggai Gobi, Inner Mongolia: A, small core; B, flake; C–E, scrapers. All approximately × $\frac{1}{3}$. (After Wang 1981.)

or any of the other items of material culture associated with even the earliest Neolithic assemblages in Inner Mongolia. It must be remembered that quarry–workshop sites rarely reflect the full range of activities and technological skills of the groups exploiting them, so the absence of even a broad spectrum of typically Neolithic artifacts must not be taken as conclusive evidence of Pleistocene antiquity.

In 1981 and 1983 the authors examined a number of quarry–workshop sites in the steppe province north of Wuchuan and in the vicinity of Baotou that have great potential for continued investigation. In the former region, small mining operations were encountered that have intruded upon flint-working stations, exposing stratified sequences of loess enclosing stone débitage and implements. Stratified quarry–workshop localities are also reported to the south in the vicinity of the Yinshan Range (Wang 1981:123); thus it is hoped that comprehensive investigations will shed light upon the chronological questions that still surround these occurrences.

The Inner Mongolian Desert: Alashan League, Yikezhao League, and the Southern Ordos

The Sino–Swedish Expeditions of 1927 to 1935 amassed a collection of at least 50,000 stone artifacts, many of which were collected in the arid expanses of what is now Alashan League, Inner Mongolia (Bergman 1945; Maringer 1950a,d, 1963). In particular, the area on the Sino–Mongolian frontier surrounding the twin saline lakes of Gashun Nur and Sugu Nur (Sogho Nor) yielded substantial quantities of prehistoric materials, as did the Ruoshui or Edsen-gol Valley south of these bodies of water (Sommarström 1956, 1958).

The Badan Jilin (Badain Jaran) Desert, which lies between the western termination of the Yinshan Range and the Ruoshui Valley, has yielded large quantities of surface finds whose antiquity has been the subject of much speculation (e.g., Dai *et al.* 1964:415; Maringer 1950a:86–88, 103–127, 175–178, 183–185, 203). Materials of Palaeolithic appearance from the basaltic region north of the Langshan have been reported since perhaps as early as the 1930s (see Maringer 1963:77, Footnote 6). More recently a collection of 41 stone implements from the vicinity of Ailiketiebuke in Alashan Banner, Alashan League, has been analyzed by Dai Erjian and his colleagues (1964). This site, located about 160 km northwest of Jilantai near the old caravan route that runs west from Shanba past the southern edge of the Langshan Range, is characterized by a series of three ancient terraces, the uppermost (first) of which produced a collection of artifacts considered by Dai and his colleagues to be of possible Palaeolithic antiquity. The assemblage on the first terrace is not accompanied by microliths, ground-stone implements, or pottery, an absence that supports the conclusion of Palaeolithic age. Because Neolithic implements were collected in the immediate vicinity, the authors have attempted to distinguish the earlier and later components of the assemblage.

The Ailiketiebuke implements are mostly fashioned on the black quartzite characteristic of the Alashan desert and those found on the first terrace include choppers, scrapers, flakes, and cores.

The choppers are relatively large and coarse with one or more unifacially flaked working edges. A single specimen (P.2981) was alternately flaked and is typical of tools discovered in Late Palaeolithic sites elsewhere in North China. This specimen also exhibits substantial eolian abrasion, or "sand-blasting," a feature that the later, presumably Neolithic implements do not share.

The choppers include those with convex and straight cutting margins and a single specimen (P.2985) with retouching around its circumference. This last implement, fashioned on a large, thick flake is similar to tools classified as multiple-edge choppers in the Dingcun, Shanxi, industry.

The scrapers from Ailiketiebuke are made on relatively small flakes and exhibit one or two nearly straight edges. Dai and his colleagues (1964:415) point out that flakes bearing large platform angles (i.e., greater than 90°) are known from other collections of lithic material from Inner Mongolia and are regarded as of "Palaeolithic appearance."

Few cores were discovered at Ailiketiebuke, although specimens with striking platforms on cortex and on previous flake scars are both known.

Maringer (1950a, 1963) has also recognized a Palaeolithic facies in the collections of the Sino–Swedish Expeditions from the Badan Jilin Desert. He reports that tools of an "Aurignacian type" comparable to specimens from Verkholenskaia Gora in southern Siberia were collected in the Alashan region.

The Hanggai Gobi Commune, in western Wulate Zhonghoulianhe Banner, is situated about 100 km north of Linhe in northern Bayan Nur League. About 4 km southwest of the main commune village an ancient river bed, up to 2 km wide, runs in a southeasterly–northwesterly direction. A 500 × 100-m ridge of flint bedrock in the bottom of the riverbed has been exposed not only to significant eolian erosion but also to the quarrying activities of the region's prehistoric inhabitants. The vicinity is littered with débitage, larger pieces of fragmented stone, and a small number of cores, flakes, and alternately flaked side scrapers. Small pillar-shaped cores (Figure 13.9A) exhibit flake-removal scars all around their circumferences. The Hanggai Gobi flakes tend to be triangular and most bear on their dorsal surfaces scars as a result of the removal of previous flakes (Figure 13.9B).

As Wang (1981) has pointed out, the Hanggai Gobi assemblage cannot confidently be assigned to the Late Palaeolithic. However, the presence of these materials in association with an ancient fluvial environment that may well have been active in the Upper Pleistocene as well as the typological character of the tools themselves suggest a pre-Neolithic antiquity.

The arid plateau within the great bend of the Huanghe incorporating south-central Inner Mongolia, northeast Ningxia, and northern Shanxi is usually referred to in Western literature as the Ordos Region. In Inner Mongolia, the administrative district of Yikezhao League includes much of the Hobq (Kubuqi) or northernmost Mu Us (Maowusu) Desert, an area of alternating thick loess deposits and extensive active dune fields (Walker 1982; Zhu *et al.* 1980:64–67).

In the spring of 1983 the authors visited Dalate Banner in northern Yikezhao League where the complex dune fields southwest of Baotou bordering the Hantaigou Valley were found to contain abundant traces of prehistoric occupation. Eolian deflation has exposed large quantities of stone and other artifacts, mostly of the late Neolithic type described by Cui (1981) and Ji and Ma (1982). Of relevance to the present discussion is that lithic implements of possible Pleistocene antiquity were also encountered in the area in a depositional context that may ultimately yield Palaeolithic materials *in situ*.

In the dunes immediately south of Wayao Village near Dalateqi on the road that links Baotou and Dongsheng, there are desiccated playa sediments around the margins of which Neolithic materials occur in great quantities. In the course of our reconnaissance it has become clear that these stratified playa deposits may represent numerous episodes of relatively mesic conditions; thus continued investigation may yield such sediments of Pleistocene antiquity accompanied by stratified occurrences of Paleolithic remains. During our examination of the area, aceramic assemblages dominated by sand-blasted flakes produced by direct percussion were noted. However, it is possible that less-durable categories of material culture, including pottery, have been eliminated through eolian abrasion. In any event, the lithic component does not appear directly comparable to the abundant Neolithic assemblages reported from the Ordos (Cui 1981; Ji and Ma 1982). It is of interest to note that although early geological investigations west of our own study area yielded surface collections of Palaeolithic implements at "Wambar-ssu" (Boule *et al.* 1928), the authors make no mention of desiccated playa deposits such as those south of Wayaocun.

The palaeoanthropological and prehistoric archaeological importance of the Ordos has been recognized since 1922 when Emile Licent discovered a fossil human limb bone at Dagouwan in the Salawusu (Sjara-osso-gol or Hongliuhe) Valley of southeast Inner Mongolia. The following year Licent, accompanied by Pierre Teilhard de Chardin, discovered at Shuidonggou in Lingwu County, Ningxia, an assemblage of Palaeolithic cultural remains, and similar materials were uncovered in excavations in the Salawusu Valley north of Xiaoqiaoban in Jingbian County, Shanxi (Jia 1955; Licent *et al.* 1926). In the 1940s Pei Wenzhong was the first to refer to the materials collected at Salawusu and Shuidonggou as representative of an *Ordos Culture* (Kozlowski 1971; Pei 1948).

Between 1956 and 1960 Wang Yuping of the Inner Mongolia Museum made three trips to the Ordos Region, where at Fanjiagouwan he discovered a Palaeolithic locality and a human femur and parietal (Wang 1957, 1963; Wu 1958).

Investigations in the Salawusu Valley were continued in 1963–1964 and 1972 by Pei Wenzhong, Jia Lanpo, and other members of the Chinese Academy of Science's Institute of Vertebrate Palaeontology and Palaeoanthropology, during which the sedimentary geology of the region was refined (Pei and Li 1964).

In 1978–1979 the Lanzhou Desert Research Institute conducted a program of investigation in the Mu Us Desert that yielded six additional *H. sapiens* fossils and a few Palaeolithic implements. The human fossils, including three frontals, a mandible, femur, and tibia, are of particular importance since four were discovered *in situ* in strata at the bottom of the Salawusu Formation, a stratigraphic provenance established for the first time by these finds (Yuan 1978).

Finally, in 1980 a research team representing several institutions under the leadership of Jia Lanpo returned to the Salawusu Valley where an additional 11 human fossils and more than 100 Palaeolithic implements were excavated. A chronology of palaeontological, geological, and archaeological investigations in the Salawusu region, as well as a complete list of human remains discovered there through 1980, may be found in Huang and Wei (1981:29).

The Palaeolithic sites of the Salawusu Valley are concentrated in two principal areas: Shaojiagouwan, discovered by Teilhard and Licent in 1923; and Fanjiagouwan, first investigated in 1956 by Wang Yuping. At the latter locality Wang's original reconnaissance yielded more than 80 stone tools and a few intentionally flaked animal bones. In 1980 extensive excavations conducted near Fanjiagouwan produced an additional collection of more than 130 stone artifacts and a large number of flaked animal bones (Huang and Wei 1981:30).

The Salawusu assemblage contains implements that may be subdivided into three basic categories: scrapers, pointed tools, and gravers. Scrapers are the most abundant tool type and many varieties distinguished on the basis of edge morphology are recognized. Pointed tools are also quite numerous and several subtypes have been proposed. Salawusu gravers are very scarce and are characterized by little typological variation.

Both the direct percussion and pressure flaking techniques are present in the Salawusu assemblage, although the indirect percussion technique is not thought to have been used (Huang and Wei 1981:31).

Perhaps the most striking characteristic of the Salawusu lithics, particularly those collected during the 1980 excavations, is their extremely small size. According to Huang and Wei (1981:31), most measure only 2 to 3 cm in length and one pointed tool was recovered measuring only 1.17 cm in length and about 1 cm in width.

The microlithic character of the Salawusu assemblages has led Huang and Wei (1981) to include them in the North Chinese Zhoukoudian Locality 1–Shiyu (keeled scraper and burin) Series. The bone implements, which include more than 300 *Procapra* or *Gazella* horn cores thought to have been utilized as weapons or digging tools, are largely a product of the 1980 investigations and are still under analysis.

The materials discovered by Teilhard and Licent in 1923 in the southwestern Ordos at Shuidonggou, Ningxia (Licent *et al.* 1926), have been supplemented by subsequent investigations conducted in the area in the early 1960s (Jia *et al.* 1964; Pei 1965). The assemblages taken as a whole are characterized by highly variable nuclei, some with prepared platforms, marginally retouched flakes, and crude pebble tools. Breuil's original analysis of the Shuidonggou lithic assemblage, which resulted in their classification in accordance with French Middle and Upper Palaeolithic typologies, has been shown by Pei Wenzhong (1965) to be fundamentally misleading. For example, Pei has asserted that true burins are not present in the Shuidonggou assemblage (Aigner 1981:255).

The cumulative results of more than 50 years of research in the Salawusu Valley indicate the region is characterized by abundant evidence of Pleistocene human occupation. The programs of investigation conducted in the southern Ordos Desert in the 1970s and 1980s have answered many questions relating to the stratigraphic occurrence of these fossil and archaeological materials (Yuan 1978) and we may expect these data to be supplemented through additional research in the region.

Conclusions

Great contributions have been made to our understanding of the Pleistocene prehistory of Inner Mongolia during the past decade. However, a number of significant questions have yet to be dealt with. Of primary importance is the refinement of a chronological framework within which the various Palaeolithic assemblages that have come to light in Inner Mongolia may be placed.

The ecological history of Inner Mongolia has provided a remarkably diverse range of depositional environments with which prehistoric sites in the region are associated. The archaeological resources of Inner Mongolia's arid zones, including the Ordos Plateau and the Badan Jilin Desert, have barely been touched by prehistorians, although cultural remains are abundant and many seem to parallel the prehistoric sequences of adjacent, continguous environmental provinces (e.g., Kozlowski 1971). It is our hope that continued archaeological exploration in Inner Mongolia will result in the clarification of the complex relationships that linked the Pleistocene cultures of this area and the environmental milieu in which they developed.

References

Aigner, Jean S.

1981 *Archaeological remains in Pleistocene China*. Forschungen zur Allgemeinen und Vergleichrenden Archäologie, Band 1. Munich: Verlag C. H. Beck.

An Zhimin

1978 Mesolithic remains in Haila'er: On the origin of the microlithic tradition. *Acta Archaeologica Sinica* 3:289–316.

Bergman, Folke

1945 Travels and archaeological fieldwork in Mongolia and Sinkiang. A diary of the years 1927–1934. History of the expedition in Asia 1927–1935, Part IV. *The Sino-Swedish Expedition Publication 26*. Stockholm: Statens Etnografiska Museum.

Berkey, Charles P. and Nels C. Nelson

1926 Geology and prehistoric archaeology of the Gobi Desert. *American Museum Novitates* 222:1–16.

Boule, M., H. Breuil, E. Licent, and P. Teilhard de Chardin

1928 *Le Palaéolithique de la Chine*. Archives de l'Institut de Paléontologie Humaine, Memoire 4: 1–138. Paris: Masson et Cie.

Cui Xuan
1981 The investigation of Shifota and other sites in Jungar Banner. In *E'erduosi Wenwu Kaogu Wenji*, edited by the Yikezhao League Cultural Relics Work Station. Hohhot: Head Office for Inner Mongolian Agriculture and Animal Husbandry. Pp. 45–57.

Dai Erjian, Gai Pei, and Huang Weiwen
1964 Chipped stone tools of the Alashan desert. *Vertebrata PalAsiatica* 8(4):414–416.

Derbyshire, E.
1983 On the morphology, sediments, and origin of the loess plateau of central China. In *Megageomorphology*, edited by R. Gardner and H. Scoging. Oxford: Clarendon. Pp. 172–194.

Dorj, D.
1971 *Neolit vostochnoi Mongolii.* Ulan Bator: Izdatel'stvo Akademii Nauk M. N. R.

Elisseeff, Vadime
1950 La Mongolie dans l'Antiquité. *Kokogaku Zasshi* 36(4):47–56.

Guangdong Provincial Museum
1959 Stone tools excavated at Hsi-ch'iao-shan, Nan-hai county, Kwangtung. *Acta Archaeologica Sinica* 4:1–15.

Huang Weiwen, Li Chunchu, Wang Honshou, and Huang Yukun
1982 Reexamination of a microlithic site at Xiqiaoshan, Nanhai county, Guangdong. *Current Anthropology* 23(5):487–492.

Huang Weiwen and Wei Qi
1981 The Salawusu Ordos Man and his culture. In *E'erduosi Wenwu Kaogu Wenji*, edited by the Yikezhao League Cultural Relics Work Station. Hohhot: Head Office for Inner Mongolian Agriculture and Animal Husbandry. Pp. 24–32.

Inner Mongolia Autonomous Region Bureau of Culture, Cultural Relics Work Group
1957 Microlithic culture sites discovered in the Inner Mongolia Autonomous Region. *Acta Archaeologica Sinica* 1:9–22.

Inner Mongolia Museum and Inner Mongolia Cultural Relics Work Team
1977 Report on the excavation of a stone workshop in the eastern suburbs of Hohhot. *Wenwu* 5:7–15.

Ji Faxi and Ma Yaoqi
1982 Survey and trial excavation of a Neolithic site at Dakou, Jungar Banner, Inner Mongolia. *Current Antrhopology* 23(5):479–486.

Jia Lanpo (Chia Lan-po)
1955 *Ordos Man*, revised edition. Shanghai: Longmen United Bookstore.

Jia Lanpo (Chia Lan-po), Gai Pei, and Li Yanxian
1964 New materials from the Shuidonggou Palaeolithic site. *Vertebrata PalAsiatica* 8(1):75–83.

Jia Lanpo (Chia Lan-po) and You Yuzhu
1973 The quarry–workshop site at E'maokou, Huairen, Shanxi. *Acta Archaeologica Sinica* 2:13–30.

Kozlowski, Janusz K.
1971 The problem of the so-called Ordos Culture in the light of the Palaeolithic finds from northern China and southern Mongolia. *Folia Quaternaria* 39:63–99. Krakow: Polska Akademia Nauk Oddzial w Krakowie Komisja Biologiczna.

Licent, E., P. Teilhard de Chardin, and D. Black
1926 On a presumably Pleistocene human tooth from the Sjara-osso-gol deposits. *Bulletin of the Geological Society of China* 5(3–4):285–290.

Maringer, Johannes
1950a Contribution to the prehistory of Mongolia. *The Sino-Swedish Expedition Publication* 34. Stockholm: Statens Etnografiska Museum.
1950b Felsbilder im Lang-shan. *Ethnos* 15:14–26.
1963 Mongolia before the Mongols. *Arctic Anthropology* 1(2):75–85.

Nelson, Nels C.
1926 The dune dwellers of the Gobi. *Natural History* 26:28–32.

1939 Archaeology of Mongolia. *Compte-rendu de Congres International des Sciences Anthropologiques et Ethnologiques, Deuxieme Session, Copenhague 1938*. Pp. 259–262.

Okladnikov, Aleksei Pavlovich

1951 Novye dannye po drevneishei istorii vnutrennei Mongolii. *Vestnik Drevnei Istorii* 4:162–174.

Pei Wenzhong (Pei Wen-chung)

1948 *The study of Chinese prehistory*. Beijing: Commercial Press.

1965 Professor Henri Breuil, pioneer of Chinese Palaeolithic archaeology and its progress after him. In *En Homenaje al Abate Henri Breuil, Volume 2*. Barcelona: Diputación Provincial de Barcelona. Pp. 251–269.

Pei Wenzhong (Pei Wen-chung) and Li Youheng

1964 Tentative opinions on the Sjara-osso-gol series. *Vertebrata PalAsiatica* 8(2):99–119.

Sommarström, Bo

1956 Archaeological researches in the Edsen-gol region, Inner Mongolia, Part 1. *The Sino-Swedish Expedition Publication 39*. Stockholm: Statens Etnografiska Museum.

1958 Archaeological researches in the Edsen-gol region, Inner Mongolia, Part 2. *The Sino-Swedish Expedition Publication 41*. Stockholm: Statens Etnografiska Museum.

Teilhard de Chardin, Pierre and Emile Licent

1924 On the discovery of a Palaeolithic industry in northern China. *Bulletin of the Geological Society of China* 3(1):45–50.

Teilhard de Chardin, Pierre and Yang Zhongjian (C. C. Young)

1932 On some Neolithic (and possibly Palaeolithic) finds in Mongolia, Sinkiang, and West China. *Bulletin of the Geological Society of China* 12(1):83–104.

Walker, Alta S.

1982 Deserts of China. *American Scientist* 70(4):366–376.

Wang Yuping

1957 A preliminary report on archaeological investigations in the Salawusu Valley, Yikezhao League. *Wenwu Cankao Ziliao* 4:22–25.

1963 Human fossils discovered in Wushen Banner, Yikezhao League, Inner Mongolia. *Vertebrata PalAsiatica* 7(2):190–191.

1979 The discovery of the Dayao Culture and its significance. *Neimenggu Ribao*, February 17, Hohhot.

1980 The Dayao Culture stone workshop in the east suburbs of Hohhot. In *Zhongguo Kaoguxuehui Diyici Nianhui Lunwenji*, edited by the Chinese Archaeological Society. Beijing: Cultural Relics Press. Pp. 1–13.

1981 Stone workshops in the Yinshan region, Inner Mongolia. *Neimenggu Wenwu Kaogu*, premier issue 1981:123–129.

Wu Rukang (Woo Ju-kang)

1958 Fossil human parietal bone and femur from Ordos, Inner Mongolia. *Gu Jizhuidongwu Xuebao* (*Vertebrata PalAsiatica*) 2(4):208–212.

Xie Junyi and Zhang Luzhang

1977 Palaeolithic artifacts in Qingyang district, Gansu. *Vertebrata PalAsiatica* 15(3):211–222.

Yuan Baoyin

1978 Sedimentary environment and stratigraphic subdivisions of the Sjara-osso-gol Formation. *Acta Geologica Sinica* 3:220–234.

Zhongshan University Investigation Group

1959 Preliminary study of the stone artifacts from Xiqiaoshan, Nanhai county, Guangdong. *Zhongshan Daxue Xuebao* 1.

Zhu Zhenda, Wu Zheng, Liu Shu, Di Xingmin, and others

1980 *An Introduction to the Deserts of China*. Beijing: Science Press.

14

On the Recognition of China's Palaeolithic Cultural Traditions

JIA LANPO AND HUANG WEIWEN

Introduction

As early as 1932 Pierre Teilhard de Chardin and Pei Wenzhong pointed out, in relation to their analysis of the stone artifacts from the Middle Pleistocene Locality 1 deposits, "the Choukoutien [Zhoukoudian] industry, by its association of choppers and an almost microlithic industry, represents a very characteristic culture type, so far unique in China" (1932:354).

Later, during their research on the Palaeolithic remains from Dingcun, Shanxi, Pei Wenzhong and Jia Lanpo uncovered artifacts different in most respects from those known from other North Chinese localities. Not only were the Dingcun tools very large, but specialized morphological types such as heavy triangular points were found. Thus, the scholars pointed out that the Dingcun and Zhoukoudian "*Sinanthropus*" industries were quite dissimilar in that the former was characterized by the employment of different stoneworking techniques and the absence of bipolar flakes. This Upper Pleistocene Dingcun Industry was considered to be in no way directly comparable to previously identified Palaeolithic manifestations within China or abroad (Pei *et al.* 1958:110–111).

The Kehe Early Palaeolithic site, located in the Yellow River valley of Shanxi, yielded an assemblage of lithic implements quite distinct from that of Zhoukoudian Locality 1. Jia Lanpo and his colleagues, Wang Zeyi and Wang Jian, pointed out (1962:40) that certain tool types identified at Kehe are also known from the Dingcun site, such as heavy triangular points and stone spheroids or bolas.

Palaeoanthropology and
Palaeolithic Archaeology in the
People's Republic of China

ISBN 0-12-601720-4

However, flaking techniques appear more developed at Dingcun and this industry as a whole is advanced in comparison to that from Kehe. In view of the parallels readily discernable between these two industries, it is likely that the Palaeolithic of Dingcun was derived through a process of gradual evolution from its predecessor at Kehe. Jia, Wang, and Qiu demonstrated in relation to the stone artifacts of Kehe that "these few stone tools look very similar to those from Dingcun. This is especially true in the case of retouched pieces, for although some are broken, the shape of the flakes and their pattern of retouching are nearly identical to the heavy triangular points of Dingcun" (1961:11).

Beginning in the 1960s Jia Lanpo conducted research on the stone artifacts fashioned by *Homo erectus pekinensis* from Zhoukoudian Locality 1 in relation to other contemporary cultural remains. Jia (1960:49) stressed that the slightly younger assemblage from Zhoukoudian Locality 15 most closely resembles those from the "*Sinanthropus*" cave, because both are predominantly flake industries fashioned on vein quartz, sandstone, hornfels, and occasionally chert. Tool types from both localities include a large variety of scrapers, points, and chopper–chopping tools.

As the amount of available archaeological data increases, our understanding of the dynamics of change within Chinese lithic traditions deepens at a corresponding rate. In his analysis of the Late Palaeolithic stone artifacts from the cave of Xiaonanhai near Anyang, Henan, An Zhimin concluded

> Some elements of this culture can be traced back to the earlier Palaeolithic industries of Zhoukoudian and even bear a certain resemblance to the so-called Ordos Culture. The Xiaonanhai site probably represents one variety of Late Palaeolithic culture in North China. The fact that some of its characteristic tool types seem to bear a relationship to later microlithic assemblages suggests it may have been a forerunner of Mesolithic and Neolithic culture in China. (1965:27)

The discovery of the Upper Pleistocene Shiyu site in Suoxian County, Shanxi, has proven especially important in the clarification of cultural divisions within the Palaeolithic of North China. The stone artifacts recovered from this site may in fact correlate best with the well-known Late Palaeolithic localities in the Salawusu (Sjara-osso-gol) Valley of southern Inner Mongolia.

Beginning in 1972 Jia and his colleagues pointed out that

> At least two traditions are apparent in the development of China's Palaeolithic cultures. One of them may be termed the Kehe–Dingcun Series and is characterized by large chopper–chopping tools made on flakes and heavy triangular points. Only a few microlithic tools of limited morphological types are known to be associated with this tradition. Typical sites include Kehe, Shanxi; localities in the Sanmen Gorge area of western Henan; and Emaokou, near Datong, Shanxi.
>
> The second tradition is referred to as the Zhoukoudian Locality 1–Shiyu (or keeled scraper and burin) Series. This tradition was typified by the use of small, irregular flakes in the production of microlithic artifacts which exhibit meticulous retouch. Characteristic sites include Zhoukoudian Localities 1 and 15; Hougedafeng, Shanxi; Shiyu, Shanxi; Salawusu (Sjara-osso-gol), Inner Mongolia; and Xiaonanhai, Henan. The Zhoukoudian Locality 1–Shiyu Series is well represented in Middle and Upper Pleistocene contexts

throughout North China and is the forerunner of the microlithic Mesolithic in the area. (Jia *et al.* 1972:54–55)

The Xujiayao Culture

In his synthesis of Chinese microlithic assemblages investigated through 1976, Jia Lanpo stressed the importance of the newly discovered Xujiayao, Shanxi, Middle Palaeolithic site in understanding the developmental history of China's small-tool industries. Jia states, "The tools from this site are basically similar to those from Shiyu. All are small tools made of vein quartz, flint, agate, and quartzite. Of particular interest is the fact that many tool types from Xujiayao are similar to those already known in microlithic assemblages elsewhere in China, Japan, Mongolia, Siberia, and North America" (1976:8).

In fact, the Xujiayao culture may prove to be the link between the chronologically remote Zhoukoudian Locality 1 and Shiyu small-tool occurrences. The excavation of the Xujiayao site not only yielded large quantities of mammalian fossils and the remains of over 10 individual humans, but tens of thousands of stone, bone, and antler implements were also recovered. Large tools were rarely encountered at Xujiayao, the assemblage being dominated by microliths. Included in the Xujiayao collection were protoprismatic cores, funnel-shaped cores, proto-Gobi cores, and thumbnail scrapers, demonstrating the extremely close relationship between this culture and those of the early Holocene microlithic tradition. Jia and Wei concluded that

> the microlithic industries of North China probably originated locally rather than in Mongolia or other parts of Central Asia as suggested by A. P. Okladnikov and others. This opinion is supported by the discovery of a primitive microlithic industry at Shiyu in Suoxian, Shanxi. The discovery of the present site [Xujiayao], with its older geological stratification and typologically more primitive microliths has lent further support to this opinion. In fact, the Xujiayao artifacts may well represent the earliest microlithic industry thus far discovered in China or neighboring regions. (1976:109–114)

The Xujiayao cultural remains are thought to extend back to the late Riss glacial period, which, at a conservative estimate, is over 100,000 years old (Jia *et al.* 1979:293).

Even in 1972 when the idea of dividing China's Palaeolithic into parallel traditions was first formally put forth (Jia *et al.* 1972), it was clear that the recognition of only two such series was probably an oversimplification of reality. In addition, it was apparent that although these traditions may have floresced and developed in a parallel fashion during the Pleistocene, they were not completely independent of one another.

The inevitable infiltration and mutual influence that must have been a vital part of these early cultural traditions undoubtedly shaped the way in which they are manifest in the archaeological record. We were only dimly conscious of the complexity of this question when we formulated the original model in 1972, thus

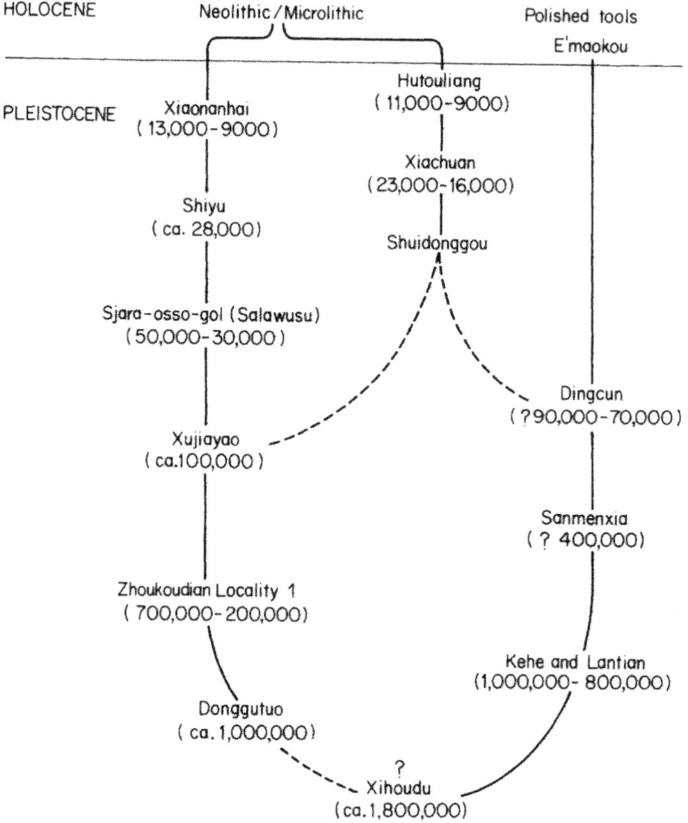

Figure 14.1 The development of Palaeolithic traditions in North China. (Dates are in years BP.)

it should not be taken as a definitive explanation but rather as a working hypothesis that has served its purpose by stimulating research and discussion (Figure 14.1). The question of China's Palaeolithic cultural traditions is an important one for us to tackle in the future, and as more data are accumulated we may begin to refine our original interpretations of the archaeological record.

The Shuidonggou Industry

A good example of this process concerns the site of Shuidonggou in the Ordos Desert of the Ningxia Hui Autonomous Region. In 1924 Pierre Teilhard de Chardin and Emile Licent described the Palaeolithic materials they recovered from this site in the following manner:

> The implements (points, scratchers, "coups de poing" . . .), made of quartzite and silicified limestones which occur abundantly in the basal conglomerate of the loess, are of

> well defined shapes and generally large size. They appear to be of Mousterian or early Aurignacian type. (1924:46)

The authors went on to state:

> The Palaeolithic implements of the Sjara Osso Gol are remarkably small—probably in consequence of the lack of a satisfactory material . . . . Chips, sometimes exceedingly small . . . are common,—true implements (scratchers, Mousterian points. . .) rather rare. An exceptionally large scratcher (7 × 5 cm) looks very similar to the Choei Tong Keou's [Shuidonggou] implements. (1924:47)

In 1960, our new investigations at Shuidonggou resulted in the following conclusions: "The stone artifacts of Shuidonggou seem to be more closely related to those from Dingcun than to any other assemblage currently known in China. Although the Shuidonggou industry seems to have inherited many of the characteristics of its Dingcun predecessor, there is nonetheless a very significant hiatus between these two" (Jia *et al.* 1964:80).

Certain typological elements common in the Xujiayao Middle Palaeolithic collection are also found at Shuidonggou. Thus we now believe this latter assemblage reflects a mixed influence including both Dingcun and Xujiayao as earlier Pleistocene precursors.

The discovery of the Xiaochangliang and Donggutuo sites in Yangyuan County, Hebei, is most exciting (You *et al.* 1980). Palaeomagnetic dates and biostratigraphic evidence suggest an antiquity somewhat in excess of 1 million years for both of these localities. The stone artifacts recovered from these two sites are rather small and bear a striking resemblance to the flake industry from Zhoukoudian's Middle Pleistocene Locality 1; so much so that we have reason to consider Xiaochangliang and Donggutuo as logical precursors of the Zhoukoudian "*Sinanthropus*" Industry.

Conclusions

Based on the totality of archaeological data available to us at present, we propose the following assessment of North China's Palaeolithic stone industries.

We still cannot positively assert in what geographic area or cultural province the roots of China's Palaeolithic traditions lie. For example, we cannot say that the origin of the Kehe emphasis on large stone tools can be traced back to the Lower Pleistocene archaeological site of Xihoudu, Shanxi, simply because it too is characterized by a lithic assemblage dominated by large tools (Jia and Wang 1978). Our investigations simply have not yet progressed far enough to state unequivocally that the Xihoudu assemblage does not contain a microlithic or protomicrolithic component. Although no microlithic tools have yet been found there, small funnel-shaped cores have been unearthed at Xihoudu, so we cannot entirely negate the possibility.

As to Palaeolithic sites south of the Yangzi River, data have been collected since the 1950s resulting in a number of known Early, Middle, and Late Palaeolithic localities. The most important of these is the Guanyindong site in Qianxi County, Guizhou, where excavations have yielded a total of over 3000 artifacts and more than 20 varieties of mammalian fossils. Although the Guanyindong lithic assemblage includes only a limited range of morphological types (scrapers, points, choppers, and gravers), the retouch apparent on these artifacts is quite different from that encountered on contemporaneous chipped-stone artifacts to the north.

In one of the first reports on South Chinese Palaeolithic materials, Pei Wenzhong (1965) drew attention to the unique character of the Guanyindong assemblage by stating:

> the style of retouch on the Guizhou artifacts is very special. Based on observations of the modified edges of the tools themselves, retouch seems to have been accomplished through the application of repeated heavy blows with a hammer stone perpendicular to the edge of the flake. . . . This technique produced a blunt edge unsuitable for fine cutting. (1965:279)

Similarly retouched artifacts have also been recovered in other Palaeolithic localities in South and West China. For example, tools unearthed in Tongliang County, Sichuan (Li and Zhang 1981), are quite similar to those from the Guanyindong locality; so much so that we have proposed the term *Guanyindong–Tongliang Tradition* to describe these related complexes.

Cultural remains excavated at the Shilongtou site in Daye County, Hubei, differ not only from their Palaeolithic contemporaries in North China, but also from the artifact assemblages from the Guanyindong and Tongliang (Li *et al.* 1974), suggesting Shilongtou and related sites may constitute yet another distinctive Chinese Palaeolithic tradition.

Advances made in Chinese Palaeolithic archaeology in the past decade have demonstrated that a simple unilinear (or bilinear) approach to the question of cultural evolution and diversification during the Pleistocene is an inadequate basis upon which to build explanatory models. We now recognize the enormous complexity of the prehistoric archaeological record in China, encompassing large geographic distinctions not only between North and South China but also within contiguous environmental zones. The dissimilarities discernable between the Shilongtou and Guanyindong sites exemplify this phenomenon. We believe additional studies of the Pleistocene prehistory of China are a major research task for the future and will continue to reveal the chronology and dynamics of this diversification.

References

An Zhimin

1965 Trial excavations of the Palaeolithic cave of Hsiao-nan-hai in Anyang, Honan. *Acta Archaeologica Sinica* 1:1–28.

Jia Lanpo (Chia Lan-po)

1960 The stone artifacts of *Sinanthropus* and its relationship with the contemporary cultures in North China. *Gu Jizhuidongwu yu Gu Renlei* (*Palaeovertebrata et Palaeoanthropologia*) 2(1):45–50.

1976 On the origin of microlithic industries in East Asia. Colloque 18, Union Internationale des Sciences Prehistoriques et Protohistoriques, IX Congres, Nice. Pp. 7–9.

Jia Lanpo (Chia Lan-po), Gai Pei, and Li Yanxian
1964 New materials from the Shuidonggou Palaeolithic site. *Vertebrata PalAsiatica* 8(1):75–83.

Jia Lanpo (Chia Lan-po), Gai Pei, and You Yuzhu
1972 Report of excavation in Shi Yu, Shanxi—a Palaeolithic site. *Acta Archaeologica Sinica* 1:39–60.

Jia Lanpo (Chi Lan-po) and Wang Jian (Wang Chien)
1978 *Hsihoutu—A culture site of early Pleistocene in Shansi province.* Beijing: Cultural Relics Press.

Jia Lanpo (Chia Lan-po), Wang Zeyi, and Qiu Zhonglang
1961 Palaeoliths of Shansi. *Memoirs of the Institute of Vertebrate Palaeontology and Palaeoanthropology,* Series A 4:1–48.

Jia Lanpo (Chia Lan-po), Wang Zeyi, and Wang Jian (Wang Chien)
1962 K'oho—An Early Palaeolithic site in south-western Shansi. *Memoirs of the Institute of Vertebrate Palaeontology and Palaeoanthropology,* Series A 5:1–40.

Jia Lanpo (Chia Lan-po) and Wei Qi
1976 A Palaeolithic site at Hsu-chia-yao in Yangkao county, Shansi province. *Acta Archaeologica Sinca* 2:97–114.

Jia Lanpo (Chia Lan-po), Wei Qi, and Li Chaorong
1979 Report on the excavation of Hsuchiayao Man site in 1976. *Vertebrata PalAsiatica* 17(4):277–293.

Li Xuanmin and Zhang Senshui
1981 On Palaeolithic culture of Tongliang county. *Vertebrata PalAsiatica* 19(4):359–371.

Li Yanxian, Yuan Zhenxin, Dong Xingren, and Li Tianyuan
1974 Report on the excavation of a Palaeolithic station known as Shilongtou at Daye, Hubei. *Vertebrata PalAsiatica* 12(2):139–157.

Pei Wenzhong (Pei Wen-chung), Wu Rukang (Woo Ju-kang), Jia Lanpo (Chia Lan-po), Zhou Mingzhen (Chow Min-chen), Liu Xianting, and Wang Zeyi
1958 Report on the excavation of Palaeolithic sites at Tingtsun, Hsiangfenhsien, Shansi province, China. *Memoirs of the Institute of Vertebrate Palaeontology and Palaeoanthropology,* Series A 2:1–111.

Pei Wenzhong (Pei Wen-chung), Yuan Zhenxin, Lin Yipu, and Zhang Yinyun
1965 Discovery of Palaeolithic chert artifacts in Kuan-yin-tung Cave in Ch'ien-Hsihsien of Kweichow province. *Vertebrata PalAsiatica* 9(3):270–279.

Teilhard de Chardin, P. and E. Licent
1924 On the discovery of a Palaeolithic industry in Northern China. *Bulletin of the Geological Society of China* 3(1):45–50.

Teilhard de Chardin, P. and Pei Wenzhong (Pei Wen-chung)
1932 The lithic industry of the *Sinanthropus* deposits in Zhoukoudian. *Bulletin of the Geological Society of China* 11:315–364.

You Yuzhu, Tang Yingjun, and Li Yi
1980 New discovery of palaeoliths in the Nihewan Formation. *Quaternaria Sinica* 5(1):1–13.

15

Pleistocene Mammalian Faunas of China

HAN DEFEN AND XU CHUNHUA

Introduction

At present no fewer than 200 localities in China have been found to produce significant quantities of Pleistocene mammalian fossils. In an effort to provide a basic synopsis of China's Quaternary mammalian faunas, we have selected for discussion a series of 27 assemblages that may be taken as representative of the broader range of fossil materials known. Each of the assemblages included here has been derived from a locality of particular human palaeontological or archaeological interest and as such constitutes an important basis for both palaeoenvironmental and chronological interpretations.

It will be noted that the diversity and abundance of these mammalian faunas has permitted intensive study of their systematic relationships and their classification into a relative chronological hierarchy. Small mammalian remains, particularly those from South China, are relatively scarce; consequently the sample size of such fossils from any given locality are commonly too small to permit accurate comparison, particularly on a quantitative basis. Because marine mammalian fossils are rarely recovered from China's Quaternary strata, remains of these animals are not treated in this synthesis.

This essay is divided into two complementary sections. First, a series of interim conclusions are offered that outline our current understanding of chronological distinctions and change within China's Quaternary mammalian assemblages. Second, a chronologically ordered series of faunal lists (Tables 15.2–

Palaeoanthropology and
Palaeolithic Archaeology in the
People's Republic of China

ISBN 0-12-601720-4

15.4, at end of chapter) are presented to provide the principal data upon which many palaeoenvironmental and zoogeographic interpretations in China have been based.

Chronological Divisions within Chinese Pleistocene Mammalian Faunas

Palaeontological research conducted in China during the past century has produced a corpus of data that permits the organization of mammalian fossiliferous assemblages into a discrete chronological framework. The following discussion illuminates the basic conclusions that have been reached regarding these questions of relative chronology. Particular attention is paid to the recognition of early Pleistocene faunas due to their importance in establishing the antiquity of human occupation of China and because many of these earlier Quaternary fossiliferous remains are derived from localities that also yield evidence of hominid activity (see Jia Lanpo, Chapter 8, this volume, and Zhang Senshui, Chapter 9, this volume).

The Lower Pleistocene

Teilhard and Piveteau were among the first to recognize the abundance of North China's Pleistocene fossil localities. Their 1930 study of mammalian remains from the lacustrine deposits at Nihewan in the Sangan River valley of northern Hebei indicated that a number of localities in this basin contained fossils attributable to the earliest phase of the Pleistocene. This Nihewan Fauna has been found to include surviving Tertiary forms such as *Proboscidipparion (Hipparion) sinense, Elasmotherium, Chalicotherium,* and *Machairodus.* In addition some recent species including *Equus, Elephas, Camelus, Bison,* and *Ovis* appear in China for the first time in the Nihewan Fauna.

Both biostratigraphic and geological evidence suggest a Lower Pleistocene age for the Nihewan Fauna, corresponding to the early Quaternary Villafranchian of Europe. Thus far, human fossils have not been discovered in the Nihewan beds but archaeological evidence indicates the basin may have been the scene of human activity in the early Pleistocene.

The analysis of the Nihewan Fauna has resolved a number of problematic points concerning the antiquity of such taxa as *Canis (Nyctereutes) sinensis, Paracamelus gigas,* and *Cynailurus (Acinonyx) pleistocaenicus,* all of which occur not only at Nihewan but also in Middle Pleistocene assemblages such as that from Zhoukoudian, near Beijing.

In the 1960s and 1970s several important new Lower Pleistocene fossiliferous localities were discovered in the heart of North China's loesslands. Most important among these are Linyi and Xihoudu in Shanxi (Jia and Wang 1978; Zhou and Zhou 1959) and Laochihe in Lantian County, Shaanxi (Ji 1975). Although all three sites contain *Proboscidipparion* and *Equus*, their ages may not all be identical and preliminary evidence suggests the Xihoudu locality may be considered the earliest.

Among the Xihoudu mammalian fossils, apparent Tertiary surviving forms include *Proboscidipparion sinense, Elasmotherium* cf. *inexpectatum, Axis,* and *Gazella* cf. *blacki*. The Lower Pleistocene deposits of Xihoudu and Nihewan hold a number of mammalian forms in common including *Elephas* (*Palaeoloxodon*) *namadicus, Equus sanmeniensis, Bison palaeosinensis, Sus lydekkeri, Elaphurus bifurcatus, Euctenoceros boulei,* and *Coelodonta antiquitatis*. However, correlation of the stratigraphic sequences at these two sites is still problematic. If one considers the faunal assemblage alone, it seems clear that Xihoudu is the earliest, with 47% of the known genera and 100% of the known mammalian species being those of extinct forms. At Nihewan only a third (33.33%) of the fossil mammalian genera and 93.35% of the species are those of extinct animals (Jia and Wang 1978:72); hence some temporal separation is apparent.

In South China, two fossiliferous localities may be taken as representative of the Lower Pleistocene. The *Gigantopithecus* Cave (Juyuandong) at Liucheng, Guangxi, contains a typical cave faunal assemblage, while lacustrine sediments in the Yuanmou Basin of Yunnan have preserved a record of early Quaternary animals adapted to that unique environment.

The Liucheng *Gigantopithecus* Cave was discovered in 1956 by a field team led by the late Professor Pei Wenzhong (Pei and Li 1958). Excavations were conducted at the site from 1956 to 1964 and yielded three mandibles and more than 1000 isolated teeth of *Gigantopithecus* (Wu 1962), in addition to a rich mammalian fossil assemblage (Han n.d.; Li n.d.; Pei n.d.). The Liucheng Fauna is of special interest since it differs from contemporary North Chinese assemblages such as those of Nihewan, Xihoudu, and Zhoukoudian Locality 18 (Teilhard 1940). The Liucheng collection is also dissimilar to other South Chinese assemblages, including typical Middle Pleistocene *Ailuropoda–Stegodon* Fauna such as that from the *Gigantopithecus* locality of Daxin, also in Guangxi Province (Pei and Wu 1956). In particular, the Liucheng Fauna includes a range of archaic taxa such as *Gomphotherium serridentoides, Nestoritherium praesinensis, Tapirus peii, Rhinoceros chiai, Dorcabune liuchengensis, Megalovis guangxiensis,* and *Cervavitus* (*Cervoceros*) *fenqii*. Based on the presence of such forms at Liucheng, it is widely accepted among Chinese palaeontologists that the Liucheng fauna is of Lower Pleistocene age.

Fossiliferous caverns in Jianshi County, western Hubei, have also produced remains of *Gigantopithecus* in association with an essentially early Quaternary fauna (Xu *et al.* 1974). In this assemblage surviving Pliocene forms include *Gomphotherium* and members of the subfamily Machairodontinae, while typical Lower Pleistocene species such as *Hyaena licenti* and *Equus yunnanensis* occur as well. Various elements of the Jianshi fauna are also morphologically larger than their counterparts elsewhere. The *Gigantopithecus* teeth follow this pattern, as do the dentition of panda and tapir, which, while being larger than *Ailuropoda microta* and *Tapirus peii* from Liucheng, are smaller than the typical Middle–Upper Pleistocene forms *Ailuropoda melanoleuca fovealis* and *Megatapirus augustus*. Because of these considerations, the Jianshi fauna is assigned to the late Lower Pleistocene, establishing it as the predecessor of the other Guangxi *Gigantopithecus* faunas such as those from the localities of Daxin, Wuming, and Bama (Han 1982; Huang 1979; Zhang *et al.* 1973, 1975).

A faunal assemblage remarkably similar to that of Jianshi has been recovered from fossiliferous cave deposits in a small hill called Bijiashan, near Liuzhou, Guangxi (Han *et al.* 1975). Although no remains of *Gigantopithecus* have yet been discovered at Bijiashan, the *Ailuropoda* and *Tapirus* dentition from the site are very similar in size and morphology to those from Jianshi, Hubei.

The recent discoveries at Jianshi and Bijiashan have caused us to reconsider the whole definition of the "*Gigantopithecus* Fauna." We now have indisputable evidence from the five known *Gigantopithecus* localities in China that indicates the mammalian faunas associated with this large primate underwent considerable change during the Lower and Middle Pleistocene. Consequently, to apply a single term such as "*Gigantopithecus* Fauna" to such a diverse array of fossiliferous remains is misleading because it does not take into account the evolution of various taxa such as *Ailuropoda* and *Tapirus* over this relatively long period of time. However, it is equally unsuitable to apply unrelated terms to each of these assemblages. For example, if the designation "*Gigantopithecus* Fauna" is reserved for the Lower Pleistocene component and its Middle Pleistocene descendant is termed the "*Ailuropoda–Stegodon* Fauna," as some palaeontologists have proposed, the essential relationship between these two assemblages is obscured.

In order to resolve this dilemma we propose that all Pleistocene mammalian faunas from South China be referred to collectively as "*Ailuropoda–Stegodon* Faunas," which may then be subdivided into discrete temporal stages. Thus, the early *Ailuropoda–Stegodon* Fauna includes the typical *Gigantopithecus*-bearing assemblages of Liucheng and Jianshi, which are of Lower Pleistocene age.

Another South Chinese locality that has produced an important Quaternary fauna is the site of Yuanmou, near Shangnabang in Yunnan Province. The Cenozoic strata of the Yuanmou Basin include abundant Plio–Pleistocene vertebrate remains that have been the subject of numerous studies (Bian 1940; Colbert 1940; Pei 1961; Zhou 1961). In 1963 two incisors identified as *Homo erectus* were discovered in geological strata whose geological age was originally thought to be late Lower Pleistocene (Hu 1973). At present, considerable controversy surrounds the absolute chronology of the Yuanmou assemblage (see Wu and Wang, Chapter 2, this volume). Liu Dongsheng and Ding Menglin (1983) have restudied the biostratigraphic, lithostratigraphic, and magnetostratigraphic data from the area and point out that the stratum yielding the hominid incisors within the Yuanmou Formation (*sensu lato*) is of Middle Pleistocene rather than Lower Pleistocene antiquity. However, the rather abundant vertebrate assemblage from the Shangnabang locality presents a somewhat different picture.

In their analysis of cervid dentition from Yuanmou, Lin and others (1978) pointed out that relatively archaic morphological features—such as the *Palaeomeryx* fold in dentition—occur frequently. Furthermore, many elements characteristic of the Upper Pliocene Yushe Fauna are found in the Yuanmou deposits, including *Muntiacus lacustris, M. nanus, Procapreolus stenos, Metacervulus capreolinus, Axis shansius, Eostyloceros longchuanensis,* and *Cervoceros ultimus.* However, remains of *Equus* are also rather abundant, demonstrating that the Yuanmou sequence extends into the early Quaternary as well. Based on biostratigraphic evidence it is suggested that the age of the Yuanmou fauna is earlier than that of Nihewan.

Clearly, the complexity of the Yuanmou Formation itself as well as its derived fauna renders interpretation of these remains problematic at best. Palaeomagnetic evidence suggests the relevant strata of the Yuanmou Formation fall entirely within the Brunhes Normal Epoch—a conclusion that is obviously at odds with the vertebrate fossil assemblage as it is now understood. It is evident that additional stratigraphic studies must be conducted in the field if these questions are to be resolved.

The Middle Pleistocene

Chinese localities at which a definite relationship between *Homo erectus* and a wide range of other vertebrate taxa have been established include Gongwangling and Chenjiawo at Lantian, Shaanxi (Hu and Qi 1978; Wu *et al.* 1966; Zhou 1964; Zhou and Li 1965); Locality 1 at Zhoukoudian, Beijing (Liu 1973; Pei 1934; Yang 1932, 1934; Zhou 1979); Hexian, Anhui (Huang *et al.* 1982); and Nanzhao, Henan (Qiu *et al.* 1982).

The mammalian fossils from the Gongwangling locality at Lantian, Shaanxi, include 42 taxa, of which surviving Tertiary forms include *Megantereon lantianensis* and *Nestoritherium sinensis* (Ji 1980). Lower Pleistocene species present at Gongwangling but absent in the faunal assemblage from the abundant Middle Pleistocene fossiliferous fissure of Locality 1, Zhoukoudian, include *Sivapanthera pleistocaenicus, Leptobos brevicornis, Myospalax tingi,* and *Ochotonoides complicidens.* However, a number of characteristic Nihewan faunal elements are not found at Gongwangling, such as *Elasmotherium, Bison palaeosinensis,* and *Proboscidipparion sinense.* In addition, the Gongwangling fauna contains fewer living species than does the vertebrate assemblage from Zhoukoudian Locality 1. Therefore it is suggested that the Gongwangling fauna is later than the Nihewan material but older than the *Homo erectus* occupation of Zhoukoudian. In addition, the Gongwangling fauna differs from this locality in its inclusion of many southern species such as *Ailuropoda melanoleuca fovealis, Stegodon orientalis,* and *Tapirus sinensis.*

The other principal Middle Pleistocene locality at Lantian, Chenjiawo, has yielded a total of 14 mammalian species, of which 11 are also known from Gongwangling: *Myospalax tingi, M. fontanieri, Apodemus, Bahomys hypsodonta, Ochotonoides complicidens, Sus lydekkeri, Pseudaxis grayi, Megaloceros (Sinomegaceros), Meles* cf. *leucurus, Hystrix,* and *Felis (Panthera) tigris.* The remaining three species—*Lepus wongi, Cuon alpinus,* and *Elephas*—are all common forms of the Middle to Upper Pleistocene. Unlike Gongwangling, the Chenjiawo locality has produced no remains of southern Chinese animals, but the totality of our data suggest the Chenjiawo assemblage is slightly younger than that of the Gongwangling locality.

The famous fossiliferous fissures of Zhoukoudian southwest of the city of Beijing have yielded a rich array of Middle Pleistocene faunal remains. In particular, the stratigraphic sequence in Locality 1, spanning a period from roughly 200,000 to 500,000 years ago, has been the subject of intensive study. In the Zhoukoudian Locality 1 fauna, only one surviving Tertiary form is present: *Megantereon inexpectatus.* It should be noted that this faunal assemblage shares a number of taxa in common with the Lower Pleistocene Nihewan deposits including *Spiroceros, Coelodonta, Paracamelus gigas, Palaeoloxodon namadicus,* and *Equus sanmeniensis.*

Vertebrate forms particularly characteristic of the Locality 1 fauna include *Hyaena brevirostris sinensis* (from the lower deposits up through Layer 3), *Trogontherium cuvieri, Ursus spelaeus, Felis youngi, Coelodonta antiquitatis yenshanensis, Dicerorhinus choukoutienensis, Pseudaxis grayi, Crocuta crocuta ultima* (Layers 3–1), *Canis lupus variabilis,* and *Bubalus teilhardi.* Numerous recent taxa also appear for the first time in North China in the Zhoukoudian fossiliferous fissures. Based on biostratigraphic evidence alone, it is clear the Zhoukoudian Locality 1 fauna is later than that found at Nihewan but retains sufficient archaic forms to obviate the possibility of its being considered Upper Pleistocene (Kahlke and Zhou 1961). The abundant Locality 1 deposits, over 40 m in thickness, represent an extraordinarily long sequence of sedimentation. Throughout the deposits one can witness evolutionary change in the resident population of *Homo erectus,* other vertebrates, and the archaeological assemblage fashioned by the cave's inhabitants.

As Pei Wenzhong (1955) pointed out, the Locality 1 deposits may be roughly subdivided into two chronological units. The Palaeolithic industry of the lower deposit exhibits a much more primitive character than that of the upper strata (see Chapter 9 this volume). Based on his examination of the Locality 1 faunal assemblage, Zhou Mingzhen (1955) concluded that the diversity of the taxa represented and the complexity of the stratigraphic context in which they occur indicate more than one period of deposition.

The fossils of *H. erectus* at Zhoukoudian are also characterized by substantial change through time. For example, the 1966 cranium, discovered in Locality 1, Layer 3, exhibits many progressive features when compared with the hominid remains from the lower deposit (Qiu *et al.* 1973). Combined geological, palaeontological, and archaeological evidence indicates the roughly 300,000-year cycle of sedimentary deposition in Zhoukoudian Locality 1 preserves a rich record of environmental and cultural change. It is hoped that the program of multidisciplinary research initiated at Zhoukoudian will result in the resolution of persistent chronological and related problems.

The rather complete *H. erectus* calvarium discovered in Hexian, Anhui, in 1980 was accompanied by a diverse and abundant fossil vertebrate assemblage. A preliminary analysis conducted by Huang Wanbo and others (1982) has identified 40 mammalian species, of which the following are also found in the Zhoukoudian Locality 1 fauna: *Megantereon, Megaloceros pachyosteus, Trogontherium cuvieri, Pseudaxis grayi, Hyaena brevirostris sinensis, Ursus arctos, Sus lydekkeri,* and *Dicerorhinus.* The Hexian locality also possesses a number of species characteristic of the South Chinese *Ailuropoda–Stegodon* Fauna: *Ailuropoda, Tapirus sinensis,* and *Megatapirus augustus.* Thus, it can be seen that the Hexian and Lantian Gongwangling faunas share features of both the Palaearctic and Oriental Realms. In consideration of the fact the Hexian fauna lacks the characteristic Gongwangling taxa, *Equus sanmeniensis* and *Nestoritherium,* and due to the relatively advanced morphology of the hominid cranium itself, it is logical to conclude that the Hexian deposit is later than that at Gongwangling and might be correlated with the upper strata at Zhoukoudian Locality 1 (Wu and Dong 1982).

A single fossil human tooth and a small collection of mammalian fossils have been unearthed in Nanzhao County, Henan Province (Qiu *et al.* 1982). The vertebrate assemblage includes only one surviving Tertiary form, a member of the Machairodontinae, but typically North Chinese Middle Pleistocene forms include *Equus sanmeniensis, Megaloceros pachyosteus,* and *Hyaena brevirostris sinensis.* The southern Chinese faunal realm is also represented at Nanzhao by *Stegodon, Rhinoceros sinensis,* and *Megatapirus augustus.* Judging from the character of this vertebrate assemblage, the age of the fossiliferous deposit is considered to be Middle Pleistocene and corresponds well with the Zhoukoudian Locality 1 fauna.

South China's most abundant Middle Pleistocene faunas are those associated with the yellow deposits in this region's numerous karst caverns and fissures. Three localities in particular, all in Guangxi Province, have yielded *Ailuropoda–Stegodon* faunas including remains of *Gigantopithecus.* Daxin (Han 1982; Pei and Wu 1956), Wuming (Zhang *et al.* 1973), and Bama (Zhang *et al.* 1975) are all typical karst cave deposits, although some variation in their faunal assemblages is apparent. At Daxin, three species are held in common with the earlier *Gigantopithecus* occurrence at Liucheng—*Dicoryphochoerus ultimus, Megalovis guangxiensis,* and *Pongo*—although none of these taxa is yet known from either Wuming or Bama. Of ancillary interest is the fact that the *Gigantopithecus* dentition recovered from each of these three localities is larger than the Liucheng series, attesting to diachronic change within the genus (see Zhang Yinyun, Chapter 4, this volume). All three localities are thought to be early Middle Pleistocene in age, and chronometric dating techniques have thus far not been able to determine the sequence of their deposition.

The Lower Palaeolithic archaeological sites of Guanyindong, Guizhou, and Shilongtou, Hubei, are associated with typical *Ailuropoda–Stegodon* faunal assemblages (Li and Wen 1978; Li *et al.* 1974). Due to the recovery of a *Gomphotherium* tooth in the Guanyin Cave, the age of the locality was originally determined to be late Middle Pleistocene. The Guanyindong deposits have subsequently been subdivided into two stratigraphic units. Group A, which includes all the upper strata at the site, resembles the Yanjinggou II Fauna of Sichuan and also bears similarities to the Trinil Fauna of Java. The Guanyindong Group B vertebrate remains, which derive from the cave's lower member, are nearly identical to the Yanjinggou I and Djetis faunas, suggesting they are considerably older than the Group A assemblage.

The collection of mammalian fossils from Shilongtou is rather small, but a preliminary analysis of the material (Li *et al.* 1974) suggests it may be contemporary with the Guanyindong Group B fauna.

The Upper Pleistocene

China is characterized by abundant late Pleistocene fossiliferous localities and archaeological sites. Because of the quantity of palaeontological specimens recovered thus far, only the most significant and thoroughly analyzed localities are discussed.

In North China the Dali site in Shaanxi Province has produced an extensive array of vertebrate fossils in addition to the cranium of an early *Homo sapiens* (Wu and You 1979). Eight fossil mammalian species have been recovered at the site in addition to *Homo,* and judging from the composition of the fauna, especially the presence of *Megaloceros pachyosteus,* the geological age of the site is thought to be early Upper Pleistocene.

Locality 100 at Dingcun, Xiangfen County, Shanxi, is also thought to preserve a record of early Upper Pleistocene deposition (Pei *et al.* 1958). Twenty-seven mammalian species have been identified from the site thus far, including *Dicerorhinus mercki, Pseudaxis grayi,* and *Coelodonta antiquitatis,* which are known from the Zhoukoudian Locality 1 fauna.

North China's widespread Upper Pleistocene Sjara-osso-gol (Salawusu) Fauna is also represented at Dingcun Locality 54.100 by taxa including *Equus hemionus, E. przewalskyi, Cervus elaphus* (*canadensis*) *asiaticus, Megaloceros* cf. *ordosianus,* and *Bos primigenius.* Living species are also well represented at Dingcun, all of which indicates a geological age nearly identical to Dali, Shaanxi.

One of China's most important Middle Palaeolithic archaeological sites, Xujiayao, located on the Shanxi–Hebei border, has yielded a range of controversial chronometric dates (Jia and Wei 1976; Jia *et al.* 1979; see also Chapter 2, this volume). Mammalian fossils associated with the Palaeolithic artifacts and *Homo sapiens* remains at Xujiayao include *Microtus brandtioides* and *Spiroceros peii,* both of which are known from the Zhoukoudian Locality 1 deposits. Consequently, biostratigraphic evidence indicates a late Middle Pleistocene or early Upper Pleistocene date for the site.

Twenty-two fossil mammalian species have been collected from the cave known as Gezidong in Liaoning Province (Gezidong Excavation Team 1975). Of interest is the recovery of dentition of *Marmota robustus,* which are morphologically similar but larger than the remains of this animal discovered in Localities 1 and 18 at Zhoukoudian. The large canid remains originally identified as *Canis* cf.

chihliensis have been reidentified as *Canis lupus* and the Gezidong fauna as a whole appears typical of many Upper Pleistocene assemblages known in northeastern China.

In the Ordos (Hetao) Region of southern Inner Mongolia and northern Shanxi, the type site of the North Chinese Upper Pleistocene fauna, Sjara-osso-gol (Salawusu), has yielded a collection of fossil vertebrates that has been the subject of numerous studies. In 1928 Boule and his colleagues identified 32 mammalian species in the Sjara-osso-gol Fauna and concluded that it was early Upper Pleistocene in age.

Extinct taxa in the Sjara-osso-gol Fauna include *Elephas* cf. *namadicus, Coelodonta antiquitatis, Megaloceros ordosianus, Spiroceros kiakhtensis, Bos primigenius, Bubalus wansjocki, Crocuta crocuta ultima,* and *Struthiolithus chersonensis*. Living species extirpated from the Sjara-osso-gol vicinity today but present in the fossil assemblage include *Equus hemionus, Cervus elaphus, Ovis ammon, Sus scrofa,* and *Gazella*. Such forms as *Canis lupus, Erinaceus,* and other small mammals still inhabit the Ordos Region today.

In 1963 and 1964 two fragmentary human femora and more than 10 species of fossil vertebrates were collected at Yangsigouwan in the Salawusu Valley. In addition to previously identified taxa, two species, *Felis* (*Panthera*) *tigris* and *Cricetulus* sp. indet., were added to the faunal list. The age of the assemblage is considered to be late Upper Pleistocene (Qi 1975).

The assemblage of vertebrate remains from the Upper Cave (Shandingdong) at Zhoukoudian is one of China's youngest Upper Pleistocene faunas. Extinct taxa include *Crocuta crocuta ultima, Ursus spelaeus, Elephas,* and *Struthio*. Living forms predominate in the Upper Cave assemblage and, in spite of its northern geographic position (approximately 40°N), a few southern faunal elements are included such as *Cynailurus* (*Acinonyx*) cf. *jubatus* and *Paguma larvata* (Pei 1940). A radiocarbon date from the cave's lower fissure of 18,865 ± 420 BP (ZK-136-0) suggests the bulk of the cavern's deposits are late Upper Pleistocene in age; the archaeological materials excavated from this locality corroborate this interpretation.

The *Ailuropoda–Stegodon* Fauna (*sensu lato*) of the Upper Pleistocene contains no archaic forms. Localities that have produced typical assemblages of this type include Maba, Guangdong (Guangdong Provincial Museum 1959); Tongzi, Guizhou (Wu *et al.* 1975); Changyang, Hubei (Jia 1957); Jiande, Zhejiang (Han and Zhang 1978); and Liujiang, Guangxi (Wu 1959). Although the mammalian fossiliferous remains from each of these localities are nearly identical, it should be noted that the hominid fossils recovered in association are of two types. Those from Maba, Changyang, and Jiande are provisionally classified as early *H. sapiens,* while the Liujiang specimen, like its close counterpart from Ziyang, Sichuan (Pei and Wu 1957), is classified as *H. sapiens sapiens*.

The relatively early placement of the Changyang fauna is based in part on the recovery of remains of *Hyaena ultima* (Jia 1957) (=*Hyaena brevirostris sinensis*) (Kurten 1958). As fossils of *Crocuta crocuta ultima* are not yet reported from

Pleistocene	South China: Zhou (1957)	South China: Kahlke (1961)	South China: Pei (1965)	South China: Huang (1978)	Present Authors	Present Authors: Cave Deposits				Present Authors: Lake Deposits	Present Authors: Mixed Deposits (North China)	North China: Ji (1980)	
Upper		*Ailuropoda* - *Stegodon* Fauna (sensu lato)	*Homo sapiens* - *Ailuropoda* - *Stegodon* Fauna	Liujiang Man Fauna	*Ailuropoda* - *Stegodon* Fauna	Ziyang Liujiang Jiande Maba Tongzi Changyang					Zhoukoudian Upper Cave Tongliang Salawusu (Sjara-osso-gol) Gezidong Xujiayao Dingcun Dali	Zhoukoudian Upper Cave Salawusu (Sjara-osso-gol) Dingcun	
Middle	*Ailuropoda* - *Stegodon* Fauna	*Ailuropoda* - *Stegodon* Fauna (sensu stricto)	*Ailuropoda* - *Stegodon* Fauna (sensu stricto)	Liuzhou - Bijiashan Fauna		Shilongtou		Guanyindong			Nanzhao Hexian	Zhoukoudian Locality 1	
		Liucheng Fauna				*Gigantopithecus* Fauna	Daxin *Giganto-pithecus* Fauna	Daxin Wuming Bama	Yunxian Yunxi		Zhoukoudian Locality 1 Chenjiawo Gongwangling	Upper	Chenjiawo
												Lower	Gong-wangling
Lower	*Gigantopithecus* Fauna		*Gigantopithecus* Fauna	Liucheng *Gigantopithecus* Fauna			Liucheng *Gigantopithecus* Fauna	Jianshi Liucheng	Bijia-shan	Yuanmou ?	Laochihe Linyi Nihewan Xihoudu	Laochihe and Zhoukoudian Locality 18 Nihewan	

Figure 15.1 Alternative subdivisions of major Pleistocene mammalian faunas in China.

Changyang, it is thought this fauna represents a cycle of deposition somewhat earlier than that of Maba, Jiande, or Tongzi.

Discussion and Conclusions

It is evident from our analysis of Quaternary mammalian faunas that the Pleistocene of China may be subdivided into three chronological units, each characterized by unique faunal assemblages (Figure 15.1).

Based principally on our own research and that of Pei (1957, 1965) and Kahlke (1961), we believe the characteristic mammalian faunas of the Pleistocene may be summarized as in Table 15.1.

The zoogeographic subdivisions of China's Quaternary faunal provinces have been the subject of considerable research (Pei 1957; Zhou 1964). Based on these previous syntheses in addition to newly acquired data, we believe China's Pleistocene zoogeography may be summarized as follows.

Due to a combination of environmental factors and accessability of terrain, most Pleistocene localities, particularly those containing hominid fossils and cultural remains, are distributed in the eastern half of the People's Republic of

Table 15.1
CHARACTERISTIC MAMMALIAN FAUNAS OF THE PLEISTOCENE

I. North China
   A. Lower Pleistocene *Proboscidipparion–Equus* (Nihewan) Fauna
      Principal localities include Xihoudu, Shanxi; Linyi, Shanxi; Nihewan, Hebei; and Laochihe, Shaanxi.
   B. Middle Pleistocene *Sinanthropus–Megaloceros pachyosteus* Fauna
      Type site is Locality 1, Zhoukoudian, Beijing
   C. Upper Pleistocene *Homo sapiens–Megaloceros ordosianus* (Sjara-osso-gol Fauna)
      Principal localities include Dali, Shaanxi; Dingcun, Shanxi; Xujiayao, Shanxi; and Sjara-osso-gol (Salawusu), Inner Mongolia
II. South China. All southern Chinese Pleistocene faunas may be designated *Ailuropoda–Stegodon* faunas.
   A. Lower Pleistocene Liucheng *Gigantopithecus* Fauna (*Ailuropoda–Stegodon* Fauna, *sensu lato*)
      Principal localities include Liucheng, Guangxi, and Jianshi, Hubei
   B. Middle Pleistocene *Ailuropoda–Stegodon* Fauna (*sensu stricto*)
      Typical assemblages include the *Gigantopithecus*-bearing localities of Daxin, Wuming, and Bama, all in Guangxi, and Shilongtou, Hubei
   C. Upper Pleistocene *Ailuropoda–Stegodon* Fauna (*sensu lato*)
      Major sites include Maba, Guangdong; Tongzi, Guizhou; and Liujiang, Guangxi
III. Transitional Zone. This as-yet-poorly defined geographic province in central China has yielded Pleistocene fossiliferous assemblages containing elements of both northern and southern faunas. Present evidence indicates the mixed character of this fauna may have begun as early as the Lower Pleistocene, although insufficient data exist to permit accurate chronological boundaries to be drawn. The principal localities where assemblages of this type have been recovered include Chaoxian, Anhui (Xu and Fang 1982); Hexian, Anhui; and Gongwangling, Lantian, Shaanxi.

China. Two broad geographic subdivisions are immediately apparent in this distribution of fossil localities: those in the South being characteristic of the Oriental Realm, and those in the North of the Palaearctic Realm. The generally agreed-upon boundary between these major faunal zones consists of a line running from the Himalayan massif in the southwest through the Qinling Mountains of east-central China to the middle and lower reaches of the Yangzi River.

Beginning in the early Quaternary the composition of the faunas of these two adjacent zones began to diverge significantly. The Lower Pleistocene Liucheng *Ailuropoda–Stegodon* Fauna is characteristic of South China and exhibits features of the present Oriental Realm. In North China, the Nihewan *Proboscidipparion–Equus* Fauna of the Lower Pleistocene contains the main taxa found in the Palaearctic Realm today.

During the Middle Pleistocene the zoogeographic distinctions between North and South China became clearer. The typical *Ailuropoda–Stegodon* Fauna of this period is more similar in character to that of the modern Oriental Realm, a trend that continued through the close of the Upper Pleistocene.

In North China the Nihewan Fauna of the Lower Pleistocene developed into the typical *Sinanthropus–Megaloceros pachyosteus* assemblage exemplified by the Middle Pleistocene fossiliferous localities at Zhoukoudian. By the late Pleistocene a new species of hominid and other mammals had formed a vertebrate assemblage essentially similar to that which characterizes the Palaearctic Realm today.

In the territory between the middle and lower reaches of the Yangzi River, the Qinling Mountains, and the Huai River a region of transition between the ancient and modern zoogeographic provinces has been discerned. To what extent this gradational zone reflects an ecotone extant throughout most of the Quaternary has yet to be thoroughly investigated.

The composition of any fauna is a reflection of its local environment. At present, only very broad palaeoenvironmental interpretations can be put forth based on extant data. What can be said is that the Quaternary faunas of North China indicate a gradual transition from principally steppe–grassland ecological zones in the Lower Pleistocene to substantially increased forest cover during the Middle Pleistocene in response to a general warming trend. North China seems to have become somewhat cooler and drier once again during the Upper Pleistocene and this shift is reflected in the composition of faunal assemblages recovered from localities such as Salawusu (Sjara-osso-gol) in Inner Mongolia, and others.

In South China, much less environmental fluctuation is apparent and the bulk of the Pleistocene seems to have been characterized in this area by the presence of tropical and subtropical forests and their associated fauna.

The application of multidisciplinary techniques in the analysis of palaeoenvironmental data is gaining impetus in China and it is hoped that in the future we will be able to refine further our understanding of the chronological and zoogeographic subdivisions of China's Quaternary fossil vertebrate record.

Table 15.2
MAMMALIAN FAUNAS OF THE LOWER PLEISTOCENE

Nihewan, Hebei

- *Ochotonoides complicidens* Boule et Teilhard
- *Erinaceus* cf. *dealbatus* Milne-Edwards
- *Allactaga* cf. *annulatus* Milne-Edwards
- *Myospalax tingi* Young
- Arvicolidae gen. et sp. indet.
- *Canis* (*Nyctereutes*) *sinensis* (Schlosser)
- *Canis chihliensis* Zdansky
- *Canis chihliensis palmidens* Teilhard et Piveteau
- *Canis chihliensis minor* Teilhard et Piveteau
- *Vulpes* sp. indet.
- *Ursus* cf. *etruscus* Cuvier
- *Mustela pachygnatha* Teilhard et Piveteau
- *Meles* cf. *leucurus* Hodgson
- *Lutra licenti* Teilhard et Piveteau
- *Hyaena brevirostris licenti* Pei
- *Hyaena* sp. indet.
- *Megantereon* (*Machairodus*) *nihowanensis* Teilhard et Piveteau
- *Felis* sp. indet.
- *Felis* (*Lynx*) sp. indet.
- *Cynailurus* cf. *pleistocaenicus* Zdansky
- *Palaeoloxodon namadicus* Falconer et Cautley
- *Hipparion* (*Proboscidipparion*) *sinense* Sefce
- *Equus sanmeniensis* Teilhard et Piveteau
- *Rhinoceros* cf. *sinensis* Owen
- *Coelodonta antiquitatis* Blumenbach
- *Elasmotherium* sp. indet.
- *Circotherium* sp. indet.
- Chalicotheridae gen. et sp. indet.
- *Sus* cf. *lydekkeri* Zdansky
- *Camelus* (*Paracamelus*) *gigas* Schlosser
- *Cervulus* cf. *sinensis* Teilhard et Piveteau
- *Cervus* (*Elaphurus*) *bifurcatus* Teilhard et Piveteau
- *Cervus* (*Eucladoceros*) *boulei* Teilhard et Piveteau
- *Cervus* (*Rusa*) *elegans* Teilhard et Piveteau
- *Cervus* (*Rusa*) sp. indet.
- *Gazella* cf. *subgutturosa* Guldenstaedt
- Antilopinae gen. et sp. indet.
- *Spiroceros wongi* Teilhard et Piveteau
- *Ovis shantungensis* Matsumoto
- Ovibovinae gen. et sp. indet.
- *Bison palaeosinensis* Teilhard et Piveteau

Xihoudu, Shanxi

- *Erinaceus* sp. indet.
- *Trogontherium* sp. indet.
- Leporidae gen. et sp. indet.
- *Hyaena* sp. indet.
- *Stegodon* sp. indet.
- *Archidiskodon planifrons* Falconer et Cautley
- *Elephas* cf. *namadicus* Falconer et Cautley
- *Coelodonta antiquitatis shansius* Chia et Wang
- Rhinocerotinae gen. et sp. indet.
- *Hipparion* (*Proboscidipparion*) *sinense* Sefce
- *Equus sanmeniensis* Teilhard et Piveteau
- *Elasmotherium* cf. *inexpectatum* Chow
- *Sus* cf. *lydekkeri* Zdansky
- *Cervus* (*Elaphurus*) *bifurcatus* Teilhard et Piveteau
- *Cervus* (*Elaphurus*) *chinnaniensis* Chia et Wang
- *Euctenoceros boulei* Teilhard et Piveteau
- *Axis rugosus* Chow
- *Axis shansius* Teilhard et Trassaert
- Cervinae gen. et sp. indet.
- *Gazella* cf. *blacki* Teilhard et Young
- *Bison palaeosinensis* Teilhard et Piveteau
- *Leptobos crassus* Jia et Wang

Gigantopithecus Cave, Liucheng, Guangxi

- *Gigantopithecus blacki* Koenigswald
- *Pongo* sp. indet.
- *Atherurus* sp. indet.
- *Hystrix subcristata* Swinhoe
- *Hystrix magna* Pei
- *Cuon dubius* Teilhard
- *Arctonyx minor* Pei
- *Ursus* cf. *thibetanus* Cuvier
- *Ailuropoda microta* Pei
- *Hyaena brevirostris licenti* Pei
- *Felis* (*Panthera*) *pardus* (Linnaeus)
- *Felis* sp. indet.
- *Felis teilhardi* Pei
- *Cynailurus pleistocaenicus* Zdansky
- *Paguma larvata* Hamilton-Smith
- *Viverra* sp. indet.
- *Gomphotherium* (*Trilophodon*) *serridentoides* Pei
- *Stegodon preorientalis* Young
- *Equus yunnanensis* Colbert
- *Nestoritherium praesinensis* Li
- *Tapirus peii* Li
- *Rhinoceros chiai* Li
- *Dicoryphochoerus ultimus* Han
- *Sus xiaozhu* Han, Xu et Yi
- *Sus peii* Han
- Suidae gen. et sp. indet. 1, 2
- *Dorcabune liuchengensis* Han
- *Muntiacus lacustris* Teilhard et Trassaert
- *Cervocerus* (*Cervavitus*) *fenqii* Han
- *Rusa yunnanensis* Lin,Pan et Lu

(*continued*)

Table 15.2 *(Continued)*

Bibos sp. indet.
Megalovis guangxiensis Han
Caprinae gen. et sp. indet. 1, 2

Yuanmou, Yunnan
Homo erectus Mayr
Ochotonoides complicidens Boule et Teilhard
Trogontherium sp. indet.
Rhizomys sp. indet.
Microtus sp. indet.
Arvicola sp. indet.
Hystrix subcristata Swinhoe
Canis yuanmoensis You et Qi
Vulpes cf. *chikushanensis* Young
Viverricula malaccensis fossilis Pei
Hyaena brevirostris licenti Pei
Hyaena sp. indet.
Megantereon nihowanensis Teilhard et Piveteau
Felis (Panthera) tigris (Linnaeus)
Felis (Panthera) pardus (Linnaeus)
Cynailurus sp. indet.
Stegodon zhaotongensis Chow et Zhai
Stegodon yuanmoensis You, Liu et Pan
Stegodon elephantoides Clift
Stegodon sp. indet.
Equus yunnanensis Colbert
Nestoritherium sp. indet.
Rhinoceros sinensis Owen
Sus scrofa Linnaeus
Sus sp. indet.
Eostyloceros longchuanensis Lin, Pan et Lu
Metacervulus capreolinus Teilhard et Trassaert
Paracervulus attenuatus Teilhard et Trassaert
Muntiacus lacustris Teilhard et Trassaert
Muntiacus nanus Teilhard et Trassaert
Cervocerus ultimus Lin, Pan et Lu
Axis shansius Teilhard et Trassaert
Axis cf. *rugosus* Chow
Rusa yunnanensis Lin, Pan et Lu
Rusa sp. indet.
Cervus (Rusa) stehlini Koenigswald
Cervus sp. indet.
Procapreolus stenos Lin, Pan et Lu
Gazella sp. indet.
Bos sp. indet.
Bibos sp. indet.

Jianshi, Hubei
Gigantopithecus blacki Koenigswald
Hystrix sp. indet.
Cuon javanicus antiquus (Matthew et Granger)
Ursus sp. indet.
Ailuropoda cf. *melanoleuca fovealis* (Matthew et Granger)
Arctonyx sp. indet.
Hyaena brevirostris licenti Pei
Felis sp. indet.
Machairodontidae gen. et sp. indet.
Gomphotheridae gen. et sp. indet.
Stegodon sp. indet.
Equus yunnanensis Colbert
Tapirus sinensis Owen
Rhinoceros sp. indet.
Sus sp. indet. A
Sus sp. indet. B
Cervus sp. indet.
Muntiacus sp. indet.
Bovinae gen. et sp. indet.
Ovinae gen. et sp. indet.

Bijiashan, Guangxi
Macaca sp. indet.
Ursus thibetanus Cuvier
Ailuropoda melanoleuca fovealis (Matthew et Granger)
Arctonyx collaris Cuvier
Hyaena brevirostris licenti Pei
Gomphotherium (Trilophodon) serridentoides Pei
Stegodon cf. *preorientalis* Young
Stegodon orientalis Owen
Tapirus sinensis Owen
Rhinoceros sinensis Owen
Sus xiaozhu Han, Xu et Yi
Sus bijiashanensis Han, Xu et Yi
Sus sp. indet.
Cervus sp. indet. 1, 2
Muntiacus sp. indet.
Bovinae gen. et sp. indet.
Rhinolophus sp. indet.

Table 15.3
MAMMALIAN FAUNAS OF THE MIDDLE PLEISTOCENE

Gongwangling, Lantian, Shaanxi
Homo erectus Mayr
Scaptochirus moschatus Milne-Edwards
Megamacaca lantianensis Hu et Qi
Ochotonoides complicidens Boule et Teilhard
Ochotona cf. *thibetana* Milne-Edwards
Cricetulus cf. *griseus* Milne-Edwards
Cricetulus (Cricetinus) varians (Zdansky)

Table 15.3 *(Continued)*

Myospalax tingi Young
Myospalax fontanieri Milne-Edwards
Myospalax sp. indet.
Arvicola terrae-rubrae Teilhard
Microtus epiratticeps Young
Bahomys hypsodonta Chow et Li
Gerbillus sp. indet.
Petaurista sp. indet.
Apodemus sp. indet.
Hystrix cf. *subcristata* Swinhoe
Canis variabilis Pei
Ursus cf. *etruscus* Cuvier
Ailuropoda melanoleuca fovealis (Matthew et Granger)
Meles cf. *leucurus* Hodgson
Hyaena brevirostris sinensis (Owen)
Felis (Panthera) cf. *tigris* Linnaeus
Felis (Panthera) pardus Linnaeus
Sivapanthera (Acinonyx) pleistocaenicus Zdansky
Megantereon lantianensis Hu et Qi
Stegodon orientalis Owen
Equus sanmeniensis Teilhard et Piveteau
Dicerorhinus cf. *mercki* Jaeger
Dicerorhinus lantianensis Hu et Qi
Megatapirus augustus Matthew et Granger
Tapirus sinensis Owen
Nestoritherium sinense Owen
Sus lydekkeri Zdansky
Elaphodus cephalophus Milne-Edwards
Pseudaxis grayi Zdansky
Megaloceros (Sinomegaceros) konwanlinensis Chow, Hu et Li
Leptobos brevicornis Hu et Qi
Leptobos sp. indet.
Capricornis sumatraensis qinlingensis Hu et Qi

Chenjiawo, Lantian, Shaanxi
Homo erectus Mayr
Lepus wongi Young
Ochotonoides complicidens Boule et Teilhard
Bahomys hypsodonta Chow et Li
Myospalax tingi Young
Myospalax cf. *fontanieri* Milne-Edwards
Apodemus cf. *sylvaticus* Linnaeus
Hystrix sp. indet.
Cuon alpinus Pallas
Meles cf. *leucurus* Hodgson
Felis (Panthera) tigris Linnaeus
Elephas sp. indet.
Sus cf. *lydekkeri* Zdansky
Pseudaxis grayi Zdansky
Sinomegaceros (Megaloceros) sp. indet.

Locality 1, Zhoukoudian, Beijing
Homo erectus pekinensis Weidenreich (*Sinanthropus pekinensis* Black)
Macaca robustus Young
Scaptochirus primitivus Schlosser
Neomys sinensis Zdansky
Neomys bohlini Young
Crocidura sp. indet.
Erinaceus olgai Young
Rhinolophus pleistocaenicus Young
Myotis sp. indet.
?*Hesperoptenus giganteus* Young
?*Pipistrellus* sp. indet.
Spermophilus mongolicus (Milne-Edwards)
Tamias wimani Young
Petaurista brachyodus (Young)
Arctomys robustus Milne-Edwards (*Marmota bobak* (Radde))
Arctomys (Marmota) complicidens (Young)
Chalicomys (Castor) anderssoni Schlosser
Trogontherium cf. *cuvieri* Fischer
Cricetulus (Cricitinus) varians (Zdansky)
Cricetulus cf. *griseus* Milne-Edwards
Cricetulus cf. *obscurus* Milne-Edwards
Micromys cf. *minutus* Pallas
Mus musculus bieni Young
Mus (Apodemus) sylvaticus Linnaeus
Rattus rattus (Linnaeus)
Gerbillus roborowskii Buchner
Clethrionomys (Evotomys) rufocanus Sundvell
?*Eothenomys* sp. indet.
Alticola sp. indet.
?*Phaiomys* sp. indet.
Pitymys simplicidens Young
Microtus brandtioides Young
Microtus epiratticeps Young
Myospalax wongi (Young)
Myospalax epitingi Teilhard et Pei
Myospalax sp. indet.
Rhizomys sp. indet.
Hystrix cf. *subcristata* Swinhoe
Lepus cf. *wongi* Young
Lepus sp. indet. A
Lepus sp. indet. B
Ochotona koslowi Buchner
Ochotona sp. indet. A
Ochotona sp. indet. B
Canis lupus Linnaeus
Canis lupus variabilis Pei
Canis cyonoides Pei
Canis (Nyctereutes) sinensis (Schlosser)
Vulpes cf. *corsac* (Linnaeus)
Vulpes cf. *vulgaris* (Linnaeus)
Cuon cf. *alpinus* Pallas
Canidae gen. et sp. indet.

(continued)

Table 15.3 (*Continued*)

- *Ursus angustidens* Zdansky (*Ursus thibetanus kokeni* Matthew et Granger)
- *Ursus arctos* Linnaeus
- *Ursus spelaeus* Blumenbach
- ?*Ailuropoda* sp. indet.
- *Meles* cf. *leucurus* Hodgson
- *Lutra melina* Pei
- *Gulo* sp. indet.
- *Mustela* cf. *sibirica* Pallas
- *Mustela* sp. indet.
- *Martes* sp. indet.
- *Hyaena brevirostris sinensis* Owen
- *Crocuta crocuta ultima* (Matsumoto)
- *Megantereon inexpectatus* Teilhard
- *Felis* (*Panthera*) *tigris* (Linnaeus)
- *Felis youngi* Pei
- *Felis* (*Panthera*) cf. *pardus* (Linnaeus)
- *Felis* sp. indet. 1, 2
- *Felis teilhardi* Pei
- *Felis* cf. *microtis* Milne-Edwards
- *Cynailurus* (*Acinonyx*) sp. indet.
- *Palaeoloxodon* cf. *namadicus* (Falconer et Cautley)
- *Coelodonta antiquitatis yenshanensis* Chow
- *Dicerorhinus choukoutienensis* Wang
- *Equus sanmeniensis* Teilhard et Piveteau
- *Sus lydekkeri* Zdansky
- *Paracamelus gigas* Schlosser
- Camelidae gen. et sp. indet.
- ?*Hydropotes* sp. indet.
- *Moschus moschiferus pekinensis* Young
- *Capreolus* sp. indet.
- *Pseudaxis grayi* Zdansky
- *Megaloceros pachyosteus* (Young)
- *Cervus* sp. indet.
- *Gazella* sp. indet.
- *Spirocerus peii* Young
- *Spirocerus* cf. *wongi* Teilhard
- *Ovis* cf. *ammon* Pallas
- *Ovis* sp. indet.
- Ovibovinae gen. et sp. indet.
- *Bubalus teilhardi* Young
- *Bison* sp. indet.

Hexian, Anhui

- *Homo erectus* Mayr
- *Macaca robustus* Young
- *Chodsigoa youngi* Zheng
- *Blarinella quadraticauda* (Milne-Edwards)
- *Anourosorex squamipes* Milne-Edwards
- ?*Scaptochirus* sp. indet.
- *Rhinolophus* cf. *ferrum-equinum* Thomas
- *Hipposideros* sp. indet.
- ?*Myotis* sp. indet.
- *Miniopterus schreiberii* Kuhl
- *Trogontherium cuvieri* Fischer
- *Cricetulus* (*Cricitinus*) *varians* (Zdansky)
- *Apodemus agrarius* Pallas
- *Rattus rattus* (Linnaeus)
- *Rattus rattus norvegicus* Berkenhout
- *Rattus rattus edwardsi* Thomas
- *Microtus brandtioides* Young
- *Canis* sp. indet.
- *Cuon alpinus* Pallas
- *Vulpes* sp. indet.
- *Arctonyx collaris* Cuvier
- *Lutra* sp. indet.
- *Hyaena brevirostris sinensis* Owen
- *Megantereon* sp. indet.
- *Felis chinensis* Gray
- *Felis* (*Panthera*) *pardus* (Linnaeus)
- *Ailuropoda* sp. indet.
- *Ursus arctos* Linnaeus
- *Ursus thibetanus kokeni* Matthew et Granger
- *Stegodon orientalis* Owen
- *Equus* sp. indet.
- *Tapirus sinensis* Owen
- *Megatapirus* sp. indet.
- *Dicerorhinus* sp. indet.
- *Sus lydekkeri* Zdansky
- *Sus* cf. *xiaozhu* Han, Xu et Yi
- *Pseudaxis grayi* Zdansky
- *Megaloceros pachyosteus* (Young)
- *Hydropotes inermis* Swinhoe
- *Elaphurus davidianus* Milne-Edwards (*Elaphurus menziesianus* Sowerby)
- *Bison* sp. indet.

Daxin, Guangxi

- *Gigantopithecus blacki* Koenigswald
- *Pongo* sp. indet.
- *Rhinopithecus* sp. indet.
- *Hylobates* sp. indet.
- *Macaca* sp. indet.
- *Hystrix subcristata* Swinhoe
- *Atherurus* sp. indet.
- *Rattus rattus* (Linnaeus)
- *Ailuropoda melanoleuca fovealis* (Matthew et Granger)
- *Ursus thibetanus* Cuvier
- *Arctonyx collaris* Cuvier
- *Cuon javanicus* (Matthew et Granger)
- *Viverricula malaccensis fossilis* Pei
- *Viverricula malaccensis* (Gmelin)
- *Paguma larvata* (Hamilton Smith)
- *Stegodon orientalis* Owen
- *Rhinoceros sinensis* Owen
- *Megatapirus augustus* Matthew et Granger

Table 15.3 *(Continued)*

Dicoryphochoerus ultimus Han
Sus bijiashanensis Han, Xu et Yi
Sus sp. indet.
Megalovis guangxiensis Han
Bibos sp. indet.
Cervus sp. indet.
Muntiacus sp. indet.
Caprinae gen. et sp. indet.

Wuming, Guangxi
Gigantopithecus blacki Koenigswald
Macaca sp. indet.
Hystrix cf. *subcristata* Swinhoe
Rhizomys sp. indet.
Rattus cf. *edwardsi* Thomas
Ailuropoda melanoleuca fovealis (Matthew et Granger)
Ursus sp. indet.
Lutra sp. indet.
Hyaena sp. indet.
Stegodon sp. indet.
Rhinoceros sinensis Owen
Sus sp. indet. 1, 2 (small)
Bovinae gen. et sp. indet.
Capricornis cf. *sumatraensis* Bechstein

Bama, Guangxi
Gigantopithecus blacki Koenigswald
Pongo sp. indet.
Hylobates sp. indet.
Macaca sp. indet.
Hystrix subcristata Swinhoe
Atherurus sp. indet.
Ursus sp. indet.
Ailuropoda melanoleuca baconi Woodward
Cuon javanicus (Matthew et Granger)
Felis sp. indet.
Rhinoceros sinensis Owen
Tapirus sp. indet.
Stegodon sp. indet.
Sus scrofa Linnaeus
Bovinae gen. et sp. indet.
Ovinae gen. et sp. indet.
Cervidae gen. et sp. indet.

Nanzhao, Henan
Homo sp. indet.
Castoridae gen. et sp. indet.
Sciuridae gen. et sp. indet.
Hystrix subcristata Swinhoe
Hyaena brevirostris sinensis Owen
Felix (Panthera) tigris (Linnaeus)
Felis sp. indet.
Machairodontinae gen. et sp. indet.
Arctonyx sp. indet.
Canis lupus variabilis Pei
Cuon alpinus Pallas
Ursus arctos Linnaeus
Stegodon sp. indet.
Equus sanmeniensis Teilhard et Piveteau
Megatapirus augustus Matthew et Granger
Rhinoceros sinensis Owen
Sus sp. indet.
Megaloceros pachyosteus (Young)
Cervus sp. indet. A
Cervus sp. indet. B
Caprinae gen. et sp. indet.
Bibos sp. indet.

Guanyindong, Guizhou
Group A
Hystrix sp. indet.
Stegodon sp. indet.
Rhinoceros sinensis Owen
Bovinae gen. et sp. indet.
Group B
Macaca sp. indet.
Hystrix cf. *subcristata* Swinhoe
Rhizomys cf. *sinensis* Gray
Vulpes cf. *vulgaris* Linnaeus
Ursus thibetanus kokeni Matthew et Granger
Ailuropoda melanoleuca fovealis (Matthew et Granger)
Mustelidae gen. et sp. indet.
Crocuta crocuta ultima (Matsumoto)
Felis (Panthera) cf. *tigris* (Linnaeus)
Gomphotheriidae gen. et sp. indet.
Stegodon guizhouensis Li et Wen
Stegodon cf. *orientalis* Owen
Equus sp. indet.
Megatapirus augustus Matthew et Granger
Rhinoceros sinensis Owen
Sus cf. *scrofa* Linnaeus
Muntiacus sp. indet.
?*Pseudaxis* sp. indet.
Cervus (Rusa) sp. indet.
Bubalus sp. indet.
Bibos sp. indet.
Capricornis sumatraensis Bechstein

Shilongtou, Daye, Hubei
Hystrix subcristata Swinhoe
Ailuropoda melanoleuca fovealis (Matthew et Granger)
Hyaena brevirostris sinensis Owen
Felis (Panthera) tigris (Linnaeus)
Stegodon orientalis Owen
Rhinoceros sinensis Owen
Sus sp. indet.
Pseudaxis sp. indet.
Cervus sp. indet.
Bovinae gen. et sp. indet.

Table 15.4
MAMMALIAN FAUNAS OF THE UPPER PLEISTOCENE

Dali, Shaanxi
Homo sapiens Linnaeus
Castoridae gen. et sp. indet.
Palaeoloxodon sp. indet.
Equus sp. indet.
Rhinoceros sp. indet.
Megaloceros pachyosteus (Young)
Megaloceros sp. indet.
Pseudaxis cf. *grayi* Zdansky
Bubalus sp. indet.

Locality 100, Dingcun, Shanxi
Homo sapiens Linnaeus
Talpidae gen. et sp. indet.
Ochotona sp. indet.
?*Castor* sp. indet.
Muridae gen. et sp. indet.
Siphneus (Myospalax) fontanieri (Milne-Edwards)
Canis sp. indet.
Canis (Nyctereutes) cf. *procyonoides* (Gray)
Vulpes sp. indet.
Ursus sp. indet.
Meles sp. indet.
Palaeoloxodon cf. *tokunagai* Matsumoto
Elephas (Palaeoloxodon) namadicus Falconer et Cautley
Elephas cf. *indicus* Linnaeus
Coelodonta antiquitatis Blumenbach (*Rhinoceros trichorhinus* Cuvier)
Dicerorhinus mercki Jaeger
Equus hemionus Pallas
Equus przewalskyi Poliakof
Sus sp. indet.
Elaphus canadensis asiaticus Lydekker
Pseudaxis cf. *grayi* Zdansky
Megaloceros cf. *ordosianus* (Young)
Megaloceros sp. indet.
?*Moschus* sp. indet.
Gazella sp. indet.
Spirocerus sp. indet.
Bubalus sp. indet.
Bos primigenius Bojanus

Xujiayao, Shanxi
Homo sapiens Linnaeus
Ochotona sp. indet.
Myospalax fontanieri (Milne-Edwards)
Microtus brandtioides Young
Canis lupus Linnaeus
Felis (Panthera) cf. *tigris* (Linnaeus)
Palaeoloxodon cf. *naumanni* Makiyama
Coelodonta antiquitatis Blumenbach
Equus przewalskyi Poliakof
Equus hemionus Pallas
Megaloceros ordosianus (Young)
Cervus elaphus Smith
Cervus nippon grayi Temminca
Spirocerus hsuchiayaocus Jia, Wei et Li
Spirocerus peii Young
Procapra picticaudata przewalskyi Büchner
Gazella subgutturosa Guldenstaedt
Gazella sp. indet.
Bos primigenius Bojanus
Sus sp. indet.

Gezidong, Liaoning
Vespertilionidae gen. et sp. indet.
Ochotona daurica Pallas
Lepus sp. indet.
Marmota robustus Milne-Edwards
Myospalax sp. indet.
Microtus epiratticeps Young
Rattus rattus Linnaeus
Cricetulus sp. indet.
Canis cf. *chihliensis* Zdansky
Vulpes cf. *corsac* Linnaeus
Felis sp. indet.
Lynx sp. indet.
Felis cf. *microtis* Milne-Edwards
Crocuta crocuta ultima (Matsumoto)
Equus sp. indet.
Equus cf. *hemionus* Pallas
Coelodonta antiquitatis Blumenbach
Cervus sp. indet.
Bos sp. indet.
Gazella sp. indet.
Pseudois cf. *nayaur* Hodgson

Sjara-osso-gol (Salawusu), Inner Mongolia Autonomous Region
Homo sapiens sapiens Linnaeus
Erinaceus sp. indet.
Scaptochirus (Talpa) moschata Milne-Edwards
Chiroptera gen. et sp. indet.
Lepus sp. indet.
Ochotona sp. indet.
Spermophilus (Citellus) mongolicus (Milne-Edwards)
Myospalax fontanieri Milne-Edwards
Dipus sowerbyi Thomas
Allactaga cf. *annulatus* Milne-Edwards
Gerbillus (Meriones) meridianus Pallas
Eothenomys sp. indet.
Alticola cf. *aricetulus* Miller
Microtus cf. *ratticeps* Keyserling et Blasius
Microtus sp. indet.
Cricetulus sp. indet.
Canis lupus Linnaeus

Table 15.4 *(Continued)*

Felis (Panthera) tigris (Linnaeus)
Crocuta crocuta ultima (Matsumoto)
Meles taxus Boddaert
Elephas (Palaeoloxodon) cf. *namadicus* Falconer et Cautley
Coelodonta antiquitatis Blumenbach
Equus hemionus Pallas
Equus cf. *przewalskyi* Poliakof
Sus scrofa Linnaeus
Camelus knoblochi Brandt
Cervus elaphus Linnaeus
Cervus mongoliae Gaudry
Megaloceros ordosianus Young
Gazella przewalskyi Buchner
Gazella subgutturosa Guldenstaedt
Spirocerus kiakhtensis Pavlov
Ovis ammon Pallas
Bubalus wansjocki Boule et Teilhard
Bos primigenius Bojanus

Upper Cave, Zhoukoudian, Beijing
Homo sapiens sapiens Linnaeus
Scaptochirus sp. indet.
Erinaceus sp. indet.
Rhinolophus sp. indet.
Myotis sp. indet. A
Myotis sp. indet. B
Chiroptera gen. et sp. indet.
Lepus europaeus Pallas
Ochotona daurica Pallas
?*Sciurus* sp. indet.
Petaurista sulcatus Howell
Cricetulus (Cricetinus) varians Zdansky
Cricetulus obscurus (Milne-Edwards)
Apodemus sylvaticus Linnaeus
Rattus rattus Linnaeus
Gerbillus sp. indet.
Microtus epiratticeps Young
Alticola cf. *stracheyi* Thomas
Siphneus (Myospalax) armandi (Milne-Edwards)
Hystrix sp. indet.
Canis lupus Linnaeus
Canis (Nyctereutes) procyonoides (Gray)
Vulpes corsac Linnaeus
Vulpes vulgaris Linnaeus
Cuon alpinus Pallas
Ursus angustidens Zdansky (*Ursus thibetanus kokeni* Matthews et Granger)
Ursus spelaeus Blumenbach
Meles leucurus Hodgson
Mustela cf. *altaica* Pallas
Mustela (Putorius) eversmanni Hollister
Paguma larvata (Smith)
Crocuta crocuta ultima (Matsumoto)
Felis (Panthera) tigris (Linnaeus)
Felis (Panthera) pardus (Linnaeus)
Felis (Lynx) lynx (Linnaeus)
Felis cf. *microtis* Milne-Edwards
Felis (Lynx) sp. indet.
Felis catus Linnaeus
Cynailurus (Acinonyx) cf. *jubatus* Walger
Elephas sp. indet.
Rhinoceros sp. indet.
Equus hemionus Pallas
Sus sp. indet.
Capreolus manchuricus Noack
Cervus canadensis Erxleben (*Elaphus canadensis* Severtzow)
Pseudaxis hortulorum Swinhoe
Gazella przewalskyi Buchner
Ovis sp. indet.
Bos sp. indet.

Maba, Guangdong
Homo sapiens Linnaeus
Hystrix sp. indet.
Lepus sp. indet.
Hyaena sp. indet.
Ursus sp. indet.
Ailuropoda sp. indet.
Felis (Panthera) tigirs (Linnaeus)
Mustelidae gen. et sp. indet.
Stegodon sp. indet.
Elephas (Palaeoloxodon) namadicus Falconer et Cautley
Tapirus sp. indet.
Rhinoceros sp. indet.
Sus sp. indet.
Cervus sp. indet.
Bos sp. indet.

Tongzi, Guizhou
Rhinopithecus sp. indet.
Hylobates sp. indet.
Pongo sp. indet.
Petaurista (Pteromys) cf. *brachyodus* Young
Rhizomys sp. indet.
Hystrix cf. *subcristata* Swinhoe
Hystrix magna Pei
Canis lupus Linnaeus
Cuon javanicus (Matthew et Granger)
Ailuropoda melanoleuca fovealis (Matthew et Granger)
Arctonyx sp. indet.
Ursus thibetanus kokeni Matthew et Granger
Crocuta crocuta ultima (Matsumoto)
Felis (Panthera) tigris (Linnaeus)
Felis (Panthera) pardus (Linnaeus)
Stegodon orientalis Owen
Megatapirus augustus Matthew et Granger
Rhinoceros sinensis Owen

(continued)

Table 15.4 *(Continued)*

Sus scrofa Linnaeus	Jiande, Zhejiang
Cervus sp. indet. A	*Homo sapiens* Linnaeus
Cervus sp. indet. B	*Macaca* sp. indet.
Muntiacus sp. indet.	*Hystrix subcristata* Swinhoe
Capricornis cf. *sumatraensis* Bechstein	*Ursus thibetanus* Cuvier
Bovidae gen. et sp. indet.	*Ailuropoda melanoleuca fovealis* (Matthew et Granger)
Changyang, Hubei	*Arctonyx collaris* Cuvier
Homo sapiens Linnaeus	*Crocuta crocuta ultima* (Matsumoto)
Hystrix cf. *subcristata* Swinhoe	*Stegodon orientalis* Owen
Rhizomys cf. *troglodytes* Matthew et Granger	*Elephas* (*Palaeoloxodon*) cf. *namadicus* Falconer et Cautley
Cuon javanicus antiquus (Matthew et Granger)	*Megatapirus augustus* Matthew et Granger
Cuon sp. indet.	*Rhinoceros sinensis* Owen
Ursus angustidens Zdansky (*Ursus thibetanus kokeni* Matthew et Granger)	*Cervus* sp. indet.
Ailuropda sp. indet.	*Muntiacus* sp. indet.
Felis (*Panthera*) *tigris* (Linnaeus)	*Sus* sp. indet.
Felidae gen. et sp. indet.	*Bubalus* sp. indet.
Meles sp. indet.	*Ovis* sp. indet.
Hyaena brevirostris sinensis Owen	Liujiang, Guangxi
Stegodon orientalis Owen	*Homo sapiens sapiens* Linnaeus
Megatapirus augustus Matthew et Granger	*Hystrix* sp. indet.
Rhinoceros sinensis Owen	*Ursus* sp. indet.
Sus sp. indet.	*Ailuropoda melanoleuca fovealis* (Matthew et Granger)
?*Bubalus* sp. indet.	*Stegodon orientalis* Owen
?*Spirocerus* sp. indet.	*Megatapirus augustus* Matthew et Granger
Cervidae gen. et sp. indet.	*Rhinoceros sinensis* Owen
	Sus sp. indet.

References

Bian, Meinian (M. N. Bien)
1940 Preliminary observations on the Cenozoic geology of Yunnan. *Bulletin of the Geological Society of China* 20:179–204.

Boule, M., H. Breuil, E. Licent and P. Teilhard de Chardin
1928 *Le Paléolithique de la Chine*. Archives de l'Institut de Paléontologie Humaine. Memoire 4:1–138. Paris: Masson et Cie.

Colbert, E. H.
1940 Pleistocene mammals from the Makai Valley of northern Yunnan, China. *American Museum Novitates*:1099.

Gezidong Excavation Team
1975 Discovery of Palaeolithic artifacts in Gezidong Cave in Liaoning province. *Vertebrata PalAsiatica* 13(2):122–136.

Guangdong Provincial Museum
1959 Preliminary report on the excavation of human and mammalian fossils at Mapa, Kwangtung. *Gu Jizhuidongwu Xuebao* (*Vertebrata PalAsiatica*) 3(2):104.

Han Defen
1982 Mammalian fossils from Daxin County, Guangxi. *Vertebrata PalAsiatica* 20(1):58–63.
n.d. Artiodactyl fossils from the *Gigantopithecus* Cave, Liucheng, Guangxi. In press.

Han Defen, Xu Chunhua, and Yi Guangyuan
1975 Quaternary mammalian fossils from Bijiashan, Liuzhou, Guangxi. *Vertebrata PalAsiatica* 13(4):250–256.

Han Defen and Zhang Senshui
1978 A hominid canine from Jiande and new Quarternary fossil mammalian materials from Zhejiang. *Vertebrata PalAsiatica* 16(4):255–263.

Hu Changkang and Qi Tao
1978 Gongwangling Pleistocene mammalian fauna of Lantian, Shaanxi. *Palaeontologia Sinica,* New Series C 21:1–64.

Hu Chengzhi
1973 Ape-man teeth from Yuanmou, Yunnan. *Acta Geologica Sinica* 1:65–71.

Huang Wanbo
1979 On the age of the cave faunas of South China. *Vertebrata PalAsiatica* 17(4):327–342.

Huang Wanbo, Fang Dusheng, and Ye Yongxiang
1982 Preliminary study on the fossil hominid skull and fauna of Hexian, Anhui. *Vertebrata PalAsiatica* 20(3):248–256.

Ji Hongxiang
1975 The Lower Pleistocene mammalian fossils of Lantian district, Shensi. *Vertebrata PalAsiatica* 13(3):169–177.
1980 Subdivisions of the Quaternary mammalian fauna of Lantian district, Shensi. *Vertebrata PalAsiatica* 18(3):220–228.

Jia Lanpo (Chia Lan-po)
1957 Notes on the human and some other mammalian remains from Changyang, Hupei. *Gu Jizhuidongwu Xuebao (Vertebrata PalAsiatica)* 1(3):247–258.

Jia Lanpo (Chia Lan-po) and Wang Jian (Wang Chien)
1978 *Hsihoutu—a culture site of early Pleistocene in Shansi province.* Beijing: Cultural Relics Press.

Jia Lanpo (Chia Lan-po) and Wei Qi
1976 A Palaeolithic site at Hsu-chia-yao, Yangkao county, Shansi province. *Acta Archaeologica Sinica,* 2:97–114.

Jia Lanpo (Chia Lan-po), Wei Qi, and Li Chaorong
1979 Report on the excavation of Hsuchiayao Man site in 1976. *Vertebrata PalAsiatica* 17(4):277–293.

Kahlke, Hans-Dietrich
1961 On the complex of the *Stegodon–Ailuropoda* Fauna of South China and the chronological position of *Gigantopithecus blacki* Koenigswald. *Vertebrata PalAsiatica* 2:83–108.

Kahlke, Hans-Dietrich and Zhou Benxiong (Chow Ben-shun)
1961 A summary of stratigraphic and palaeontological observations in the lower layers of Choukoutien Locality 1 and on the chronological position of the site. *Vertebrata PalAsiatica* 3:212–240.

Kurten, Bjorn
1958 A note on the hyaenid remains from the Langdong cave described by Chia. *Gu Jizhuidongwu Xuebao (Vertebrata PalAsiatica)* 2(2–3):164.

Li Yanxian and Wen Benheng
1978 The discovery and significance of the Guanyindong Palaeolithic culture, Qianxi, Guizhou. In *Gurenlei Lunwenji (Collected Papers of Palaeoanthropology)*, edited by the Institute of Vertebrate Palaeontology and Palaeoanthropology, Chinese Academy of Sciences. Beijing: Science Press. Pp. 77–93.

Li Yanxian, Yuan Zhenxin, Dong Xingren, and Li Tianyuan
1974 Report on the excavation of a Palaeolithic station known as Shilongtou at Daye, Hubei. *Vertebrata PalAsiatica* 12(2):139–157.

Li Youheng
n.d. Perissodactyl fossils from the *Gigantopithecus* Cave, Liucheng, Guangxi. In press.

Lin Yipu, Pan Yuerong, and Lu Qingwu

1978 The Lower Pleistocene mammalian fauna from Yuanmou, Yunnan. In *Gurenlei Lunwenji* (Collected Papers of Palaeoanthropology), edited by the Institute of Vertebrate Palaeontology and Palaeoanthropology, Chinese Academy of Sciences. Beijing: Science Press. Pp. 101–125.

Liu Dongsheng and Ding Menglin

1983 Discussion on the age of "Yuanmou Man". *Acta Anthropologica Sinica* 2(1):40–48.

Liu Houyi

1973 Fossil horses in Peking Man site. *Vertebrata PalAsiatica* 11(1):86–101.

Pei Wenzhong (Pei Wen-chung)

1934 On the carnivora from Locality 1 of Choukoutien. *Palaeontologia Sinica,* Series C 8(1):1–116.

1940 The Upper Cave fauna of Choukoutien. *Palaeontologia Sinica,* New Series C 10.

1955 The Palaeolithic cultures of China. *Kexue Tongbao* 1:30–45.

1957 The zoogeographical divisions of Quaternary mammalian faunas in China. *Gu Jizhuidongwu Xuebao (Vertebrata PalAsiatica)* 1(1):9–24.

1961 Fossil mammals of early Pleistocene age from Yuanmo (Makai) of Yunnan. *Vertebrata PalAsiatica* 1:16–30.

1965 Excavation of Liucheng *Gigantopithecus* Cave and exploration of other caves in Kwangsi. *Memoirs of the Institute of Vertebrate Palaeontology and Palaeoanthropology* 7.

n.d. Rodent, carnivore, and proboscidean fossils from the *Gigantopithecus* Cave, Liucheng, Guangxi. In press.

Pei Wenzhong (Pei Wen-chung) and Li Youheng

1958 Discovery of a third mandible of *Gigantopithecus* in Liucheng, Kwangsi. *Gu Jizhuidongwu Xuebao (Vertebrata PalAsiatica)* 2(4):193–200.

Pei Wenzhong (Pei Wen-chung) and Wu Rukang (Woo Ju-kang)

1956 New materials of *Gigantopithecus* teeth from South China. *Gushengwu Xuebao (Acta Palaeontologica Sinica)* 4(4):477–490.

1957 Tzeyang Man. *Memoirs of the Institute of Vertebrate Palaeontology and Palaeoanthropology,* Series A 1:1–71.

Pei Wenzhong (Pei Wen-chung), Wu Rukang (Woo Ju-kang), Jia Lanpo (Chia Lan-po), Zhou Mingzhen (Chow Min-chen), Liu Xianting, and Wang Zeyi

1958 Report on the excavation of Palaeolithic sites at Tingtsun, Hsiangfenhsien, Shansi province, China. *Memoirs of the Institute of Vertebrate Palaeontology and Palaeoanthropology,* Series A 2:1–111.

Qi Guoqin

1975 Quaternary mammalian fossils from Salawusu River district, Nei Mongol. *Vertebrata PalAsiatica* 13(4):239–249.

Qiu Zhonglang, Gu Yumin, Zhang Yinyun, and Zhang Senshui

1973 Newly discovered *Sinanthropus* remains and stone artifacts at Choukoutien. *Vertebrata PalAsiatica* 11(2):109–131.

Qiu Zhonglang, Xu Chunhua, Zhang Weihua, Wang Rulin, Wang Jianzhong, and Zhao Chengfu

1982 A human fossil tooth and fossil mammals from Nanzhao, Henan. *Acta Anthropologica Sinica* 1(2):109–117.

Teilhard de Chardin, Pierre

1940 The fossils from Locality 18 near Peking. *Palaeontologia Sinica,* New Series C 9:1–94.

Teilhard de Chardin, P. and J. Piveteau

1930 Les mammifères fossiles de Nihowan (Chine). *Annales de Paléontologie* 19.

Wu Maolin, Wang Linghong, Zhang Yinyun, and Zhang Senshui

1975 Fossil human teeth and associated fauna from northern Guizhou. *Vertebrata PalAsiatica* 13(1):14–23.

Wu Rukang (Woo Ju-kang)
1959 Human fossils found in Liukiang, Kwangsi, China. *Gu Jizhuidongwu Xuebao (Vertebrata PalAsiatica)* 3(3):109–118.
1962 The mandibles and dentition of *Gigantopithecus*. *Palaeontologia Sinica*, New Series D 11:1–94.
Wu Rukang (Woo Ju-Kang) and Dong Xingren
1982 Preliminary study of *Homo erectus* remains from Hexian, Anhui. *Acta Anthropologica Sinica* 1(1):2–13.
Wu Xinzhi and You Yuzhu
1979 A preliminary observation of Dali Man site. *Vertebrata PalAsiatica* 17(4):294–303.
Wu Xinzhi, Yuan Zhenxin, Han Defen, and Qi Tao
1966 Report of the excavation at Lantian Man locality of Gongwangling in 1965. *Vertebrata PalAsiatica* 10(1):23–29.
Xu Chunhua and Fang Dusheng
1982 New discovery of human fossils in Anhui. *Acta Anthropologica Sinica* 1(2):206.
Xu Chunhua, Han Kangxin, and Wang Linghong
1974 Discovery of *Gigantopithecus* teeth and associated fauna in western Hupei. *Vertebrata PalAsiatica* 12(4):293–309.
Yang Zhongjian (C. C. Young)
1932 On the artiodactyla from the *Sinanthropus* site at Choukoutien. *Palaeontologia Sinica*, Series C 8(2):1–100.
1934 On the insectivora, chiroptera, rodentia, and primates other than *Sinanthropus* from Locality 1 at Choukoutien. *Palaeontologia Sinica*, Series C 8(3):1–139.
Zhang Yinyun, Wang Linghong, Dong Xingren, and Chen Wenjun
1975 Discovery of a *Gigantopithecus* tooth from Bama district in Kwangsi. *Vertebrata PalAsiatica* 13(3):148–153.
Zhang Yinyun, Wu Maolin, and Liu Jinrong
1973 New discovery of *Gigantopithecus* teeth from Wuming, Kwangsi. *Kexue Tongbao* 18(3):130–133.
Zhou Benxiong (Chow Ben-shun)
1979 The fossil rhinocerotids of Locality 1, Zhoukoudian. *Vertebrata PalAsiatica* 17(3):236–258.
Zhou Mingzhen (Chow Min-chen)
1955 Inferred living environments of Chinese fossil humans from vertebrate fossils. *Kexue Tongbao* 1:15–22.
1961 An occurrence of *Enhydriodon* at Yuanmou, Yunnan. *Vertebrata PalAsiatica* 2:164–167.
1964 Mammals of "Lantian Man" locality at Lantian, Shensi. *Vertebrata PalAsiatica* 8(3):301–311.
Zhou Mingzhen (Chow Min-chen) and Li Chuankuei
1965 Mammalian fossils in association with the mandible of Lantian Man at Chen-chia-ou, in Lantian, Shensi. *Vertebrata PalAsiatica* 9(4):377–393.
Zhou Mingzhen (Chow Min-chen) and Zhou Benxiong (Chow Ben-shun)
1959 Villafranchian mammals from Lingyi, S.W. Shansi. *Gushengwu Xuebao (Acta Palaeontologica Sinica)* 7(2):89–98.

Index

F

G

H

I

J

K

L

M

N

O

P

Q

R

S

T

U

W

X

Y

Z

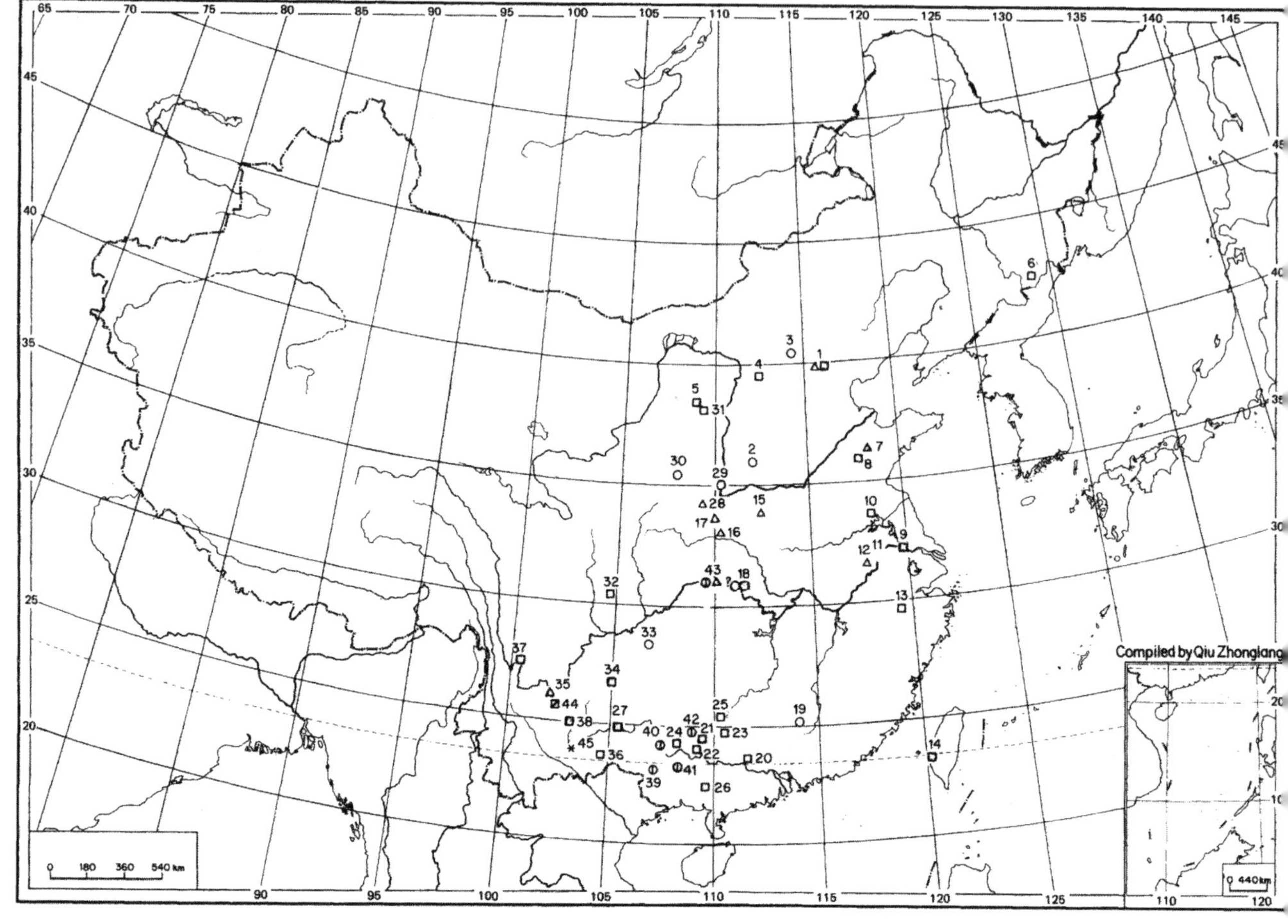

Localities in China yielding remains of fossil primates and humans

1. Zhoukoudian, Beijing
2. Dingcun, Shanxi
3. Xujiayao, Shanxi
4. Suoxian, Shanxi
5. Salawusu (Sjara-osso-gol), Inner Mongolia
6. An'tu, Jilin
7. Yiyuan, Shandong
8. Xintai, Shandong
9. Dantu, Jiangsu
10. Sihong, Jiangsu
11. Hexian, Anhui
12. Chaoxian, Anhui
13. Jiande, Zhejiang
14. Zuozhen, Taiwan
15. Nanzhao, Henan
16. Yunxian, Hubei
17. Yunxi, Hubei
18. Changyang, Hubei
19. Maba, Guangdong
20. Fengkai, Guangdong
21. Liujiang, Guangxi
22. Laibin, Guangxi
23. Lipu, Guangxi
24. Du'an, Guangxi
25. Guilin, Guangxi
26. Lingshan, Guangxi
27. Longlin, Guangxi
28. Lantian, Shaanxi
29. Dali, Shaanxi
30. Changwu, Shaanxi
31. Hengshan, Shaanxi
32. Ziyang, Sichuan
33. Tongzi, Guizhou
34. Shuicheng, Guizhou
35. Yuanmou, Yunnan
36. Xichou, Yunnan
37. Lijiang, Yunnan
38. Chenggong, Yunnan
39. Daxin, Guangxi
40. Bama, Guangxi
41. Wuming, Guangxi
42. Liucheng, Guangxi
43. Jianshi, Hubei
44. Lufeng, Yunnan
45. Kaiyuan, Yunnan

* *Dryopithecus*
▨ *Sivapithecus* and *Ramapithecus*
⦶ *Gigantopithecus*
△ *Homo erectus*
○ Early *Homo sapiens*
□ *Homo sapiens sapiens*